Thinking and Reasoning

To our sons:
Robin and Thomas

Thinking and Reasoning

Alan Garnham
Jane Oakhill

BLACKWELL
Oxford UK & Cambridge USA

First published 1994
Reprinted 1995

Blackwell Publishers, the publishing imprint of Basil Blackwell Ltd
108 Cowley Road
Oxford OX4 1JF, UK

Basil Blackwell Inc.
238 Main Street
Cambridge, Massachusetts 02142
USA

British Library Cataloguing in Publication Data
A CIP catalogue record for this book is available from the British Library.

Library of Congress Cataloging-in-Publication Data
Garnham, Alan, 1954–
    Thinking and reasoning / Alan Garnham, Jane Oakhill.
        p.   cm.
    Includes bibliographical references and index.
    ISBN 0–631–17002–2 (alk. paper). — ISBN 0–631–17003–0
(pbk. : alk. paper)
    1. Thought and thinking.   2. Reasoning (Psychology)   I. Oakhill,
Jane.   II. Title.
BF441.G38   1994
153.4—dc20
                                                            93–39084
                                                            CIP

Typeset in 10 on 12 pt Sabon by Graphicraft Typesetters Ltd., Hong Kong
Printed in Great Britain by Hartnolls, Bodmin

This book is printed on acid-free paper

Contents

Preface

Thinking and Reasoning is a text intended primarily for intermediate and advanced undergraduate courses, though it might also be suitable for beginning postgraduates. The book is organized along traditional lines. Those who know our background will not be surprised to see a slight bias in favour of the mental models view of thinking and reasoning, but we have tried to present a fair overview of the field. As we explain in the final chapter, we do not believe the world is quite ready for a text on thinking and reasoning that takes an exclusively mental models line!

We have kept the chapters fairly brief, so that they can be consumed at the rate of either one a week or two a week, depending on the intensity of the course, and the level at which it is taught. Some pairings of chapters are self-selecting, for example 5 and 6, 7 and 8, 9 and 10, 16 and 17; others are at the instructor's discretion. Some chapters, such as chapter 4, can be omitted if they are not thought suitable for a particular class.

We would like to thank Phil Johnson-Laird, not only for reading the entire manuscript for Blackwell, but for his continued support more generally. His comments on the manuscript were, as usual, detailed and incisive. If we had had more time, and wider expertise, we would have followed more of his suggestions. Other friends and colleagues who provided comments on or help with parts of the book were Jane Beattie (chapters 9 and 10), Ted Ruffman (on children's hypothesis testing) and Josef Perner (on children's theory of mind).

The book was first mooted with Philip Carpenter in 1987, but has been delayed by, among other things, the arrival of our two children in the meanwhile. This book is dedicated to them, not in acknowledgement of that delay, but for adding a new dimension to our lives. Since 1991, we have been coaxed along by Alison Mudditt. We would like to thank both Philip and Alison for their patience. We would also like to thank Caroline Richmond for her work in the later stages of the production of the book.

Laboratory of Experimental Psychology
University of Sussex
August 1993

Acknowledgements

The authors gratefully acknowledge permission from the sources listed below to reproduce the following figures:

Figure 2.2: From R. Shepard and J. Metzler, Mental rotation of three-dimensional objects. *Science*, 171 (1971), 701–3; © AAAS.

Figure 2.3: From S. M. Kosslyn, T. M. Ball and B. J. Reiser, Visual images preserve metric spatial information: evidence from studies of image scanning. *Journal of Experimental Psychology: Human Perception and Performance*, 4 (1978), 47–60; © 1978 by the American Psychological Association. Reprinted by permission.

Figure 12.1: From A. Garnham, *Artificial Intelligence: an Introduction* (London: Routledge & Kegan Paul, 1988).

Figures 16.1, 16.2: From R. S. Siegler, Information processing approaches to cognitive development. In W. Kessen, ed., *Handbook of Child Psychology*, vol. 1. Copyright © 1983 by John Wiley & Sons, Inc. Reprinted by permission.

Figure 16.3: From *Thinking, Problem Solving, Cognition* by Richard E. Mayer. Copyright © 1983 by W. H. Freeman and Company. Reprinted with permission.

Figure 16.4: From R. S. Siegler, *Children's Thinking*, 2nd edn (Englewood Cliffs, NJ: Prentice-Hall, 1991).

1

Historical Background

Of all our ploys to distinguish ourselves from the rest of the animal kingdom, perhaps the most enduring has been our identification of ourselves as *rational* animals. Our capacity for reasoning and other complex thought processes appears to set us off from other animals, and, partly for this reason, thinking and reasoning have always been regarded as crucial, if not always central, topics in empirical psychology. Perhaps because thinking is so complex a topic, widely different approaches to its study have been advocated, and very different theories have been put forward to explain it. Furthermore, more than in most areas of psychology, historical ideas remain both interesting and important. In this chapter we set out the major approaches to the study of thinking, and introduce the information processing approach that underlies much of the modern research we discuss throughout the rest of the book.

1.1 Introspectionism

The existence of experimental psychology as a discipline separate from philosophy is usually dated to the founding of a psychological institute in Leipzig by Wilhelm Wundt in 1879. Wundt's goal was to analyse consciousness into elementary sensations, and one of the methods he advocated was the method of 'pure observation' or introspection. An experimental psychologist engaged in introspection is observing his or

her own mind at work: the idea is to carry out a mental task while trying to observe the mental processes that underlie its performance. Wundt
himself was doubtful whether higher thought processes could be studied
experimentally, but his pupil Külpe believed that they could be. In 1896
Külpe founded the Würzburg School at that university, which soon became the best-known centre for psychological research after Leipzig.
This school included Marbe and Bühler, and it was known primarily
for its research on thinking.

Perhaps the best-known doctrines of the Würzburg School were that
thought is often 'imageless' and that it frequently occurs without conscious awareness. This idea, which has as a consequence that introspection
is severely limited as a tool for examining mental processes, is a commonplace within the current information processing approach. At the
time it was seen as dangerous, and as possibly undermining the existence
of experimental psychology. Wundt attacked it sharply, and Edward
Titchener, an Englishman who had studied with Wundt and subsequently founded a psychology laboratory at Cornell University in 1892,
repeated the empirical work of the Würzburgers, but claimed that images
accompanied all the kinds of thought processes that had been studied
in Würzburg. With hindsight, it is clear that both theoretical prejudices
and individual differences in styles of thought led to different reports
about whether thought could be imageless. The immediate consequence
was the attempt, mainly by North American psychologists, to find a
more objective way of studying behaviour than that proposed by introspectionists.

1.2 Behaviourism, Associationism, Neo-Behaviourism

Modern philosophy started with the French philosopher René Descartes
(1596–1650), and, for more than two centuries following Descartes,
epistemology – the theory of knowledge – was the central topic in philosophy. The most important debate at the time was about the source of
knowledge: do we learn everything we know from experience, as the
Empiricists argued, or is some knowledge present in us at birth, as the
Rationalists believed? For experimental psychology, the more important
question is about the nature of knowledge: what is it that we know
when we know something? Indeed Robert Thomson (1968: p. 89)
identifies the goal of early experimental psychology as 'to make the old

associationist-empiricist philosophy of mind into an empirical and experimental science'.

As this quote from Thomson makes clear, psychologists took their
account of knowledge from the Empiricist side of the Empiricist–
Rationalist debate. In fact, the Empiricists had discussed in greater depth
the question of what knowledge consisted in. Their thesis was that
knowledge is built up out of what they called 'ideas'. Since all knowledge is learned through experience, ideas must somehow get into
people's minds, and the principal route into minds is through the senses.
In philosophy much of the discussion centred around the distinction
between primary and secondary qualities of objects. Primary qualities
are those qualities, such as colour, that give rise to their corresponding
ideas directly. Secondary qualities give rise to ideas only indirectly.
Indeed, on one view, espoused, for example, by John Locke (the philosopher with whom this distinction is usually identified), secondary
qualities are not qualities of bodies at all. They are powers that bodies
have to produce ideas in minds. However, the distinction that is important for experimental psychology is that between simple and complex
ideas.

According to the Empiricists all the complexities of human cognition
can be explained in terms of one relation between ideas – that of association. Associations between ideas in the mind are brought about by
experience of the things that produce ideas in the mind occurring together in the world. Associations can vary in strength, depending on
how often the associated ideas occur together and how often they occur
separately, but apart from that they are all basically similar. Associations stamped in by experience reflect relations between objects in the
real world. However, the mind also has the power to create its own
associations – to rearrange and recombine the ideas it holds. So the idea
of a unicorn, which corresponds to nothing actually experienced, is
created by combining ideas that include horse, twisted and horn. What
the mind cannot do, however, is to create new simple ideas. Although
a detailed account was never presented, it was assumed by the Empiricists
that all the complexities of human thought could be explained in terms
of ideas and the associations between them.

As we have already said, early experimental psychologists had the
specific goal of converting this empiricist theory of knowledge and
philosophy of mind into an exact scientific account of human thought.
The introspectionists attempted to find, by looking into their own minds,
the basic building blocks of thought, and to observe the processes that
combined and recombined them. However, the associationist legacy
was most strongly felt in the movement that grew up, particularly in

the United States, as a reaction to the failings of introspectionism – behaviourism.

As is well known, behaviourist psychology is couched in terms of learning rather than in terms of thinking and reasoning. Part of the reason was that behaviourism arose largely from the work of Edward L. Thorndike, one of the first major figures in experimental psychology to be trained in the United States rather than in Europe. From the start, Thorndike's primary interest was in learning, and indeed much of his later work was in educational psychology, where he had a major influence on the development of intelligence testing. In his earlier work with animals, Thorndike reacted against the anthropomorphism that he detected in much writing about animal behaviour, particularly that of Darwinians. Thorndike aimed to discover more mechanistic explanations of animal behaviour.

Thorndike's best-known contribution to learning theory is the Law of Effect, which states that if an animal acts in a particular way in a given situation, and if the outcome is positive, the same action will be more likely in the same situation in the future. Conversely, if the outcome is negative the action will be less likely. Thus, the Law of Effect is a law about how situations and actions become more or less strongly associated with one another. Another aspect of Thorndike's theorizing is his claim that learning typically occurs by trial and error. The Law of Effect changes the association between situation and action, once a suitable action occurs, but faced with a problem to which it does not know the solution an animal will select actions at random until one of them has a positive outcome. Thorndike based this idea partly on experiments in which cats had to escape from 'puzzle boxes', which were designed so that arbitrary actions released a lock. Since the early part of this century, the Law of Effect has been challenged as a general account of learning. Thorndike's account of problem solving as basically a process of trial and error has also been questioned. Trial and error may be an appropriate method to tackle a totally unfamiliar problem, but most problems we encounter are not like that. Nevertheless, Thorndike's ideas have had a profound influence on subsequent work in experimental psychology.

The ideas of Thorndike, and those of Ivan Pavlov, the Russian physiologist who identified and studied the phenomenon of classical conditioning, influenced the thinking of J. B. Watson, who systematized the doctrines of behaviourism and popularized them among psychologists. Watson saw physics as the model for psychology, and thought that both experimental work and theory should focus on observable aspects of behaviour. Introspection was rejected as an experimental method, and mentalistic concepts were struck out of the vocabulary of experimental psychology. Complex thought processes were not a popular topic among behaviourists, who believed that the laws of learning were the same for all animals ('organisms', as they were usually called in behaviourist writings), and were more conveniently studied in animals. However, Watson himself made some rather bizarre observations on thinking from the behaviourist perspective. He claimed that, to study thinking, psychologists should study sub-vocalization, for example, by measuring muscle activity in the throat while people were engaged in solving problems.

Watson's behaviourism is sometimes referred to as 'naive', and many of the psychologists who were influenced by Watson's ideas developed their own, more complex, versions of behaviourist theory. While some, notably B. F. Skinner, rigorously eschewed unobservables in their theories, others, in particular Clark Hull and Edward Tolman, advocated the inclusion of variables intervening between stimulus and response in their accounts of learning. The views of Hull and Tolman were opposed in many ways. Nevertheless, both held that behaviour is *mediated*. The idea of mediation was developed in the mediation hypothesis of Charles Osgood, who attempted to reconcile the ideas of Hull and Tolman and to introduce some aspects of Gestalt psychology (see §3 below) into behaviourist theory. Osgood conceived external stimuli (in the world) as producing not behavioural responses, but mediating responses within the animal. These mediating responses then produce mediating stimuli, which may produce overt responses, or further mediating responses, resulting in an internal chain of such responses.

Such mediational learning theories can be combined with Hull's idea of a *habit-family hierarchy* to produce a behaviourist account of problem solving. In problem solving (or learning), the animal's natural response is, by definition, the wrong one. Otherwise it would have nothing to learn or no problem to solve. The animal will, however, have various responses available to it – a family of habits it can fall back on. These responses will have different strengths of association, and hence will form a hierarchy. In order to learn, an animal must reorder the strengths of the associations. In simple (S-R) learning theory, the animal will have available a number of overt responses. However, in a mediational theory, any particular stimulus may be associated with several mediational responses, arranged in a habit-family hierarchy. The rearrangement of the habit-family hierarchy at each point in the chain corresponds to thinking in such theories.

In the study of cognitive functions, particularly in humans, behaviourist theories were replaced by cognitive (information processing) theories in the late 1950s and early 1960s. These theories will be discussed in more detail later in this chapter. For the moment, we will simply point out a crucial contrast between cognitive theories and behaviourist theories. Obviously cognitive theories differ from theories of the kind favoured by Skinner and his followers, which eschew mental notions, including the intervening variables postulated by Hull and Tolman. However, cognitive theories also differ from mediational theories. Mediational theories retain the basic associationist assumption that internal representations of aspects of the world (ideas in traditional associationist philosophy; stimuli, responses and reinforcers in learning theory) are related to one another via associations. Cognitive theories postulate a richer structure for the human mind, one in which not all relations are associations, and in which there are many constraints on the form that knowledge can take. As Fodor and Pylyshyn (1988: p. 48) point out, if one relation between bits of (mentally stored) information holds, others automatically will.

> You don't . . . get minds that are prepared to infer *John went to the store* from *John and Mary and Susan and Sally went to the store* and from *John and Mary went to the store* but not from *John and Mary and Susan went to the store.*

On an associationist account there is no reason why you should not.

It is on these grounds that Fodor and Pylyshyn criticize connectionist or parallel distributed processing (PDP) accounts of higher mental processes. Some proponents of PDP have suggested that it provides a new approach to modelling mental processes – one that can, and should, replace the cognitive approaches of the last twenty years. Fodor and Pylyshyn point out that the limitations of connectionism are just those of associationism, and that connectionist models, in their current form, cannot provide a satisfactory account of mental abilities that depend on highly structured representations – the ability to use language, for example, or the ability to solve problems.

PDP models may change in the future, so that they are less wedded to associationist assumptions. They may also be hybridized with more traditional symbolic models, as they already have been to some extent by researchers who want the best of both worlds. There will, therefore, be some discussion of PDP models, and models with PDP components, in this book, though there are still comparatively few PDP models of complex thought processes. Here, we will give a brief account of the principal assumptions underlying connectionism.

PDP models are constructed from simple units – often very many of them – with properties, at an abstract level, like those of brain cells or groups of brain cells. They resemble such cells in that each unit receives excitatory and inhibitory inputs from other units, combines them according to a fixed rule, and then passes its excitation or inhibition on to other units, weighted according to the strength of the connections between them. The units are arranged in layers. One layer encodes inputs, which must be translated into patterns of excitation and inhibition in the input units (just as sensory inputs are encoded in transducer cells, such as the rods and cones in the retina). In many models, inputs are 'hand coded' but, in principle, the pattern of excitation in the input layer could be produced directly by external stimulation, as it is in the retina. Another layer of units is the output layer, in which the pattern of excitation represents the output. This layer may comprise a single unit, which represents a 'yes' response when excited and a 'no' response when inhibited, or it could be more complicated. Between the input and the output layer there may optionally be one or more other layers, which are usually referred to as *hidden layers*. Hidden layers allow for complexities in the transformation of the input into the output. The strengths of connections between the units encode the knowledge stored in a PDP system. Such a system can learn to perform new tasks by altering those strengths. The most important method of learning in PDP networks is *back propagation*, in which the difference between the actual output of the system and the intended output (which must be provided) is used to adjust the connections.

PDP models differ considerably from the cognitive models that are common in many branches of psychology. (Traditional models are often referred to *symbolic*, in contrast to PDP models, which are *subsymbolic*.) Nevertheless, it can be proved that any traditional symbolic model will work on a PDP network. One way of thinking about what this proof means is the following. A working version of a symbolic model can be made to run on a computer by writing a program in one of the traditional programming languages used in artificial intelligence (AI) research (LISP, POP11 or PROLOG, for example). Such programs are frequently written by AI researchers. What the proof says is that if, instead of an ordinary computer, one had a 'connectionist machine' – a computer made up of many PDP-style units working in parallel, rather than a few complex units all governed by one serial central processing unit (as in a normal computer) – one would still be able to write programs that embodied symbolic models, and run them on that machine.

This result is important, because by design connectionist machines share properties with the human brain. So although the brain is different from the kind of computer on which cognitive models are typically programmed, those cognitive models could be embodied in the human brain. But if the brain is, roughly speaking, a connectionist machine, and if connectionist machines can support cognitive models of higher mental processes, what are Fodor and Pylyshyn arguing about? To understand what they dislike, it is necessary to distinguish between two ways that connectionism could be related to cognitive psychology. The one we have focused on so far is the idea that the brain is a connectionist machine and that, therefore, whatever the right account of human thought, it must be compatible with the highly parallel architecture of the brain. Fortunately, as we have seen, although cognitive models look as though they are designed to run on a different kind of system (a serial computer), they will also run on a connectionist machine. A different claim is that *theories* about, say, thinking and reasoning, should be constructed using PDP concepts. Of course, if a theory is constructed using connectionist concepts, it will be compatible with the architecture of the brain, but the kinds of concept available for theory construction will be different from those available to cognitive modellers in the symbolic tradition. Indeed, since connectionist theories are associationist in nature, as theories of higher cognitive functions they suffer from the same problems as behaviourist accounts. The single relation of association is not capable of describing the rich structure of human thought.

1.3   Gestalt Psychology

Associationism regards all thoughts as built out of simple ideas, related to one another via associations of varying strength. Wundt specifically identified one of the tasks of experimental psychology as the empirical analysis of the contents of the mind into its building blocks. We have also seen that behaviourism is closely related to associationism. However, not all psychologists accepted that mental functioning can be studied satisfactorily by finding and describing the building blocks of thought. Thinkers as diverse as Külpe, William James and Lloyd Morgan had already suggested that complex mental contents had properties that could not be deduced from their components – that wholes were more than the sum of their parts, and that their properties could not be discovered by the kind of analysis that Wundt had proposed. This doctrine became one of the central tenets of the Gestalt school of psychology, which flourished in Central Europe from about 1910 until the 1930s, when many of its members, being Jewish, were forced to flee Europe and settle in the United States. There the school, as such, disappeared, though many of its ideas and empirical findings remain influential today.

Gestalt psychology focused on two topics: perception and thinking. It regarded Gestalts, or directly perceived groupings of elements, as crucial in both. Much of the theoretical work within the Gestalt school was directed to the discovery of laws of good form, which determined how readily a Gestalt was perceived. The formulation of many of these laws is vague and depends, in some cases, on incorrect assumptions about the workings of the brain. Furthermore, the mere formulation of laws does not necessarily explain the phenomena that the law describes. Nevertheless, some of the more specific ideas of Gestalt psychology remain useful in describing how people solve complex problems.

One set of ideas relates to why people often fail to solve problems that they ought to be able to solve. Duncker (1935) introduced the idea of *functional fixity* as one factor that can prevent a person from seeing a solution to a problem. Functional fixity occurs when an object needed to solve a problem is perceived as having a different use from the one to which it must be put to solve the problem. The problem solver becomes fixed on its previous use, and is unable to consider using it in the way required to solve the problem. To give a concrete example, one problem that Duncker set his subjects was to fix a candle to a door so that it could be lit. The intended solution was to fix a small box to the door with a drawing pin and to stand the candle in the box. This problem was more difficult to solve if the box was used as a container for the candle and drawing pins. The subjects saw its function as being fixed as a container, and failed to think of it as part of the solution to the problem. If the box was presented separately, not as a container, the problem was easier to solve.

A related idea is *set*, in which people come to think that problems of a certain kind should be solved in a certain way. This may lead them to fail to solve a superficially similar problem which requires a different method of solution. A more benign effect of set can be illustrated in so-called jugs problems, in which the subject has to discover how to measure out a given amount of water with jugs of various sizes. Consider the problem of how to measure 5 units, given jugs of 18 units (A), 43 units (B) and 10 units (C) together with a supply of water. The solution, to fill jug B, then to pour out 18 units into A and 10 units into C twice, can be represented as B − A − 2C. Luchins (1942) gave subjects a series of jugs problems to which the answer was of this form; then he asked them how to measure 25 units from jugs of 28 units (A), 76 units (B) and 3 units (C). Many people gave the B − A − 2C solution, following the established pattern (set), which works, but which is more complex than the solution A – C. The idea of set was generalized by the Gestalt psychologists, under its German name of *Einstellung*, to describe a more general carry-over effect from one piece of thinking to another. It is, of course, often useful to tackle new problems in ways that have previously proved successful, but Einstellung effects are likely to be deleterious when searching for novel solutions, or when solving problems that are fundamentally different from ones that have been encountered before.

The Gestalt psychologists regarded functional fixity, set and Einstellung effects in general as hindrances to problem solving. The positive ideas from the Gestalt School that still retain some importance come mainly from Max Wertheimer's posthumously published *Productive Thinking* (1945). Wertheimer contrasted productive thinking with reproductive thinking. Productive thinking brings about a recognition of the relations between the problem's elements – the Gestalt that they form – and the restructuring of those elements into a new Gestalt, in which the problem is solved. Restructuring is aided by a tendency to *pregnance* (or good Gestalt), and if it is successful it can lead to a flash of insight as the new Gestalt is grasped. Reproductive thinking, on the other hand, is based on the repetition of learned responses to individual problem elements, and a failure to take account of the Gestalt that they form.

The ideas of Gestalt psychology continue to be important not only in the field of thinking and reasoning, but also in visual perception, the other main area of Gestalt work. For example, some of the Gestalt laws of grouping of perceptual elements are reflected in the general principles of David Marr's (1982) account of visual perception.

1.4   Psychometrics

Modern approaches to thinking and reasoning focus primarily on the mental representations and processes that underlie our ability to think, and the limitations on it. However, for much of this century, a different approach – the psychometric approach – was more prominent. Psychometrics, which means measurement of the mind, is intimately connected with mental testing. Psychometric tests, of which IQ tests are a particularly important example, produce scores that are interpreted as measures of mental characteristics. So, although IQ tests provide directly a measure only of how good people are at solving problems of certain kinds under test conditions, they have, albeit controversially, been taken to measure a more fundamental mental ability. What they do not provide, and what they are not intended to provide, is an account of the processes by which people solve those problems.

Psychometrics is interestingly poised between theoretical and applied psychology. Much of the impetus for mental testing came from a desire to select people, for jobs or educational opportunities, in an objective way. In Britain, for example, Cyril Burt used IQ testing to identify children from disadvantaged backgrounds who might benefit from a more academic 'grammar school' education. And, in both world wars, mental testing was used in personnel selection to identify the most appropriate people for difficult jobs: fighter pilots in the Second World War, for example. Indeed, the importance of mental testing can be attributed largely to its perceived success in personnel selection for the United States armed forces in the First World War.

A good test for selecting fighter pilots is one that gives higher scores to people who actually turn out to be better pilots. Such a test, with a specific objective, is comparatively easy to *validate*. Validation of IQ tests is harder, since criteria for determining intelligence that are both objective and independent of IQ tests are difficult to find. For children, subsequent scholastic achievement provided an imperfect criterion, but for adults no obvious criterion suggested itself. This problem led to the idea that the tests themselves might provide the only useful insights into the nature of intelligence. On the basis of this somewhat unsatisfactory proposal an attempt was made to discover the structure of human mental abilities from an analysis of the results of psychometric testing. One of the major controversies was whether intelligence had a central component (*g*, for general intelligence) that helped people to solve all the kinds of problem that are found in IQ tests, as originally suggested by Spearman, or whether there were, for example, separate abilities to solve the spatial problems and the verbal ones, as Thurstone had proposed. The technique used to answer such questions is a complex development of correlational techniques, called factor analysis. If the ability to answer the spatial questions on IQ tests and the ability to answer the verbal ones arise from a general ability, there should be a high positive correlation between scores on the spatial items and scores on the verbal items. As with any psychological data, scores on IQ tests vary for reasons that the investigator cannot control. Factor analysis, therefore, examines a large range of correlation coefficients and tries to find a small number of factors that can account for the scores of many subjects on many test items. There are several variants of factor analysis, and some are more likely to find a single predominant factor (general intelligence, in the analysis of IQ tests) whereas others are more likely to find sets of independent abilities (verbal IQ and visuo-spatial IQ). The is no simple way of deciding which factoring is best.

Psychometrics is not concerned solely with IQ tests. Tests of 'personality' are also popular. In Britain the best known is the Eysenck Personality Inventory (EPI), in the United States, the Minnesota Multiphasic Personality Inventory (MMPI). Most of these tests are not directly relevant to the study of thinking and reasoning, though there are some that attempt to identify people with different thinking styles. From our point of view, the most interesting of these tests are those that attempt to measure a person's capacity for divergent or creative thinking, as distinct from IQ. These tests, which will be discussed further in chapter 13, have not been wholly successful. Either their scores have been highly correlated with IQ scores for the same people, or they do not correlate with any independently measurable ability.

In recent years some theorists, notably Sternberg (1985), have tried to combine ideas from the psychometric and cognitive approaches to intelligence. Sternberg takes from the psychometric approach the idea that intelligence might be broken down into separate abilities (corresponding to the factors of Thurstone, Guilford and others), and also a preoccupation with the explanation of differences between individuals. However, the kinds of theories he favours are cognitive in nature, and they focus on the mental processes that underlie intelligent behaviour.

1.5   The Information Processing Approach

The advent of digital computers and information theory in the late 1940s led, in a matter of years, to a new way of thinking about mental processes – the information processing approach. The computational metaphor for the mind is not the first mechanical metaphor for it. One of its predecessors was the idea that the mind is like a telephone exchange. However, the computer metaphor may be different. Certain abstruse results in higher mathematics suggest that it is the most general mechanical metaphor of all, and that any mechanical device can be described in computational terms.

Shannon's (1948) concept of information was a specific one that quantified the notion of a reduction of uncertainty. The characterization of a computer, and hence of the human mind, as an information processing device is more general. The idea, at least in traditional rather than connectionist models, is that the mind is what Newell (1980) calls a *physical symbol system*. Its contents are symbolic in nature – they hold information about something outside the mind, which they stand for (or represent). When reasoning and other mental processes take place, the mind performs transformations on the symbols. The term *physical* in the phrase 'physical symbol system' is used to contrast the mind with other kinds of symbol systems, for example those used in certain kinds of art.

In an information processing model of a mental process, mental contents take the form of structured sets of symbols, and operations on those contents are structural operations on those symbols. High-level computer programming languages are, therefore, particularly suitable for formulating and implementing information processing models. All such languages allow logical operations, such as negation ('not'), conjunction ('and') and disjunction ('or'), to be performed on sets of symbols. In addition, the list processing languages of AI, which were specifically developed by Newell for formulating information processing models, allow symbols to be represented in a convenient list structure format. As we will see in chapter 4, logic is used to analyse arguments, and it has often been proposed (for example, by George Boole, 1854, almost a century before electronic computers were invented) that human thought can be modelled using these logical operations. On this view, the operations on symbols that can be performed in high-level programming languages correspond directly to the mental operations that comprise thinking.

In AI, the idea that the laws of thought corresponded to the laws of logic was quickly rejected in the work of Newell, Shaw and Simon (1957). Nevertheless, their alternative suggestion, that thinking depends on heuristic, rule-of-thumb methods of problem solving, remained firmly within the information processing tradition. It has continued to be one of the major influences on models of problem solving. In psychology, Miller, Galanter and Pribram's (1960) book *Plans and the Structure of Behavior* was particularly important. Miller et al. conceived of mental functioning as carried out by a hierarchy of TOTE (test, operate, test, exit) loops. Such a loop tests to see if it needs to do any work; if it does it performs the required operation, after which it retests, and then exits if all is satisfactory. Since the loops are organized in a hierarchy, exiting from one loop will usually mean stepping back into the main body of a loop at a higher level.

The effects of the cognitive revolution have been all-pervasive in human experimental psychology, and most of the work we will describe in the rest of this book falls in the information processing tradition. Nevertheless, even within that tradition, there are widely different opinions about what kind of (cognitive) model best characterizes human thought. Perhaps the major disagreement is about the nature of the processes that manipulate the symbols encoding mental contents. In chapter 4 we will introduce the distinction between proof-theoretic and model-theoretic approaches to logic. In the proof-theoretic approach one piece of information is transformed into another by applying formal rules – formal in the sense that their application depends only on the form of the information to which they are applied. On one view human thought proceeds in this way. More specifically, the mental operations postulated on this view correspond directly to the inference rules of a standard logical system. The best-known example of such a rule is *modus ponens*, which says that, whatever P and Q may be, if you know that P and you know that P implies Q then you can deduce that Q. According to the proof-theoretic view, a person represents, for example, a problem situation in their mind, and then applies formal rules, such as modus ponens, to the representation to try to produce a solution to the problem.

In the model-theoretic approach, arguments are assessed according to a basic semantic principle, which states that a conclusion is valid if it is true whenever the premises from which it is drawn are true. There are rules, indeed rules that can be implemented in a computer program, for establishing whether a conclusion is valid, but they are different from the rules needed for a proof-theoretic solution to the same problem. Nevertheless, for simple logics, the model-theoretic and the proof-theoretic approaches are, in a deeper sense, equivalent – anything that one approach shows to be a valid argument will be shown to be valid by the other. A view of human reasoning that is closely related to this model-theoretic approach is embodied in the theory of *mental models* (Johnson-Laird, 1983). This theory focuses on the way mental representations are interpreted as models of part of the real world or an imaginary one. It claims that people work out what follows from information represented in their minds by using information about the meaning of the representation. The mental models theory has been developed within the information processing framework, and it is hard to see how things could have been otherwise. Nevertheless, the approach has many antecedents, in particular Wittgenstein's (1922) picture theory of meaning, Barlett's (1932) early work on schemata, and Craik's (1943) idea that thinking depends on internal models of parts of the world.

Although we will consider both proof-theoretic and model-theoretic approaches in this book, we will tend to favour the second, particularly as an account of everyday thinking. It is consistent with three facts about human thought that will recur throughout the book:

1   People prefer to reason about concrete situations. They find abstract reasoning (including logic and mathematics) more difficult.
2   Because reasoning requires the interpretation – often the rich interpretation – of mental contents, information stored in long-term memory plays a crucial role in human thought. Problems are easier

to solve if we can relate them to what we already know, partly because we may have solved similar problems before.

3 Thinking becomes difficult when we have to develop alternative models from the same (under-specified) pieces of information. We prefer to reason from a single model, presumably because of limitations on the capacity of short-term stores that are used to manipulate mental models.

In the rest of this book we shall see how these three ideas – the preference for concrete reasoning, the importance of content (because of relations with what we already know) and the difficulties posed by multiple possibilities – apply to specific domains of human thought.

1.6 Methods of Studying Thinking

In our historical overview we mentioned several ways thinking and reasoning can be studied. Within the information processing approach on which we will be focusing, the primary research tool is the controlled experiment. Cognitive psychology has sometimes been criticized for being 'paradigm driven' – for allowing the availability of neat experimental techniques to drive the choice of research topics. The implication of this criticism is that experiments ought, rather, to test critical predictions from theories, since it is theories, and their truth or falsity, with which scientists are primarily concerned. This criticism is to some extent justified, but it is less valid now than it was twenty years ago. Although it is possible to cite instances of paradigm-driven research, throughout this book we will present many experiments testing specific predictions that distinguish between different theories of thinking and reasoning.

In our discussion of the origins of behaviourism, we saw how and why the introspective method of studying thinking fell into disrepute. Nevertheless, a related technique known as *protocol analysis* has been widely used by some proponents of the information processing approach. Protocols are usually collected as part of an experimental study, in which subjects are asked to 'think aloud' as they engage in, say, problem solving. Analysed protocols can provide useful experimental data, whatever assumptions one makes about their relation to thought processes. Indeed, there is no single agreed account of how what people say relates to what is going on in their minds. Nevertheless, Ericsson and Simon's (1980, 1984) account has been particularly influential. According to Ericsson and Simon, what a subject reports when thinking aloud reflects what is happening in short-term working memory at the time the report is made. This idea is linked to Newell and Simon's (1972) theory of thinking and reasoning based on production systems. On this account, thinking is modelled using productions, which are 'if . . . then' rules stating that *if* certain conditions are satisfied *then* certain (mental) actions are to be performed. When a production's conditions are satisfied, it is transferred to working memory and, hence, into consciousness. So, according to Ericsson and Simon, a protocol provides information about the problem-solving rules that subjects are currently using.

In addition to these experimental techniques with human subjects, computer programming can help us to understand thinking and reasoning, in three main ways. First, research in artificial intelligence attempts to produce machines that behave intelligently, though not necessarily by mimicking human intelligence. There may, indeed, be an attempt to surpass it. Nevertheless, a general understanding of intelligent processes is useful in understanding the nature, and perhaps the limitations, of human reasoning. Second, often within artificial intelligence, there can be a deliberate attempt to create programs that model human thinking. Such research is sometimes dubbed 'the computer simulation of behaviour'. Much of the work by Allen Newell, Herbert Simon and their colleagues, referred to at various points in this book, comes under this head. For example, what is generally regarded as the first AI program, Newell, Shaw and Simon's (1957) Logic Theory Machine – the one that led to the idea of rule-of-thumb methods of reasoning – is an attempt to simulate human problem solving. Third, and more rarely, theories about human thinking and reasoning may be expressed in the form of computer programs, so that their consequences can be more readily discerned.

Experimental research and computer modelling are the main ways in which thinking and reasoning have been studied. However, they should not be thought of as exhausting the possibilities. Indeed, we will give examples of other methods at various places in this book. For example, in chapter 8 we will discuss the (auto)biographical approach to the study of creative thinking, in which accounts of the work of creative artists and scientists, either biographical or autobiographical, are used as a source of data for the construction and testing of theories about creativity.

Summary and Outline of the Book

The nature and complexity of our thought processes, if not the mere ability to think, appear to set people apart from other animals. For this reason, the psychology of thinking and reasoning assumes an important place within psychology as a whole. In its comparatively short history, empirical psychology has seen several major schools of thought that have made important contributions to the study of thinking and reasoning. The early introspectionists thought psychologists could determine the workings of their own minds by observing them in action. This line of research degenerated into a sterile debate about the possibility of imageless thought. More recently psychologists have started to collect other people's comments on their thought processes as data.

Behaviourism arose in part as a reaction to the futility of debates about introspective data. It combined an emphasis on observable behaviour, particularly by animals learning to perform tasks, with the idea, taken from empiricist philosophy, that learning is the formation of associations between ideas. Some forms of behaviourism countenanced only associations between stimuli and responses, but others allowed for a complex process of mediation between stimulus and response. Modern parallel distributed processing (PDP) models of learning inherit the associationist assumptions of behaviourism.

Behaviorism flourished primarily in the United States. In Germany, at least before the upheavals of the 1930s, introspectionism was replaced by Gestalt psychology. Gestalt psychology emphasized the importance of patterns, and of finding new patterns. However, it failed to produce a convincing account of how such patterns were discerned. Nevertheless, the Gestalt notions of functional fixity, set and Einstellung remain important, if still unexplained, aspects of thinking and reasoning.

Psychometrics represents a tradition separate from either behaviourism or Gestalt psychology. It was, nevertheless, greatly concerned with questions about thinking and reasoning and, in particular, with the explanation of abilities in terms of notions such as IQ. Psychometrics pays little attention to the representations and processes needed for thinking and reasoning. However, it is not incompatible with the search for such representations and processes, and there have recently been attempts to combine psychometric and mainstream cognitive approaches to thinking and reasoning.

These latter approaches are based on the notions of information processing and physical symbol systems. They developed from work in artificial intelligence and are based on the analogy between minds and computer programs. Indeed, computer programs may be constructed as models that embody particular theories of how people think and reason. However, such theories must also be tested using experimental and other empirical techniques.

The rest of the book is organized as follows. Chapter 2 discusses two sets of building blocks of thought: concepts and images, and chapter 3 considers the vexed question of the relation between language and thought. Logic, an attempt to formalize valid arguments, is described in chapter 4, and the following chapters (5 and 6) deal with psychological research on deductive reasoning. Chapter 7 looks at induction, and chapter 8 considers the related topic of hypothesis testing. Statistical reasoning and decision making are analysed in chapters 9 and 10, and in chapters 11 and 12 we consider problem solving and expertise. In chapter 13 we ask how creative thinking differs from ordinary thinking. Chapter 14 is devoted to the study of thinking in everyday life, and chapter 15 to the question of whether thinking skills can usefully be taught. Chapters 16 and 17 discuss the development of thinking. Finally, in chapter 18 we outline a framework for thinking about thinking.

Further Reading

Sternberg, R. J. (1990). *Metaphors of Mind: Conceptions of the Nature of Intelligence*. Cambridge: Cambridge University Press.
Watson, J. B. (1925). *Behaviorism*. New York: Norton.
Wertheimer, M. (1945). *Productive Thinking*. New York: Harper & Row.

2

The Building Blocks of Thought

2.1 Concepts and Categorization

In one of psychology's best-known aphorisms, William James described the young child's world as a 'blooming buzzing confusion'. Although James's ideas about children are no longer regarded as correct, the point he was making is that we cannot make sense of the world unless we can *impose* order on our perceptual experiences. James assumed that young children have not learned to impose order on what they perceive – hence the confusion. Modern experiments have shown that even neonates have a more structured world than James imagined.

James's claim was based on the fact that what a person sees at any moment, to focus on the most important sense for human beings, is never exactly the same as what he or she, or anyone else, has seen before. Yet we relate our perceptual experiences to one another by recognizing the recurrence of both individual people and things, and of types of people and objects, as well as of types of events, states and process. In other words, we *categorize* our perceptual experiences into, for example, experiences of (photographs of) William James, of American psychologists, of chairs, of sleeping.

The major problem that would be caused by James's 'blooming buzzing confusion' would be the inability to act consistently. If people could not recognize recurring patterns in their experience, they could not react in a consistent way to things that it makes sense to act consistently to. We can be sure, therefore, that the perceptual world of adult animals, at least, is not a 'blooming buzzing confusion'. If a zebra did not respond in a similar way to all the lions it encountered, it would not live very long. Animals categorize, if only implicitly.

Although many animals can make discriminations that people cannot make, there is a sense in which human categorization is more complex than that of animals. This complexity arises from the link between categorization and language. Concepts allow categorization, and human language allows us to give names to concepts, to express relations between them, and to construct more complex concepts out of simpler ones: many concepts do not have a single word associated with them, though many do. 'American psychologist' is a perfectly good concept, even though it must be expressed in two words in English. Whether a particular concept is *lexicalized* varies from one language to another.

2.1.1   Philosophical problems about categorization

Our ability to categorize and form concepts poses many philosophical questions. A psychology textbook is not the place to discuss these questions in detail, but we will mention the most important ones. We will not, of course, provide definitive answers to them: they are still the subject of intense philosophical debate. The most general of these questions is whether the categories embodied in our conceptual schemes reflect structure in the world that is independent of people's ability to form concepts. *Realists* believe that the structure in the world is independent of human conceptual abilities, whereas *anti-realists* or *constructivists* find the realist claim inconsistent, at least in part because there is no way it can be made without using concepts from a human conceptual scheme.

The second question is about the most general categories, which reflect the kinds of thing we see the world as being made up of – our *ontology* to use the technical philosophical term. For example, virtually all philosophers believe that objects are one of the basic categories in our ontology. But there is disagreement about whether events are basic in the same sense, or whether events should be regarded as being made up of objects and relations between them.

The third philosophical question is the analytic one: what *is* a concept? This question has a direct counterpart in cognitive science: how is our conceptual knowledge mentally represented? A popular answer to the philosophical question – one that appeals to formalists – is that a concept is a set of *necessary and sufficient conditions* for membership of the category to which the concept corresponds, with each condition being individually necessary for membership, and the whole set jointly sufficient. So, for example, the concept of a triangle might be analysed as that of a three-sided plane figure. If something is a triangle it must be a plane figure and it must be three-sided – each of those conditions is *necessary* for trianglehood. Furthermore, anything that has both those properties will automatically be a triangle – they are *sufficient* for trianglehood as well. For some concepts with straightforward definitions, such mathematics concepts, kinship concepts and some legal concepts, the notion of a set of necessary and sufficient conditions for class membership is quite appealing. However, when the idea is applied to everyday concepts, it works less well. Although philosophers of a formal bent assumed for many years that such concepts could be defined by sets of necessary and sufficient conditions, they made no attempt to demonstrate that fact by producing such definitions. Dictionary definitions take a wide variety of forms – very few comprise sets of necessary and sufficient conditions. Within philosophy, the strongest challenge to the formalists' assumption came from the later work of Ludwig Wittgenstein (see especially *Philosophical Investigations*, 1953), who pointed out that everyday concepts have a looser structure than that suggested by the model of necessary and sufficient conditions. The members of a category are often related to one another by overlapping sets of features, rather than by any set of features they have in common. To use an analogy introduced by Wittgenstein, they bear *family resemblances* to one another. Wittgenstein illustrated this idea in his discussion of the concept of a *game*, and it is worth thinking about exemplars of a concept of this kind in order to convince oneself that the notion of necessary and sufficient conditions does not work. If you need help, look at *Philosophical Investigations*, Part 1, section 66.

Johnson-Laird (1993, chapter 2) groups concepts such as game with concepts such as chair and table, as they correspond to different types of *artefact*. He claims that such concepts 'have no objective correlates in the physical world' and that they 'depend on mental constructs that are imposed upon the world by their use in the design of artefacts' (1993: p. 95). For such concepts, the anti-realist account is most plausible.

A further problem for the idea of necessary and sufficient conditions for category membership is posed by a third major class of concepts identified by Johnson-Laird (1993), those, for example, that correspond to species of animal. Animal concepts are an example of a type of concept known as a *natural kind*. Natural kinds are types of things that naturally occur in the world – animals, plants, minerals. The philosophers Saul Kripke (1972) and Hilary Putnam (1975) have worked extensively on the meaning of natural-kind terms. Putnam, in particular, has come to some rather surprising conclusions. For example, he made a claim that he formulated in the provocative phrase 'meanings ain't in the mind'.

Putnam's analysis of what people know about natural kinds makes use of the concept of a *stereotype*, which is closely related to that of a prototype (see §2.1.2.b below), but far removed from that of a set of necessary and sufficient conditions for category membership. Putnam argued that a person's idea of, say, a lemon is embodied in a description of a stereotypical lemon. Stereotypical members of natural kinds share many properties. This fact is sometimes expressed by saying that natural-kind concepts have a highly correlated structure – most of the stereotypical properties of the exemplars of a natural kind go together most of the time. So, stereotypes are in the mind, but, according to Putnam, they don't represent the meaning of natural-kind terms. So, how should the meaning of natural-kind terms be characterized? Putnam and Kripke argue that there are core properties of, for example, lemons that made them lemons (biological properties – the genetic make-up of lemons according to current scientific thinking – that are not part of the stereotype). These properties must be discovered by scientists, though scientists can never be sure they have correctly identified them. What we mean by 'lemons' is all the things that have the same core properties as those things that were originally called lemons, whatever those properties might be. That original dubbing lies at the beginning of a *causal chain* that links through to our current use of the term 'lemon', and that justifies it. However, it is not necessary to accept this causal theory of the meaning of natural-kind terms to recognize, as Johnson-Laird (1993) points out, that concepts corresponding to natural kinds are dependent upon scientific theories of the world (and their precursors in our everyday theories).

Another crucial aspect of Putnam's theory is his idea of the *division of linguistic labour*. Putnam points out that his own stereotypes of a beech and a larch are so impoverished that he cannot identify the two kinds of tree – a position that many people find themselves in. However, he knows that there are experts who can tell the difference, and that justifies his belief that the two concepts are different. Thus, the difference in the mental representation of the two concepts lies not in specific information about what the two types of tree look like – Putnam knows nothing more than that they are trees. The concepts are distinguished for Putnam merely by the fact that he knows that someone else knows that beeches and larches differ and, hence, that they have different core properties.

2.1.2   Psychological theories of categorization

2.1.2.a   Network and feature models

As we mentioned earlier, the guiding question in psychological work on concepts and categorization is: how are concepts mentally represented? This question began to attract attention in the late 1960s (though see, e.g., Smoke, 1932, for some important earlier work). At that time, two kinds of theory were proposed – network-based theories and feature-based theories. These theories were referred to as theories of semantic memory, since our knowledge about the meaning of words is one of the things that is supposed to be held in that memory store. Network theories were based on work in artificial intelligence research by Ross Quillian (1968), and imported into psychology in his collaboration with Allan Collins (e.g., Collins and Quillian, 1969, 1972). According to network models, each concept is represented by an unanalysed node, and relations between concepts are represented by the links that bind the nodes into a network. Meaning is determined by the overall place of a node in the network. The most important aspect of network representations is their ability to represent in an appealing way the taxonomic relations that hold among object concepts (that dogs, cats, horses, cows, zebras and so on are types of animal and that labradors, alsatians, cocker spaniels and bull terriers are types of dog). These relations are represented by ISA links – the ISA link between the dog node and the animal node, for example, represents the fact that dogs are a subset of animals. Collins and Quillian also proposed that ISA hierarchies could be used to store information economically. If the property of barking is represented at the 'dog' level in the hierarchy (linked to the dog node by a HASPROP link), it need not be represented for each kind of dog, since that property can be inherited by concepts, such as labrador, that are below it in the hierarchy – hence the name *inheritance hierarchy*. Figure 2.1 shows a semantic network encoding some of the relations we have just been discussing.

Feature models (e.g., Schaeffer and Wallace, 1969; Smith, Shoben and Rips, 1974) represent taxonomic information in a different way. They are based on the idea that the meaning of a word can be represented as a collection of features, drawn from a set that are used repeatedly to specify the meaning of different words. Features are usually bivalent – something either has the feature or it does not. So, a feature such as +/−ANIMATE distinguishes between the meaning of words that name animate objects (+ANIMATE) and those that name inanimate ones

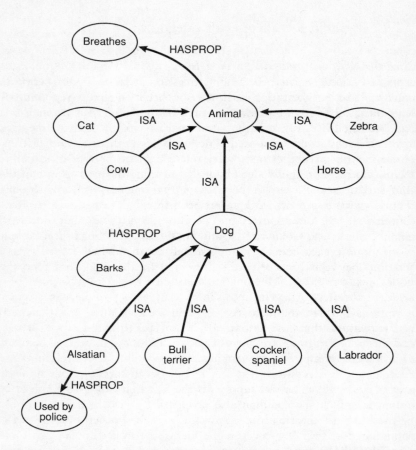

Figure 2.1   Part of a semantic network showing relations between animal concepts: ISA links represent subclass relations; HASPROP links represent property relations. The representation of properties in this network illustrates the principle of cognitive economy

(−ANIMATE). In this scheme, specific concepts, or the words corresponding to them, have more features than general ones − a labrador has all the features of dogs and some others specific to labradors. So, taxonomic relations are represented implicitly in the relations between the sets of features that correspond to the concepts.

These early models generated a substantial amount of research, but much of it is only of historical interest. Formally, the two models are equivalent (Hollan, 1975), and both are closely related to the philosophical idea of sets of necessary and sufficient conditions (most clearly so in the case of feature theories). Both also focused on concepts expressed by concrete nouns, a limitation shared by other psychological theories of categorization. In particular, neither dealt directly with relational concepts, expressed primarily by verbs, that are crucial in linking concepts together to form thoughts, though networks that encode the meaning of sentences can readily accommodate such relations (see Garnham, 1985: pp. 141–5). Processing models based on network and feature theories might well lead to different predictions (Rips, Smith and Shoben, 1975). However, this possibility rapidly became irrelevant, in the early to mid-1970s, as interest rapidly shifted to an issue that had not been considered in the early research, *typicality*. In an average Westerner's conceptual scheme, a robin is a more typical bird than a penguin or an ostrich. Yet this fact has no place in either the network or the feature models. Neither can the idea of necessary and sufficient conditions explain it – if an object satisfies the conditions, it is a member of the category, and that is all there is to it.

2.1.2.b Prototype theories

It was quickly demonstrated, largely by Eleanor Rosch, that typicality had profound effects on a wide variety of judgements about concepts and their exemplars. Network and feature theories were quickly adapted to accommodate the basic typicality effects (Collins and Loftus, 1975; Smith et al., 1974; Glass and Holyoak, 1975). However, typicality raised a host of questions about the mental representation of concepts that became apparent only over a period of years.

Rosch's own account of typicality effects was based on the imprecisely defined notion of a *prototype*, or most typical example of a category. The most obvious ambiguity in this term is whether it refers to a real example – (North American) robin for the category of bird, as determined by the ratings of North American students – or an imaginary bird that is even more typical than a robin – one that takes the most typical value on every feature a bird can have. Another serious problem is exactly how the prototype theory claims the meaning of words is mentally represented. If the representation of the category of birds is organized around a prototype that bears a close resemblance to a robin, how do we make the judgement that an ostrich is a bird, or a sparrow for that matter? In fact, this problem is soluble, and later versions of prototype theory have indicated how it might be solved (see Smith and Medin, 1981). In these theories there is a subtle shift of perspective – the question becomes: how do we decide which of two (or more) categories an object belongs to? If the prototypical exemplars of the two concepts can be characterized using similar measures – for example, size and colour, among other things, for animals – any particular animal can be classified as more similar to the prototypical horse than the proto-typical zebra, or vice versa, and hence assigned to one category or the other, if appropriate. There is an obvious link between Putnam's idea that mental representations are based on stereotypes (see §2.1.1 above) and the idea that category membership might be based on some kind of similarity judgement. Since ordinary people do not know the core prop-erties of, say, lemons, they cannot judge whether something is a lemon by checking whether it has the core properties of a lemon, but they can judge its similarity to a stereotypical lemon.

The most popular way of measuring similarity is Tversky's (1977) contrast model. However, tests of this model led to an alternative *exemplar-based* view of the representation of concepts (Medin and Schaeffer, 1978; Medin and Smith, 1981; Nosofsky, 1986; Estes, 1986). On this view, there is no abstract prototype in semantic memory, but a collection of representations of particular examples of a concept. In the original versions of this theory the person formulating the model had to specify the similarity metric. However, recent work, in one of the few instances in which PDP models have been successfully applied to higher thought processes (Gluck and Bower, 1988a, 1988b; Shanks, 1990), has shown that similarity metrics may be better learned by the connectionist models described in chapter 1. Such models will, over a series of learning trials in which clear examples of horses and zebras are presented, discover which features distinguish between them, and how much weight should be given to the discriminatory power of each such feature. Human judgements about the discriminatory power of features – on the part of people setting up exemplar-based theories – are less reliable.

Further evidence in favour of exemplar-based representations comes from work by Brooks (e.g., 1978, 1983) on the learning of artificial concepts. Brooks compared two learning strategies. The first encour-aged subjects to discover the (deliberately complex) rule that distin-guished between two artificial concepts (i.e., to figure out the conditions for membership of each of the two corresponding categories, for exam-ple, made-up diseases that have to be diagnosed on the basis of symp-toms in fictitious patients). The second group effectively had to learn the exemplars. In the second part of the experiment, the two groups had to classify new examples. The second group had not been told about the two categories, and protested that they would not be able to carry out the task. Nevertheless, and quite surprisingly, they performed better than the first group. Just learning examples can, under certain circumstances, be a better way of learning concepts than deliberately trying to figure out defining conditions. It leads to *implicit learning* of the concepts. However, this result may not generalize to the learning of natural concepts, rather than the deliberately obscure artificial concepts used in these studies.

2.1.2.c Theory-based theories

Putnam's ideas have not been fully incorporated into psychological theorizing, but many psychologists have recognized that the idea of a prototype is not sufficient to describe the mental representation of natural-kind concepts. Even non-scientists know, for example, that whether a cat is a pedigree Siamese depends not on what its looks like – whether it fits the Siamese stereotype – but on its lineage. One way of expressing this idea is to say that people have 'lay theories' about what makes something what it is, and that these lay theories determine the core properties of natural kinds. The importance of lay theories in classification has been emphasized in work by Medin (e.g., Murphy and Medin, 1985), and the way that developing theories of the natural world influence categorization in children is a key idea in the work of Susan Carey (1985) (see chapter 17). Smith (1988) suggests that the representation of a natural-kind concept comprises both a prototype and a set of core properties, which depend on an underlying theory of the domain from which the concept is drawn. He further claims that neither represents its meaning.

An idea that *has* been imported into psychological theory, in an attempt to account for some of the complexity in the mental representation of natural categories, is Wittgenstein's concept of family resemblance (see, e.g., Rosch and Mervis, 1975). Rosch failed to make explicit her views on the relation between prototypes and family resemblance structure, though Lakoff (1987) presents some interesting ideas about how one might be more specific on this point. The idea that concepts have family resemblance structure is popular among psychologists (see, e.g., Markman, 1989). But, as Markman herself points out, the psychological evidence in favour of this notion is not entirely conclusive. Detailed linguistic analyses, such as those presented by Lakoff, are more convincing.

2.1.3 Conceptual combination

We are still not through with the problems of prototype theory. On the classical account of concepts – that they comprise sets of necessary and sufficient conditions – combination of simple concepts to produce complex concepts is straightforward. For example, the concept of a fish can be combined with the concept of a pet to give the concept of a pet fish. A pet fish is something that satisfies all the conditions for being a fish *and* all those for being a pet. With prototypes there are two problems. How do we combine the prototype for fish and the prototype for pet? And how do we get the right results about typicality? The prototypical pet fish is a goldfish, but a goldfish is far from being either a prototypical fish or a prototypical pet. One suggestion, which initially appeared appealing to Rosch and others, was that prototype theory might be formalized using Zadeh's (1965) fuzzy set theory. However, Osherson and Smith (1981) showed that fuzzy set theory led to incorrect predictions about prototypicality. For example, fuzzy set theory predicts that the typicality of a goldfish as a pet fish cannot be greater than its typicality as a fish or its typicality as a pet, whichever is greater. More recently, alternative formalizations that do not suffer from this problem have been proposed, for example, by Smith and Osherson (1984; Smith, Osherson, Rips and Keane, 1988) and by Jones (1982).

These proposals have been directed primarily to solving the problem of typicality, not the problem of how meanings, perhaps stored in the form of prototypes, can be combined. Indeed, there is a separate literature, both in psychology and in formal semantics, on the problem of conceptual combination. This literature addresses problems such as why 'tin can' has a different kind of meaning from 'tin mine', and how a uniform account can be given of the way that an adjective such as 'good' modifies nouns. We will not discuss this problem in detail here, but it may well be that, whatever the processes that effect conceptual combination, they operate on core meanings rather that prototypes.

The typicality problem for 'pet fish' is separate from the question of how 'pet' modifies 'fish'. Similarly, Larry Barsalou's (1983, 1985) work on what he calls *ad hoc* concepts and *goal-derived* concepts is usually seen as distinct from work on conceptual combination, though concepts of these kinds are expressed by phrases rather than by single words. Ad hoc categories are ones that are not stored in memory, but are created on the fly, in response to a particular situation. A goal-derived category is a special kind of ad hoc category, in which all the members are related to the fulfilment of a particular goal. Barsalou's examples include 'things to take on vacation' and 'things to save in the event of a fire'. Since ad hoc categories are not stored in memory, they are not automatically activated by their exemplars. Barsalou found that, unless there was a preceding story to cue an ad hoc concept, such concepts do not help people to learn lists of their exemplars. Ordinary concepts do – a list of fruits is easier to learn than a list of unrelated words, even if the category 'fruit' is not mentioned.

A theory of conceptual combination attempts to explain how the meaning, and hence the set of objects in the corresponding category, is determined by the parts of an expression such as 'things to take on vacation', together with its syntactic structure. For these types of category this process is of little interest. What is of interest is the fact, demonstrated by Barsalou, that ad hoc and goal-derived categories show typicality effects, just like ordinary concepts. However, since ad hoc categories are not stored in memory, these typicality effects cannot arise because of similarity between exemplars and a stored prototype. Barsalou argues that with an ad hoc concept such as 'foods not to eat on a diet' there is a crucial feature, in this case calorific value, that determines whether something belongs to the class. He argues that it is an item's value on this dimension that determines how typical it is. Resemblance, in any straightforward sense, to the most typical member of the category, chocolate, is not at stake. Smith (1988) argues that such effects arise from the core of ad hoc concepts, not from their prototype. However, this analysis, although compelling for this one ad hoc concept, is not so convincing for others.

Smith suggests a similar explanation for an interesting finding by Armstrong, Gleitman and Gleitman (1983) that has also been seen as problematic for prototype theory. Armstrong et al. showed that concepts which everyone agrees have classical definitions, such as 'odd number', show typicality effects. For example, 7 is rated a more typical odd number than 193. Thus, empirically observed typicality effects may have little, if anything, to say about whether a concept's meaning is represented by a prototype, since it is not clear that there is a prototypical odd number. Smith argues that the explanation of Armstrong et al.'s finding may lie in the fact that people find it easier to decide that 7 is odd than 193. In other words, they find it easier to determine that 7 has the properties specified in the core of the concept of an odd number (the necessary and sufficient condition for being odd, namely not being divisible by 2). However, this idea is not entirely convincing, since there is a simple way of telling whether a number is odd – by looking at the last digit.

In early psychological work on semantic memory, based on network and feature theories, relations between concepts were of great importance: those theories at least recognized the need for an overall picture of our *conceptual scheme*, though they restricted their attention to taxonomic (hierarchical) relations among concepts expressed by concrete common nouns. Interest in typicality shifted attention to individual concepts, though if prototype theory is to be a complete theory of the mental representation of concepts, it, too, must answer broader questions about our conceptual scheme. Indeed, psychological theories of categorization and conceptualization need to take these general questions more seriously. On the one hand, they have barely noted that, although hierarchical relations are most important among concepts that are expressed by concrete common nouns, they also exist among abstract concepts (democracy and dictatorship are types of government) and among concepts expressed by verbs (roasting and grilling are types of cooking). On the other hand, they have, by and large, ignored other types of relations between concepts. To give just one example, one view of certain very abstract concepts, such as those expressed by *and, or* and *if . . . then*, which are important in deductive reasoning (see chapter 5), is that they should be treated *syncategorematically*. That is to say, they should not be regarded as expressing concepts themselves, but as having meaning only in so far as they can be used to relate other concepts to one another. However, the relations they stand for are not the kind of hierarchical relations captured by network and feature theories.

2.1.4   Basic level categories

Despite the tendency to focus on individual concepts and hierarchical relations between them, two other aspects of the organization of our conceptual scheme have received attention within psychology: basic level categories and mutual exclusiveness of category membership. The idea of a basic level category, which depends on the existence of hierarchical organization, is another of Eleanor Rosch's many contributions to the psychology of categorization (see, e.g., Rosch, Mervis, Gray, Johnson and Boyes-Braem, 1976). The relation to taxonomic organization is that 'level' in the phrase 'basic level category' refers to a level in an ISA hierarchy such as that shown in figure 2.1. The basic level is, in some sense, the most natural level. For example, in categorizing foodstuffs, basic level categories might include apple, pear and banana. Higher levels, such as one where fruit contrasts with vegetable, are called superordinate by Rosch. Lower levels, such as one where Golden Delicious contrasts with Granny Smith and Jonathan, are called subordinate.

Basic level categories provide the labels that people spontaneously give to objects or pictures (when they are not obviously trying to suggest a contrast), and they readily invoke concrete images, unlike superordinate terms such as fruit. Subordinate terms also invoke concrete images, but if a higher level term, such as fruit, evokes an image, it will usually be of a particular kind of fruit (i.e., one at the basic level). In many experimental classification tasks, Rosch et al. showed that categories at the basic level were processed faster and more accurately. As part of her explanation of the importance of basic level categories, Rosch introduced the notion of *cue validity* (which she took from Brunswik, 1956). Objects at the basic level share many features with other objects in the same category, but few with those in contrasting categories. Two apples are similar, but an apple and a banana are readily distinguishable. In contrast, at the superordinate level two randomly chosen exemplars of a category such as fruit are likely to have few features in common, and those features may not be particularly helpful in distinguishing fruit from vegetables. At the subordinate level, exemplars in contrasting categories (Granny Smiths and Golden Delicious) have many features in common. Basic level categories are, therefore, distinguished by high within-category similarity and high between-category contrast. Hence, at the basic level there are many features that are valid cues for membership of a category, and the categories are easy to learn, image and work with.

Tverksy and Hemenway (1984) have suggested that objects at the basic level might have parts in common rather than features in common, and other problems with Rosch's definition of cue validity have been pointed out by Medin (1983; Murphy & Medin, 1985). Medin argues that what is important about the basic level is that the strongest *correlational structure* among features of objects belonging to categories is found at that level. Correlational structure is the tendency of features, such as the ability to fly and being feathered, to go together (i.e., for their appearance to be correlated). Medin argues that this correlation of features provides the basis for the lay theories that he and Murphy claim to underlie categorization.

2.2   Images

Concepts are important building blocks of thoughts, particularly those thoughts that are expressed in language. But are there any kinds of higher-order thinking that do not depend on language? Any kind of problem solving that animals can engage in is an obvious contender, and one of the most complex problems that animals can solve is learning to learn (Harlow, 1949). In learning to learn, an animal learns a series of simple (pairwise) discriminations between objects that never appear again in the study. For example, the animal might have to learn, in one part of the experiment, that the container behind a key always contains food, whereas the one behind a watch does not. Chimpanzees find the first pairs of objects difficult, because they are unsure whether it is the object that signals the food, or the position (left-hand container vs. right-hand container) or some other aspect of the experimental situation. However, a chimpanzee will eventually realize that, in each part of the experiment, it just needs to know which object signals food. It can learn the answer to this question in a single trial, picking one object at random when the pair is first presented, and learning from that trial whether that object is or is not a signal for the food.

Learning to learn is an example of transfer of learning from one problem to another, and it can only be readily demonstrated with the simplest kind of discrimination learning (learning to discriminate a key from a watch is very easy). A more difficult type of learning is matching to sample, in which an animal is shown one object and then has to choose between two others in order to get food. It has to choose the one that is the same as the 'sample' it has just been shown. Transfer of matching to sample has only been reliably demonstrated in language-trained chimpanzees (Premack, 1976; Premack and Premack, 1983). Research of this kind begins to map the boundaries between what is and what is not possible without language. It suggests that recognizing the recurrence of higher-order relations (such as the relations of sameness and difference between objects) requires a language that allows one to label such relations. Premack's best-known chimp subject, Sarah, did learn words for 'same' and 'different'.

Some kinds of thinking require natural language, but are there kinds of complex thinking that are possible without language? One of the oldest debates in the psychology of thinking is about the role of images in thought. Often the debate has been fruitless. Indeed, it was the impossibility of resolving the 'imageless thought' debate at the turn of the century that provided part of the impetus to the extreme empiricism of behaviourist psychology, and its refusal to consider anything that could not be observed (see chapter 1). However, thought in the form of images is a prime candidate for a kind of higher-order thinking that does not depend on language.

The idea of imageless thought arose out of attempts to study thinking by introspection (see chapter 1). Introspectionists considered that the correct way for psychologists to study thinking was to sit in an armchair and think, and, at the same time, to introspect on their thought processes. Some people who adopted this technique reported thinking in images and others did not, even when they were thinking about similar problems. Since it was widely assumed that thought had a single nature, it followed that both kinds of report could not be correct. Yet there was no objective way of deciding which party was right. Partly for this reason, imagery became a taboo subject within the broadly behaviourist tradition that dominated experimental psychology in the English-speaking world in the first half of this century. It was not taken seriously again until the work of Paivio in the late 1960s (see Paivio, 1971, for a summary).

Paivio's work was carried out in the verbal learning tradition. He showed that, when their other attributes were matched, concrete words, naming easily imagined objects, were remembered better than abstract words. To explain this result Paivio put forward the *dual coding hypothesis*. This hypothesis suggests that concrete words are remembered better because they can be encoded into memory in two ways – using either a verbal or a visual (imaginal) code. Abstract words can only be encoded verbally.

Once imagery research had been rehabilitated within psychology, further work was soon underway. In Roger Shepard's 'mental rotation' experiments (e.g., Shepard and Metzler, 1971), subjects saw pairs of pictures of simple three-dimensional objects and they had to say whether they were pictures of the same object or of an object and its mirror image. When the objects were the same, the object in one of the pictures was rotated with respect to its position in the other picture (see figure 2.2). Shepard found that the time to make the same/mirror image judgement was directly related to the angle through which the shape had been rotated in the second picture. Indeed, a graph of judgement time against angle of rotation was a straight line. He suggested that subjects performed the task by creating an image-like mental representation of the pictures, and then rotating one of the representations until it could (or could not) be superimposed on the other – hence the name 'mental rotation'. Shepard's results suggested that the mental rotation took place at a constant rate.

The most vociferous champion of the idea that mental images play a central, functional role in thinking is Stephen Kosslyn (e.g., 1980). In one of Kosslyn's best-known experiments (Kosslyn, Ball and Reiser, 1978), subjects studied a map of an imaginary island until they could remember all the landmarks on it (a hut, a tree, a rock, a well, a lake, some sand and some grass; see figure 2.3). They then had to imagine moving between two of the landmarks. The time that these imagined movements took was proportional to the distance between the landmarks. Kosslyn takes this result to indicate that subjects perform the task using a representation of the map that shares certain spatial properties with a percept of the map. In particular, the representation

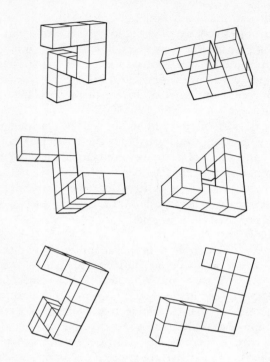

Figure 2.2   Stimuli used in experiments on mental rotation by Shepard and Metzler (1971)

is analogue, and is not a set of mental sentences ('propositions') about the positions of the objects. Other experiments that suggest similar conclusions include one in which subjects were asked to imagine an animal coming towards them and to judge when its image filled their visual field (the judged time depended on the size of the animal), and one in which subjects had to judge the relative size of two animals. Judgements were faster when the animal differed more in size (Kosslyn, 1975).

Kosslyn has sometimes been taken to be proposing a 'homunculus' theory of performance in his map experiment. A homunculus theory would say that subjects perform the task by looking at a mental 'picture' of the map with their mind's eye. This kind of theory has no place in psychology, since it tries to explain human abilities by postulating a little man (or parts of a little man – his eyes in this case) inside the head. But such an explanation is useless, since it leaves unexplained the abilities of the man in the head, and those abilities are, *ex hypothesi*, the same in crucial respects as the human abilities we are trying to explain.

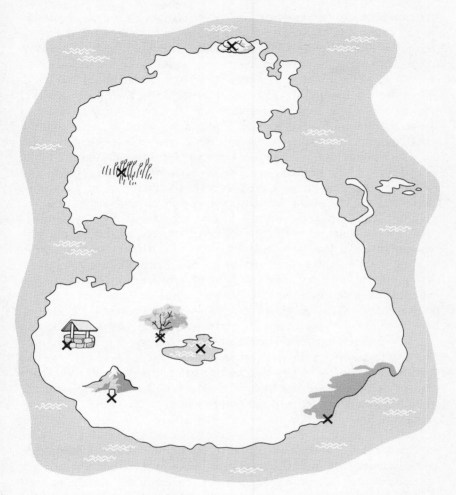

Figure 2.3   Map of an island used in an experiment by Kosslyn, Ball and Reiser (1978)

This misinterpretation of Kosslyn is partly explained by his use of the term 'image', which suggests something seen by the mind's eye. However, in response to critics such as Pylyshyn (e.g., 1973), Kosslyn has made it clear that what is important about images, on his account, is not their phenomenal nature – how they appear to the mind's eye – but the way they function in producing behaviour. Among their important properties are their analogue (as opposed to digital) nature, and the relation between their structure and the structure of what they represent (also, Palmer, 1978). On this view, Kosslyn's 'images' need not be images at all, in the everyday sense. They are simply representations of parts of the real, or of some imaginary, world – representations with certain properties. Our experience of images, in the everyday sense, might be the by-product of using a propositional (or language-like) representation, but they might also be a by-product of using an imaginal representation, in Kosslyn's sense. There is, however, evidence that the use of imagery, in Kosslyn's sense, depends on the same brain mechanisms as visual perception (e.g., Farah, Perronet, Gonon and Giard, 1988).

Pylyshyn (1981) has further argued that data on mental rotation and map scanning can be explained as task specific, and, in particular, dependent on the particular instructions that subjects are given. For complex, and largely invalid, reasons he argues that imagery theorists should not countenance the possibility of strategic effects on the way images are used. It is true, as Pylyshyn argues, that the information in a Kosslyn-style 'image' of a map of an island could be expressed in a set of propositions, but that fact is of little interest in itself. It is also true that the kind of representation used may be under strategic control. However, as psychologists we are not so much interested in how information *might* be represented, but in how it *is* represented in the human mind. In order to answer the question of how information is represented, we have to ask about the way a person behaves when set a certain task. One kind of representation will make certain types of judgement easy and others hard; one will predict that a task (say, mental rotation) should have certain properties, another will not. Or, rather, it will not naturally.

Seen from this perspective, the work of Shepard and of Kosslyn is part of a wider body of work on spatial representation, which suggests that spatial layouts are mentally represented in a format that reflects their spatial properties, not the properties of sentences that might be used to describe them. This phenomenon in turn reflects the fact that mental models encode the structure of the part of the world that they model, not the structure of the text that was used describe that part of the world. Spatial layouts happen to be a domain in which the differences between the structure of the world and the structure of a text describing it are most readily apparent.

The work of George Potts in the early 1970s (e.g., Potts, 1972) showed that descriptions of one-dimensional spatial arrays, which might comprise sentences such as:

the apple is to the left of the banana
the banana is to the left of the orange

are encoded to reflect the structure of the array, not the structure of the sentences. For example, it is easier to make judgements about objects far apart in the array, even when all the sentences are about adjacent objects. Phil Johnson-Laird produced similar findings for two-dimensional arrays. In addition, he has shown (Mani and Johnson-Laird, 1982) that 'indeterminate' descriptions, consistent with more than one layout, tend to be held in memory in a verbatim form. This finding reflects a natural preference for working with a single model. He and his colleagues have also shown (Ehrlich and Johnson-Laird, 1982; Oakhill and Johnson-Laird, 1984; Oakhill and Garnham, 1985) that, although the linguistic properties of the description are not encoded into mental models, they affect how easily those models are constructed. It is easier to construct a model for a continuous description, in which each sentence refers back to an object mentioned in the last, than for a discontinuous description, in which adjacent sentences do not always have referential links.

Our spatial knowledge of larger 'layouts' appears to be encoded in *mental maps*. Mental maps of areas in which we live, or around which we frequently travel, are used to guide our movements. There is evidence (e.g., Byrne, 1979) that these maps resemble network maps rather than survey (or scale) maps. Network maps, such as the standard map of the London Underground, represent the important features of, say, a road or rail system for someone trying to get around it, but do not attempt to be accurate in their representation of distance, for example. Byrne found that distances along routes with many turns or landmarks tended to be overestimated compared with those along routes with few of them. This finding suggests that mental maps are encoded in term of important features and choice points, rather than physical distance. However, later work (e.g., Thorndyke, 1981) has found similar errors when real (scale) maps are used, so the original results do not favour mental network maps as strongly as was originally supposed.

Knowledge of larger areas is notoriously inaccurate, and people's judgements can most readily be explained on the assumption that they engage in 'propositional' reasoning rather than using an accurate spatial representation. For example, Stevens and Coupe (1978) found that people incorrectly claim Los Angeles is west of Reno, because they think of California as being west of Nevada (see figure 2.4 for the true relation between the two cities). One way of explaining this finding is to assume that information about large-scale geography is encoded in a hierarchical network structure. So, for example, information about the geography of the United States might be divided first into information about individual states. Information about particular towns would then be encoded according to the state they are in. The judgement about

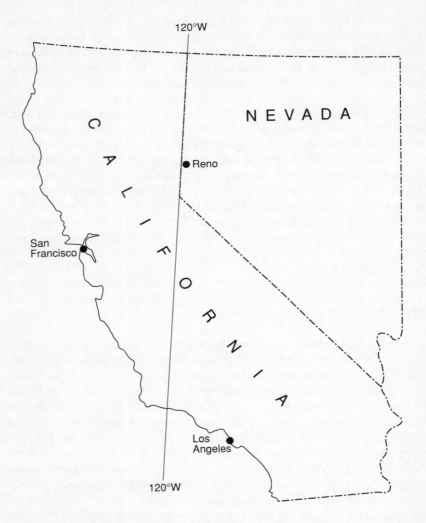

Figure 2.4 Map of California and Nevada showing the relative positions of Los Angeles and Reno

Reno and Los Angeles would then be based on the following pieces of information from the network: Reno is in Nevada; Los Angeles is in California; Nevada is (for the most part) to the east of California. The conclusion that Reno is east of LA would then be derived by 'propositional' reasoning, as mentioned above.

This explanation assumes that the only spatial relations directly encoded are those between locations at the same level of the hierarchy. It assumes, further, that only relations between items that fall under the same superordinate node are encoded. So, relations between states are encoded, and relations between cities within a state, but not relations between cities in different states. It has also been suggested that, even within a natural grouping (cities in a state, for example), only some relations are directly encoded – relations between so-called *landmarks*, and between those landmarks and locations near to them. So, for example, in someone's 'mental map' of London the distance between landmarks such as Trafalgar Square and Oxford Circus might be encoded directly, but the distance between lesser known locations such as St Martin-in-the-Fields church and the Selfridge's department store might be encoded indirectly. Each of these locations can be encoded with respect to a landmark (St Martin-in-the-Fields is just north-east of Trafalgar Square and Selfridge's a little west of Oxford Circus, along Oxford Street).

2.3   Building Thoughts and Trains of Thought

Concepts allow us to categorize things we experience, but a typical thought comprises more than a simple categorization. Some concepts are relational: prototypically, though not exclusively, those expressed by verbs. So a verb such as *hit* can be used to describe an act relating two people or things, which, in turn, can be classified using concepts expressed by nouns (as, for example, in *the hammer hit the nail*). Thus, individual thoughts can be built out of concepts by making use of the relational structure inherent in some of those concepts. Those thoughts can then be expressed in language using the words that express those concepts (or phrases, if the concepts are not lexicalized), together with the rules of grammar for the language. An individual thought might be about a small part of the real world (a hammer hitting a nail), a fictional world, or an abstract domain. To think about a more substantial part of such a world or domain (the building of a house, of which the hitting of the nail was just one small part, for example), we may need more, or more complex, thoughts, or thoughts at a different level of abstraction. Thus, we can think about complex situations, and store information about them in our long-term memories. Images also allow us to think about complex situations and events. But they are composed out of a different type of element than concepts, more akin to the elements of a complex perceptual experience.

The rest of this book deals not primarily with individual thoughts, or thoughts of complex situations, but with trains of thought of various kinds. Trains of thought are built out of individual thoughts, and much of our attention will be on how people move from one thought to another in such trains of thought. Some trains of thought, those of daydreams for example, have no clear direction. Indeed, daydreaming appears to be one of the few kinds of complex thinking in which association (see chapter 1) plays a crucial role. However, although many people spend a large proportion of their time daydreaming, and although there has been a certain amount of psychological research on that topic, there appears to be little of interest for cognitive psychologists to learn about it, and we will not discuss it further in this book. Instead, our focus will be on more directed forms of thinking, in which people move, purposefully, from information they already have to other information that they can derive from it in one way or another. We will be addressing such questions as:

- How do people work out what, if anything, follows from 'some insects are dangerous' and 'some insects are killed by aerosol sprays'? (chapter 6)
- How do chess players decide what move to make? (chapter 11)
- How did Charles Darwin come up with the theory of natural selection? (chapter 13)

In each case the general answer is: by engaging in trains of thought in which the individual thoughts are built out of the components discussed in this chapter.

Summary

If we are to think, we must have thoughts. Many of our thoughts are built from concepts, which we use to categorize things in the world. It is hard to elucidate the notion of a concept, as philosophers can attest. This problem is reflected in the wide variety of ideas about the mental representation of concepts that psychologists have put forward. Early models were based on semantic networks or sets of semantic features, though these apparently dissimilar approaches were shown to be formally equivalent. Both had to be modified to accommodate the typicality effects that inspired a rival theory based on the notion of a prototype, together with information about how far something can differ from the prototype and still exemplify the same concept. A further possibility is that a concept is not represented by an abstract prototype, but simply by its exemplars. Yet another view, which applies primarily to natural kind concepts, is that theories play a crucial role in categorization, and that concepts are not independent of theories of the domains in which they apply.

A theory of concepts also has to provide a mechanism of conceptual combination that explains, for example, how the concept of a pet fish relates to those of a pet and of a fish. It also has to explain general properties of our conceptual scheme, such as why some concepts are more basic than others. Strong correlations among the attributes of objects belonging to basic level categories explain why they are easy to learn.

Some kinds of thought are mediated not by language, but by images. Paivio argued that many ideas can be encoded both verbally and imaginally. Shepard (mental rotation) and Kosslyn (map scanning) suggested that some tasks are performed using an image-like, rather than a language-like, representation. However, their use of the term image does not imply a 'mind's eye' scanning images. What is crucial is that the representation preserves spatial properties of what it represents. However, people do not always represent two- or three-dimensional space accurately. Research on mental maps suggests that network-like maps are sometimes used rather than scale maps, and that some spatial information is represented verbally rather than spatially.

Further Reading

Kosslyn, S. M. (1980). *Image and Mind*. Cambridge, MA: Harvard University Press.

Rosch, E., Mervis, C. B., Gray, W. D., Johnson, D. M. and Boyes-Braem, P. (1976). Basic objects in natural categories. *Cognitive Psychology*, 8, pp. 382–439.

Smith, E. E. and Medin, D. L. (1981). *Categories and Concepts*. Cambridge, MA: Harvard University Press.

3

Language and Thought

In the previous chapter we argued that concepts are one kind of building block of thought. More so than images, concepts are firmly rooted in language, and we considered questions about categorization and the relation between categories, concepts and words. However, we did not consider in detail the question of whether language is shaped by the kinds of concepts we have, and the way we can put those concepts together to form thoughts; or whether the kinds of concepts, and more generally the kinds of thoughts, we have are shaped by the language we speak. Before moving on to a detailed study of the directed trains of thought we mentioned briefly at the end of the last chapter, we will consider, in this chapter, the general question of how language and thought are related.

According to the realist view, things in the world *really* belong to certain categories, independently of the existence of human minds. So, other things being equal, people do best if their concepts match categories in the world. On this view, all languages will be forced to fit the same mould, so that their speakers can say the same things about the same objective reality. It might, however, be thought that an anti-realist or constructivist who sees categorization as dependent on the existence of minds, and inconceivable without them, would favour the opposite view that concepts are moulded by language. But this view is by no means a consequence of the anti-realist position. Given their broadly similar genetic make-up and the broadly similar environments in which people find themselves, it is likely that they will construct similar conceptual schemes, which will be reflected in similarities between their languages. Of course, languages show differences as well as similarities, and either view must be able to accommodate them. Realists can claim that different cultures adopt different subsets of the set of concepts. However, this view is less plausible when different cultures seem to carve up the same part of the natural or social world in different ways. Here the constructivist view is more plausible. If categories are made by people to fulfil their needs, and if different cultures have different real or perceived needs, there is no reason why they should not adopt different classificatory systems.

3.1 The Traditional View

Both realism and constructivism are compatible with the traditional view about the relation between language and thought. This view, which can be traced back at least as far as the Ancient Greek philosopher Aristotle, is that *thought is prior to language*, and that languages have the properties they have so that they can express the kinds of thoughts people have. This view is not only the traditional one, it has also been the most popular one in modern times. However, as we will see later in this chapter, it has not gone unchallenged. It is a view that is reflected in different ways in the works of thinkers as diverse as the developmental psychologist Jean Piaget, the linguist Noam Chomsky, and the artificial intelligence researcher Roger Schank.

In Piaget's influential theory of cognitive development (see, e.g., Boden, 1979, and chapter 16 below), a child's thinking passes through a fixed sequence of stages. At the broadest level there are four stages – sensorimotor, preoperational, concrete operational and formal operational – though each is divided into a number of sub-stages. At each stage the child's thought has characteristic properties. So, in the preoperational stage, children do not realize that, when objects or sets of objects are transformed, certain of their properties remain invariant. They do not realize, for example, that when a ball of plasticine is rolled out, the amount of plasticine in it remains the same. Within any stage, the child's thinking is refined by being expressed in words. But development is driven by changes in the way a child thinks. It is not until a child moves from the preoperational stage to the concrete operation stage that he or she can begin to express the idea that the amount of material is conserved in a transformation of its shape. So, in Piaget's theory, the way of thinking changes first, then language changes so that the child can express the new way of thinking.

One of the main goals of Chomsky's linguistic theory is to discover properties that all human languages have in common, and that any other human language that has existed or might exist had or would have to have (see, e.g., Chomsky, 1972, 1975). These properties reflect the structure of the human mind. Chomsky himself prefers to express these properties formally and to claim that they reflect the structure of a special part of the mind called the language faculty. He also believes that this faculty is largely separate from the part of the mind that gives us our ability to think. Other linguists do not necessarily adhere to this 'modular' view of the mental location of these so-called *linguistic universals* as Chomsky. They argue that our linguistic ability is part of our general cognitive ability. Nevertheless, even in Chomsky's theory, we can see a version of the theory that languages are the way they are because of the way the human mind is – because of the way people think.

Roger Schank is an artificial intelligence researcher whose goal was to write computer programs that could 'understand' texts, in the sense that they could paraphrase them, translate them, and answer inferential questions about them. One aspect of his theory was that the meaning of all sentences should be represented in a universal notation, which he called *conceptual dependency* (Schank, 1972). He chose that name because he thought that a representation of meaning should be a representation of relations (or dependencies) among concepts. Conceptual dependency provides a way of representing the ideas that people have. One of its important properties is that ideas expressed in natural language should be readily convertible into conceptual dependency (in language understanding) and vice versa (in language production). Hence the idea, once again, is that properties of human languages depend on properties of human thought. Languages are the way they are so that they can express the ideas that we represent to ourselves (mentally) in the conceptual dependency notation.

3.2　Vygotsky

The traditional view that thought has logical priority over language is not only a plausible one, but one that has considerable support among contemporary thinkers. Nevertheless, it is not one that is universally accepted. One potential problem with the idea is that it postulates a very simple relation between two complex aspects of human life. It was partly this thought that motivated the Russian psychologist Lev

Vygotsky's account (1986, but originally published in Russian in 1934) of the relation between thought and speech.

Like Piaget, Vygotsky was interested primarily in developmental questions. He proposed that, as a child grows older, three main stages can be discerned in the relation between thought and speech. However, Vygotsky's concept of a developmental stage is less rigid, and much closer to the everyday notion, than Piaget's.

In the first stage thought and speech are unrelated. The kinds of thought that very young children have are much the same as those of the higher animals. An ability to use language is not required for such thoughts. The 'speech' of these children begins as prelinguistic babbling, whose role is complex, but unrelated to the expression of thoughts. Neither is the first use of words related to complex thought processes, but to naming (and learning names), and to issuing requests.

In the second stage thought and speech become connected. At first what the child says is only loosely related to what it does in order to solve problems. For example, Luria (1959) tells the story of a child who, when a blue light came on, had to say the words 'don't press' and refrain from squeezing a rubber bulb (the child had to press when a red light came on). However, as the child said 'don't press', it pressed the bulb harder than when the red light came on. A further feature of this second stage is that, at its beginning, the child's verbal comments tend to *follow* the actions to which they relate. However, as the stage progresses, the verbalizations come earlier in relation to the actions and they become more accurate descriptions of the actions.

The talking to oneself that the child engages in during this second state is what Piaget called *egocentric speech*. Such speech is readily observed in children from about two to six years old, but Vygotsky and Piaget had strongly opposing views on its function. Piaget's view was that egocentric speech was related to the preoperational child's general egocentricity (hence the name 'egocentric speech') and that it disappeared, along with other aspects of egocentricity, when the child moved on to the stage of concrete operations. Vygotsky, on the other hand, thought that egocentric speech was transformed into the internal speech that characterizes much of our complex thinking.

Thus in Vygotsky's third stage in the developing relation between thought and language (from about seven years on) egocentric speech has become internal speech, and complex thoughts are made possible by the fact that they can make use of a linguistic medium. However, Vygotsky was careful never to identify thought with internal speech. He always allowed the possibility that some kinds of thought did not depend on internal speech.

As a theory of the developing relation between language and thought Vygotsky's theory appears more plausible than Piaget's. However, it is not incompatible with the traditional view of how the two are related at the end of development. The form of languages may, indeed, be determined by the nature of the thoughts that they, in their role as inner speech, have to express. However, Vygotsky's views would also be compatible with an alternative theory, to which we now turn.

3.3   The Sapir–Whorf Hypothesis

A more radical alternative to traditional ideas about language and thought is the diametrically opposed view that language is logically prior to thought, and that the kinds of thought a person can have are determined by the language they speak. This view has been mooted at several times in the past, for example, by the German critic and poet Johann Gottfried von Herder (1744–1803) in the eighteenth century and by the German philologist Wilhelm von Humboldt (1767–1835) in the nineteenth. However, it has received its most detailed exposition in the present century, in the work of the linguist Edward Sapir and, more especially, his admirer Benjamin Lee Whorf (1956).

In the early part of this century a primary concern among many American linguists was to record and preserve the languages of the native American Indians. Sapir contributed to this work and Whorf, though not himself a professional linguist, drew heavily on the American Indian languages to support his twin hypotheses of *linguistic determinism* and *linguistic relativity*.

Whorf worked for a fire insurance company. Legend has it that he was first led to consider the effect language has on thinking when he processed fire insurance claims for fires that started when cigarette ends were thrown into empty fuel cans. Whorf argued that the label 'empty' led people to believe that these cans were safe, whereas they were really filled with explosive vapour. The idea that linguistic labels shape our thought underlies the doctrine of linguistic determinism which, in its strong form, states that language wholly determines thought. Whorf derived his second hypothesis, that of linguistic relativity, largely from his study of the American Indian languages. This study convinced him that the American Indian languages were significantly different from European languages, and led him to believe that the Indians thought in different ways from the newer European peoples of North America. So not only does language determine thought, different languages force their speakers to think in different ways. Whorf then set out to show how the different features of, on the one hand, American Indian languages and, on the other hand, what he came to call Standard Average European (SAE) produced different thought processes in their speakers.

Whorf believed that speakers of different languages thought in different ways at both a specific and a general level. One of his best-known examples revolves around the Eskimo words for snow, of which there are several (but see Pullum, 1989, for an account of how the actual number has been greatly exaggerated in the secondary literature). These words are names for types of snow that are important in the (traditional) Eskimo way of life. Some, for example, are names of types of snow that are suitable for building different parts of igloos. Whorf argued that the existence of these different words in the Eskimo language led Eskimos to think about snow in a different way from Europeans. At a more general level, Whorf argued that American Indians had different ideas about such fundamental concepts as space, time and causality from speakers of European languages. For example, he claimed that the Hopi thought that time was circular and that the basic constituents of the world were events rather than objects. Of course, it is not unusual for anthropologists to attribute unusual beliefs to the people they study. What was unusual about Whorf was that he claimed that these heterodox beliefs could be explained by properties of the Hopi language.

Whorf's writings are somewhat vague and inconsistent, and this fact has led commentators to identify at least two, and sometimes three, versions of the hypothesis of linguistic determinism. On the strong view, speaking a particular language forces you to think in a particular way. And the only way to find out how speakers of a different language speak is to learn that language. This idea leads to the implausible conclusion that translation between languages is impossible. A further feature of the strong form of linguistic determinism is that it implies that language affects all of cognition, including the way that the world is perceived. Although some of Whorf's writings suggest this strong form of the hypothesis, his own practice of translation and of explicating the thought processes of American Indians in English does not seem consistent with it. The weak form of the hypothesis states that a particular language makes some ways of thinking easier than others, but does not actually compel its speakers to think in one way rather than another. Sometimes a very weak form of the hypothesis is also identified in which the only cognitive effects are on memory, and they arise because the length and frequency of the name for something determines how easy it is to remember.

For some years, in the 1950s and 1960s, Whorf's ideas were seen as a real challenge to the traditional view, particularly as some early ex-perimental work appeared to lend support to them. More recently, however, it has become apparent that there are both theoretical and experimental reasons for rejecting his hypotheses. We will consider the theoretical reasons first.

3.3.1   Theoretical problems with the Sapir–Whorf hypothesis

Whorf's observations about languages and the thought processes of their speakers, and his arguments from those observations to his twin hypotheses of linguistic determinism and linguistic relativity, have been criticized on several counts. Sometimes his arguments are circular – his only evidence that a certain people think about the world in a non-European way comes from his analysis of their language. But to support his hypotheses he needs to find independent evidence for a different way of thinking, and then to show how it can be explained in terms of prop-erties of the language of the people who think that way. More specifically, perhaps because he was only an amateur linguist, Whorf's linguistic arguments are often fallacious. One of his favourite techniques is to pro-vide a putative translation of an American Indian sentence into English, to point out that the result is not at all like ordinary English, and to conclude that speakers of the American Indian language think differ-ently from speakers of English. However, his approach to 'translation' is a simplistic, word-by-word one that would produce bizarre results even when translating between closely related languages, such as Eng-lish and German. Whorf also tends to assume that any syntactic or morphological marking on a word is reflected in the way people think about what it denotes. American Indian languages tend to have more complex inflectional morphology than English – the beginnings and ends of the words change, depending on their role in a sentence, what other words are in the sentence, and so on (like verb endings or agree-ment between nouns and adjectives in French). So, for example, Navaho verbs have endings that indicate the shape of an object on which an action is carried out (e.g., round vs. long and thin vs. flat). But Whorf's argument is rather like claiming that if we say in English 'a dog of Mary's' we are indicating some kind of double possession, because both the word 'of' and the apostrophe 's' indicate possession.

Whorf's arguments about the effect of Eskimo words for snow on the thought patterns of Eskimos are also invalid, since English speakers could describe the kind of snow suitable for the walls of an igloo differently from snow suitable for its roof. Indeed, a subgroup of English speakers (skiers) also have a rich vocabulary for different types of snow, though the distinctions they make are not the same as the Eskimos'. English speakers would not, however, be able to use single words for the types of snow that Eskimos distinguish, but they could use longer phrases. Of course, most English speakers would have to be taught to make the (perceptual) distinction between the two types of snow, but this fact points to the most telling argument against Whorf. If English speakers and Eskimos think about snow differently, it is not because they speak different languages. It is because they come from different cultures, and have different concerns. In putting forward his arguments, Whorf failed to take account of the cultural differences that always go along with linguistic differences, and of the fact that cultural differences are more likely that linguistic ones to influence the way people think.

3.3.2 Empirical investigations of the Sapir–Whorf hypothesis

Whorf's attempts to show that language determines thought were unsuccessful. However, it does not follow that his twin hypotheses are disproved, only that he himself did not provide adequate evidence to support them. Other, more psychological, lines of research have also attempted to test Whorf's hypotheses. In one early experiment Carroll and Casagrande (1958) tried to show that the existence of the Navaho verb endings that encode the shape of objects would be reflected in a greater tendency of Navaho speaking children to group objects by shape. This finding was confirmed for Indian children who spoke either Navaho or English, but was made difficult to interpret by the fact that English-speaking children from Boston showed just as strong a tendency as the Navaho-speaking Indians to classify by shape.

3.3.2.a Experiments on colour
A central topic in research on language and thought has been the perception of and memory for colours. It may, at first, seem that this is an odd place to look for an effect of language on thought. However, there is one very good reason for selecting it. Colours can be characterized in a way that is independent of how human languages standardly describe them. Physicists describe colours as lying in a colour space that has three dimensions, of wavelength, amplitude and spectral composition. The values that any particular colour has on these dimensions can be established by physical measurement, but, to give an intuitive idea of

what they mean, they correspond roughly to the psychological dimensions of hue (or apparent colour), brightness and saturation (or purity of colour: pink, for example, is an unsaturated red, diluted, or made impure, by the addition of white).

The first colour experiments related to Whorf's hypotheses were carried out by Brown and Lenneberg (1954). Surprisingly, these investigators tested speakers of only one language, English. Brown and Lenneberg tried to show that English colour names affected the way speakers of English divided up the (continuous) colour space, and hence how they thought about colours. They first established what they called the codability of various colours, which basically amounted to agreement about their names. The most highly codable colours were the so-called *focal* reds, blues, greens and yellows – the ones that people chose as the best examples of those colours. Then, in the main part of the experiment, subjects had to pick out from an array of colour chips one that had previously been presented on its own. Choice time was predicted by codability, with highly codable colours picked out fastest. In-between colours, bluish reds, for example, are both less codable and less easy to reidentify in Brown and Lenneberg's experiment. These results were taken to support Whorf's hypothesis of linguistic determinism, since they showed that colours for which there are short common names are easiest to process in psychological tasks.

In 1964 Lantz and Stefflre showed that *communication accuracy* was a better predictor of choice time than codability. Communication accuracy is a measure of how easily one person can get another to pick a single colour from an array of chips when both are looking at the same set of chips, arranged differently, and neither can see the other. Although focal reds, blues, greens and yellows are both highly codable and communicated accurately, some of the non-focal colours score considerably higher on one measure than the other.

Despite Lantz and Stefflre's minor caveat, the original interpretation of the Brown and Lenneberg study was not challenged until the publication of experiments by Eleanor Rosch (e.g., Heider and Olivier, 1972 – Heider is Rosch's former name). Rosch considered the possibility that the colours English speakers find easy are easy for speakers of all languages, and that Brown and Lenneberg's results do not reflect the fact that English has short common words for red, blue, green and yellow. Perhaps the results reflect, rather, properties of the human visual system. To test this idea Rosch repeated the experiment with speakers of many languages.

Rosch's choice of languages was based in part on Berlin and Kay's (1969) work on colour vocabulary. Although there had been much

Table 3.1 Basic colour terms

black	white		
red			
yellow	blue	green	
brown			
purple	pink	orange	grey

anthropological work on colour terms, and it was known that colour vocabulary was highly variable from one language to another, no systematic variation between languages had been discovered. By concentrating on *basic colour terms* – those that are not also names of objects (e.g., in some languages the word for sky might also be used for other blue objects) – Berlin and Kay were able to show that languages behave systematically with respect to which basic colour terms they contain. All languages have at least two basic colour terms, black (or dark) and white (or light). The other basic terms may or may not be found in any particular language. However, if a language has one of the basic colour terms given in table 3.1, it will have all the others above it in that table. It may have some or all or the terms in the same row. So a language with five basic colour terms will have black, white and red and two of yellow, blue and green.

One language in which there are only two colour terms is that of the Dani, a tribe from Papua New Guinea. In the Brown and Lenneberg task, the Dani were slower and less accurate overall than English speakers, but the pattern of their results was the same – they were more accurate for the focal reds, blues, greens and yellows, even though they did not have basic terms for these colours. In a wider study (see, e.g., Rosch, 1974), involving speakers of 23 languages, the only difference from the original Brown and Lenneberg pattern of results was among certain tropic-dwellers whose blue–green discrimination was abnormal. This result has a simple physiological explanation – these people have a dense yellow pigment in their eyes as a result of high exposure to UV light, and this pigment absorbs light in the blue–green region of the spectrum.

Rosch also performed experiments with geometrical shapes on the Dani. Their language does not include words for these shapes, yet they were better at recognizing circles, squares and equilateral triangles, in a version of the Brown and Lenneberg task, than distortions of those shapes. Rosch concluded that the experimental evidence that had been seen as favouring linguistic relativity did not, in fact, support that idea, and that there was no reason to reject the traditional account of the relation between language and thought.

One reason for being slightly cautious in accepting this conclusion is that linguistic relativity is least likely to be correct for 'perceptual' concepts, such as those corresponding to colour terms, which are probably strongly constrained by our biological make-up. A better place to look for evidence of linguistic relativity is among abstract concepts. Bloom (1981) tried to show that Chinese speakers had more difficulty than English speakers with the concept of counterfactuality because English signals the concept linguistically (by using the subjunctive mood: 'if I were to come . . .') whereas Chinese does not. Although Bloom found differences between speakers of English and Chinese, he was unable to circumvent Whorf's problem that language and culture always vary together, and that differences in ways of thinking are more likely to be explained culturally than linguistically. Other problems with Bloom's study were pointed out by Au (1983) who, as a native speaker of Chinese, detected problems in the Chinese translations of the passages that Bloom had used to investigate understanding of counterfactuality.

Apart from speakers of different languages, there are other groups that might be compared in an attempt to elucidate the relation between language and thought. Among the comparisons that might be made are:

1 deaf vs. hearing: a comparison made by Piaget, who was unable to detect any abnormality in the cognitive development of the deaf
2 aphasic vs. normal
3 animal vs. human: attempts to teach language to apes might be relevant to determining the relation between language and thought, as might some of the more complex cognitive abilities of apes, such as learning to learn (see pp. 31–2).
4 monolinguals vs. bilinguals
5 different social classes
6 different ethnic groups.

3.3.2.b Language and thought in bilinguals

All these comparisons produce data that are difficult to interpret. We will look very briefly at some data from bilinguals, and then in a little more detail at comparisons between different social classes and ethnic groups. From the perspective of the question about the relation between language and thought, the interesting question about bilinguals is: do they have shared or separate cognitive systems for their two languages? The Whorf hypothesis suggests that they should have separate systems, though those systems might overlap for related languages. Unfortunately, most bilinguals speak related languages. A further complication arises from the distinction between compound bilinguals, who learned their two languages at the same time, and co-ordinate bilinguals, who learned one of them first, and whose knowledge of their second language might well be contaminated by knowledge of their first.

There is clear evidence that compound bilinguals who speak related languages, for example English and French, have a single conceptual system that underlies their use of both languages. For example, repetition of words in lists in a single language makes those lists easier to remember. Kolers (1966) showed that repetition of translations (window – fenêtre) does too. In another experiment, Kolers (1968) showed that memory for the content of a story that switched from one language to another was independent of memory for which part was in which language. Furthermore, people were not very good at remembering which part was in which language. Preston and Lambert (1969) demonstrated Stroop colour naming interference between the two languages of bilinguals. In the standard Stroop task, naming the colour of the ink of a word is made difficult if the word itself is the name of a different colour (e.g., it is hard to respond 'blue' to the word 'red' printed in blue ink). In Preston and Lambert's experiment the words were in a different language from the language in which the ink colour had to be named.

One slightly different result comes from an experiment by Ervin-Tripp (1964). She showed that English-Japanese bilinguals produced different word associations in the two languages. She explained this difference by appealing to the different social contexts in which the languages were used. The subjects were living in the United States, and tended to use Japanese at home and with close friends, and to use English in more public situations, for example, when shopping. Research on bilinguals, therefore, suggests a common conceptual core that underlies the use of the two languages (*pace* Whorf). However, the connotations that words have depend on the particular language and its associated social milieu.

3.3.2.c Social and ethnic groups

A strong argument for a Whorfian view of the relation between language and thought was made by the English sociologist Basil Bernstein (1971), who studied differences between the languages of different social classes and claimed that those differences had 'cognitive consequences'. He described the language of the working classes as a 'restricted code' with the following properties:

1 short grammatically simple sentences
2 frequent shifts of attention, which he saw as producing 'illogical structure' in working-class dialogue.

3   frequent calls for feedback, reflected in the use of tag questions such
    as 'don't they?' and 'ok?'
4   context boundness – references to both space and time are not encoded
    linguistically, but rely on speaker and hearer sharing the same context
5   limited vocabulary and limited number of grammatical constructions.

Middle-class language, on the other hand, is an 'elaborated code', which
does not suffer from the same limitations as the 'restricted code' of the
working classes. According to Bernstein, the class system restricts access
to the elaborated code of the middle classes. Furthermore, since most
teachers are middle class, working-class children do not understand
them properly, which exacerbates their problems at school.

The evidence that is supposed to support Bernstein's contentions is
poor. It is true, as Bernstein pointed out, that working-class children
tend to have depressed verbal IQ scores. However, there is no evidence
that verbal IQ is related to mastery of aspects of language that are
available only in the elaborated code of the middle classes. Another
piece of evidence cited by Bernstein comes from a questionnaire study
(Bernstein and Henderson, 1969) in which mothers were asked what
they would do if their child became dumb. Middle-class mothers foresaw
more problems, indicating a better ability to describe the importance of
language in interactions with the child, but there was no attempt to
show that the results reflected the behaviour of mothers who really had
dumb children, nor any explicit detailing of the relation between this
result and the alleged problems created by lack of access to the restricted
code.

Bernstein's conclusions have been subjected to much criticism, in
particular by the American sociolinguist William Labov (e.g., 1970).
Three of Labov's criticisms are particularly important. The first we have
already alluded to. One of the most important pieces of information on
which Bernstein bases his argument is the depressed verbal IQ of working-class children, as compared with their own visuo-spatial IQ. Verbal
IQ is measured by items such as verbal analogies on IQ tests. Ironically,
Bernstein's own data show that verbal IQ, thus defined, bears little if
any relation to the linguistic abilities that he believed to vary between
social classes. A second problem with Bernstein's work identified by
Labov is that, even given that Bernstein identified linguistic differences
between working-class and middle-class children, and given that the
differences in educational achievement were real, Bernstein produced no
evidence that the linguistic differences *caused* the differences in educational achievement. That idea was an unsupported speculation. Thirdly,
Labov questioned whether the differences between working-class and

middle-class language were really as Bernstein described them. Bernstein had used middle-class informants to collect samples of speech from both middle-class and working-class children. The samples from the working-class children may have been impoverished not because of any linguistic disability, but because of an inability of the working-class children to relate to the middle-class interviewers. Like Whorf, Bernstein had failed to see that differences he took to be linguistic might have been primarily cultural in nature.

Labov and others (e.g., Dillard, 1972) have compared the dialects of English spoken by blacks and whites in the USA. For each group of subjects they used informants from that group's ethnic community to collect language samples. This work has shown that Black English has different syntactic rules and different word formation rules (morphology) from White English. However, the rules for each dialect are equally clear, and are used consistently by speakers of that dialect. There are no grounds for claiming that one is superior to the other. Any argument that can be expressed in one dialect can be expressed in the other. There is no reason to suppose that being a speaker of Black English restricts the power of one's thought. It remains true, of course, that many black children in the United States are educationally disadvantaged. Labov's conclusion is that we should not try to explain this educational disadvantage by characteristics of the language the blacks speak. The problem lies elsewhere, and we are doing everyone a disservice if we focus on the wrong explanation for the problem.

3.3.3   The Sapir–Whorf hypothesis: conclusions

There is no experimental evidence that supports the strong version of Whorf's hypothesis – that speaking a particular language determines the kinds of thought a person can have. Indeed, it is not clear that there could be. The strong version seems to make comparisons between languages impossible – in what language could the comparison be stated? It may, therefore, be incoherent. The weak form of the hypothesis – that speaking a particular language makes some kinds of thinking easier than others – is certainly not incoherent, but it remains extremely difficult to test, because linguistic differences always go along with cultural ones. Most of the experimental evidence discounts the strong form, but is probably compatible with the weak form. Indeed, it could be argued that, for example, the fact that the Dani were slower in the Brown and Lenneberg task than English speakers, overall, could be explained by their impoverished colour vocabulary. However, it could also be explained culturally, by their lack of familiarity with experimental procedures. Some anecdotal evidence appears to favour the weak version, for example Whorf's 'fuel can' story, where cultural differences are not at stake. Furthermore, the vital importance of mathematical notation (a mathematical language) for thinking mathematically also suggests that a particular language can make some kinds of cognition possible.

Summary

The traditional view of the relation between language and thought, which can be traced back at least as far as Aristotle, is that thought has priority over language. Versions of this view can be found in modern theorists as diverse as Piaget, Chomsky and Schank. Vygotsky argued that speech and thought are initially independent of one another, but become more closely entwined as a child grows older, when most complex thinking depends on internal speech. Sapir and Whorf argued for the opposite of the traditional view in putting forward their twin hypotheses of linguistic determinism – that language determines thought – and linguistic relativity – that speakers of different languages think in different ways. Experimental work has provided little support for this idea, though the clearest data comes from domains, such as perception of and memory for colours, in which an influence of language on thought is implausible on biological grounds. Similarly, attempts to show that the language of the working-class (in the UK) or of blacks (in the USA) impairs their ability to think have not been successful.

Further Reading

Labov, W. (1970). The logic of nonstandard English. In F. Williams (ed.), *Language and Poverty* (pp. 153–89). Chicago: Markham.

Rosch, E. (1974). Linguistic relativity. In A. Silverstein (ed.), *Human Communication: Theoretical Perspectives* (pp. 95–121). New York: Halstead Press.

Vygotsky, L. S. (1986). *Thought and Language* (rev. edn). Cambridge, MA: MIT Press.

Whorf, B. L. (1956). *Language, Thought and Reality: Selected Writings of Benjamin Lee Whorf* (ed. J. B. Carroll). Cambridge, MA: MIT Press.

4

Logic

After our discussion of the relation between language and thought in chapter 3, we begin, in this chapter, our account of the trains of thought that comprise human reasoning, which we mentioned briefly at the end of chapter 2. We start by describing logic, which provides a yardstick for assessing whether certain trains of thought amount to valid *arguments*.

Once a person knows some facts, others follow from them with certainty, and a train of thought leading from the known facts to those that follow will often be useful. For example, if I know it's snowing and if I know that whenever it snows the air temperature is low, then I am led to the conclusion that the air temperature is low, which might prompt me to put on a coat and scarf before I go out. However, not all pieces of reasoning are as easy to assess as this one. Consider the following two arguments, discussed by Fisher (1988). The first is adapted from a leaflet produced by the Campaign for Nuclear Disarmament (CND).

> If the civil population cannot be defended in the event of nuclear war, we do not need a civil defence policy. But we *do* need a civil defence policy if 'deterrence' is to be a convincing strategy. Therefore, deterrence is *not* a convincing strategy.

The second comes from the philosopher John Locke's *Second Treatise of Government*.

> The materials of nature (air, earth, water) that remain untouched by human effort belong to no one and are not property. It follows that a

thing can become someone's property only if he works and labours on it to change its natural state. From this I conclude that whatever a man improves by the labour of his hand and brain belongs to him and to him alone.

Are either of these pieces of reasoning valid? How can we tell? And how can we explain why they are or are not valid? In this chapter we address these questions, and in the next two we consider the corresponding psychological question of how to explain people's ability or inability to deduce one fact from others.

In fact, neither piece of reasoning is correct as it stands, though one of them is correct given a reasonable assumption that might be made by its intended audience. To justify these statements we need to draw on the discipline of logic, in which philosophers try to distinguish systematically between valid and invalid arguments. We will return to the two arguments above at the end of the chapter.

4.1   Deduction

One kind of thinking is simply thinking about something – a person, an animal, a place, a particular topic or whatever, with no attempt to initiate a train of thought. But once we know at least one fact about something we may be able to reason from that fact, and add other facts to our knowledge. Indeed, in deciding whether one thing follows from another, it doesn't really matter if the facts are facts. They can be mere suppositions. We can reason about fictional or hypothetical worlds, and we can reason from mistaken beliefs, just as well as we can reason about the real world. Some conclusions follow with certainty from a set of facts or suppositions. If the facts are facts, there is no way that certain conclusions from them can be false. And if the suppositions were facts there would be no way that those conclusions could be false. In such cases the conclusions can be *deduced* from the facts or supposed facts. In other cases the conclusions do not follow with absolute certainty, but they are very likely to be true.

Since conclusions can follow equally from true facts and from suppositions, a distinction must be drawn between an argument (from facts to conclusion) being *valid* and its having a true conclusion. It is likely, though by no means certain, that a valid argument from premises that are not actually true, but merely supposed to be true, will lead to a false conclusion. However, by definition, a deductively valid argument can *never* lead from true premises to a false conclusion.

It is an undeniable truth that people do not always draw the conclusions they should draw from the facts that they know. Sometimes they fail to draw a conclusion that they are entitled to draw. Sometimes they draw a conclusion that does not follow from what they know. This inability to reason properly can be irritating (in others at least), but it has prompted attempts to characterize what makes an argument correct. The philosophers of Ancient Greece addressed this question, and the high point of their work is to be found in the collection of Aristotle's works known as the *Organon*, especially the *Peri Hermeneias* (or *De Interpretatione*, as it is usually known), and the *Prior Analytics*, in which he expounded the doctrine of the syllogism. As we will see in chapter 6, syllogisms are a highly circumscribed form of argument, for example:

> Some beekeepers are artists
> All beekeepers are chemists
>
> so,   Some artists are chemists.

However, for over two millennia the syllogism remained the only type of argument that had been systematically formalized.

The study of argument in Ancient Greece, and in the Roman world, was never far removed from the practical concerns of rhetoric and persuasion. Modern formal logic, the heir to Aristotle's doctrine of the syllogism, is regarded by its practitioners in a more abstract light. In particular, many modern logicians regard formal logic as a branch of mathematics, and are content to create formal systems without worrying, at least in the first instance, about their relation to human thought. This approach would have been totally alien to Aristotle and his contemporaries, who were squarely concerned with human reasoning, and saw their work as giving a precise account of how people think – or at least of how they ought to think.

Formal logicians have created many hundreds of logical systems. Nevertheless, one of these systems, the predicate calculus, has remained pre-eminent. Predicate calculus was first formalized by Gottlob Frege in the 1870s. Frege (1879/1972) called his system by the German name *Begriffsschrift*, which is usually translated as 'conceptual notation'. However, Frege's name for the system and his arcane symbolism are not now in common use. The first 'modern' treatment of the predicate calculus was developed by Whitehead and Russell in their *Principia Mathematica* (1910–13). However, as we shall see shortly, there are many (mathematically equivalent) ways of formalizing predicate calculus, and this fact makes its relation to the mental apparatus used in reasoning difficult to determine.

4.2   The Propositional Calculus

We will simplify the following discussion by restricting our attention to
a part of the predicate calculus known as the propositional (or sentential)
calculus. It is so called because it formalizes arguments that depend only
on relations between propositions (the meanings of simple sentences),
and not on the internal structure of the sentences that express them.
Sentences do have internal structure, but that structure need not be
important for the purposes of arguments in which those sentences are
used. More particularly, the propositional calculus formalizes arguments
that depend on the words *not, and, or, if . . . then* and *if and only if*, or
at least on precisely defined propositional operators with interpretations
that bear a reasonably close relation to the meanings of these ordinary
language words. The term operator indicates that these words take (or
operate on) one (in the case of *not*) or two (in the case of the other
words) sentences and make a new sentence out of them (other uses of
these words, for example, to join two proper names, as in 'John and
Mary' are not considered in the propositional calculus). If the word
operator appears to have a mathematical flavour, it does so because
modern formal logic, as opposed to traditional syllogistic logic, is regarded very much as part of mathematics.

There are two main ways in which propositional calculus can be
formalized. Both are formal in the sense that they are precise and well
defined, but one is formal in the additional sense that it characterizes
a valid argument in terms of the *form* of sentences, and makes use of
rules that can be applied to sentences on the basis of their form, while
the other characterizes such arguments in terms of the *meaning* of
sentences. The first of these methods is known as the *proof-theoretic
method*, the second as the *model-theoretic method*. The reason for these
names will become clearer shortly. We will describe the two methods
at some length. From a psychological view, the details are not crucial.
What is important, however, is that the complexity of the formalizations
has implications, albeit indirect, for the complexity of the mental processes
that underlie our ability to reason.

4.2.1   Well-formed formulas

Before looking at the methods of deciding whether an argument is valid
in the propositional calculus we need to say what counts as a correctly
structured sentence, or *well-formed formula*, to use the technical term,
in that system. This is rather like saying what counts as a proper sentence

Table 4.1 Operators of the propositional calculus

Logical operator	Approximate equivalent in ordinary English	Alternative symbols
¬	not	~
∧	and	& , .
∨	or	
→	if . . . then	⊃
↔	if and only if	≡

of English before saying anything about whether those sentences are true or false, plausible or implausible, and before deciding which arguments that can be expressed in ordinary English are valid ('the rat ate the bed' is a structurally well-formed sentence, 'rat bed ate the the' is not). The difference is that the rules for propositional calculus are much simpler than those for English. The 'words' of propositional calculus are the simple sentences and the operators we mentioned above. The operators form a fixed set, but the sentences do not. So to state the rules for well-formed formulas of propositional calculus we need to use variables that can stand for any sentence. It is usual to choose the letters p, q, r, . . . for these variables. The letters are variables in just the same way that x, y, z, . . . are variables in the kind of simple algebraic formulas that are encountered in high-school mathematics. So the repetition of p means definitely the same sentence (for example, the two occurrences of p in $((p \lor q) \land (r \rightarrow p))$ stand for the same sentence), whereas the use of different letters indicates possibly different sentences (p and q may turn out to be the same, just as in an algebra problem x and y might turn out to be the same number). The operators of the propositional calculus are represented by the (constant) terms ¬, ∧, ∨, → and ↔. As we mentioned above, these operators correspond roughly to the English words *not, and, or, if . . . then* and *if and only if*, as shown in table 4.1. Different logicians use different symbols for these operators, and some alternatives, which may be encountered in other texts, are shown in table 4.1. Finally, opening and closing parentheses ('(' and ')') are used to 'punctuate' sentences.

The rules for what counts as a correct sentence are straightforward.

1 Any single letter (a simple sentence) is a well-formed formula.
2 The sign ¬ followed by any well-formed formula is a well-formed formula.

3   An opening parenthesis followed by any well-formed formula followed
    by one of the signs ∧, ∨, →, ↔ followed by another well-formed
    formula followed by a closing parenthesis is a well-formed formula.

These rules are said to be *recursive*, since a formula that results from
applying one rule can be further elaborated by another rule. Both rule
(2) and rule (3) can be applied to *any* well-formed formulas. So, starting
with the single letters p, q, r, . . . we get all of the following (among
others) as well-formed formulas: ¬p, (p ∧ q), (p ∨ q), (p → q), (p ↔
q). Further application of the rules gives us more complex sentences
such as (p ∧ ¬q), ((p ∨ q) → r), ((p ∧ ¬q) ∧ (¬r ↔ s)). Indeed this small
set of rules can produce an infinite number of well-formed formulas. In
writing down well-formed formulas it is usual to omit the outermost
parentheses. Logic textbooks often adopt further conventions that allow
more parentheses to be omitted, but we will not describe these conventions here.

4.2.2   Proof-theoretic formalizations of the propositional calculus

We return now to methods of showing that arguments in the propositional calculus are valid. We begin by discussing proof-theoretic
methods. Most people are familiar with the idea of a mathematical
proof, if only from high-school geometry. In such a proof, certain things
are given (e.g., 'let ABC be an isosceles triangle . . .'), and others are
shown to follow from them (e.g., 'prove that angle DBX is a right
angle'), by the application of a set of rules of inference. The proof-
theoretic approach to logic extends this idea to arguments. The propositions (facts) that are given are referred to as the *premises* of the
argument, and any valid conclusion must be derived from them using
rules for manipulating the sentences expressing them. The goal of
formalizing propositional calculus is to characterize all those arguments
and only those arguments that depend just on the words *not, and, or,
if . . . then, if and only if*, or their formal equivalents. There are two
main types of proof-theoretic formalization of the propositional calculus:
the axiomatic method and the method of natural deduction.

4.2.2.a   *The axiomatic method*
This first proof-theoretic method parallels the method that Euclid developed to formalize geometric proofs. Euclid selected a small set of independent, but mutually consistent, *axioms* together with a set of rules
for proving other formulas (called *theorems*) from those axioms. The

Table 4.2 Definitions of →, ∧, ↔ in *Principia Mathematica*

Simple formula containing operator	English equivalent	Formula providing the definition	English equivalent
p → q	if p then q	¬p ∨ q	not p or q
p ∧ q	p and q	¬(¬p ∨ ¬q)	not (not p or not q)
p ↔ q	p if and only if q	(p → q) ∧ (q → p)	if p then q and if q then p

axioms include the notion that a straight line can be drawn between any two points, and the famous parallel axiom (take a straight line and a point not on the line: there is one and only one line through the point that is parallel to the first line). Euclid thought his axioms to be self-evident, and the reason why the parallel axiom is famous is that it was shown in the nineteenth century that 'non-Euclidean' geometries could be developed in which the parallel axiom was not true. In one kind of non-Euclidean geometry there are no lines parallel to a given line that pass through a point outside it, in another there are infinitely many. The development of non-Euclidean geometries was one of the principal factors that caused mathematicians to rethink the role of axioms in mathematics. They are now no longer regarded as self-evident. Rather, they are taken to be assumptions that may, on the one hand, lead to interesting mathematical systems and, on the other hand, allow those systems to be applied to 'real-world' problems, just as Euclidean (and non-Euclidean) geometry can be used in calculations about real-world space.

The best-known axiomatization of the propositional calculus is that of Whitehead and Russell in *Principia Mathematica*. Just as Euclid had taken certain concepts, such as line and point, as undefined within his system, Whitehead and Russell were forced to take certain concepts as primitive in their formulation of propositional calculus. The ones they chose were ¬ and ∨, which are supposed to correspond roughly to the ordinary language concepts *not* and *or* (in the sense of either p or q or both). The other operators are then introduced by the definitions in table 4.2. In this system →, ∧ and ↔ are used only as a sort of shorthand. They can be eliminated from proofs altogether (at the expense of making the proofs longer) using the definitions in table 4.2. The axioms of Whitehead and Russell's system, with their names on the right, are shown in table 4.3. The reasonableness of these axioms can be assessed by substituting the appropriate English words for the

Table 4.3   Axioms of the system of *Principia Mathematica*

Formula	Name
$(p \vee p) \rightarrow p$	Tautology
$q \rightarrow (p \vee q)$	Addition
$(p \vee q) \rightarrow (q \vee p)$	Permutation
$(p \vee (q \vee r)) (q \vee (p \vee r))$	Association
$(q \rightarrow r) \rightarrow ((p \vee q) \rightarrow (p \vee r))$	Summation

connectives and arbitrary (true or false) statements for the variables. Addition, for example, says that if some statement is true then that statement or some other statement is true (e.g., 'if grass is green then snow is white or grass is green').

The system contains three rules for deriving one well-formed formula from another:

1   The rule of *substitution of variables* allows one variable (letter) to be substituted for another (e.g., q for p) provided that the substitution is made consistently throughout a formula.
2   The rule of *inference* states that from the formulas p and p → q the formula q can be derived. This rule is often referred to by its Latin name *modus ponens*.
3   The rule of *definitional substitution* allows a formula to be replaced by one that it is defined as being equivalent to.

In fact, Whitehead and Russell's axiomatization of the propositional calculus can be improved on. The axioms do not satisfy the condition of independence. The principle of association can be shown to follow from the others, and so it can be dropped. The system can be further simplified by the introduction either of an operator that can be translated as 'not both p and q' or of one that can be translated as 'not p and not q'. In either case this new operator is usually written | (pronounced 'stroke'), and all the other operators (¬, ∧, ∨, →, ↔) can be defined in terms of the stroke operator. Only the stroke operator need remain undefined. Furthermore, with stroke as the only undefined operator, the number of axioms can be further reduced.

4.2.2.b   Natural deduction systems
The alternative proof-theoretic method of formalizing propositional calculus is to treat it as a *natural deduction system*, with one or more

Table 4.4 Lemmon's natural deduction system for propositional calculus

assumption	
modus ponens	from formulas of the form p and p → q infer q
modus tollens	from formulas of the form ¬q and p → q infer ¬p
double negation	from a formula of the form ¬¬p infer p
conditional proof	from a proof of q on the assumption p infer p → q
'and' introduction	from a proof of p and a proof of q infer p ∧ q
'and' elimination	from a formula of the form p ∧ q infer p
'or' introduction	from a formula of the form p infer p ∨ q
'or' elimination	from a formula of the form p ∨ q, a proof of r on assumption p and a proof of r on assumption q infer r
reductio ad absurdum	given a proof of q ∧ ¬q on assumption p infer ¬p

rules of inference for each of the main logical operators. In a natural deduction system there are no axioms. The first rule of such a system, the so-called rule of assumption, states that any proposition (strictly, the sentence expressing it) can, at any point in a proof, be introduced as an assumption. In this way we can show that one sentence follows from one or more others (the premises of an argument) by introducing those premises as assumptions. Of the other rules of a natural deduction system, Whitehead and Russell's rule of inference (modus ponens), associated with the operator →, is just one among several. The rules in table 4.4 (taken from Lemmon, 1965) can be used to formalize the propositional calculus as a natural deduction system. In every case assumptions carry over from the premises to the conclusion in the expected way.

To demonstrate how the rules of a natural deduction system are used in proofs, we will show that the formula ¬p → (p → q) (if it is not the case that p then if p then q) is a theorem of predicate calculus. Although we may have to make assumptions in proving the formula (introduced into the proof using the rule of assumption), those assumptions are eventually eliminated (by conditional proof, or reductio ad absurdum), so no assumptions have to be made to show that the formula is true. In the first part of the proof we show that ¬(p ∧ ¬q) follows from ¬p. The reason for this step is that p → q follows from ¬(p ∧ ¬q) – in fact, each follows from the other, though we do not need to prove that here. So, if ¬(p ∧ ¬q) follows from ¬p, so does p → q.

1	¬p	assumption
2	p ∧ ¬q	assumption
3	p	from 2, by 'and' elimination
4	p ∧ ¬p	from 3 and 1, by 'and' introduction
5	¬(p ∧ ¬q)	from 2 and 4, by reductio ad absurdum on assumption 1.

In the next section of the proof we show that p → q does, indeed, follow from ¬(p ∧ ¬q). For this part of the proof we make some additional assumptions, which are quickly eliminated, so that the conclusion does not rest on them.

6	p	assumption
7	¬q	assumption
8	p ∧ ¬q	from 6 and 7, by 'and' introduction
9	(p ∧ ¬q) ∧ ¬(p ∧ ¬q)	from 8 and 5, by 'and' introduction on assumptions 1, 6 and 7
10	¬¬q	from 7 and 9, by reductio ad absurdum eliminating assumption 7
11	q	from 10, by double negation
12	p → q	from 6 and 11, by conditional proof on assumption 1, eliminating assumption 6.

Finally, we conditionalize (11) on (1) to prove the theorem, eliminating all the assumptions.

13	¬p → (p → q)	from 1 and 12, by conditional proof

4.2.3 Model-theoretic formalizations of the propositional calculus

The model-theoretic method of formalizing the propositional calculus is known as the method of truth tables. In general, model-theoretic methods of formalizing logical calculi are based on semantic notions, traditionally the semantic notion of truth and a more technical semantic notion called satisfaction, but other semantic notions have become important in some recent developments. Model-theoretic formulations of logical systems are based on a definition of a valid argument that is similar to

Table 4.5 Possible combinations of truth
values for three sentences, p, q, r

p	q	r
true	true	true
true	true	false
true	false	true
true	false	false
false	true	true
false	true	false
false	false	true
false	false	false

an informal one we have used above. A valid argument is one in which
there is no (consistent) way of interpreting the premises and conclusion
so that the premises are true and the conclusion false. At first glance the
new parts of this definition look a little odd. Surely, in ordinary language
at least, the premises and conclusion of an argument have only one
interpretation, unless there is some hidden ambiguity. However, it must
be remembered that this definition of validity is intended to apply to
argument *forms*. So, for example, we want to be able to show that any
argument of the form:

Premises: $p \vee q, p \rightarrow r, q \rightarrow r$
Conclusion: r

is valid. Since p, q and r are variables that might stand for any sentence,
this argument is only valid if, no matter what values we choose for p,
q and r, the premises cannot be true when the conclusion is false.

Because there are indefinitely many sentences in the propositional
calculus, it may seem a daunting task trying to find out whether an argument in the propositional calculus is valid using a semantic method.
However, whatever proposition the sentence p (or q or r) expresses, it
is assumed that it can have only two semantically distinct values, true
or false. (By distinguishing between sentences and propositions, we can
allow that some sentences fail to express a proposition, and so the
question of whether such a sentence expresses a true proposition or a
false proposition need not arise.) So, for an argument whose premises
and conclusion contain n distinct propositional variables, there will be
2^n interpretations to consider (8, for example, for the argument above).
These possibilities are shown in table 4.5.

Table 4.6a   Truth table for ¬p

p	¬p
true	false
false	true

Table 4.6b   Truth tables for p ∧ q, p ∨ q, p → q, p ↔ q

p	q		p ∧ q	p ∨ q	p → q	p ↔ q
true	true		true	true	true	true
true	false		false	true	false	false
false	true		false	true	true	false
false	false		false	false	true	true

Table 4.7a   Truth values of ¬p and p → q on the four possible assignments of truth and falsity to p and q

p	q	¬p	p → q
true	true	false	true
true	false	false	false
false	true	true	true
false	false	true	true

To find out whether an argument is valid we next need a method of deciding whether a complex formula is true (or false) given the truth or falsity of its components. The model-theoretic approach to propositional calculus does this by providing a truth table for each operator of the system. These truth tables are shown in tables 4.6a and 4.6b. These truth tables can be used to determine the truth or falsity of a well-formed formula of any complexity, provided that they are used in a manner that parallels the way the formula was constructed. So, for example, for the formula ¬p → (p → q), which we showed to be a theorem of propositional calculus using the natural deduction method, the truth values of ¬p and p → q are first determined for the four possible assignments of truth and falsity to p and q, as shown in table 4.7a. The truth table for → is then used to work out the truth values of the formula as a whole. So, for the first line in table 4.7b the first part of

Table 4.7b Use of truth table to show that ¬p →
(p → q) is a theorem of propositional calculus

p	*q*	*¬p*	*→*	*(p → q)*
true	true	false	true	true
true	false	false	true	false
false	true	true	true	true
false	false	true	true	true

the overall formula (¬p) is false and the second (p → q) is true. This configuration corresponds to the third line of the truth table for →. So, with p true and q true the formula ¬p → (p → q) is true. The complete derivation is shown in table 4.7b. The completed table shows that no matter what the truth values of p and q this formula is always true. It is, as we previously showed, a theorem of the propositional calculus. These theorems are sometimes called tautologies. They are true in virtue of the meanings of the operators of the propositional calculus (*not*, *and*, etc.). To find out whether an *argument* is valid using truth tables one constructs the truth tables for the premises and for the conclusion and then looks to see if there is any combination of truth values that makes the premises all true and the conclusion false. If there is not then the argument is valid.

4.3 Predicate Calculus

Predicate calculus is an extension of propositional calculus. We will not describe it in detail here, but we will give a very brief outline of its most important features. Propositional calculus says nothing about the internal structure of sentences (propositions). It cannot, therefore, be used to formalize arguments that depend on that internal structure. The predicate calculus recognizes that a simple sentence can be analysed into a *predicate*, usually expressed by the verb in an ordinary language sentence, or by a noun or adjective following the verb *to be* (e.g., 'is asleep', 'is a dog'), and a number of *arguments* – the people, animals, things, places, or whatever that are related to one another by the verb. So, in the sentence 'John is tall', 'tall' is the predicate and 'John' its argument, and in 'Mary likes Paris', 'likes' is the predicate and 'Mary' and 'Paris' are the arguments. Predicates can take any number of arguments, but the usual numbers are one, two or three. The first, second and third arguments usually correspond to the subject, direct object and indirect object of a simple sentence. Simple sentences in predicate calculus are written in a form that corresponds to likes(Mary, Paris). So, following the usual convention of using the letters F, G, H, ... as variables that can stand for predicates and x, y, z, ... as variables that can stand for arguments, the form of a simple sentence comprising a predicate and two arguments is 'F(x, y)'.

The second important idea in predicate calculus is that sentences can make general claims as well as specific ones. Generality is conveyed in predicate calculus by the device of *quantification*. Two kinds of generality are recognized in predicate calculus, one corresponding to statements about any thing (or all things) of a certain kind and one corresponding to statements about some things (taken in the broad sense of at least one thing and possibly all things) of a certain kind. In *first order predicate calculus*, which is the most important system, only generalizations about arguments are allowed, not generalizations about predicates. So, one can formalize arguments that depend on statements such as 'some cows are brown' (there is at least one object to which the predicate 'cow' applies, and to which the predicate 'animal' also applies), but one cannot formalize arguments from statements such as 'Mary has all the same personal qualities as John' (take any predicate expressing a personal quality; if it can be applied to John, it can be applied to Mary). The two quantifiers of the predicate calculus are called the universal quantifier (∀, corresponding to 'any') and the existential quantifier (∃, corresponding to 'some'). Quantifiers are combined with variables when they are used in predicate calculus formulas. In first-order predicate calculus those variables must be variables that stand for arguments, not predicates. The statement 'some cows are brown' would, therefore, be written as:

$(\exists x)(cow(x) \wedge brown(x))$
there is something x, such that x is a cow and x is brown.

which corresponds reasonably closely to the above gloss on the simple English sentence.

Aristotle's theory of the syllogism, which we will outline in more detail in chapter 6, formalizes a small subset of arguments that depend on these notions of generality. Since it does allow general statements, syllogistic reasoning goes beyond the kind of arguments that can be expressed in propositional calculus. Predicate calculus, however, is more powerful than the system of syllogisms.

4.4 Why is Deduction Important?

One question that arises from the discussion so far is why deductive reasoning is considered to be so important. We have seen that, on the one hand, the study of deductive reasoning focuses on a small number of logical operators corresponding to a minute proportion of all the words in a language such as English. On the other hand, however, logicians set great store by arguments that depend on the behaviour of those operators. Why should this be so?

Most logicians believe that (roughly speaking) the rest of the words of English fall into two classes. First, there are a few more words that deserve special logical treatment. Just as the propositional calculus can be extended to form the predicate calculus by including methods of treating arguments based on *any* and *some*, further extensions can cope with other words (or phrases) with interesting properties. Examples of other words that have been selected for logical treatment include *most, few, a few, necessarily, possibly, it is permissible to, it is obligatory to, know, believe*. The remaining words, by far the majority in a language such as English, do not have properties that deserve a specific logical treatment. Nevertheless, information about the meaning of those words can be captured in formulas of predicate calculus – formulas that can be stipulated to be true, even though they cannot be shown to be true on the basis of their logical properties. Such formulas are called *meaning postulates* (Carnap, 1952). For example, the meanings of the English words *haddock* and *fish* are such that anything that is a haddock is also a fish. This statement can be formalized in the predicate calculus as a statement to the effect that anything to which the predicate 'haddock' applies is one to which the predicate 'fish' applies:

$(\forall x)(haddock(x) \rightarrow fish(x))$
for any thing x, if x is a haddock then x is a fish.

Thus, arguments that rest on the fact that haddock are fish can be couched within a system of deductive logic. Given these ways of extending deductive logics, it is clear why logic is of such potential importance to the psychology of reasoning. Indeed, it has been suggested, particularly in artificial intelligence, that much of human reasoning and problem solving is deductive in the strong sense of making use of a theorem prover for predicate calculus. This view was influential in the late 1960s after the invention of a readily implemented theorem prover for predicate calculus (Robinson, 1965) based on a method known as *resolution* (see Garnham, 1988: p. 118ff., for a brief account). However, the failure of this method to solve any but trivial problems in a reasonable amount of time has meant that the view of reasoning as mental deduction has not been the dominant view in AI in the last twenty years. In psychology the mental deduction theory has remained more popular. For a recent exposition of a theory of this kind see Rips (1988).

4.5 Why might Deduction not be so Important?

Deductive systems, such as the propositional and predicate calculi, can be used to analyse some everyday arguments (see the end of this chapter). However, much of our everyday reasoning has a property, technically known as *non-monotonicity*, that appears to put it outside the scope of such analysis. In the propositional and predicate calculi, if a conclusion follows from a set of premises, it follows from any larger set of premises that includes them. New information cannot overturn an old conclusion, unless it is inconsistent with what was previously known. In everyday life, however, we are always revising our conclusions when we get new evidence. If someone knows I am very particular about locking my windows and doors when I go out, and they call round and find my door open, they will assume I am at home. But if they cannot find me anywhere, they will revise this opinion. If I then come out from under a manhole cover in my driveway, they will change their mind again.

There is some debate about the correct characterization of the mental processes that underlie such reasoning. Is my acquaintance drawing probabilistic conclusions? Or engaging in arguments that can be analysed using a non-standard type of logic (a *non-monotonic* logic)? Is that person making ordinary deductions based on unstated premises that are false, and that are, hence, discarded in the drawing of the second and third conclusions (i.e., they are not simply enlarging the set of premises from which they are arguing)? The second of these ideas has been the most popular, though it has been pursued largely in artificial intelligence, rather than in experimental psychology. However, the attempt to formulate a non-monotonic logic that even approximately captures the inferences that people readily draw in everyday life has proved extraordinarily difficult (see, e.g., Oaksford and Chater, 1991). Furthermore, Oaksford and Chater argue that, even if such a logic could be formulated, it could not explain how people perform simple everyday inferences. Our everyday reasoning can draw on virtually any piece of knowledge we have, and, claim Oaksford and Chater, it is impossible that mental machinery characterized in terms of a logical system could find the right bits of knowledge quickly enough – their argument is a technical one that draws on the notion of computational complexity.

Oaksford and Chater hint that a connectionist model of everyday reasoning might solve this problem, but they do not explain how. Garnham (1993) argues that Oaksford and Chater are wrong about how knowledge is used in everyday reasoning. For example, if someone is trying to calculate when an egg will be soft-boiled, they do not usually consider the possibility of an earthquake disrupting the boiling process. A typical non-monotonic logic would give the conclusion: the egg will be soft-boiled four minutes from when it was put into boiling water, or there will be an earthquake and it will never be soft-boiled, or an orang-utan that has run away from the local zoo will snatch it out of the water and it will never be soft-boiled, or . . . , or. . . . Such possibilities are not considered unless something in the environment (the tell-tale trembling of the ground, the appearance of a large red-furred ape) or something in the reasoner's mind makes them salient. Garnham outlines an account of everyday reasoning, along these lines, within the mental models framework mentioned in chapter 1.

Summary

To decide if a piece of reasoning is good, we need a standard against which to assess arguments. Logic attempts to provide such a standard. It distinguishes between a valid argument, the conclusion of which must be true *if* its premises are true, and an argument that, in fact, has a true conclusion. Logic has its origins in Ancient Greece, and in particular in Aristotle's doctrine of the syllogism. However, the most important modern logical systems are the propositional and, more especially, the predicate calculus. Propositional calculus attempts to formalize arguments based on *and*, *or*, *not* and *if . . . then*. Predicate calculus adds the multiple generalities that can be expressed using *any* and *some*. In doing so, it is forced, unlike propositional calculus, to take into account the internal structure of sentences. These systems can be regarded as languages in which ideas (propositions) are expressed in sentences. The rules for what counts as a good (well-formed) sentence are much simpler than the corresponding rules for English.

There are two types of method for describing valid arguments: proof theoretic and model theoretic. Proof-theoretic methods show how one sentence (or formula) of a logical language can be derived from certain others by constructing proofs rather like those found in high-school geometry. Model-theoretic methods attempt to show directly that, given the meaning of the premises and the meaning of the conclusion, the latter cannot be false when the former are all true.

At the end of the chapter we considered the question of how large a subset of arguments propositional calculus, predicate calculus and extensions of them might encompass. Their limitations are not so great as they might at first seem, given the limited number of English words to which their operators correspond. However, many everyday arguments have a property, non-monotonicity, that makes it difficult to formalize them using systems of these kinds. Reasoning is non-monotonic if its conclusion can be overthrown in the light of new information that does not contradict the original premises. Whether such arguments can be captured in an extension of predicate calculus remains to be determined.

Appendix: Analysis of the Everyday Arguments

At the beginning of this chapter we presented two everyday arguments from Fisher (1988), which we repeat here for convenience.

1 If the civil population cannot be defended in the event of nuclear war, we do not need a civil defence policy. But we *do* need a civil defence policy if 'deterrence' is to be a convincing strategy. Therefore, deterrence is *not* a convincing strategy.
2 The materials of nature (air, earth, water) that remain untouched by human effort belong to no one and are not property. It follows that a thing can become someone's property only if he works and labours on it to change its natural state. From this I conclude that whatever a man improves by the labour of his hand and brain belongs to him and to him alone.

We will now analyse these arguments using the apparatus of the propositional calculus. To formalize the first, we will use the natural deduction system for propositional calculus. For this particular argument the premises can be considered to have the form 'if p then not q' and 'if r then q', where:

$\quad$ p = the civil population cannot be defended in the event of a nuclear war
$\quad$ q = we need a civil defence policy
$\quad$ r = 'deterrence' is a convincing strategy.

The argument is invalid, as it stands, but it is valid if it is assumed that the civil population cannot be defended in the event of a nuclear war. This additional assumption is 'p'. So, from this assumption plus the first premise we conclude 'not q' (i.e., we do not need a civil defence policy) by the rule of modus ponens (from 'p' and 'if p then q' conclude 'q'). And from this conclusion plus the second premise we conclude 'not r' ('deterrence' is not a convincing strategy) by the rule of modus tollens (from 'not q' and 'if p then q' conclude 'not p'). In the USA and in the UK the additional assumption is reasonable, since it is enshrined in government policy. However, in Switzerland there are enough shelters for all the civilian population, and so the argument cannot be validly made in that country.

The second argument is a little more tricky to formalize, partly because the way each simple proposition is expressed varies from sentence to sentence, and partly because it contains quantifier phrases, such as 'whatever', that might suggest the need for the predicate calculus to formalize it, but which are irrelevant to the structure of the argument. The argument has two steps. Both are doubtful, and for similar reasons. We will focus on the second step, in which Locke starts with a premise of the form 'p only if q' and concludes 'if p then q', where:

p = a thing can become someone's private property
q = he works and labours on it to change its natural state.

'p only if q' is equivalent to 'if q then p', which is far from being equivalent to 'if p then q'. This fact is obvious from the truth table for 'if p then q' (see table 4.6b). More intuitively, Locke's 'p only if q' gives a condition that must be fulfilled if 'p' (if the person is to own the thing), but there may be other conditions that have to be fulfilled as well. So simply by working on something a person cannot establish ownership of it. It might already belong to someone else, for example. The second argument, therefore, despite being that of a philosopher, is invalid!

Further Reading

Barwise, J. and Etchemendy, J. (1989). Model-theoretic semantics. In M. I. Posner (ed.), *Foundations of Cognitive Science* (pp. 207–43). Cambridge, MA: MIT Press/Bradford Books.

Fisher, A. (1988). *The Logic of Real Arguments*. Cambridge: Cambridge University Press.

Lemmon, E. J. (1965). *Beginning Logic*. London: Nelson.

5

Deductive Reasoning

In the last chapter we considered how a valid argument might be characterized. In the next two chapters we look at people's ability to reason deductively. This chapter considers first the idea that people have the rules of a mental logic in their minds. It goes on to discuss psychological research on simple reasoning tasks. Chapter 6 presents research on syllogistic reasoning, the most extensively investigated type of deduction, and examines the effects of belief on reasoning – a topic that has been studied almost entirely in the context of syllogistic reasoning.

5.1   The Idea of a Mental Logic

As we mentioned in the previous chapter, Aristotle and other Greek philosophers believed that, in studying forms of argument, they were studying the way people think. This idea was reflected in the first writings of what can be regarded as modern logic, and in particular in those of the British mathematician George Boole, the most important of which was his book *The Laws of Thought* (1854). However, this 'psychological' way of thinking about logic was rejected by Frege, the inventor of predicate calculus, who argued that logic was part of mathematics.

It has always been recognized that people make errors when they reason, and so the psychological view of Aristotle and Boole is, roughly, that logic characterizes the way that people think when they can avoid mistakes. In modern terms, logic is a *competence* theory, which captures people's underlying ability to reason, not a *performance* theory, which would describe their reasoning in real situations, as affected by memory limitations, lapses of concentration, lack of interest, and so on. However, Frege was more impressed by people's muddleheadedness than by their abilities, and part of his argument was that human thought is so muddled and error-prone that identifying the study of logic with the study of thought introduced unnecessary complications – complications that he thought would render impossible a precise account of what constitutes a valid argument.

Frege wanted to abstract away from the vagaries of actual thought, and to talk about ideal rational thinking. He adopted a doctrine called Platonism, also dating back to Ancient Greece, which is still popular with mathematicians. Platonists hold that mathematical entities, such as numbers, exist in an abstract realm that is independent of human thought, but accessible to it. One can take a similar view about logical operators and forms of argument. These ideal operators (with the simple definitions provided by truth tables) and ideal forms of argument exist in an abstract Platonic realm. Logicians can study them, just as mathematicians study the properties of numbers. However, when ordinary people engage in argumentation, and try to follow these ideal forms of argument, they are likely to get in just as much of a muddle as when they try to solve complex mental arithmetic problems.

Mathematicians and logicians may find it useful to talk about Platonic abstractions. Psychologists, however, are interested in the actual thought processes of ordinary people engaged in ordinary reasoning. One perennially popular proposal about the mechanism underlying this ability is that, despite the mistakes that they make, people have rules of logic in their head, and that they use this *mental logic* in reasoning. The developmental psychologist Jean Piaget (e.g., Beth and Piaget, 1966) was one of the principal proponents of this idea. Contemporary advocates include Lance Rips (1983) and Martin Braine (e.g., 1978; Braine, Reiser and Rumain, 1984; Braine and Rumain, 1983). There are three major problems with this idea. First, as should be apparent from the previous chapter, there are many ways of formalizing even the simplest logical system – the propositional calculus. The idea of a 'mental logic' is, therefore, not a clear one. A theory claiming that people's reasoning abilities are based on a mentally embodied natural deduction system would make very different predictions from one claiming they use mental truth tables, for example. This problem, of course, in no way counts against the possibility of a mental logic. It simply highlights the fact that a bald claim that reasoning is based on a mental logic is not specific enough to count as a theory of how people reason. In fact, when people talk about a mental logic, what they usually have in mind is a mental logic, *proof-theoretically formulated*. Most modern advocates of mental logic propose a mental natural deduction system. Indeed, mental models theory, which claims, roughly speaking, that reasoning is based on semantically formulated principles of reasoning, has frequently be contrasted with the doctrine of mental logic.

The doctrine of mental logic can, therefore, be characterized roughly as follows. People store information in their minds in the form of propositions. To deduce conclusions from what they know, they apply rules such as modus ponens to propositions in their mind. The propositions to which the rules are applied must have the form specified by the premises of those rules, and the propositions that are derived have the form of conclusions of those rules. In saying that mental logicians advocate a mental natural deduction system, we are not saying that they believe the ten rules of Lemmon's system (which we stated in the previous chapter; see table 4.4) are all mentally encoded. There are alternative natural deduction systems, and, in any case, there are problems in suggesting that people use the introduction rules, particularly 'or' introduction. We outline below Johnson-Laird's account of why people do not use the rule of *or* introduction. However, writers who favour the mental logic approach must simply stipulate that introduction rules are not part of mental logic (see, e.g., Sperber and Wilson, 1986, chapter 2). Another problematic rule is *modus tollens* (from 'p → q' and '¬q' infer '¬p'). The reason it is problematic is that people find modus tollens more difficult than modus ponens, but, if both were rules of a mental natural deduction system, both inferences should be equally easy. It has, therefore, been proposed that modus tollens inferences are made indirectly, as follows:

1	p → q	premise
2	¬q	premise
3	p	by the rule of assumption
4	q	from (1) and (3), by modus ponens
5	q ∧ ¬q	from (2) and (4), by ∧ introduction
6	¬p	from (3) and (5), by reductio ad absurdum

Because this argument is more complex than a simple application of modus ponens, people find modus ponens easier than modus tollens. However, this account cannot explain a recent finding described by Girotto (1993). He found that modus tollens is easier when the '¬q' premise is presented first than when the 'p → q' premise is presented first. This finding can be explained by the mental models theory (see §5.2.3 below).

The second problem with the idea of a mental logic also focuses on a lacuna in the theory. If we are to explain how people reason, we must explain why they reach some conclusions, but not others. For example, one of the rules of Lemmon's natural deduction system for the propositional calculus is 'or' introduction. This rule states that 'p ∨ q' can be inferred from 'p'. Yet people almost never draw conclusions such as 'snow is white or grass is green' from a premise such as 'snow is white'. However, omitting the rule of 'or' introduction from a natural deduction system has far-reaching consequences. Johnson-Laird and Byrne (1991) have suggested a simple, but quite different, solution to the problem of characterizing which inferences people draw. It is a solution that is most naturally cast within a semantic (model-theoretic) approach to logic, and it lends support to the idea that any mental logic is likely to be semantically based. Johnson-Laird and Byrne's idea is that people use three extra-logical principles when making deductions. The first principle is that a conclusion should not contain less semantic information than the premises from which it is drawn. An increase in semantic information corresponds to a decrease in the number of situations that are compatible with the conclusion as compared with the number that are compatible with the premises. This constraint explains immediately why people do not draw a conclusion of the form 'p ∨ q' from a premise of the form 'p'. Of the four possible combinations of truth values for 'p' and 'q' (true/true, true/false, false/true, false/false), 'p ∨ q' is consistent with the first three, but 'p' is consistent only with the first two. 'p', therefore, contains more semantic information than 'p ∨ q'. Johnson-Laird and Byrne's second principle is that the conclusion should result in a simplification of the information. People do not simply join premises together with '∧'s, though if they did they would be led to a valid conclusion by the law of ∧ introduction. The third principle is that a conclusion should not repeat something that was explicitly stated in one of the premises.

The final problem with the idea that reasoning is based on a (proof-theoretically formulated) mental logic is one that we hinted at in our discussion of Girotto's finding about modus tollens. The theory does not give a satisfactory account of experimental findings on deductive reasoning. Most importantly, it provides no satisfactory account of why the content of a problem exerts so strong an influence on how easy it is to solve. We will mention some more specific problems in the rest of this chapter and in the following chapter.

5.2   Psychological Studies of Deductive Reasoning

As we explained in the last chapter, a deductive inference is one in which one statement follows from a set of other statements, in the sense that there is no way that the set of statements could be true and the conclusion false. A typical deduction is:

> All swans are white
> This bird is a swan
> _____
> so,   This bird is white.

Deduction can be contrasted with other kinds of reasoning, primarily induction and abduction (see chapter 7). In (one type of) inductive inference one moves from specific cases to a general law, rule or description. Induction is not 'safe' in the way that deduction is, because cases that are examined after the generalization has been formulated may be inconsistent with it. This 'problem' is illustrated in the following example of an induction:

> All swans that I have ever seen are white
> _____
> so,   All swans are white.

Before the discovery of Australia, an induction similar to this one had been made in Europe. Australia's black swans showed the induced generalization to be false. Abduction is the working out of the reason or cause of an event or state, often on the basis of an induced generalization. The reason why abduction is not deduction is that the same event may be caused in various ways. A broken glass lying on the floor might have been dropped, or it might have been hit with a hammer.

Do people engage in deductive reasoning in everyday life? At first one might be tempted to answer: no, deductive reasoning is much more formal than everyday reasoning. But people do come to conclusions that can be characterized as deductions from what they know. For example, if a person is told that there is a swan on the river, and if they are interested in seeing it, they will go out and look for a white bird. Why? Because they know that (European!) swans are white and that the bird they are looking for is a swan. What is not so clear is *how* people make such 'deductions'. They do not usually go explicitly through a process of deduction. But, as we saw in the discussion of mental logic, some psychologists have proposed that the unconscious procedures responsible for generating such conclusions are directly related to the explicit rules of inference (such as modus ponens) that logicians have described. Thus, the psychological question about deductive reasoning divides into two parts. First, are (some of) the inferences that people make best characterized as ones that lead to deductively valid conclusions? Second, what mental mechanisms are responsible for people's ability to make such inferences, and how do they relate to the formal accounts of deduction provided by logicians? Given that people's actual reasoning diverges from the prescriptions of logic, part of what is at stake in trying to answer these questions is whether people's underlying ability is basically a logical one, but one that can be disrupted by other influences, such as inattention or prejudice, or are they reasoning by some non-logical, and perhaps in some sense irrational, method that happens to produce the 'right' results in a proportion of cases.

5.2.1 What aspects of deduction do psychologists study?

We have given a broad definition of deduction above: a deductive inference is one that cannot lead from true premises to a false conclusion. We have also seen, in the previous chapter, that, in the two most important logical systems (propositional and predicate calculus), logicians study inferences that depend on (formal operators corresponding to) the words *not, and, or, if . . . then, if and only if, any, some.* The body of psychological research that is usually regarded as work on 'deductive inference' is closely related to this narrower definition of deduction. In addition, it focuses on relatively simple inferences that do not require many deductive steps. However, it should be borne in mind that much of the reasoning required to test hypotheses (see chapter 8) is deductive, that solutions to some, but by no means all, of the problems that psychologists have studied (see chapter 11) are naturally characterized deductively (though it is a moot question whether people try to solve them deductively). Furthermore, even though mathematics cannot be reduced to the simple logics discussed in the previous chapter, as Frege and others hoped it could, mathematical reasoning has much in common with deductive reasoning.

Turning to empirical research in psychology, a large, but fairly old, set of studies investigated people's ability to understand negation, the *not* of the predicate calculus. A rather more interesting line of research investigates conditional reasoning. One question that has to be faced in this research is what relation the ordinary language conditional *if . . . then* bears to the so-called *material conditional* ($\rightarrow$) of the propositional calculus. Work on three-term series problems, in which three people or objects are linked to one another by a relation such as 'is taller than' or 'is to the left of', reflects an interest among logicians in the properties of relations of these kinds. These properties can be expressed in predicate calculus formulas, just as the information that all dogs are animals can. However, they are not part of the predicate calculus proper. Finally, work on the understanding of quantifiers – both the *all* and *some* of the predicate calculus and other quantifiers such as *few* and *most* – and on syllogistic reasoning looks at (a small part of) our ability to reason about generalities.

Before we discuss this work in detail, we should perhaps comment on why we have not mentioned psychological work on people's understanding of *and*, *or* and *if and only if*. Work on *if and only if* comes under the head of conditional reasoning and, indeed, one of the questions in this research is whether the natural language *if . . . then* is sometimes interpreted to mean 'if and only if'. In so far as psychologists have concerned themselves with *and*, it has been mainly in the context of text comprehension (but see Braine, Reiser and Rumain, 1984). As with *if . . . then*, one of the most interesting questions has been how the divergence between the natural language term and the logical operator should be explained. 'p ∧ q' is true if 'p' is true and 'q' is true, and that it all there is to it. So, for example, there is no logical difference between 'p ∧ q' and 'q ∧ p'. In ordinary language, the difference between 'he fastened his seat belt and drove straight into the wall' and 'he drove straight into the wall and fastened his seat belt' is that between taking a sensible precaution and shutting the barn door after the horse has bolted.

The case of *or* is different. Research on thinking and reasoning has shown that people are very bad at dealing with disjunctions – alternatives of the kind presented by statements containing 'or's. Indeed, one of the fundamental tenets of the mental models theory is that people prefer to reason from a single model. However, much of the work on disjunctions has been either explicitly or implicitly carried out under the head of 'hypothesis testing' (see chapter 8), where people are given problems that contain implicit 'or's, or 'problem solving' (see chapter 11). One exception is the work of Johnson-Laird, Byrne and Schaeken (1992). As expected, these authors report that people find reasoning from double disjunctions, such as:

June is in Wales, or Charles is in Scotland, but not both.
Charles is in Scotland, or Kate is in Ireland, but not both.

very difficult. The valid conclusion in this case is:

June is in Wales, and Kate is in Ireland,
  or Charles is in Scotland, but not both.

Interestingly, the difficulty of such problems increases with the number of models required to solve them, and incorrect conclusions are almost always compatible with a subset of the legitimate models, a fact that cannot be explained on the hypothesis that deductive reasoning depends on a mental natural deduction system. Bauer and Johnson-Laird (1993) have shown that reasoning with double disjunctions can be improved with certain kinds of diagrammatic representations, based on electrical circuit diagrams, of the premises.

5.2.2 Negation

We saw in the last chapter that one of the operators of the propositional calculus is the negation operator ($\neg$), which corresponds roughly to the word *not*. To understand negation in the propositional calculus is to understand that if a sentence is true its negation is false, and that if a sentence (p) is true, so is its double negation ($\neg\neg p$).

In fact, the psychological investigation of how people understand negation lies partly within the study of thinking and reasoning and partly within psycholinguistics. On the one hand, to understand a negative sentence is not really to make a deduction (see the definition above). On the other hand, it is part of ordinary sentence comprehension. The reason why psycholinguists are particularly interested in negation, or why they were interested in it in the 1960s, is because the negation of a sentence was thought to be derived from the affirmative form by a rule known as a transformation. The use of transformations to describe the relation between sentences was popularized by the linguist Noam Chomsky (e.g., 1957, 1965), and Chomsky's ideas were crucially influential in the early days of psycholinguistics, when it was thought that negative sentences were understood by unpicking the transformation and keeping a record of the fact that this operation had been performed.

The psycholinguistic work on negation was based on how quickly people could confirm sentences such as:

Twenty-four is not an odd number.

or decide whether sentences such as:

The car is not behind the truck.

were accurate descriptions of simple pictures. It led to processing models in which the number of negatives, either explicit (the word *not*) or implicit (mismatch with reality or picture), increased the difficulty of verifying the sentence, because of a fixed formal operation that each negative called for (e.g., Clark and Chase, 1972; Trabasso, Rollins and Shaughnessy, 1971). However, this idea that negatives make a fixed contribution to the difficulty of understanding a sentence had already been shown to be incorrect by Peter Wason (1965), who demonstrated that in certain contexts, which he called 'contexts of plausible denial', the difficulty of negative sentences was considerably reduced. If, in a row of five circles, all but the fourth are blue, the sentence:

The fourth circle is not . . .

can be completed fairly rapidly with the word 'blue'.

5.2.3 Conditionals

Much of our everyday reasoning is conditional in form. We argue that if so and so is true then something else must be. However, in the study of deductive reasoning, conditionals (*if . . . then* statements) pose a number of problems. We gave the truth table for the material conditional ($\rightarrow$) of the propositional calculus in the previous chapter. This conditional has a number of properties that seem at odds with the behaviour of *if . . . then* in ordinary language.

1 Any material conditional with a false antecedent is deemed to be true. So, if *if . . . then* were to be identified with the material conditional, statements such as the following would be true:

If snow is black, grass is purple.

2 Any material conditional with a true consequent is deemed to be true, for example:

If snow is black, grass is green.

3 The material conditional is purely truth functional, but *if . . . then* statements are almost always made in natural language either when some relation (e.g., causal, inferential, deontic) is known to hold between the antecedent and the consequent, or where some as yet unknown relation is assumed to hold. People do not say:

If snow is white, grass is green

or base deductive arguments on such a statement, even though, as a material conditional, it would be deemed to be true.

4 Natural language conditionals are traditionally divided into ordinary conditionals and counterfactual conditionals – those that carry a presupposition that their antecedent is false – for example:

If snow were black, it wouldn't look so pretty.

These two kinds of conditional appear to have different properties, which cannot be captured if we have only a single material conditional operator to formalize them.

5 Some natural language conditionals, for example:

If you need some money, there's $10.00 in my purse

have truth values that seem to depend only on the truth of their consequents.

In fact, ordinary conditionals are usually judged to be irrelevant (rather than true) if their antecedent is false, unless the antecedent is negative, when they are judged to behave (more or less) like material conditionals.

The philosopher Paul Grice (1975) attempted to explain some of the deviations of the meaning of natural language *if . . . then* sentences from the material conditional in terms of *pragmatic principles* governing what it is appropriate to say when. This idea can explain why we normally expect there to be a stronger relation between the antecedent and the consequent than simply a truth-functional one, and why conditionals are deemed irrelevant when their antecedents are false (to save the material conditional account, it can be claimed that they are irrelevant but true). Johnson-Laird (e.g., 1986) has also shown how the idea that deductions should not discard semantic information (see §5.1 above), which can be regarded as a more specific version of one of Grice's maxims (quantity), can explain why some inferences that are valid for material conditionals are never drawn in ordinary reasoning.

Nevertheless, a full account of conditional reasoning within the mental models framework requires some additional theoretical apparatus (see Johnson-Laird and Byrne, 1991). Johnson-Laird's goal is a uniform semantics for the natural language conditional. To distinguish between ordinary and counterfactual conditionals he contrasts actual, really possible, really impossible, and counterfactual states of affairs. 'Counterfactual situations . . . were once real possibilities, but are so no longer because they did not occur' (Johnson-Laird and Byrne, 1991: p. 66).

They can, therefore, form the basis for counterfactual antecedents. Ordinary conditionals implicitly contrast the actual state of affairs with real possibilities, whereas for counterfactuals the implicit contrast is between the actual and the counterfactual, as defined above. Given this background, a uniform account of conditionals can be given, as follows. For any conditional, the antecedent describes a state of affairs which is to be presupposed in interpreting the consequent. The consequent then has the same interpretation as it would if it were said unconditionally in the situation described by the antecedent. So, the conditional as a whole is true if the consequent must be true whenever the antecedent is. This account is consistent with the truth table definition of the material conditional, but uses pragmatic principles, such as the fact that a sentence is not usually labelled as true or false when its presuppositions are unfulfilled, to bridge the gap between the truth-table definition and the behaviour of ordinary language conditionals.

Johnson-Laird and Byrne (1991) present a detailed theory of conditional reasoning within the mental models framework. The theory is closely related to their theory of syllogistic reasoning (see chapter 6), since a syllogistic statement of the form 'all A are B' is equivalent to a conditional statement that if something is A then it is B. The theory explains some well-established facts, such as the greater difficulty of modus tollens as compared with modus ponens. According to the theory, 'if p then q' is initially encoded in two models, one of which explicitly represents the occurrence of p and q.

$$[p] \qquad q$$
$$\ldots$$

The square brackets mean that there can be no other types of situation (and hence no other types of model) in which p is true. If another model in which p is true has to be constructed in the course of reasoning, q will have to be true in it as well. The second initial model of a conditional premise, the *implicit* model, has no explicit content. It merely indicates that other types of situation are possible. It is usually represented by three dots. Thus, modus ponens is easy, because the additional premise 'p' means that there are no models in which p is not true. The explicit model represents the only type of situation consistent with the premises, and hence 'q' must be true. Modus tollens ('if p then q', 'not q', therefore 'not p') is harder, because it requires the fleshing out of the implicit model, which, it will turn out, can represent situations of two kinds.

$$\neg p \qquad q$$
$$\neg p \qquad \neg q$$

The premise '¬q' rules out the (original) explicit model and the first implicit model, leaving only:

¬p   ¬q

Hence, it follows that '¬p'.

Johnson-Laird and Byrne's theory also makes some new predictions, for example, that modus tollens should be easier with a biconditional ('if and only if p then q') than with an ordinary conditional. The biconditional requires only two models, the original explicit model and the second of the implicit models, whereas the ordinary conditional requires the consideration of three. These predictions have been empirically verified (Johnson-Laird, Byrne and Schaeken, 1992). Furthermore, the theory explains Girotto's (1993) finding (see §5.1 above) that modus tollens is easier when the '¬q' premise is presented first. This premise forces the explicit representation of the possibility of ¬q, and hence helps subjects to avoid the most common error with modus tollens, which is to say that nothing follows.

In addition to the two valid inferences with conditionals, modus ponens and modus tollens, there are two invalid patterns, which many experimental subjects accept. Inferring 'p' from 'if p then q' and 'q' is known as the fallacy of *affirming the consequent*. Inferring '¬q' from 'if p then q' and '¬p' is known as the fallacy of *denying the antecedent*. People can be quite readily made to accept fallacious arguments of these kinds (see, e.g., Evans, 1982, chapter 8). At first, this result appears problematic, especially for people who believe that reasoning proceeds according to the rules of a mental natural deduction system. However, since the inferences are valid on a biconditional reading of *if ... then*, and since they can be suppressed by information that shows the biconditional reading to be incorrect, it has been claimed that their occurrence can be readily explained (e.g., Rumain, Connell and Braine, 1983; Markovits, 1985). For example, Markovits (1985) showed that the occurrence of fallacious reasoning with a rule such as:

If there is a snow storm in the night then the school will be closed the next day

was considerably reduced if it was embedded in a paragraph describing alternative reasons why a school might be closed (e.g., a teachers' strike, or a plumbing fault).

However, Byrne (1989) has shown that information about additional requirements can suppress the valid inferences, modus ponens and modus tollens. For example, given the premises:

If she meets her friend she will go to the play
She meets her friend

almost all subjects conclude that she will go to the play. However, if an additional premise is added:

If she has enough money she will go to the play

subjects no longer conclude, just from the fact that she meets her friend, that she will go to the play. Byrne suggests that, given two conditionals with the same consequent, the relation between their antecedents determines how they will be represented. So, given alternative reasons (snow storm = p, teachers' strike = r) for closing a school (q), the combined model effectively represents 'if (p or r) then q'. Given multiple requirements (p = meeting a friend, r = having enough money) for going to a play (q), the combined model effectively represents 'if (p and r) then q'. In this latter case, if the individual premise 'if p then q' is not retained separately, the additional premise 'p' will not license the conclusion 'q', and modus ponens will apparently be suppressed. This account, however, raises the question of what the premises of a particular argument are. In propositional calculus the three premises 'if p then q', 'if r then q' and 'p' imply 'q' by modus ponens from the first and third premises. Indeed, subjects draw this conclusion from these premises and, effectively, withdraw it given the second premise as a further piece of information. A natural interpretation of this result is that subjects simply reject the simple ('if p then q') conditional on the basis of their new information ('if p and r then q') (see Politzer and Braine, 1991). However, Johnson-Laird and Byrne (1993) report that subjects do not reject the simple conditional. Thus their reasoning is apparently non-monotonic (see chapter 4).

5.2.4   Three-term series problems

Another kind of deductive reasoning problem that psychologists have studied is the three-term series problem. A three-term series problem has two statements about three people or objects that can be ordered according to a relation such as height, for example:

Ann is taller than Barbara
Barbara is taller than Carol.

The problem is to draw a conclusion about the two people or objects that are not explicitly related to one another, for example:

Ann is taller than Carol.

These problems are easier than syllogisms (see chapter 6). Psychologists have, therefore, been interested primarily in how quickly people can solve them, although the number of errors people make is also an indication of how difficult they find the problem. Much of the work on three-term series problems was carried out in the late 1960s, and some even earlier. However, it is still of interest because it led to theoretical ideas that have continued to be important in the study of deductive reasoning.

Three main theories were proposed to explain how people solve three-term series problems. The oldest, Ian Hunter's (1957) operational theory, had a crucial influence on the mental models theory of deductive reasoning. Hunter proposed that, in order to integrate information from the two premises of three-term series problems, two types of operation had to be performed in a short-term memory store. The first operation is conversion, in which the order of the two people or objects is swapped around, and the relation is replaced by its converse. Thus,

Ann is taller than Barbara

converts to:

Barbara is shorter than Ann.

The second operation is reordering the two premises, so that the two occurrences of the so-called middle term are adjacent to one another and can be combined to produce an integrated representation. So, if the premises in the problem above were presented in the reverse order:

Barbara is taller than Carol
Ann is taller than Barbara

A representation of the form:

B > C   A > B

would have to be changed into one of the form:

A > B   B > C

before integration produced A > B > C. According to this theory, each operation adds to the difficulty of the problem. Hunter traces the idea of operations on the premises of deductions back to Aristotle.

The second theory, the imagery theory, was once favoured by Johnson-Laird (1972), among others. It shares with the mental models theory the idea that the premises are integrated into a single array, though the mental models theory is not committed to the idea that even spatial mental models are images. The third theory (Clark, 1969) identified two linguistic properties of three-term series problems that affect their difficulty. First, in a pair of terms such as *long* and *short*, *long* is neutral in the sense that the question 'how long is that piece of material?' does not imply that it is either particularly long or particularly short. The question 'how short is that piece of material?', however, implies that it is short. Problems that use the neutral *unmarked* terms are easier than those that use their *marked* converses. Second, congruence between premises and conclusion (i.e., use of the same relational term, rather than its converse) makes a problem easier. Johnson-Laird (see, e.g., Johnson-Laird and Byrne, 1991: p. 93) showed that these ideas can be incorporated into a model-type theory as assumptions about how models of spatial arrays are built, and how information is preferentially read out of them.

5.2.5   Quantifiers

We have already discussed psychological research on the operators of the propositional calculus. In the last chapter we saw that the principal additions to the propositional calculus in forming the predicate calculus are the quantifiers $\forall$ and $\exists$, which are roughly equivalent to the ordinary language terms *any* (or *all*) and *some*. We will see in the next chapter that people can have great difficulty with what appear to be simple arguments with quantifiers (syllogisms). In this section we will consider the question of how people interpret the two quantifiers of the predicate calculus, *all* and *some*, and also how they interpret other natural language quantifiers.

As with some of the propositional connectives, there is a *prima facie* mismatch between the meanings of the quantifiers of the predicate calculus and of the corresponding words in ordinary language. For example, the universally quantified sentence '$(\forall x)(Fx \rightarrow Gx)$' (for any thing x, if x is F then x is G) is true if nothing is F, whereas it would be somewhat bizarre to say that 'any F is G' if there were no Fs (and more bizarre to say that 'all Fs are Gs'). Similarly, the existentially quantified

'(∃x)(Fx ∧ Gx)' (there is something x, such that x is F and x is G) is true if only one F is G and true if all F are G, but it would be inappropriate to say that 'some F are G' if they all were, and somewhat odd to say it if only one was.

Again, as with the propositional connectives, Gricean principles governing what it is and is not appropriate to say go a good way towards explaining these discrepancies. For example, it would be misleading for someone who knew that 'all F are G' to say that only some were. The question therefore arises as to whether people interpret sentences containing quantifiers, given as premises of logical arguments, according to Gricean principles. And if they do, can that fact explain why some of the conclusions they draw are not those expected from a logical analysis of those arguments? The results of research on this topic are, at present, somewhat difficult to interpret. There is clear evidence that quantifier statements are interpreted according to Gricean principles (e.g., Newstead and Griggs, 1983). However, Gricean interpretations contribute to only a small proportion of the errors people make (Newstead, 1989).

Apart from *all* and *some*, ordinary language contains many terms that express quantities. As well as numbers, these terms include *few*, *a few*, *only a few*, *no many*, *several*, *many*, *lots*, *most*. There are also terms that indicate frequencies, such as *occasionally* and *often*. Such terms can be treated as logical constants, within a framework called *generalized quantifier theory* (see Barwise and Cooper, 1981). However, it is difficult, and sometimes impossible, to state axioms or natural deduction rules that capture the properties of these quantifiers. Thus, the only satisfactory treatments of such quantifiers are semantic, and extensions of the predicate calculus that include such quantifiers are problematic for a number of technical reasons. Furthermore, many of these quantifiers do not support interesting classes of deductively valid inferences, though those that include a numerical component do. For example, the following inference is an example of a valid type of inference for quantifiers of the form 'less (fewer) than N': if fewer than six people finished the race, fewer than six people finished the race within three hours.

Although many of these quantifiers have imprecise interpretations, so that, for example, the proportion of a set that corresponds to 'many' may vary from context to context, psychological research has established that they can be ranked in a reasonably consistent way. Pollard, Hunter and Service (1992), for example, report the following order: *all*, *most*, *lots*, *many*, *some*, *several*, *a few*, *none*.

Moxey and Sanford (1987; Moxey, Sanford and Barton, 1990) argue that quantifiers in sentences of the form '*Quantifier* of the A are B' focus attention on one of two sets of things. These sets are those As that are

Bs, the *reference set*, and those As that are not Bs, the *complement set*. For example, it is natural to continue a passage beginning:

Many of the fans went to the match

with a sentence such as:

They thought it would be an exciting game.

They refers to the fans who went to the match, and the use of a pronoun to refer to this set suggests that it is *in focus*. However,

Few of the fans went to the match
They thought it would be an exciting game

sounds decidedly odd. A more appropriate continuation would be:

Few of the fans went to the match.
They thought it would be an boring game.

In this version, *they* refers to the fans who did not go to the match. Moxey and Sanford (1993) argue that focus on the complement set is related to the need to explain why a significant proportion of the larger set (the fans, in the examples above) do *not* have a certain property (going to the match).

Summary

Deductive reasoning is reasoning from information that is given to information that follows from the given information with certainty. One way that people might carry out such reasoning is by having rules of logic in their minds. However, there are many versions of this idea, and many aspects of reasoning that the idea, by itself, cannot explain – facts, for example, about which of several conclusions people prefer to draw.

Psychologists have studied many types of deductive reasoning, and have tried to explain why people often find such reasoning difficult. The most important studies have been of negation, conditional reasoning, three-term series problems, the interpretation of quantifiers, and syllogisms. The most important idea to emerge from work on negation was that of a context of plausible denial, in which a negative statement is understood more readily than an affirmative one. Such contexts provide an example of the more general phenomenon of context determining the difficulty of a piece of reasoning.

The study of conditionals highlights the problem of identifying the operators of logic (in this case →) with ordinary language terms (*if . . . then*). Nevertheless, the differences between the two can be explained largely by pragmatic considerations, and a uniform theory of conditional reasoning, within the mental models framework, has been developed on this basis.

The study of three-term series problems suggested the role of a model-like representation in deductive reasoning, but also highlighted the influence of the language in which the problem was presented.

The interpretation of ordinary language quantifiers *any* (or *all*) and *some* is also governed, at least in part, by Gricean principles. However, these principles account for only a small number of errors in deductive reasoning. Ordinary language contains many other quantifiers, such as *most* and *a few*. Moxey and Sanford have shown that these quantifiers focus attention on one of two sets of items, either As that are Bs, or As that are not Bs (given a sentence of the form '*Quantifier* of the As are Bs').

Further Reading

Grice, H. P. (1975). Logic and conversation. In P. Cole and J. L. Morgan (eds), *Syntax and Semantics*, Vol. 3: *Speech Acts* (pp. 41–58). New York: Seminar Press.

Johnson-Laird, P. N. and Byrne, R. (1991). *Deduction*. Hove, East Sussex: Lawrence Erlbaum Associates.

Moxey, L. M. and Sanford, A. J. (1993). *Communicating Quantities: A Psychological Perspective*. Hove, East Sussex: Lawrence Erlbaum Associates.

6

Syllogistic Reasoning

In the previous chapter we introduced the idea of a mental logic, and described psychological research on several aspects of deductive reasoning: negation, conditional reasoning, three-term series problems and quantifiers. In this chapter we cover the most extensively studied aspect of deductive reasoning: the ability to solve syllogisms. We also consider how prior beliefs affect reasoning, a topic that has been studied almost exclusively in the context of syllogistic reasoning.

6.1 What are Syllogisms?

As we mentioned in the previous chapter, from Ancient Greece to the middle of the last century, the only type of argument whose properties were well understood was the syllogism. Syllogisms have two premises, each of which must be in one of the four forms shown in table 6.1. The traditional names A, I, E, O, which are referred to as the *moods* of premises, are derived from the first two vowels of the Latin words AffIrmo and nEgO (premises of type A and I are affirmative, and those of type E and O are negative). The moods are also cross-classified as universal (A and E) and particular (I and O). The conclusion of a syllogism must also be in one of these four moods. The premises of a syllogism relate A and B and B and C, and the conclusion, if there is one, must relate A and C. The theory of the syllogism was developed in great detail, though often without Aristotle's insight, by medieval

Table 6.1 The four moods of the syllogism

All A are B	(A)
Some A are B	(I)
No A are B	(E)
Some A are not B	(O)

Table 6.2 The four traditional figures of the syllogism

M–P	P–M	M–P	P–M
S–M	S–M	M–S	M–S
S–P	S–P	S–P	S–P

logicians. In this 'traditional' development, the premise that contains the subject (S) or first term of the conclusion is called the major premise, and the one that contains the predicate (P) of the conclusion is called the minor premise. The term eliminated from the premises to form the conclusion is referred to as the middle term (M). In this system the minor premise is always placed before the major premise. However, this 'traditional' presentation of the syllogism is not always a useful one for psychological purposes. As Johnson-Laird discovered, when subjects are asked to draw their own conclusion from a pair of syllogistic premises, rather than to evaluate one or more possible conclusions (as they had been asked to in previous research), there is no guarantee that they will take the subject of their conclusion from the second premise (see Johnson-Laird and Steedman, 1978). For this reason we will, for the most part, follow Johnson-Laird's method (e.g., 1983; Johnson-Laird and Bara, 1984a; Johnson-Laird and Byrne, 1991) of describing syllogisms, which uses the more neutral A, B and C rather than S, M and P for the terms, and which differs in other ways from the traditional system.

According to the traditional method of describing syllogisms there are four patterns in which the S, M and P can be arranged, which are independent of the moods of the premises and the conclusion. These arrangements, shown in table 6.2, are known as the four figures of the syllogism. In Johnson Laird's system the four figures are identified only by their premises, as shown in table 6.3:

Table 6.3 Johnson-Laird's four figures of the syllogism

A–B	B–A	A–B	B–A
B–C	C–B	C–B	B–C

Table 6.4   The 24 valid syllogisms of the traditional system

First figure:	AAA	EAE	AII	EIO	AAI	EAO
Second figure:	EAE	AEE	EIO	AOO	EAO	AEO
Third figure:	AAI	IAI	AII	EAO	OAO	EIO
Fourth figure:	AAI	AEE	IAI	EAO	EIO	AEO

Johnson-Laird's four figures map onto figures 4, 1, 2, 3, respectively, in the traditional system. In each case the conclusion in the traditional system would be C–A. However, as we have already said, when people draw a conclusion from syllogistic premises, they do not necessarily take the subject of the conclusion from the second premise. In fact, Johnson-Laird's first figure strongly favours A–C conclusions, his second favours C–A, and there is no strong preference for one order over the other in the other figures. Thus, not only do people shun syllogisms in the traditional fourth figure, the easiest syllogisms are of the form:

$$
\begin{array}{c}
\text{A–B} \\
\underline{\text{B–C}} \\
\text{A–C}
\end{array}
$$

which is not even recognized in the traditional system. Aristotle, however, not only recognized it, but claimed it to be the perfect figure.

The traditional system contains 256 syllogisms. Each premise and the conclusion can be in one of four moods, and there are four figures ($4 \times 4 \times 4 \times 4 = 256$). Of these, the 24 shown in table 6.4 are traditionally recognized as valid. Johnson-Laird allows twice as many syllogisms, calculating the figure of 512, as follows. Premises and conclusion can each be in one of four moods. In addition, there are four patterns (or figures) for the two premises. Finally, there are two orders of terms in the conclusion, A–C and C–A ($4 \times 4 \times 4 \times 4 \times 2 = 512$). In this system each syllogism in the first figure is logically, though not necessarily psychologically, equivalent to one in the second figure, but with the premises in the reverse order. For example,

$$
\begin{array}{c}
\text{All A are B} \\
\underline{\text{All B are C}} \\
\text{All A are C}
\end{array}
$$

so,

is the same as:

All B are A
All C are B
so,   All C are A

with A and C interchanged and the premises in the opposite order. In contrast, each syllogism in the third and fourth figures is equivalent to another in the *same* figure, with the premises in the other order. So, in the second figure,

Some A are B
No C are B
so,   Some A are not C

is equivalent to:

No A are B
Some C are B
so,   Some C are not A

A calculation based on the idea that there are only three figures, with order of premises being a factor that varies *within* each figure, and with the first and last figures taken to be the same, leads to the same total of 512 syllogisms, but in a more roundabout way. In the four-figure system, the order of the premises is not independent of the figure and the order of the terms in the conclusion, so it does not enter explicitly into the calculation.

We have already presented a list of the syllogisms traditionally taken to be valid. However, simply presenting a list does not explain why these syllogisms are valid. Two methods for determining the validity of syllogisms, both proof-theoretic, have been developed. One method parallels the axiomatic method of formalizing logical calculi (see chapter 4). It takes some syllogisms to be obviously valid, and gives rules for reducing any other valid syllogism to one of them. This method was first developed by Aristotle. The reduction of one syllogism to another can be interpreted as a demonstration that the reduced syllogism follows (as a theorem) from the one to which it is reduced by the laws of inference that are embodied in the method of reduction. Aristotle showed that all syllogisms could be reduced to those in the first figure, which he claimed could be evaluated directly using a principle called the *dictum de omni et nullo*. This principle states that anything that can be predicated (positively or negatively) of a *distributed* term can be predicated in the same way of anything that falls under that term.

Table 6.5 Distribution of subject and predicate terms in the four moods of the syllogism

Type of statement		Subject term	Predicate term
All A are B	(A)	Distributed	Undistributed
Some A are B	(I)	Undistributed	Undistributed
No A are B	(E)	Distributed	Distributed
Some A are not B	(O)	Undistributed	Distributed

To understand Aristotle's dictum we need to define the technical concept of distribution, which applies to the terms (the As, Bs and Cs) in the premises and conclusions of a syllogism. A term is said to be distributed when the premise or conclusion is about all members of the corresponding class. For each type of statement A, E, I, O, we must, therefore, decide whether the subject term is distributed and whether the predicate term is distributed. The subject terms are easy. Obviously a statement about all A or no A (= all A are not) is about all members of the class A. So the subject terms of statements of type A and E are distributed, whereas those of type I and O are not. For predicate terms Aristotle argued as follows. A statement of the form 'all A are B' is not about all Bs, because there may be some Bs that are not As. This conclusion holds even more clearly for statement of type I ('some A are B). However, the negative statements (E and O) do distribute their predicate terms, since 'no A are B' excludes all Bs from being As, and 'some A are not B' excludes some of the As from all of the Bs. It appears, at first, that this definition of distribution refers to the meanings of the logical terms (all, some, none, not) in a syllogism, in which case it ought to be part of a model-theoretic development of the syllogistic system. However, a purely formal definition of distribution can be given, as in table 6.5, which simply sets out, for statements in each mood, whether the subject and predicate terms are distributed or not. A variation of this technique is to show that all valid syllogisms can be reduced to a single one, usually AAA in the first figure.

> All A are B
> All B are C
> ───────────
> so,   All A are C

The alternative method of formalizing syllogistic reasoning is to give a set of criteria that any valid syllogism must meet. This method also makes use of the concept of distribution, and requires a set of axioms for syllogisms. There are five axioms, two of quantity (or distribution) and three of quality.

Axioms of quantity
- The middle term must be distributed at least once.
- No term can be distributed in the conclusion if is not distributed in the premises.

Axioms of quality
- If both premises are negative, there is no valid conclusion.
- If one premise is negative, the conclusion must be negative.
- If neither premise is negative, the conclusion must be be positive.

Let us see how these axioms work on a valid syllogism and on an invalid one. IAI in the third (traditional) figure is a valid syllogism.

> Some B are A
> All B are C
> ───────────
> so, Some A are C

Axiom 1 – the middle term (B) is distributed in the second premise
Axiom 2 – neither term is distributed in the conclusion
Axiom 3 – both premises are positive, so not applicable
Axiom 4 – ditto
Axiom 5 – conclusion is positive.

So this syllogism meets all five criteria, and is, therefore, valid. IAE (or IAO) in the third figure meets the first four criteria, just as IAI does, but fails the fifth, and is, therefore, invalid. From 'some B are A' and 'all B are C' it does not follow that 'no A are C' (or that 'some A are not C'). The five axioms can also be used to generate theorems, some general and some specific to particular figures, that can be employed to check more easily for the validity or otherwise of a syllogistic inference, without having to work through all the axioms for each syllogism.

A major problem in formulating the doctrine of the syllogism is deciding on the so-called *existential import* of statements in each of the four moods: which of the kinds of thing that a syllogistic premise mentions does it assume the existence of? Does, for example, the statement 'all A are B' imply that there are any As or Bs? And similarly for the other four moods. Universal propositions (A and E) are generally assumed not to imply the existence of any members of the classes denoted by their subject terms, whereas particular propositions (I and O) are assumed to have existential import. From a logical point of view this decision is not entirely satisfactory (see Strawson, 1952, chapter 6), but we will not pursue this point here. We will simply note that in some experimental work on syllogisms statements of a modified form have been used.

All of the A are B
Some of the A are B
None of the A is (are) B
Some of the A are not B

By using the definite description *the* A, one implies that there are As, independently of which quantifier is used. However, when statements in this form are used, the valid conclusions that follow from a pair of premises may change. For example, with the traditional wording, 'no A are B' and 'all B are C' do not entail that 'some C are not A', because the premises are consistent with their being no Cs at all. However, 'all of the B are C' presupposes the existence of Bs (and hence Cs), so that the conclusion 'some of the C are not A' is valid (see the exchange between Boolos, 1984; and Johnson-Laird and Bara, 1984b).

6.2   Models of Syllogistic Reasoning

In psychology, there is a long history of work on syllogistic reasoning, from which a set of empirical findings has emerged, together with ideas about the processes underlying people's ability or lack of ability to solve syllogisms. One of the main findings is that syllogisms range from the very easy to the very difficult. For example, about 90 per cent of subjects are able to generate the valid conclusion 'all of the artists are chemists' from the premises:

All of the artists are beekeepers
All of the beekeepers are chemists.

On the other hand, less than 10 per cent correctly conclude that 'some of the artists are not chemists' from:

All of the beekeepers are artists
None of the chemists are beekeepers

(Johnson-Laird and Byrne, 1991, table 6.1). A wide range of theoretical ideas have been put forward to account for how people solve syllogisms. In the following sections we consider some of the most important.

6.2.1 The atmosphere hypothesis

In early work on syllogistic reasoning, subjects were asked to assess conclusions presented to them, rather than to generate their own conclusions. Although this task is somewhat easier, people still make many errors. In an attempt to account for such errors, Woodworth and Sells (1935) proposed that people's assessment of the conclusions was influenced by what they called the *atmosphere* of the premises, which derives from the mood of the premises. Their claims, which were originally presented in a more complex way, can be stated as follows (see Begg and Denny, 1969):

1 Any negative premise (E or O) creates a negative atmosphere, in which negative conclusions tend to be accepted.
2 Any particular premise (I or O) creates a particular atmosphere, in which particular conclusions tend to be accepted.

These two rules are related to the axioms of quality and quantity for evaluating syllogistic conclusions. In particular, the first rule is related to the fourth axiom: if either premise is negative, any valid conclusion must be negative. However, it does not, of course, follow from this axiom that any negative conclusion will be valid. To conclude that it will be, would be to be guilty of an invalid conversion of the kind described in the next section! Atmosphere makes no distinction between valid and invalid conclusions. The second rule bears a more complex relation to the second axiom, but again makes no distinction between valid and invalid conclusions.

The atmosphere hypothesis had some success in explaining the results of experiments in which subjects evaluate conclusions. However, there are other, and perhaps better, explanations of the same findings. It has considerable difficulty explaining the results of experiments in which subjects generate their own conclusions, since some conclusions that are consistent with the hypothesis are rarely, if ever, produced, whereas others are generated frequently. The mental models theory attempts to explain syllogistic inference without recourse to the notion of atmosphere, though other model-based theories still retain the notion (e.g., Newell, 1990).

6.2.2   Conversion

A syllogistic premise is said to have been *converted* if the two terms (A and B) are swapped around. For statements in mood I and E, conversion represents a valid inference. If 'some A are B', 'some B are A', and if 'no A are B', 'no B are A'. For statements in the other two moods, A and O, conversion is not valid. It has been suggested (Chapman and Chapman, 1959) that some errors in syllogistic reasoning can be explained on the assumption that people illicitly convert one or both of the premises of an argument, and then argue from the converted premises. In some cases, the nature of the A and B may make it clear that conversion is invalid. For example, from 'all dogs are animals', one would not expect people to infer that 'all animals are dogs'. However, in other cases, the conversion may appear valid. For example, from 'all ticket holders may enter the exhibition' it may be reasonable to conclude that 'all the people who are allowed to enter the exhibition are ticket holders' or, to put it more naturally, 'only ticket holders are allowed to enter'. When people are asked to say what follows from individual syllogistic premises, conversion errors are common when they are not blocked by content (Newstead, 1990).

A more extreme view, that people routinely convert all syllogistic premises before they start reasoning, has been suggested by Revlin and Leirer (1978). These authors do allow that if conversion leads to a patently false statement, such as that 'all animals are dogs', it will be blocked. Nevertheless, their theory is *prima facie* highly implausible, and it fails in one of the principal tasks that Revlin and Leirer assign to it: to provide a systematic account of effects of belief bias in syllogistic reasoning (see §6.2.3.d below). The reason is that, as Revlin and Leirer's own data show, belief bias effects are still found even when both premises of a syllogism can be validly converted.

6.2.3   Model-based theories

Apart from theories of syllogistic reasoning based on the proof-theoretic notion of a mental logic, there are three types of theories that could be broadly described as *model-based*: theories based on Euler circles, theories based on Venn diagrams, and the mental models theory itself. All these theories claim that reasoning has three main stages.

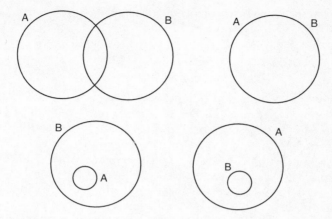

Figure 6.1   The four Euler circle representations of 'Some A are B'

1   Construct a representation of the first premise. Add in information from the second premise.
2   Look for a conclusion interrelating the end terms.
3   Search for alternative representations of the premises that support different conclusions.

If there is a conclusion that holds for all possible representations, subjects should respond with that conclusion. If there is no such conclusion, they should respond 'No valid conclusion'. We outline these three types of theory in the next three sections.

6.2.3.a   Euler circles

Syllogisms are about 'sets of entities' – the As, Bs and Cs (or whatever) mentioned in the premises. One way that mathematicians represent sets of entities is to let enclosed areas stand for them. The simplest such area is a (roughly drawn) circle, known as an Euler circle, after the eighteenth-century Swiss mathematician Leonhard Euler, though Euler circles were first invented by the philosopher Leibniz. When syllogistic premises are represented using Euler circles, the relation between the circles stands for the relation between, for example, the As and the Bs of the premise. Each of the four types of syllogistic statement can be represented in more than one way. For example, since 'some A are B' is taken to mean 'some and possibly all A are B', there are four different arrangements of the A and B circles that are compatible with this statement, as shown in figure 6.1. The Euler circle representations of the other three types of

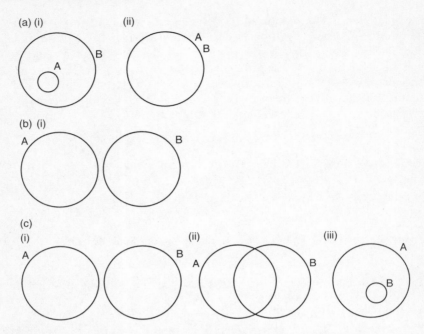

Figure 6.2   Euler circle representations of (a) 'All A are B'; (b) 'No A are B'; (c) 'Some A are not B'

statement are shown in figure 6.2. Euler circles can be used to discover what conclusions can be drawn from pairs of syllogistic premises. To do so, the diagrams representing the A–B and B–C premises must be combined by identifying the B circles in the two sets of diagrams. If there are M diagrams for the first premise and N for the second, there will be at least M × N possible combinations. In general there will be more, since there can be more than one way of combining two diagrams. The valid conclusions, if there are any, are those that are true in all of the diagrams representing all possible ways of combining the premises.

At least three psychological theories of syllogistic reasoning have been based on the assumption that people use (the mental equivalent of) Euler circles (Erickson, 1974; Guyote and Sternberg, 1981, whose theory based on a notation that represents set/subset relations is equivalent to one based on Euler circles; Stenning and Oberlander, in press). The problem with the first two of these theories is that they predict that the difficulty of a syllogism should depend on the number of different diagrams needed to represent the combination of its premises. However, this prediction is not supported by the experimental evidence. Some of the easiest syllogisms need a large number of diagrams. Stenning and Oberlander's theory, which uses just one Euler circle representation for each kind of premise, is equivalent to the mental model theory described below. Johnson-Laird and Byrne (1991) argue that, unlike the mental models theory, theories based on Euler circles do not readily generalize to represent statements containing more than one quantifier, such as:

All of the nurses were in the same place as some of the doctors.

Stenning and Oberlander's method of using Euler circles also suffers from this problem.

6.2.3.b Venn diagrams

A Venn diagram (named after the British mathematician John Venn, 1834–1923) is another geometrical method of representing sets. In a Venn diagram a single representation is used, which, in a certain sense, is maximally general. So, in a Venn diagram representing the sets A, B and C each set is (initially) shown as overlapping with both of the others, and the overlap of all three sets is also represented (those things that are A and B and C). The circles representing the sets in a Venn diagram are shown inside a box that represents the universal set – the set of everything there is. For geometrical reasons, it is only possible, in two dimensions, to draw 'pleasing' Venn diagrams for up to three sets. Syllogistic reasoning with Venn diagrams can be modelled by adopting the convention that areas of the diagram shaded in one way definitely have no members, and that areas shaded in another way definitely do have members. For example, a premise of the form 'no A are B' states that the overlap of the sets of As and Bs has no members, so that area might be blacked out. Figure 6.3 shows a Venn diagram shaded in accordance with two syllogistic premises. Since there is only one diagram, any conclusion that is true in the diagram is valid. The theory of syllogistic reasoning proposed by Newell (1981) is equivalent to a theory based on Venn diagrams. However, like the theories based on Euler circles, this theory cannot account for the difficulty of different types of syllogism.

6.2.3.c The mental models theory of syllogistic reasoning

Theories of syllogistic reasoning based on Euler circles or Venn diagrams represent sets of things – the As, Bs and Cs of the premises – by

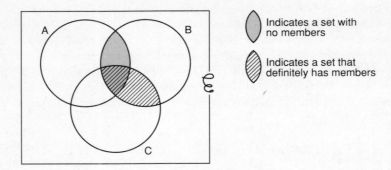

Figure 6.3   Venn diagram representation of 'No A are B, some B are C'

Table 6.6   Mental model representations of statements in the four moods of the syllogism according to Johnson-Laird and Byrne (1991)

All A are B		Some A are B		No A are B		Some A are not B	
[a]	b	a	b	[a]		a	
[a]	b	a	b	[a]		a	
...		...			[b]	a	[b]
					[b]		[b]
				...		...	

spatial extents. The mental models theory represents these sets by representative members – with 'a' standing for a representative member of the set of As, 'b' of the set of Bs and so on. The representations of premises in the four moods, as proposed by Johnson-Laird and Byrne (1991, chapter 6), are shown in table 6.6. Each line shows a representative individual with a particular combination of properties (just A, just B, or both A and B). Some types of individual whose existence is compatible with the premises are shown explicitly. However, the dots under each representation indicate that there might be other types of individual. For example, the existence of individuals that are not A and not B is compatible with the premise 'all A are B'. The square brackets place restrictions on what properties these *implicit* individuals can have. They indicate that individuals with certain properties are *exhaustively* represented in the model, so there cannot be other types of individual with those properties. In the model for 'all A are B', for example, there can be no other kinds of individual that are A, other than those in the model (i.e., each one must also be B, as the premise states). The number of individuals in the model is arbitrary, but is kept small in these examples to avoid wasting space! The Bs in the model for 'all A are B' are not exhaustively represented, so there can, but there need not necessarily, be other types of individual that are B (i.e., ones that are not A). Thus, a single representation includes the two possibilities captured by the two different Euler circle representations of premises in this mood.

The representations above, which leave some possibilities implicit, can be *fleshed out* in a number of ways, so as to represent all the types of individual that exist in a particular situation. For example, for 'all A are B' there are three possible fleshed-out representations, assuming existential import (i.e., that there are some individuals with property A). For brevity, only one example of each type of individual is shown in each fleshed-out representation. (Note that −a represents an individual who is not a member of the set of As.)

```
a   b      a   b      a   b
          −a   b     −a   b
                     −a  −b
```

Without existential import there are three further models with no individuals who are both a and b, the first of which has no kinds of individual in it.

To draw a conclusion from two premises, their mental models must first be combined by identifying the b's in the models of the two premises. The procedure for deriving the conclusions is based on the (model-theoretic) idea that an argument is valid if there is no way that its premises can be true and its conclusion false. Indeed, just as the method of truth tables for the proposition calculus can be regarded as a method for setting out all relevantly different states of affairs, the mental models theory allows a specification of all the relevantly different ways in which the premises of a syllogism can be true. The valid conclusions, if there are any, are those statements linking the A and C terms that are true in all models that represent different ways of combining the premises.

With the partly implicit representation and the square bracket notation described by Johnson-Laird and Byrne, there are at most three relevantly different ways of combining two syllogistic premises. So, some syllogisms have one model, some have two models, and some have three models. For example, the syllogism with premises in mood AA in Johnson-Laird's first figure has only one model. The models of the premises are:

All A are B	All B are C
[a] b	[b] c
[a] b	[b] c
. . .	. . .

These two models can be combined to produce:

```
[[a]   b]   c
[[a]   b]   c
       . . .
```

In the combined model the square brackets on the b's are extended around the a's because, when the b's in the second model are identified with those in the first model, they must remain exhaustively represented with respect to the c's (i.e., no b's that are not c's can be introduced). We also know from the first model that these b's must be a's as well. There is no way of producing an explicit version of this model that leaves the premises true, but which leads to a different conclusion. Therefore, there is no alternative model, and so the conclusion that the model supports, namely 'all A are C', is valid.

An example of a three-model syllogism is IE in the third figure:

	Some B are A
	No B are C
so,	Some A are not C

The models of the premises are:

Some B are A	No B are C
b a	[b]
b a	[b]
. . .	[c]
	[c]
	. . .

The simplest way of combining these premises, by identifying the b's in the two models, is:

```
a   [b]
a   [b]
        [c]
        [c]
    . . .
```

Note that, in this combined model, the a's are not exhaustively represented with respect to the c's, because the model of the first premise does not show them to be exhaustively represented with respect to the b's. This model suggests the conclusion that 'no A are C', or conversely 'no C are A'. However, there is no reason why one of the c's should not also be an a, though it cannot be a b, if the second premise is to remain true. So, there is a second model:

```
a   [b]
a   [b]
a           [c]
            [c]
    . . .
```

This model suggests the conclusions 'some A are C', 'some C are A', 'some A are not C', and 'some C are not A', though only the last two of these four are compatible with the first model. However, it is possible that all the c's might be a's, as the third model makes clear.

```
a   [b]
a   [b]
a           [c]
a           [c]
    . . .
```

In this model 'some C are not A' is not true, and 'some A are not C' remains as the only conclusion compatible with all three models. It is, therefore, the only valid conclusion.

As we have described it so far, the theory of mental models is a non-standard model-theoretic development of the doctrine of the syllogism. It can be used to decide, for every pair of syllogistic premises, which conclusions follow validly from them. However, the theory is also explicitly intended, unlike other formal developments of logical systems, to form the basis of a psychological account of syllogistic reasoning. Thus, it is intended to explain individual differences in ability to solve syllogisms, the relative difficulty of different types of syllogism, the kinds of mistakes people make in solving syllogisms, and the effects of content and prior beliefs on syllogistic reasoning. Furthermore, not only is the mental models theory of syllogistic reasoning part of a more general theory of deductive reasoning, it is also part of a broader cognitive theory that accounts for other types of reasoning, and for the way representations of the world are derived from perception and language understanding. In this respect it is different from theories of syllogistic reasoning based on Euler circles and Venn diagrams, which at first sight it might appear to resemble. Such accounts do not even extend naturally to other types of reasoning, let alone to other cognitive abilities.

The mental models theory identifies two major determinants of the difficulty of syllogisms. First, and most obviously, the number of models affects how easy it is to find a valid conclusion. Since mental models are constructed, manipulated and compared in working memory, and since working memory has a limited capacity that must be shared between storage and processing, the more models there are, the more difficult a syllogism will be. Second, the figure of a syllogism influences both its difficulty, and whether the conclusion is more likely to be A–C or C–A. The explanation of these figural effects is based on the idea, from Ian Hunter's (1957) operational theory of three-term series problems (see pp. 89–90), that the more manipulations of the premises in working memory that are needed to create an integrated model, the harder a problem will be. In the three-model syllogism that we analysed above, for example, the a's and b's had to be reversed before the b's could be put together.

The difficulty of syllogisms in Johnson-Laird's four figures increases as follows:

A–B	B–A	A–B	B–A
B–C	C–B	C–B	B–C

The A–B, B–C figure, which requires no additional operation to integrate the premises, is the easiest, and it strongly favours A–C conclusions, even when both A–C and C–A conclusions are valid. This fact is explained by assuming that conclusions are read off from models in the same direction as the premises were read in. The simplest way of solving syllogisms in the B–A, C–B figure is to discard the first encoding of the first premise and to reread it following the second premise. This produces C–B, B–A, which favours C–A conclusions. The A–B, C–B figure is harder still, because it requires the model of its second premise to be 'spatially' reversed before an integrated model of the two premises can be formed. Finally, the B–A, B–C figure is the hardest of all, since it requires either the first premise to be reversed, after the second has been read and seen not to fit with it, or for the model of the second premise to be reversed and then the first premise to be reread. Experimental evidence supports the mental model theory's predictions about the relative difficult of the figures, and about the strong preferences for A–C and C–A conclusions, respectively, in the first two figures (see, e.g., Johnson-Laird and Byrne, 1991).

Multi-model problems are, according to the mental models theory, more difficult than single-model problems. Many of the errors that occur on these problems can be explained by assuming that subjects choose a conclusion that is compatible with one of the models, but not with the others. For example, for the three-model syllogism that we discussed above, a common error is to claim that 'no A are C' or that 'no C are A', either of which is consistent with the first model we presented. Conclusions that are compatible with none of the models, such as 'all A are C', are never drawn. Individual differences can be explained in terms of working memory capacity, which determines how many models a person can consider and how easily operations can be performed on models. Belief bias can arise if a person accepts a believable conclusion which is compatible with one, but not all, of the models of a multi-model problem (Oakhill, Johnson-Laird and Garnham, 1989). However, once a conclusion has been formulated it may be subject to a process of 'filtering', in which it is assessed for believability, independently of its relation to the premises. These effects of beliefs on reasoning are discussed in more detail below.

6.2.3.d The effect of content

Like other kinds of reasoning, syllogistic inference is affected by content. The classic study of the effect of content is that of Wilkins (1928), who showed that having familiar words instead of As and Bs, or nonsense words (e.g., epilobium), improved syllogistic reasoning. Wilkins also showed that when the validity of a syllogistic conclusion conflicted with the subjects' beliefs, their ability to reason was poorer than in the familiar words condition, but not as bad as in the abstract and nonsense words conditions.

There are a number of studies showing that subjects are affected by beliefs and prior knowledge when they assess whether a given conclusion follows from the premises. For example, given the premises:

All of the Frenchmen are wine drinkers
Some of the wine drinkers are gourmets

many subjects draw the invalid, but highly plausible, conclusion:

Some of the Frenchmen are gourmets.

Although this conclusion is empirically *true*, it does not *validly* follow. By substituting 'Italians' for 'gourmets' the fallaciousness of the argument becomes apparent (see Oakhill, Johnson-Laird and Garnham, 1989).

All of the Frenchmen are wine drinkers.
Some of the wine drinkers are Italians.

so,   Some of the Frenchmen are Italians.

In the 1980s there was a revival of interest in the effects of beliefs on reasoning, and in particular, in the *mechanisms* by which beliefs have their effect. There are three aspects of the reasoning process that beliefs could affect. First, beliefs could distort the interpretation, or representation, of the premises. Second, they could influence the deductive *process*: affecting which conclusions are derived from the premises. Third, they could induce response biases: beliefs could be used to accept or reject conclusions presented for evaluation without any reasoning taking place, or they could be use to filter conclusions derived by the deductive process.

The idea that beliefs influence the interpretation of premises is held by some to be the main or even the only way in which beliefs affect reasoning. Henle (1962), for example, argued that since deductive principles are based on the rules of logic, they cannot be influenced by beliefs. One possibility is that beliefs affect how likely a premise is to be converted. As we discussed above, familiar content will block a conversion from, for example, 'all spaniels are dogs' to 'all dogs are spaniels', but similar premises with abstract or unfamiliar content may well be converted. Conversion can, therefore, lead to reasoning errors unless it is *blocked* by content, or unless the converted premises happen to lead to the same conclusion as the originals.

Although there is no doubt that beliefs do affect subjects' interpretation of premises, it is unlikely that this is the only locus of their effect (see Oakhill, Garnham and Johnson-Laird, 1990). Indeed, Oakhill and Johnson-Laird (1985) showed that subjects are still susceptible to the biasing effects of their beliefs when conversion does not alter the valid conclusion. And, as we mentioned above, Revlin and Leirer (1978) found a similar result, even though their own theory claimed that *all* effects of belief arise through conversion. Illicit conversion cannot provide a complete account of bias effects in reasoning. Nor can Revlin and Leirer's idea of the 'perfect rationality' of the deductive process be sustained.

Revlin and Leirer's theory implies that beliefs will be overridden when they cannot produce effects by illicit conversion. However, their data provided only weak support for this claim. For example, their subjects chose 'Some Arabian sheiks are not US Senators' rather than 'No Arabian sheiks are US Senators' as the conclusion of the syllogism:

No US Senators are members of the Harem club
Some Arabian sheiks are members of the Harem club.

In this syllogism both premises can be validly converted, so illicit conversion cannot lead to an invalid, but perhaps more believable, conclusion. However, although only the first of the above conclusions is valid, both are true and believable, though the first would be a somewhat odd thing to say, given that the second is also true. So, Revlin and Leirer have not shown that an unbelievable conclusion is accepted when it cannot be blocked by conversion, only that a pragmatically odd one may be.

Further evidence that beliefs affect reasoning was provided by Evans, Barston and Pollard (1983). Their subjects had to assess the validity of a *single* conclusion. For example:

> No addictive things are inexpensive.
> Some cigarettes are inexpensive.
> ──────────────────────────────
> so,   Some cigarettes are not addictive.

As well as finding an effect of beliefs, Evans et al. showed that they had a bigger effect when the given conclusion was *invalid*. This result suggests that subjects accept believable conclusions uncritically, but are more likely to check the validity of unbelievable ones. Evans et al. suggested two models that might explain this pattern of results, and these models were developed in more detail by Evans (1989). Their primary purpose is to explain how subjects evaluate given conclusions, but they can be adapted to explain conclusion generation as well.

The *Selective Scrutiny* model assumes that the effects of belief arise through *pre-reasoning* heuristics, rather than in the course of deduction. Indeed, the model has nothing to say about the nature of the deductive process itself. In essence it proposes that subjects examine a conclusion and, if it is believable, they accept it without engaging in any reasoning. Only if it is unbelievable will they attempt to 'scrutinize' the logic, to see whether the conclusion follows validly from the premises.

The alternative *Misinterpreted Necessity* model is based on the assumption that subjects fail to understand what is meant by *logical necessity*. In this model, subjects attempt to reason but, when a conclusion is neither definitely true nor definitely false, given the premises, they base their response on the conclusion's believability, rather that claiming, correctly, that it does not follow from the premises. So, for example, all pairs of syllogistic premises from which no valid conclusion follows, and many others, have two or more conclusions which are *compatible* with the premises, but which are not *necessitated* by them. However, this model is not supported by the data. It wrongly predicts that, if the subjects are given instructions in which the principle of logical necessity is stressed, then they should be be more accurate in their decisions and less swayed by their beliefs (see Evans, 1989).

In Evans et al.'s studies the subjects were asked to assess the validity of presented conclusions. As the Selective Scrutiny model proposes, a trivial explanation of the results is that people accept or reject that conclusion depending on whether it accords with their beliefs. But if beliefs override or prevent reasoning, such results have little to say about how it occurs. Oakhill and Johnson-Laird (1985) showed that beliefs also affect performance when subjects draw conclusions for themselves. However, the results were stronger for conclusions that were false because of the definitions of the words in them, for example, 'some of the actresses are not women', than when the conclusions merely violated general knowledge, for example 'some of the athletes are not healthy people'. With the definitionally false conclusions (and their true converses) the results were parallel to those of Evans et al.: where a potential conclusion (whether valid or invalid) was believable, subjects tended to produce it uncritically, but when it was unbelievable, they took more care to establish whether their reasoning was correct.

As Oakhill and Johnson-Laird point out, their data are compatible with the mental models theory of syllogistic reasoning, though the data do not provide a strong test of that theory. However, the theory has an important advantage over the Selective Scrutiny and Misinterpreted Necessity models in that it provides an account of the reasoning *process*, and how errors in (unbiased) reasoning might occur. As we have argued elsewhere (Oakhill and Garnham, 1993), if the Selective Scrutiny and Misinterpreted Necessity models were to be developed fully as accounts of reasoning bias, they too would need an account of the reasoning process. Furthermore, a series of experiments by Newstead, Pollard, Evans and Allen (1992), investigating in detail the earlier finding of Evans et al. (1983) that beliefs have a greater effect when the presented conclusion is invalid, have provided evidence that favours the mental models theory over the other two.

Oakhill and Johnson-Laird's results provided no information about the *locus* of belief bias effects. To investigate this matter Oakhill, Johnson-Laird and Garnham (1989) carried out a series of experiments with three types of problem:

1 Single-model problems (all of which have a valid conclusion)
2 multiple-model problems with a valid conclusion ('determinate')
3 multiple-model problems without a valid conclusion ('indeterminate')

Apart from their effect on the interpretation of premises, beliefs can have two other kinds of effect, according to the mental models theory. They can affect which models of the premises are considered, and they can act as a final 'filter' on conclusions, causing subjects to reject or alter conclusions that do not fit with their beliefs. The first type of effect should be found only with multiple-model problems. If a conclusion compatible with an initial model of the premises is consistent with a person's beliefs, they might accept it without trying to find alternative models. An initial unbelievable conclusion, however, might trigger a thorough search for alternative representations of the premises. For single-model problems, there are no alternatives and, hence, beliefs should have no effect on what conclusions are drawn. This idea is related to what David Perkins (e.g., Perkins, Farady and Bushey, 1991) calls the naive reasoner's *makes-sense epistemology*: in everyday reasoning (see chapter 13), conclusions are expected to make superficial sense. In more formal reasoning problems this criterion might also be applied. So, if a conclusion concurs with world knowledge, subjects might be more inclined to accept it. The second possibility – that subjects 'filter' their conclusions – allows for beliefs to affect both single-model and multi-model problems. Reasoners who produce an unbelievable conclusion might alter it to one they find more acceptable, with no further reference to the premises, or they might respond that nothing follows.

Oakhill et al. found that, in the case of single-model problems, there was a tendency for performance to be better when the conclusions were believable than when they were unbelievable. This result cannot be explained on the assumption that believability has its effect only on the process of constructing alternative models, because there are none. The obvious explanation is in terms of conclusion filtering. However, the results for the multiple-model problems, especially the indeterminate ones, suggested that filtering is not the only locus of bias effects. For the indeterminate problems, if a conclusion compatible with an initial model was believable, it was frequently produced in error but, if such a conclusion was unbelievable, subjects more often correctly concluded that there was no valid conclusion. These results support the idea that a believable conclusion curtails the examination of alternative models of the premises. They cannot be reconciled with the idea that belief effects arise only at the stage of conclusion filtering. The multiple-model determinate problems were all difficult, and there were too few correct responses to detect believability effects, even in an experiment where subjects assessed, rather than produced, conclusions. Taken together, these results suggest that, where beliefs do have an effect, it can occur in two different ways: by curtailing the examination of alternative models, or by influencing how conclusions are assessed.

Summary

Reasoning with the quantifiers *all* and *some* has been studied mainly in the context of syllogistic reasoning. Syllogisms have two premises and a single conclusion, each of which can come in four moods. There are four figures in which the terms of the syllogism can be arranged, though a psychologically useful characterization of these figures differs from the traditional one. Aristotle devised a method for showing which syllogisms are valid, in which syllogisms that are hard to assess are reduced to easier ones. An alternative, axiomatic, method for determining the validity of syllogisms is also available.

Early experimental work on syllogistic reasoning identified effects of content, and tried to explain errors in assessing conclusions in terms of the 'atmosphere' created by negative and particular premises. A later idea was that errors arose because of illicit conversion of the premises, by swapping around the terms. Although theories of mental logic are intended to apply to syllogistic reasoning, those theories that have been developed specifically to account for syllogistic reasoning have been model-based. These theories have been based on Euler circles, Venn diagrams, and mental models. The mental models theory predicts figural effects that had not been previously noted.

The effects of content, and particularly that of the believability of the premises and conclusions of syllogisms, are complex. They cannot be explained, as Revlin and Leirer suggested, by illicit conversion. The mental models theory recognizes three points at which beliefs could have their effect: in the interpretation of the premises, in deciding whether to search for alternative models, and in filtering conclusions.

Further Reading

Evans, J. St. B. T. (1989). *Bias in Reasoning: Causes and Consequences*. Hove, East Sussex: Lawrence Erlbaum Associates.

Johnson-Laird, P. N. and Byrne, R. (1991). *Deduction.* Hove, East Sussex: Lawrence Erlbaum Associates. (chapter 6).

Oakhill, J. V., Garnham, A. and Johnson-Laird, P. N. (1990). Belief bias effects in syllogistic reasoning. In K. Gilhooly, M. Keane, R. Logie and G. Erdos (eds), *Lines of Thinking: Reflections of the Psychology of Thinking* (Vol. 1, pp. 125–38). Chichester: John Wiley & Sons.

7

Induction

In the last three chapters we have discussed a kind of reasoning –
deductive reasoning – that allows people to draw conclusions with certainty from facts they know to be true, or from suppositions that they
make. In a sense, a deduction 'simply' rearranges given information,
without going beyond it. That is not to say deductive reasoning is easy,
or that it cannot lead to unforeseen conclusions. However, one way of
characterizing deductive reasoning (e.g., Johnson-Laird and Byrne, 1991)
is to say that it cannot increase *semantic information*. In other words,
the conclusion of a piece of deductive reasoning cannot rule out more
possibilities than the premises from which it is derived. Reaching the
conclusion might make it apparent to the reasoner what possibilities are
ruled out, and what must, therefore, be true. But the ruling out is
inherent in the premises, and is simply drawn out by the reasoning.

Not all reasoning is deductive – if it were, people would be hopelessly
restricted in the conclusions they could draw. Often they need to go
'beyond the information given'. The price they pay is that they lose the
guarantee that the conclusion they have drawn follows from the premises.
Of course, mistakes in deductive reasoning are possible. But care can
eliminate them, so that if someone can establish that their premises are
true, they know their conclusion must be true as well. Non-deductive
types of reasoning include *inductive reasoning*, *abductive reasoning*,
reasoning by analogy, some kinds of *probabilistic* (or *statistical*) reasoning, and *practical reasoning* (including *decision making*). Much
everyday reasoning, in which previously established conclusions are
overthrown by new information, appears not to be deductive, at least

in the sense that its conclusions could be false, even if its premises are true. Non-monotonic logics attempt to define a more restricted sense of validity according to which this kind of everyday reasoning is deductively valid, though many instances of everyday reasoning fall under other heads, such as induction, or probabilistic reasoning. Everyday reasoning is the topic of chapter 13, and chapters 9 and 10 deal with statistical reasoning and decision making, respectively. In this chapter we will focus on inductive reasoning. We will also briefly describe abductive reasoning, which can be regarded as a form of induction, and analogical reasoning. In the next chapter we will look at methods of assessing conclusions, particularly general conclusions, that have been derived non-deductively.

7.1 Types of Induction

In *inductive reasoning*, even if a person knows the premises are true, and knows that they have reasoned as they intended, they cannot be sure that their conclusion will be true. Thus, the conclusion of an induction might be regarded as a *hypothesis*, which may have to be tested to see if it is correct (see the next chapter). Inductive reasoning is important both in everyday life and in academic, in particular scientific, investigation. In science, a hypothesis, whether it is derived by induction or some other method, *must* be subjected to formal experimental tests.

Unfortunately, there is no generally agreed definition of inductive reasoning and, indeed, the term *induction* is used in several ways in the psychological literature on thinking and reasoning. Some psychologists have adopted a broad definition that identifies 'all inferential processes that expand knowledge in the face of uncertainty' as inductive (Holland, Holyoak, Nisbett and Thagard, 1986: p. 1). Indeed, these authors effectively attempt to include deduction as a form of induction (!), since the reasoner may be uncertain of the outcome of a deduction, even though, in another sense, the conclusion is contained within the premises. On this broad view, induction 'interrelates most of the topics in the psychology of thinking' (Holyoak and Nisbett, 1988: p. 50). In this book we will *not* adopt this very broad view of induction, but will adopt Johnson-Laird's suggestion that an induction is 'any process of thought yielding a conclusion that increases the semantic information in its initial observations or premises' (1993: p. 60; and see p. 79, above, for a discussion of semantic information). Within this definition, Johnson-Laird identifies three main types of induction: specific inductions (or abductions), general descriptive inductions, and general explanatory inductions.

7.1.1   Abduction

In conditional reasoning (see chapter 5), statements of the form 'p' and 'if p then q' support the conclusion 'q'. This kind of reasoning corresponds to the logical rule of modus ponens (see chapter 4). In most real cases of conditional reasoning, the statement of the form 'if p then q' derives from knowledge of the world, typically from a theory of causation, or a theory of how people act – either an everyday theory or a scientific one. Thus we expect the truth of 'p' to provide an explanation for the truth of 'q'. For example, if someone knows that a blown fuse prevents an electrical appliance from working, and knows that the fuse in their hair dryer has blown, they can conclude that the hair dryer will not work, and they can explain the fact that it will not work by the fact that its fuse is blown.

Normally, however, people have to argue the other way round. Faced with a hair dryer that will not work, they have to find an explanation for its malfunction. They do not know the state of its fuse. Some authors (e.g., Johnson-Laird, 1993, chapter 2) classify the generation of an explanation for an event from a theory of how the world works, as a specific induction. A more common term, especially in artificial intelligence, is *abduction*. Formally, it can be characterized as an inference of the form:

$$\frac{\begin{array}{l} q \\ \text{if p then q} \end{array}}{\text{so,} \quad p}$$

In propositional calculus this form of argument is invalid, and is known as affirmation of the consequent. It is fallacious because there could be other reasons for q other than p. Its plausibility depends, in large part, on the number and the likelihood of the alternative explanations.

Because abductions are not deductively valid, they need to be checked. It is necessary to look at the hair dryer's fuse to see if it is blown. They are, however, obviously useful, in that they generate possible explanations of events, and hence (at least potentially) allow us to control the world in which we live. If the fuse has blown it can be replaced. If it has not, another explanation for the malfunction of the hair dryer is needed, and abduction can provide one. Abduction can also be used to learn about the world. Researchers in artificial intelligence (e.g., de Jong, 1988) have suggested the importance of *explanation-based learning*, in which a single event or episode, of a kind not previously encountered, is explained on the basis of a theory about the relevant aspects of the world. That explanation is then generalized so that it will be useful in other situations. As this idea shows, the distinction between specific inductions and learning the general rules that underlie them (the 'if p then q' rules in the schema above) is not entirely clear-cut. Using a rule to explain a specific example may lead to a refinement or modification of the rule. Nevertheless, the primary purpose of an abduction is to generate an explanation against a background of previously established theory.

7.1.2 General inductions

A general induction might be roughly characterized as an inference of the following form.

$$\text{so,} \quad \frac{F(a),\ F(b),\ F(c),\ \dots}{(\forall x)F(x)}$$

That is to say, from observing that a series of individual objects or events (a, b, c, ...) have the property F, it is concluded that all objects or events in the same class have that property. The general belief is formed by explicit generalization over observations of specific instances. However, it is apparent from this characterization of induction that, both in everyday life and in academic investigation, not all general beliefs or hypotheses are formed in this way. Some, for example, are produced by imaginative leaps, others by the use of analogy. Indeed, analogical reasoning is often crucial in the formation of scientific theories – many scientists mention the use of analogy when they describe their methods of working. In science, therefore, analogy appears to be one method of generating the hypotheses whose predictions are subsequently deduced and tested (see chapter 8). We will discuss the role of analogy in creative thinking in a little more detail in chapter 13. However, the use of analogy by working scientists is difficult to study in the laboratory. Most psychological research on analogy has been on problem solving, and it will be discussed in chapter 11.

Some general inductions are purely descriptive. For example, Johnson-Laird (1993) suggests that someone who had taken several air journeys within the United States might conclude that internal flights are usually late. However, descriptive inductions should be treated with care. A person who knew the reasons why internal flights are late in the USA would be in a stronger position to judge whether they should induce that all flights will be late, or just some subset of those flights, to which the ones they have taken happen to belong (those in and out of Chicago's O'Hare airport, for example). Indeed, people usually assume that an *explanation* underlies an induction, even if they cannot discover that explanation, and even if they do not try to find it. In science, in particular, explanation rather than mere description is crucial. Scientific hypotheses, and the interrelated collections of them that constitute scientific theories, take the form of general statements. Those statements that are referred to as scientific *laws* tend to have assumed a descriptive status, and are explained in terms of more fundamental ideas. However, part of what counts as progress in science is the explanation by more fundamental ideas of what previously had to be taken for granted.

A further distinction within general inductions is that between inductions of general statements (on which we have focused so far) and inductions of concepts. The two are, however, intimately related (Johnson-Laird, 1983). For example, the induction of the general statement that internal flights are late in the United States is directly related to the concept of a late internal flight, which might then be used in formulating a further (induced) general statement (e.g., late internal flights could be prevented by the building of more runways). As Johnson-Laird puts it, 'concepts are used to construct thoughts, which in turn are used to construct concepts, and on and on' (1983: p. 89).

7.2   Some Philosophical Considerations about Induction

The idea that induction, in the sense of generalization from instances, is one of the cornerstones of scientific enquiry was first set out in detail by Francis Bacon (1561–1626), who claimed that scientific laws were derived by the process of induction. For three centuries following Bacon the idea of induction as *the* scientific method was the predominant one in the philosophy of science. David Hume (1711–76) pointed out the problems that arise because inductions are not deductively valid arguments, and started a fruitless chase for a 'justification for induction'. Given the ground rules set by Hume, such a justification eluded even John Stuart Mill (1806–73), who devoted a great deal of philosophical effort to the systematization of what was known about induction (enshrined in his canons of induction). Indeed, given Hume's ground rules, such a justification was impossible.

We have described induction as a process of generalization and, indeed, this aspect of induction has been emphasized by philosophers of science after Bacon. Bacon himself, however, recognized that there are two sides to induction. On the one hand, generalizations should be couched as broadly as possible. By definition, induction should produce a general rule that describes not only the set of instances that have actually been examined, but as many other instances as possible, too. On the other hand, no generalization can be expected to apply without restrictions, and overgeneralization must be avoided. For example, too much watering may, in general, be bad for house plants, but there may be some such plants that are not adversely affected by it. It would, therefore, be misleading to claim without qualification that too much water was bad for house plants. These two aspects of induction are usually referred to as *generalization* and *specialization*, respectively. Thus, the standard view of induction is that a scientist starts by examining a finite (though perhaps large) set of cases that he or she feels should be subsumed under a general law. On the basis of what the cases have in common, the scientist proposes such a law. The law may be made more general by finding further (positive) instances, with different features, that can be grouped with the original ones. This further generalization is based on the features that all positive instances have in common. However, it may also be necessary to specialize the law, to exclude negative instances that do not obey the law but which, nevertheless, share some features with things that do obey it.

Even if there were no 'problem' of justifying induction, the procedure described by Bacon and his successors appears to describe neither the actual practice of research scientists nor the logical reconstruction of that practice that is presented in scientific treatises and research papers. For these reasons, the twentieth century has seen a number of critiques of the idea that Baconian induction is the method of science. The most important of these attacks have come from, on the one hand, Karl Popper (1959), who argues that The Logic of Scientific Discovery (to give the English title of his book) is better characterized as *hypothetico-deductive* rather than inductive, and, on the other hand, from philosophers such as Thomas Kuhn and Paul Feyerabend, who have drawn conclusions about how science works from examining in detail actual scientific practice. We will deal with the second type of attack first, before turning to Popper's ideas, which have strongly influenced psychological research on hypothesis testing, particularly that type of research instigated by Peter Wason, and described in detail in the next chapter.

Kuhn (1970) agrees with Popper that the production of general laws is only a small part of science, and that what is done with those laws by scientists is more important. He distinguishes *normal science*, in which a dominant theory is used to generate explanations of those phenomena that it can explain while recalcitrant data is ignored, from *scientific revolutions*, in which a dominant theory is overthrown. If there is a great deal of recalcitrant data, the dominant theory in a particular field of science will feel the strain, but it cannot be replaced until a sufficiently able scientist produces a viable alternative. The new theory produced in a scientific revolution will use different concepts from the old theory, and will have different concerns. Although there may be a general sense in which the new theory can be seen as making progress, detailed comparisons of the successes and failures of the old and new theory are made difficult by the fact that they are to some extent *incommensurable*. Feyerabend (1975) takes the more radical view that there is no scientific method, and that scientists should use any means that they can (well almost!) to support their theories.

Both Kuhn and Feyerabend direct some of their arguments against Popper's views. However, as we have already indicated, Popper is concerned primarily with the logical status of scientific hypotheses, rather than with how scientific research is carried out. Popper's first important claim is about the process of induction as described by Bacon and others. He points out that, while general hypotheses *might* be produced by detailed consideration of individual cases, there is no reason why they should be. They might pop into a scientist's head in the bath, for example. Furthermore, the genesis of a hypothesis has no (logical) bearing on its truth or usefulness. Wherever a hypothesis comes from, it can be tested in the same way. So what is important in science is not inducing a hypothesis, in the Baconian sense, but simply having one – hence Popper's term *hypothetico*-deductive method. The *deductive* in hypothetico-deductive reflects Popper's view that the way hypotheses should be tested is to deduce specific consequences from them, and then find out whether those consequences are true. The testing of a general hypothesis can show it to be definitively false, but can never show it to be certainly true. Intuitively, the reason is as follows. Consider a general statement such as 'no machine can allow a person to fly in the air'. The flight of the Montgolfier balloon – a single instance – falsified this statement for good. But all the previous instances of failed attempts to fly did not show it to be true. More formally, given 'if hypothesis then consequence' and 'not consequence' (i.e., the prediction fails) we can derive 'not hypothesis' by the rule of modus tollens (see chapter 4). However, from 'if hypothesis then consequence' and 'consequence', nothing follows. Concluding that the hypothesis is true would be to commit the fallacy of affirming the consequent.

Popper, therefore, proposed falsifiability as a *demarcation criterion* for science. If a hypothesis is to count as scientific, it must be falsifiable. However, because of the interrelations between scientific hypotheses, it is not always easy to decide when a hypothesis has been falsified. For this reason, the example about machine flight is misleading, because there is only a single isolated statement to consider. In science, what usually happens is that, if the predictions of a theory are not confirmed, the main hypothesis is saved, but one of more of the auxiliary assumptions (perhaps even an assumption about how the data relate to the theory) is discarded.

Popper has often been taken as claiming, also, that scientists should try to falsify their theories. There are two variants of this claim. One is that scientists should try to falsify their own theories. In practice they rarely do. They become attached to them, and try to find evidence that supports them. The other is that scientists should try to falsify the theories of other (rival) scientists, and this they often do attempt. In either case, if a theory is worth trying to falsify, it must be able to explain a broad range of phenomena, and establishing that it does have this explanatory power will take considerable effort. In a sense, this effort is devoted to showing that the theory is, or at least might be, correct. So, even if the logical reconstruction of an extended piece of scientific endeavour is: a theory was formulated, consequences were deduced from it, and it was shown to be false, it cannot be concluded that attempts to confirm theories are unimportant in science. Indeed, we will see in the next chapter that people have considerable difficulty in applying the idea of attempted falsification when they try to assess hypotheses.

7.3   Empirical Studies of Induction

There has been almost no empirical work on induction in the Baconian sense within experimental psychology, although, as we will see in the next chapter, there has been a great deal of work on hypothesis testing. However, Johnson-Laird (1993a, in press) has proposed a theory of induction within the mental models framework. As we mentioned at the beginning of this chapter, Johnson-Laird defines an inductive inference as one that increases semantic information. Hence, it is one in which the conclusion rules out more states of affairs than the premises. Thus, to perform an induction, a reasoner must mentally model the premises, eliminate some of the models that are consistent with them, and then formulate a description of the remaining models (the induced conclusion). However, the number of combinations of models that can be eliminated increases exponentially with the total number of models. Johnson-Laird, therefore, proposes four constraints on inductive generalization: the choice of the most specific hypothesis compatible with the data, parsimony, the use of existing knowledge, and the availability of that knowledge (in the sense of Tversky and Kahneman, 1973 – see chapter 9).

One advantage of Johnson-Laird's account is that it regards induction as a process that acts on and produces sets of models. It is not a process that acts on linguistic statements, though a description of the set of models produced by the process will almost always be formulated. Often this set of models can be described straightforwardly, but in some cases it may suggest a new way of thinking or a new concept. In science, in particular, new theories often call for new concepts (such as gene), or new interpretations of old concepts (energy in relativity theory, in which it is interchangeable with mass, as compared with classical physics, for example). In this respect, Johnson-Laird's theory has an advantage over the other main body of research on induction – the study of machine learning in artificial intelligence. Furthermore, there are a variety of forms of generalization based on linguistic considerations, but in Johnson-Laird's scheme they all arise via the same basic mechanism of eliminating a subset of models consistent with the premises.

Patrick Winston (1975) introduced into artificial intelligence the idea of *induction heuristics*, which perform the two Baconian tasks of generalization and specialization. Winston's program learned concepts corresponding to structures made of small wooden blocks (such as arch) from positive examples and 'near misses', structures that were almost arches, but not quite. It required a set of simpler concepts (such as pillar and lintel) to work from, and a 'teacher' to present a series of instances (of arches) in a helpful order. In subsequent work, particularly that of Ryszard Michalski (e.g., 1983), the teacher is dispensed with, and quite powerful automatic induction is made possible. Two principal innovations underlie this development. First, induction is characterized as a search for the *maximally specific conjunctive description* (MSC) of the positive instances (Dietterich and Michalski, 1981). An MSC joins together with 'and's (hence, conjunctive) all the predicates that the instances have in common. Thus the MSC for the following two cows:

A: old and brown and lame and owned by John
B: young and white and lame and owned by John

is 'lame and owned by John'. Disjunctions must be excluded, otherwise a more specific description that applied to both cows could be generated: '(old and brown and lame and owned by John) or (young and white and lame and owned by John)'. The disadvantage of characterizing induction as a search for MSCs is that it severely constrains the form of permitted generalizations, thus losing the advantage of Johnson-Laird's proposal. The second innovation is the treatment of induction as a search problem (see chapter 11), in which a set of possible generalizations is searched for the right or best one. Tom Mitchell (1982) showed how the search could be made considerably simpler by ordering (or at least partially ordering) the generalizations in terms of their specificity, and arranging them in what he called a *version space*. Johnson-Laird also stresses the importance of ordering generalizations so that the most specific can be considered first. An alternative is to construct a decision tree for classifying objects as instances, or not, of concepts, as in Quinlan's (1983) ID3 induction algorithm. Constructing the right decision tree can be thought of as finding that decision tree from among all possible decision trees.

Although methods of machine induction have their limitations, they have met with some surprising successes. After its learning phase, Michalski and Chilausky's (1980) soybean disease diagnosis system proved at least as effective as a human expert (more than 99 per cent correct on 376 new test cases), and considerably more efficient than an expert system (see chapter 12) embodying rules explicitly laid down by a human expert (83 per cent correct). The program is widely used by government departments in Illinois. Quinlan's ID3 has partly solved the problem, previously too difficult for human chess masters, of classifying positions that lead to a win in the king and pawn vs. king and rook end-game in chess (see Michie and Johnston, 1984: pp. 121–5).

Much of the work on machine induction has examined the induction of concepts, rather than the induction of rules. The programming languages of artificial intelligence allow concepts that are already known to be put together using the logical relations (*not, and, or, if . . . then, if and only if*) that those languages make available. Johnson-Laird (1983) argues that the ability to build *recursive* functions is also crucial to explaining how people can construct new concepts from old. Programming languages provide the tools for building such functions, and they can, therefore, be used to model human abilities. New concepts are often needed in everyday life, but they are particularly important in the development of new scientific ideas. Psychologists have yet to analyse this process. Their studies of the role of concepts in induction (e.g., Rips, 1975; Osherson, Smith and Shafir, 1986; Osherson, Smith, Wilkie, López and Shafir, 1990) have been concerned primarily with how the properties of exemplars of one concept (e.g., sparrow) were generalized to those of another, related concept (e.g., ostrich). In particular, Rips investigated the role of typicality (see chapter 3), and Osherson et al. (1990) suggested that category-based inductions will be psychologically compelling if they satisfy two conditions. First, members of the two categories (e.g., sparrow and ostrich) should be perceived as similar. Second, members of the premise category (sparrow) should be perceived as similar to members of the lowest superordinate category that includes the premise and conclusion categories (bird contains both sparrow and ostrich). Osherson, Smith and Shafir (1986) identified seven plausible mechanisms for what they called *belief transmission* from one concept to another, though none applied to all of the wide variety of argument types they considered.

Summary

In one sense, deductive reasoning does not take us beyond what we already know. Inductive reasoning, in which, roughly speaking, we generalize from our experience, does allow us to derive genuinely informative conclusions, but the result is that the guarantee of validity, in the sense defined in chapter 4, is forfeit.

Specific inductions, also called abductions, generate explanations for particular events, based on a background theory of how the world works. General inductions may be primarily descriptive, or they may also embody a search for an explanation. Inductions of general statements and inductions of concepts are closely related. Explanation is particularly important in science, though not all scientific theories and laws are derived by induction.

The absence of deductive validity in induction has often troubled philosophers, who have worried that our inductions are groundless. These worries have prompted some, notably Karl Popper, to argue that induction, as traditionally characterized, is not important in science. Rather, scientists make conjectures and test predictions that they deduce from them. Popper's theory, interpreted as a hypothesis about how scientists actually work, has prompted criticism from philosophers of science such as Kuhn and Feyerabend. However, although these critics have made some interesting observations about the sociology of science, Popper's ideas are better interpreted as providing a rational reconstruction of what scientists are trying to do, and not as describing what they actually do.

Johnson-Laird has proposed a theory of induction, in the mental models framework, in which all generalizations (however they might be described linguistically) are derived by a single process of eliminating models consistent with the premises. Work on machine induction, in artificial intelligence, has been based primarily on linguistically formulated generalizations. It has met with some successes, for example, in soybean diagnosis, and the analysis of chess end-games.

Further Reading

Holland, J. H., Holyoak, K. J., Nisbett, R. E. and Thagard, P. R. (1986). *Induction: Processes of Inference, Learning, and Discovery*. Cambridge, MA: MIT Press.
Johnson-Laird, P. N. (1993). *Human and Machine Thinking*. Hillsdale, NJ: Lawrence Erlbaum Associates, chapter 2.
Kuhn, T. S. (1970). *The Structure of Scientific Revolutions* (2nd edn). Chicago: Chicago University Press.
Popper, K. R. (1959). *The Logic of Scientific Discovery*. London: Hutchinson.

8

Hypothesis Testing

In the previous chapter we discussed induction – a process that allows people to generate hypotheses that are plausible, but which may, nevertheless, not be true. Such hypotheses, therefore, need testing. In this chapter we will consider how people evaluate general statements – how they decide whether their hypotheses are correct. This topic has attracted considerable attention within psychology. In hypothesis testing, deductive reasoning (see chapters 4–6) is important. Hypothesis formation may (at least sometimes) be an inductive process, but working out the specific consequences of a hypothesis, which can then be subject to empirical test, requires deductive skills. We have seen in chapters 5 and 6 that people make many mistakes in deductive reasoning, so it will come as no surprise that they make mistakes in assessing their hypotheses.

8.1 Wason's Three Tasks

Most of the psychological research on hypothesis testing has been inspired, directly or indirectly, by the work of Peter Wason, who invented three apparently simple problems – the selection task (or 4-card problem), the THOG problem, and the 2–4–6 task – for studying the way that people evaluate hypotheses. Wason was influenced by Popper's idea (see previous chapter) that hypotheses should be tested by the hypothetico-deductive method, and so the research on hypothesis testing reported below also bears on questions about deductive reasoning. We will begin by discussing Wason's three tasks, before turning to other research on hypothesis testing which has attempted to model more directly the way that scientists work.

8.1.1 The selection task

Of Wason's three tasks, the selection task (Wason, 1966) has generated the most research. Indeed, it can fairly be described as the principal tool used to investigate how people find out whether general statements are true. The original, abstract, version of the selection task is as follows. The subject is shown one face of each of four cards, and told that each card has a letter on one side and a number on the other side. The subject is also presented with a general statement that may or may not apply to the cards. The general statement, which refers to those four cards only, is: if a card has a vowel on one side, it has an even number on the other side. Although this general statement (or hypothesis) is in the form of a conditional (if . . . then) statement, every *if . . . then* statement corresponds to an *all* statement that makes the generality of its claim more obvious. 'If a card has a vowel on one side, it has an even number on the other' is equivalent to 'all cards with a vowel on one side have an even number on the other'. The cards are placed on the table in front of the subject with the following letters and numbers on the uppermost faces.

The task is to select those cards that must be turned over to find out if the rule is true, that is to say: to see if it correctly describes all the cards. As indicated above, the four cards are usually referred to as the P, ¬P, Q and ¬Q cards. The reason is that logicians refer to conditional (if . . . then) statements as having the form 'if P then Q' (see chapter 4). If we abbreviate the rule in the selection task as 'if vowel then even number', P becomes 'vowel' and Q 'even number'. The relevant contrasts are consonants (things that are not vowels, ¬P) and odd numbers (things that are not even numbers, ¬Q).

Before you read on you should decide which cards you think should be turned over. Most undergraduates who were asked this question selected the either just the P card (E), or the P and Q cards (E and 4). A few chose the ¬Q card (7) as well. If you made any of these three choices you were wrong. The Wason selection task is deceptively simple, but the greater part of even a group of well educated people gets the answer wrong.

The correct answer is that the cards that must be turned over are the E and the 7. To see why this answer is correct, we must remember Popper's discussion of the confirmation of a hypothesis by specific instances that conform to it (which is not possible), and its falsification by instances that do not conform (which is) (see pp. 124–5). Since one confirming instance, or even a great many, of one hypothesis can be consistent with many other hypotheses, these instances do not show that any one of these hypotheses is true, though there will usually be other reasons for preferring one hypothesis to another. Popper's ideas about confirmation and falsification and be applied, relatively straightforwardly, to the selection task. In this task, the rule, or hypothesis, is not a completely general one, but only a statement about the four cards on the table. It remains true, however, that the fact that one particular card conforms to the rule cannot show the rule to be correct. One of the other cards might disobey the rule. Obviously, in this case, the rule could be tested by checking that each card satisfies the rule. However, the subjects' task is to pick only those cards that *must* be turned over to see whether the rule correctly describes all the cards.

In analysing the selection task, a complication arises because only one side of each card can be seen. The subjects, therefore, have only partial information about each possible instance of the rule, and they have to consider two possibilities for each card. The two possibilities have different implications for the status of the card, at least for three of the four cards. In relation to a general hypothesis, specific instances fall into three classes. The first are those that are irrelevant. An example of a completely irrelevant case might be a blue cow as potential evidence for the general claim that all swans are white. In the selection task a card with an odd number and a consonant would be irrelevant in this sense. The ¬P card and the ¬Q card could both turn out to be irrelevant, depending what is on the unseen side of the card. The other two kinds of case are confirming instances, which satisfy the rule, and falsifying instances, which are inconsistent with it. The cards that might be confirming instances are those that might have both a vowel and an even number on them (the P card and the Q card). Those that might be falsifying instances are those that might have a vowel and odd number on them (the P card and the ¬Q card). These considerations show that the selection task is not a simple deductive reasoning task, in which subjects have to construct a straightforward deductive argument. For this reason, Wason (1968) called one of his early papers on the selection task 'reasoning about a rule'.

We will now go through the cards in turn, to explain the correct solution. The P card might have either an even number or an odd number on the back. If it has an even number, it conforms to the rule. It would, however, be consistent with many other rules, and it would not show the given rule to be true, since one or more of the other cards might not conform to it. On the other hand, if the P card has an odd number on the back, say a 5, then the rule is definitely not true. So, the P card must be turned over because it can show the rule to be incorrect. Almost no one picks the ¬P card. It can only be irrelevant, since the rule does not say anything about what is on the back of cards with consonants – it it does not matter whether the K has an even number or an odd number on the other side.

We have already seen that many subjects choose the Q card in the selection task, and therein lies their error. The Q card has 4, an even number, on it. On its reverse side there may be either a vowel or a consonant. If there is a vowel, the card is a confirming instance of the rule, which is consistent with the rule, but does not prove it to be correct. If there is a consonant, the card is irrelevant. So, the Q card cannot be a disconfirming instance. Whatever is on the other side, if the other cards satisfy the rule, the Q card will not disconfirm it. There is, therefore, no point in turning it over. Finding out what is on the back of the Q card should not make any difference to the subject's decision about whether the rule correctly describes the four cards.

For the ¬Q card the case is different. Again the card could have a vowel or a consonant on its reverse. If it has a consonant, it is irrelevant, just as any other card with a consonant is. However, if it has a vowel, it is a falsifying instance of the rule. To see if the rule is true it is, therefore, vital to turn the ¬Q card over. The correct response in the selection task is to turn over the P and ¬Q cards. The ¬P card is certainly irrelevant, and whether the Q card is irrelevant or a confirming instance of the rule cannot affect whether the rule provides a correct description of the four cards.

The possible types of letter and number on the reverse of the four cards in the selection task, together with their implications for the status of the card, are summarized in table 8.1.

Now that we have described the typical response pattern in the Wason selection task, and explained the correct solution, we should point out a firmly established finding that has often been glossed over in the literature (see Manktelow and Over, 1990a). If, after subjects have made their selection, the cards are actually turned over (or, equivalently, if the experimenter asks, for example, 'if the 7 had on E on the back, would the rule be true or false?'), subjects are quite able to judge

Table 8.1   Possible types of letters and numbers on the reverse of cards in the selection task, and their implications for the status of the cards

card	type of number of letter on reverse and status of card			
P (E)	even number	confirming	odd number	falsifying
¬P (K)	even number	irrelevant	odd number	irrelevant
Q (4)	vowel	confirming	consonant	irrelevant
¬Q (7)	vowel	falsifying	consonant	irrelevant

what the consequences for the rule are, even if they have selected the wrong cards. Indeed, some subjects tie themselves in knots trying to reconcile their selections with what is now obvious to them (see Wason, 1983, for a particularly vivid example). So, the problem that people have is not in assessing the relation between (fully specified) instances and a hypothesis but, in the abstract version of the selection task at least, in relating the incompletely specified instances to the hypothesis.

A series of experiments (summarized by Wason and Johnson-Laird, 1972) showed that the typical level of performance among undergraduates in the selection task, about 15 per cent correct selections, remained approximately constant across a wide range of instructional variations, such as asking subjects to select cards that they had to turn over to find out if the rule was *false* (following the Popperian focus on falsification) rather than true. To account for these findings Johnson-Laird and Wason (1970) proposed that the primary determinant of success in the selection task was the *insight* into the logical structure of the task shown by the subject. Their *insight model* claimed that subjects can show three levels of insight. At the first level subjects focus on the possibility of confirming the rule, and choose only cards that might turn out to be confirming instances (P alone, the more obvious potentially confirming instance, or P and Q). At the second level they realize that falsification is important, but they fail to see that confirmation is not; they therefore choose both cards that might be confirming instances and those that might be falsifying instances (P, Q and ¬Q). And, at the third level, complete insight, they choose only cards that might turn out to be falsifying instances (P and ¬Q). In experiments in which subjects are put through various training regimes, they may progress, within the course of an experimental session, from the first to the third level of insight. However, as we have already seen, simple changes to the instructions do not produce changes in insight.

The fact that so many subjects make choices that indicate only the first or the second level of insight has often been taken to reflect a confirmatory bias. Such a bias would mean that when people are testing hypotheses, and are allowed to select data that might be relevant to testing those hypotheses, they tend to choose confirming instances, which can only be consistent with the hypothesis, rather than falsifying instances, which might show that the hypothesis is definitely false. However, because of the complex nature of the selection task, it provides only indirect evidence for confirmatory bias under normal circumstances, for two main reasons. First, as we have already seen, it does not require subjects to choose fully specified instances to test a hypothesis. The subjects also have to reason about what kind of an instance an underspecified card might be. Second, in its standard form the selection task calls for reasoning about highly abstract materials. As we will see below, performance on the selection task can improve dramatically when the materials are made more concrete. However, the idea that people try to confirm, rather than to falsify, hypotheses is one that is suggested by other evidence, and we will return to it later.

A different account of the poor performance in the abstract version of the selection task has been proposed by Jonathan Evans (Evans and Lynch, 1973; Wason and Evans, 1975). Evans's *matching bias model* claims that subjects chose cards in the selection task in two ways. The first is by correct logical reasoning, and leads to the selection of the P and ¬Q cards. In the abstract version of the selection task very few subjects select cards in this way. The second method is by looking at the items explicitly mentioned in the rule and choosing cards that match those items. On Evans's account, if the word *not* appears in either part of the rule, it is discounted by the matching process, so that, for example, a rule containing the phrase 'not a vowel' is taken to match a vowel. In the standard version of the task ('if vowel, then even number') matching bias leads to the choice of the card with the vowel (P) and the card with the even number (Q), which explains why most subjects choose the P and Q cards in this version of the task. However, the matching bias model makes different predictions when *not*'s are introduced into the rules. For example, Evans carried out experiments with all four of the following rules:

1 If there is a vowel on one side of the card, there is an even number on the other side.
2 If there is a vowel on one side of the card, there is not an even number on the other side.
3 If there is not a vowel on one side of the card, there is an even number on the other side.

Table 8.2   Status of the E, K, 4, 7 cards for the four rules used by Evans

	P card	¬P card	Q card	¬Q card
Rule 1	E*	K	4*	7
Rule 2	E*	K	7	4*
Rule 3	K	E*	4*	7
Rule 4	K	E*	7	4*

* matching cards

4   If there is not a vowel on one side of the card, there is not an even
   number on the other side.

If we take rule 3, for example, to be of the form 'if P then Q', Q is 'even
number' as in the standard version (rule 1), but P is 'not a vowel' (i.e.,
P is 'a consonant'). So what was the P card for rule 1 (E), becomes the
¬P card for rule 3 and vice versa. However, for all of the rules the
matching cards are the vowel (E) and the even number (4). The complete situation is summarized in table 8.2. The asterisked cards in table
8.2, E and 4, are those explicitly mentioned in the rule. As can be seen
from the table, the matching bias hypothesis claims that the pattern of
choices, classified as P, ¬P, Q, ¬Q, will vary from rule to rule, and that,
in particular, matching bias will lead to the choice of the P and ¬Q cards
with rule 2, thus increasing the number of correct choices. Evans found
this result in a number of experiments, and he took it as evidence for
his matching bias hypothesis. In fact, he found more evidence of matching bias for the Q and ¬Q cards than for the P and ¬P cards, and more
recently (1989) he has proposed a different ('if') heuristic (*if* focuses
attention on the P card) to explain the rarity of ¬P choices with all of
the rules. Evans also asked subjects to justify their choice of cards. He
found than not only did the subjects' choice of cards (classified as P,
¬P, Q, ¬Q) change from trial to trial, their justification of their choices
did as well. So a subject who gave a justification in terms of how a card
might confirm a rule on one trial would give a justification in terms of
how a card might falsify a rule on the next. Evans concluded that these
justifications were largely post hoc. They did not reflect the processes
used to select the cards (matching), but were constructed after the cards
had been selected.
   In subsequent work, Evans has developed his dual process (matching
and logical reasoning) theory for the selection task into a more general
dual process theory of human reasoning. In recent versions (e.g., Evans,

1984, 1989), he distinguishes between *heuristic* and *analytic* processes, claiming that the former have temporal priority over the latter. So, when a person is trying to solve a problem, preattentive, largely automatic, heuristic processes select certain aspects of a problem as potentially *relevant* to its solution. Sometimes these heuristic processes effectively determine the solution to a problem, for example, for subjects who show pure matching bias in the selection task. In other cases, analytic processes work on what has been selected by the preattentive processes. Thus, even if the analytic processes work properly, their results may reflect biases in reasoning because of what they have been allowed to work on. Although Evans's description of these two kinds of process needs further clarification, and independent evidence about what is processed preattentively is urgently needed, there seems little doubt that people represent, in their mental models, those things that are explicitly mentioned to them. When drawing the correct conclusion requires the consideration of things that are not explicitly mentioned (consonants in the standard selection task rule, for example) people have difficulties.

Even highly educated people do badly when trying to solve the original, abstract version of the selection task. However, it was soon established that performance on problems with the same logical structure, but with less abstract rules, was much better. We have already mentioned the pervasive facilitatory effect of familiar content on reasoning in our discussion of syllogistic reasoning (chapter 6). The occurrence of a similar effect in the selection task means that this well-studied paradigm can be used to elucidate its nature. In the first study of content (or *thematic*) effects in the selection task, Wason and Shapiro (1971) presented subjects with the following version of the task. The rule was: every time I go to Manchester, I go by car, and the cards were:

Manchester	Leeds	Car	Train
P	¬P	Q	¬Q

The subjects were told that each card represented a particular journey made by the experimenter, with the destination on one side and the means of transport on the other. With this version of the task over 60 per cent of the subjects correctly selected the Manchester (P) and Train (¬Q) cards only. Apparently, in this version of the task, they found it easier to see that if the Train card had Manchester on the back, the rule would be false. Ironically, although content effects in the selection task are now very well documented, and there is no doubt about the effect in general, this original demonstration of such effects has proved difficult to replicate, and, according to one current theory, such effects should not be found with this rule (see below).

In another concrete version of the selection task Johnson-Laird, Legrenzi and Legrenzi (1972) made use of a rule formerly used in the British postal system. In the old two-tier system of postal charges, sealed envelopes cost 5d (5 old pence) to post, and unsealed envelopes (containing cards or other printed material) 4d. The rule used by Johnson-Laird et al. was: if a letter is sealed, then it has a 5d stamp on it (there was also an Italian version). The 'cards' were sealed and unsealed envelopes and envelopes with 5d and 4d stamps on them. Again, this version of the task made it easier for subjects to see the potential relevance of the ¬Q card. If the envelope with the 4d stamp on it is sealed, the rule has been broken. An important difference between the rule used in this version of the task and the one used in the original version (and also Wason and Shapiro's rule) is that the rule is a social rule, or norm, that can be broken or violated, while the original version uses a descriptive rule that may or may not correctly describe the world. We will return to this point below.

In addition to the postal rule, other demonstrations of thematic effects in the selection task include d'Andrade's 'Sears' problem (reported in Rumelhart, 1980 – if any purchase exceeds $30, the receipt must have the signature of the department manager on the back) and Griggs's drinking law problem (Griggs and Cox, 1982 – if anyone is drinking beer, then that person must be over nineteen years old). In these versions of the selection task subjects are usually given a scenario that sets the rule in a suitable context.

The original explanation of thematic effects in the selection task was the *memory cueing hypothesis*, which stated that familiar concrete content can remind a person of a similar problem that they have solved, or seen solved, in the past. A strong version of this hypothesis is falsified by d'Andrade's Sears problem, since not all subjects who solve it have worked in a department store. Neither do they necessarily know, before they are given the task, that department stores operate such systems. However, d'Andrade's result is compatible with a weaker version of the memory cueing hypothesis, since his rule relates to common ideas, such as the need to be careful about large financial transactions. The memory cueing hypothesis also explains the failure of Manktelow and Evans (1979) to find a facilitatory effect of arbitrary concrete content. They discovered that arbitrary pairings of concrete terms was of little help in the selection task. Subjects did about as badly with a rule such as: 'every time I eat haddock I drink gin' as they did with the original abstract version of the task. This result stands in stark contrast with versions that reliably produce content effects. However, people do not typically have experience of preferences for gin with haddock, and cannot relate such preferences to anything they do know about. So memory cueing cannot help to solve this version of the selection task.

Recently, the memory cueing hypothesis has been challenged by several authors. Cheng and Holyoak (1985; Cheng, Holyoak, Nisbett and Oliver, 1986) have discovered an abstract version of the selection task (if one is to take action 'A' then one must first satisfy precondition 'P') on which subjects perform well. They have suggested that, in a variety of deductive reasoning tasks including hypothesis testing, people use context-dependent rules of inference called *pragmatic reasoning schemas*. Cheng and Holyoak mention three schemas, but they devote most attention to the so-called *permission schema* (the other two are obligation and causation, though some authors, e.g., Manktelow and Over, 1990b, argue that the 'permission' schema actually applies to conditional obligations). This schema is used for reasoning about situations that involve permissions, and comprises four rules about actions that have preconditions (i.e., in this case, actions that require a permission to be granted). The rules are:

1 If the action is to be taken the precondition must be satisfied
2 If the action is not to be taken the precondition need not be satisfied
3 If the precondition is satisfied the action may be taken
4 If the precondition is not satisfied the action must not be taken.

Cheng and Holyoak's 'abstract permission rule', given above, invokes the permission schema, which allows subjects to solve the corresponding version of the selection task. The standard abstract version invokes no such schema and, hence, people find it difficult. Cheng and Holyoak claim, more generally, that versions of the selection task which show thematic effects are ones that activate the permission schema. They further claim that a rationale can make subjects see a rule as permission-granting rather than arbitrary. A rationale can either be provided explicitly by the experimenter, or it can be worked out by the subject relating the content of the problem to past experience with similar rules. Thus, Cheng and Holyoak can explain the findings that have traditionally been taken as evidence for memory cueing, but can also explain why subjects can succeed in versions of the selection task based on rules of which they may have had no direct experience, but which can be rationalized as giving permissions. For example, in one of their own experiments, subjects performed well with a rule about cards that stated on one side whether a person was granted entry to a country, and on the other listed diseases that that person had been inoculated against. However, like Griggs and Cox (1982), they found that American subjects, who were unfamiliar with a two-tier postal system, failed on the sealed envelope version of the selection task unless provided with an explicit rationale.

On one view, pragmatic schemas can be seen as a compromise between the mental logic view that people use context-independent rules of inference, and the memory cueing hypothesis that many apparently deductive tasks are solved simply by using the solution to a similar problem, stored in memory. However, we will discuss another interpretation of the theory shortly.

Cosmides (1989) presents a different analysis of successful performance in the selection task. Her analysis is based on the idea of *social contracts*, which specify that, in social exchanges, if one takes a benefit one is expected to pay a cost. Social contracts are important for the survival of human social groups, and Cosmides takes an evolutionary perspective on why people are good at reasoning about social contracts and, in particular, at detecting attempts to cheat on them. Cosmides, therefore, claims that people will perform well on versions of the selection task in which the rule can be interpreted as a social contract, and in which detecting a card with P on one side and ¬Q on the other (in particular, realizing that the ¬Q card might be of this form) is akin to detecting a cheater who is trying to take the benefit of the contract (P) without paying the cost (¬Q). Indeed, there is growing evidence that instructions to search for violators of rules facilitates performance in the selection task (e.g., Gigerenzer and Hug, 1992). Thus, Cosmides obtained thematic effects with the rule: 'if a man eats cassava root, then he must have a tattoo on his face', which was deliberately chosen to refer to an unfamiliar social context. However, with a rule such as: 'if a man has a tattoo on his face, then he eats cassava root', which Cosmides refers to as a *reversed social contract*, she found a choice of the no tattoo (¬P) and cassava root (Q) cards! Cosmides explains this unusual choice of cards as follows. A reversed social contract has the form: if you pay the cost, you take the benefit. Since a cheater is someone who takes the benefit without paying the cost, the ¬P card must be checked to see if someone who hasn't paid is trying to take the benefit, and the Q card must be checked to ensure that someone who is taking the benefit has paid.

Intriguing as this theory is, it is incorrect as it stands, since, as several authors have pointed out (Cheng and Holyoak, 1989; Manktelow and Over, 1990a; Pollard, 1990), many of the best established facilitatory contexts do not involve costs and benefits that are socially exchanged. For example, in Griggs's drinking law problem, being nineteen is not a cost that people pay for being able to drink beer. Or, with a rule such as: 'if you clean up spilt blood, you must wear rubber gloves' (Manktelow and Over, 1990b), cleaning up spilt blood is not a benefit for which one pays the cost of wearing rubber gloves.

Manktelow and Over (1990a, 1990b) have suggested that facilitation in the selection task can occur only when the reasoning required is practical rather than theoretical. They argue that in all the clearly established cases of facilitation, the rules are *deontic* (i.e., they are about permissions and obligations). These authors further suggest that facilitation is more likely when the rationale for a rule is obvious or is made known to the subject – hence the importance of scenarios in which the rules are presented. However, as is also true of Cheng and Holyoak's and Cosmides' accounts, familiar content is not a prerequisite for facilitation of performance in the selection task.

Like Cosmides, Manktelow and Over (1991) have shown that there are circumstances under which subjects regularly choose the ¬P and Q cards. With a genuinely permission-granting rule such as: 'if you tidy your room, when you may go out to play' (said by parent to child), subjects select the P and ¬Q cards when checking whether the parent has broken the rule, but they select ¬P and Q when checking whether the child has. The reason for these choices is as follows. There are four ways in which a permission can be violated. The agent (or person who grants the permission) can be unfair or weak-willed, and the actor (or person to whom the permission is granted) can be self-denying or can cheat the agent. The first and third of these possibilities correspond to the combination of P (room tidied) and ¬Q (no playing). The second and fourth correspond to ¬P (room not tidied) and Q (playing). Manktelow and Over's instructions focus on the case in which the agent behaves unfairly, so subjects need to be sure there are no cards with P on one side and ¬Q on the other – hence the choice of P and ¬Q – and on the case in which the actor cheats, which calls for a choice of ¬P and Q.

Gigerenzer and Hug (1992) present a revised version of Cosmides' social contract theory, which brings many of these results together. Empirically, they showed that the instruction to search for cheaters, and not just the use of a social contract rule, was essential to produce facilitation. Theoretically, by shifting the focus to cheating rather than paying costs and taking benefits, they circumvent some of the problems of Cosmides' account. Furthermore, they distinguish between social contracts in which only one side can cheat (e.g., drinking rules, postal rules) and social contracts in which both sides can cheat (e.g., Manktelow and Over's room tidying rule). Only the latter produce selection changes from P and ¬Q (when the person laying down the rule cheats) to ¬P and Q (when the person to whom the rule is directed cheats). This shift, according to Gigerenzer and Hug, can be explained in terms of the meaning of the deontic operators and of conditional rules in which they occur. Similarly, Johnson-Laird and Byrne (1992) propose that the set of mental models constructed for such a conditional differs from the set constructed for an 'ordinary' indicative conditional.

We started this section with the idea that the selection task could be used to investigate the kind of hypothesis testing that is found in the sciences. The studies described above have moved away from that idea since, as Aristotle recognized, practical reasoning is different from theoretical reasoning. The choice of the ¬P and Q cards could never be justified in a theoretical reasoning task, but there is no question that Manktelow and Over's subjects are making a rational choice. Manktelow and Over argue that the study of deontic reasoning should be more closely integrated with work on decision making (see chapter 10), because it needs to make use of notions of preference and utility, and with work on the theory of mind (see chapter 17), because permissions are granted against a background of other rules and norms, which we understand other people to be adhering to (see also Kamp, 1973). For example, a child confined to its room by a parent could reasonably expect the prohibition on leaving the room to be overthrown by a fire in the house – and that is, in a sense, understood when the ban is imposed.

Although the idea that people really come to terms with the selection task only when it causes them to engage in practical (deontic) reasoning is an attractive one, it is not universally accepted. Johnson-Laird and Byrne (1991) argue that not all contents that produce facilitation invoke deontic reasoning, although the strongest cases are ones that do. For example, Wason and Green (1984) found that by making a rule apply to two aspects of a single figure (if triangle, then red) performance was improved. However, this result was obtained in a modified version of the selection task, which produces much higher levels of performance, even with the standard abstract rule. Johnson-Laird and Byrne explain facilitation in terms of a mental models theory of the selection task. On this account people encode explicitly stated information into their models, but tend to leave other possibilities implicit. So, the rule in the abstract version of the Wason selection task leads to an explicit model in which there is a card with a vowel on one side and an even number on the other, but not necessarily to one of the other possibilities (consonant/

even number and consonant/odd number), nor to an explicit representation of the disallowed combination (vowel/odd number). Johnson-Laird and Byrne propose that any manipulation that leads to these other models becoming explicitly represented will lead to facilitation. In addition, they suggest that it may be necessary to represent explicitly that certain combinations (corresponding to vowel and odd number in the abstract version of the selection task) are impossible.

8.1.2 The THOG problem

Another problem invented by Peter Wason for the study of hypothesis testing is the THOG problem (Wason and Brooks, 1979), whose name was taken from a list of nonsense syllables in Woodworth (1938). Like the selection task, the THOG problem is deceptively simple in form, but difficult to solve correctly. The THOG problem is about geometric figures with different shapes and colours, for example:

black square   black circle   white square   white circle

Unlike the experimenter in the selection task, the person administering the THOG problem does *not* present a rule or hypothesis directly to the subject. Instead, he or she makes the following statement: 'I am thinking of one colour (black or white) and one shape (square or circle). Any figure that has either the colour I am thinking of, or the shape I am thinking of, but not both, is a THOG. Given that the black square is a THOG what, if anything, can you say about whether the other figures are THOGs?'

Again, before you read on, you should try and work through this problem for yourself. Like the selection task, the THOG problem is complicated by the fact that the subject is not given full information, but has to consider various alternatives. In the THOG problem the subject has to consider two possible rules that the experimenter might have in mind. Given that the black square is a THOG, the rule for what is a THOG could be either of:

A THOG is either black or circular but not both
A THOG is either white or square but not both.

Furthermore, deriving these possible rules from the information given by the experimenter is not entirely straightforward. In particular, it is

Table 8.3   Classification of the four figures in the THOG problem by the two possible rules that the experimenter might have in mind

	Figures			
Rule	*black square*	*black circle*	*white square*	*white circle*
black or circle	THOG (black)	non-THOG (both)	non-THOG (neither)	THOG (circle)
white or square	THOG (square)	non-THOG (neither)	non-THOG (both)	THOG (white)

well established that people have difficulty dealing with arbitrary disjunctions, such as 'black or circular' or the more complex '(black or circular) or (white or square)'.

After figuring out what rules the experimenter might have in mind, the subject has to work through the consequences of each possibility to see how it classifies the other figures. The final answer to the problem depends on whether each possibility leads to the same classification for any of the figures other than the black square. Table 8.3 shows how the two possible rules classify the figures. The table shows that the two rules classify all three remaining figures in the same way. So, whichever rule the experimenter has chosen, the black circle and white square are not THOGs and the white circle is a THOG.

As with the selection task, most undergraduate students get the THOG problem wrong. The most common answer is that the white circle is not a THOG and that the other two figures are THOGs, or that their status is indeterminate. Wason and Brooks called this error the 'intuitive error'. The white circle and black square share no features in common, so it is likely that they belong to different categories. The white square and the black circle, on the other hand, both share one feature with the known THOG. The abstract nature of the problem, and the presence of disjunctions both in the set of possible definitions of THOGs and in each candidate definition, obviously contribute to the difficulties of the problem. However, subsequent research has identified some more specific problems that subjects have in attempting to solve the THOG problem.

First, some subjects confuse the two properties of the exemplar THOG (black and square) with the properties that the experimenter has in mind (e.g., O'Brien, Noveck, Davidson, Fisch, Brooke Lea and Freitag, 1990). Second, unless they are prompted, most subjects fail to construct the two possible definitions of a THOG (again see O'Brien et al., 1990). According to Newstead and Griggs (1992), both these difficulties arise from a failure of subjects to distinguish, in their thinking about the problem, the level of data (the figures) from the level of hypotheses. This problem is compounded by the fact that each hypothesis about the definition (e.g., black and circle) can be interpreted as a description of a figure (e.g., the black circle). Newstead and Griggs's account explains why realistic content does not necessarily help subjects to solve THOG problems. For example, Smyth and Clark (1986) found no facilitation when they used the everyday concept *half-sister*, one of the few that is defined, like THOG, using an exclusive disjunction (a female with either my mother or my father, but not both, as a parent). Realistic scenarios are useful only if they help subjects to separate data and hypotheses (Girotto and Legrenzi, 1989; Newstead and Griggs, 1992). Newstead and Griggs, for example, presented subjects with a problem in which a person gives cards to each of four friends and keeps one for himself. He says he will buy a dinner for those friends who have a card with a same shape or same colour as his, but not both. Then he says, 'by this rule I must buy a dinner for X; can you work out who else I must buy one for?' In this scenario, the main character's card corresponds to the hypothesis (though the subject has to conjecture as to what might be on it), and the four friends' cards correspond to the data. Subjects are additionally helped in this task if they are explicitly asked to consider what might be on the main character's card (i.e., to form the hypothesis explicitly). Further evidence of the importance of separating hypothesis and data has been provided by Girotto and Legrenzi (1993). They showed that performance in the abstract THOG task was facilitated by giving another nonsense name (SARS) to the card corresponding to the colour and shape the experimenter has in mind.

Newstead and Griggs argue, more generally, that the THOG problem places a high load on working memory. Any manipulation that reduces this load, for example, an external method of distinguishing data and hypothesis, or a 'lexicalization' of the hypothesis, as in Girotto and Legrenzi's (1993) study, will help subjects. In everyday reasoning, we often do not bother to use external aids to thinking, but in academic reasoning they are common. There is no reason, therefore, to suppose that problems with the complexity of THOG cannot be dealt with in scientific hypothesis testing.

8.1.3 The 2–4–6 problem

A third infuriating problem invented by Wason (1960) is the 2–4–6, or reversed twenty questions, problem. In the 2–4–6 problem the subject is given almost no information about the pertinent general statement, except that it is a rule governing sequences of three numbers. The other piece of information that the subject is given is that the sequence 2–4–6 obeys the rule. The task is to discover the rule that the experimenter has in mind. To do so the subject can ask the experimenter whether other sequences of three numbers obey the rule. The experimenter answers only 'yes' or 'no'. When the subject is sure of the rule they are to announce it and, again, the experimenter will tell them whether they are right or wrong. The rule that the experimenter works with is the very general one: any three numbers in ascending order. Part of the point of this choice is that there are many specific rules all of whose instances are also instances of the experimenter's rule. Examples of such rules are: any three numbers ascending in twos, and any three even numbers in ascending order. So, if the subject asks about a sequence such as 100–102–104 and the experimenter says 'yes, that sequence obeys my rule', the subject cannot tell which of these rules (or many others) the experimenter has in mind. This point is, of course, just the point we made earlier about confirming instances. These instances are merely consistent with the experimenter's rule. They do not show it to be the correct rule, and they are consistent with many others. Such data are not, of course, completely uninformative. Even the initial 2–4–6 rules out whole classes of rules – those that allow only descending sequences, for example. Furthermore, the subject will probably (correctly) assume that the experimenter is thinking of a straightforward rule, rather than any of the complex and counterintuitive ones that are consistent with the sequences that have elicited 'yes' responses.

Although the 2–4–6 task is simply described, its logic is complex. The subject must form a hypothesis about the rule in the experimenter's mind, but this hypothesis is not itself a general hypothesis such as 'if a card has a vowel on one side it has an even number on the other'. It is a hypothesis about a specific, but unknown, fact, namely what (general) rule the experimenter has in mind. So, it is a hypothesis about a hypothesis. We have seen that there is a sense in which general hypotheses should be tested by attempting to falsify them. But specific hypotheses are not tested in this way. They are checked against the the specific state of affairs to which they pertain. So, if I think ('hypothesize') your new car is red, I can go and look at it to see if it is. However, in the

2–4–6 task subjects cannot directly inspect or ask about what is in the experimenter's mind. They can investigate only indirectly by asking whether sequences of numbers conform to the rule. And because, in hypothesizing what rule is in the experimenter's mind, they need to formulate general rules, they have to use procedures for testing general rules. At this point a further complication arises. General hypotheses can only be falsified via possible instances, never conclusively confirmed. So the subjects are never going to get conclusive evidence that they have chosen the right rule. Once they have a hypothesis about the rule in the experimenter's mind, they can falsify that hypothesis by finding a sequence that the experimenter accepts, but which does not fit the hypothesized rule. For example, if they had conjectured that the rule was numbers ascending in twos, they could try to falsify this conjecture by asking about the sequence 3–6–9. If the experimenter answers 'yes, this sequence does obey my rule' (as, indeed, happens), the subject will know that the experimenter's rule is not numbers ascending in twos. The subject's hypothesis will also be falsified by a sequence that the experimenter rejects, but which does fit the hypothesized rule. With the rule of numbers ascending in twos, there are no such sequences, but for other rules, there are. However, no matter how many rules a subject eliminates, there are still indefinitely many that the experimenter may have in mind. How should the leap be made from eliminating rules to the actual rule? Either the subject can make a guess, taking into account information about rules that have already been eliminated, or they can defy the logic of hypothesis testing, and try to support the conjecture that they make by finding evidence consistent with it – by asking the experimenter about positive instances of the rule.

Although the logic of the 2–4–6 task is complex, it produces some straightforward findings. Typically, subjects are asked either to note down the sequences they ask about and their reasons for doing so, including their current hypothesis, or they are asked to verbalize the same information, which is then recorded on a tape recorder. Most subjects ask about sequences that conform to the rule that is their current hypothesis. Furthermore, subjects who announce a rule and are told that it is wrong often continue to produce sequences that conform to it. Wason described the results of his original studies as indicating a 'failure to eliminate hypotheses'. In much of the subsequent literature, the 2–4–6 task is said to provide further evidence for the confirmation bias that was hypothesized to explain performance in the selection task. Furthermore, choosing instances that conform to the current hypothesis is often referred to as a *confirmatory* strategy. However, because of the complex logic of the 2–4–6 task, asking about positive instances of a hypothesized rule is not the same as asking to see what can only be either positive instances of a rule or irrelevant cases in the selection task. If you ask about what you take to be a positive instance of a rule in the 2–4–6 task and the experimenter answers 'no', what was supposed to be a confirming instance is turned into a falsifying instance, and you know for sure that your rule is not the one the experimenter had in mind. So someone who knew about falsification might deliberately ask about positive instances of the currently conjectured rule in the 2–4–6 task on the grounds that, if they had the wrong rule, they should eventually get a 'no' from the experimenter. This strategy will not always work, because all instances of a general rule, such as the one the experiment entertains in the 2–4–6 task, will also be instances of numerous more specific rules. However, its existence means that subjects who choose positive instances are not necessarily attempting to confirm their conjectured rule. To 'behave sensibly' in the 2–4–6 task, subjects need to know not only that confirming instances do not show a hypothesis to be true, but also that all confirming instances of a specific hypothesis are also confirming instances of a more general hypotheses.

Considerations of this kind led Klayman and Ha (1987) to a more general analysis of the relation between a *positive test strategy* and confirmation and disconfirmation. It is not, in general, possible to know what relation holds between a hypothesized rule and the 'real rule'. The 2–4–6 task is rigged so that the experimenter's rule is almost certain to be more general than the subject's hypothesized rule. In these circumstances, as we have already seen, only negative instances of the hypothesized rule can lead to conclusive falsification of it. However, Klayman and Ha show that, if the relation between the real rule and the hypothesized rule is the other way round, with the hypothesized rule being more general than the real rule, the hypothesized rule can only be conclusively falsified by positive instances which fall under that rule, but outside the scope of the real rule. So, if the real rule were 'three adjacent even numbers' and the subject hypothesized that the rule was 'any three even numbers in ascending order', a positive test of '4–8–10' (which satisfies the hypothesized rule) would lead the experimenter to say 'no' (since it does not satisfy the real rule). Hence, the hypothesized rule would be disconfirmed. In these circumstances a positive test strategy leads to falsification, so that a naive identification of positive testing with confirmation bias is incorrect. More generally (and not just in artificial situations such as the 2–4–6 task), the relation between a real rule and a hypothesized rule can take a variety of forms. Klayman and Ha argue that the positive test strategy, although it has shortcomings, is a useful one to adopt in many real-world hypothesis testing tasks. For example, when studying rare phenomena, it can be relatively unilluminating to focus on the very many circumstances in which they do not occur, since it will be hard to say something useful about what they have in common.

In the original version of the 2–4–6 task, instructions that explicitly focus on disconfirming the current hypothesis do increase the number of disconfirmatory sequences generated, but they do not increase the probability of solving the problem (e.g., Tweney, Doherty, Worner, Pliske, Mynatt, Gross and Arkkelin, 1980). However, Gorman and Gorman (1984) found that disconfirmatory instructions did help when the experimenter did not say whether subjects' guesses about the rule were correct. Gorman and Gorman explain this result in terms of the importance of making an *active* decision about whether the hypothesized rule is the correct one, rather than relying on the experimenter for feedback. However, this result did not replicate with a rule that was even more general that Wason's original rule (three different numbers) – subjects found it difficult to obtain disconfirming evidence for such a general rule. Performance on this more general rule is, however, facilitated by using the so-called DAX-MED version of the 2–4–6 task (Gorman, Stafford and Gorman, 1987) as it is with the standard rule (Tweney et al., 1980, Experiment 4). In the DAX-MED version of the task, the experimenter is said to be thinking of two rules, with the nonsense labels DAX and MED. DAX is the original rule and MED is its complement (all sets of three numbers that do not obey the original rule). Although subjects are not explicitly told about the relation between DAX and MED, it becomes obvious that every triple is either a DAX or a MED, but not both. Gorman et al. (1987) argue that the DAX-MED instructions help subjects to solve 2–4–6 type problems by letting them form a better representation of the problem.

8.2 Artificial Science Studies

As we have already mentioned, research using the selection task and the 2–4–6 task suggests a *confirmation bias* in the testing of hypotheses. We have also discussed why this might or might not be a good thing. One important question is whether confirmation bias can be demonstrated in working scientists, or in experimental situations that come closer to simulating scientific research than do Wason's tasks. Mitroff (1974), in an observational study of NASA scientists, presents convincing evidence that, at least in this group, confirmation bias is rife.

Mynatt, Doherty and Tweney (1977, 1978) conducted a series of experiments with a computer-simulated 'miniworld' in which particles could be fired at figures, some of which were protected by invisible boundaries (those presented, roughly speaking, at half intensity). The subjects' task was to discover the laws governing the motion of the particles. Instructions to confirm, disconfirm, or simply test current hypotheses had no effect on performance. However, when subjects were presented with data that disconfirmed their hypotheses (regardless of what instructions they received), they were able to make use of that data. Mynatt et al. argue that, contrary to a suggestion made by Wason (1968), people understand the logic of falsification. However, if a person's initial hypothesis focuses on wholly irrelevant aspects of a situation (for example, the shape of the objects as a determinant of whether they have invisible boundaries), that hypothesis may never be eliminated. This finding highlights the importance of the formation of several alternative hypotheses to increase the chances of an initial hypothesis that is at least partly correct, and hence amenable to falsification. This aspect of scientific investigation has been stressed by Platt (1964) in his description of the *strong inference* strategy. Strong inference requires the formulation of alternative hypotheses, the devising and carrying out of an experiment that eliminates all but one of them. Alternative versions of the remaining hypothesis are then derived, and the procedure continues.

In the later study (Mynatt, Doherty and Tweney, 1978), the complexity of the miniworld was increased in an attempt to mirror the complexity of the real world. None of the subjects derived the laws of the system in the ten hours that was allowed to them. The small number of subjects who were strongly influenced by the disconfirmatory instructions fared more poorly that the others. This result led Mynatt et al. to suggest that attempts to falsify hypotheses could be detrimental, particularly in the early stages of a scientific investigation. The idea that, in the early stages, people should try to establish a reasonable hypothesis by finding confirmatory evidence for it is compatible with the account of scientific investigation that we presented above.

An important aspect of real science, which has not been investigated in the studies mentioned so far, is that data may be misleading or in error, for a variety of reasons. Gorman (1986) has investigated the effects of unreliable data in hypothesis testing using the New Eleusis task, invented by Martin Gardner (1977). In this task a rule is formulated to describe sequences of playing cards. Typically the chosen rule will be a simple one, for example, 'alternating red and black cards'. Cards are dealt from the pack. If the current card can follow the last one in the rule-governed sequence, it is placed to the right of that card.

Otherwise it is placed underneath. Thus, correct cards continue in a straight line and incorrect ones go off at right angles. The cards on the table correspond, roughly, to a record of a sequence of experiments. Gorman, Gorman, Latta and Cunningham (1984) had previously established that, as in the standard 2–4–6 task, disconfirming instructions facilitate performance in the New Eleusis task. However, when subjects were told that there might be random errors in the feedback they received on 0 to 20 per cent of the trials, performance was severely disrupted. In fact feedback was 100 per cent accurate. The subjects worked in groups. Some groups ignored evidence that disconfirmed their hypotheses by treating it as error. The few groups that did succeed used a combination of disconfirmation and replication, thus highlighting another important feature of scientific research.

Summary

Psychological work on hypothesis testing, and most notably that of Peter Wason, has been strongly influenced by the Popperian notion of falsification. Wason devised three tasks for the study of hypothesis testing: the selection task, the THOG problem and the 2–4–6 task. In the selection task, subjects have to decide which of several cards to turn over to see if a rule relating what is on their two faces is true. It appears simple. Nevertheless, very few subjects succeed in selecting the right cards. Wason himself proposed that subjects focused on cards that might confirm the rule rather those that might falsify it. Evans suggested that subjects tend to choose cards that are explicitly mentioned in the rule. The original selection task is abstract in form. Concrete versions of the selection task are simpler. Griggs suggested that concrete rules cued memories of rule-governed situations that helped subjects solve the problem. More recent work, however, has indicated that rules about permissions and obligations are handled much more easily than rules of other kinds. Two possible explanations focus on the relation between such rules and social contracts and practical reasoning, respectively.

The THOG problem, which is about the classification of simple geometric shapes, has been much less widely studied than the selection task. Again people find it very difficult. A large part of the explanation is that it requires the consideration of a considerable number of alternative possibilities which bear no systematic relation to one another. Another is that, because of the structure of the task, subjects find it difficult to distinguish hypotheses and data.

The 2–4–6 problem requires subjects to discover a rule governing sequences of three numbers, by asking whether or not particular sequences obey the rule. The logic of the task is complex, but subjects' protocols indicate that they choose sequences that fit the rule that they currently have in mind. Wason argues that this behaviour is another instance of the confirmation bias that he identified in the selection task. However, Klayman and Ha have shown that the relation between a positive test strategy and confirmation (or falsification) is not as simple as Wason assumed. Furthermore, artificial science studies, using more complex tasks, have suggested that people understand the logic of falsification, even if they do not always apply a falsification strategy in the face of complex, and possibly inaccurate, data.

Further Reading

Tweney, R. D., Doherty, M. E. and Mynatt, C. R. (eds) (1981). On *Scientific Thinking*. New York: Columbia University Press.

Wason, P. C. and Johnson-Laird, P. N. (1972). *Psychology of Reasoning: Structure and Content*. London: Batsford.

9

Statistical Reasoning

People have great difficulty with arguments that depend on statistics or probability. For example, psychology undergraduates find that their intuitions are of little help in learning about probability theory and statistical hypothesis testing. Presumably this experience reflects the problems that people have with statistical concepts in everyday life. To take a simple example, many people fail to see that the fact that they have known smokers who have lived to ninety has no tendency to disprove the (statistical) connection between smoking and fatal diseases. A slightly more complex example from the same domain underlines this point. About ten times as many smokers as non-smokers die from lung cancer and about twice as many smokers as non-smokers die from heart disease. Nevertheless, giving up smoking reduces a person's chances of dying from heart disease more than it reduces their chances of dying from lung cancer, because the absolute number of people dying from heart disease is so much larger (in the UK, about 300,000 per year vs. about 50,000 per year).

As these examples show, statistical reasoning is often important in practical reasoning about how to conduct our everyday lives – whether or not to give up smoking. Our decisions do not, of course, depend on the statistical aspects of the problem alone, but on factors such as how much we value avoiding a premature, and possibly painful, death. In this chapter we consider people's ability to make use of statistical evidence, independently of its role in decision making. We ask the question 'how good are people as *intuitive statisticians*?', and we survey some statistical concepts with which people have difficulty. In the following chapter, we will discuss decision making, including risky decisions (where the outcome is not known, but the probabilities of the outcomes are) and decisions under uncertainty (where the probabilities are not). In making decisions people combine their beliefs about the outcomes of their actions with their preferences, in order to choose between various courses of action.

9.1   Probability Theory

Both descriptive and inferential statistics are founded on the notion of probability. In the study of deductive reasoning, logic provides a way of formalizing arguments and, hence, a standard against which particular arguments can be judged. In a similar way, the mathematical theory of probability can be used to formalize arguments from statistical evidence. Probability theory can also be used as a standard against which to compare everyday arguments. Evaluating arguments against the standard of logic is problematic, because it can be difficult to justify the identification of a formally defined logical constant, such as ¬ or ∧, with its natural language counterpart, 'not' or 'and'. Similar problems arise in judging everyday statistical reasoning against the yardstick of probability theory. In particular, do the judgements people make about the likelihood of events have the properties of probabilities as defined in probability theory?

A fundamental question, therefore, is: what is a probability? Three types of answer have been given to this question. According to one view (championed, for example, by John Venn, the inventor of Venn diagrams; see chapter 6), probabilities are defined in terms of long-term (relative) frequencies. So, to take a simple example, the probability of a fair coin coming down heads is one-half, because, in the long run, the number of tosses of such a coin that come down heads will be one half of the total number of tosses. Although this theory is appealing when applied to gambles, it runs into problems for more mundane events where the comparison class (in the coin-tossing example, times when the coin does *not* come down heads) is less obvious. How, for example, should the probability of a happy marriage be assessed? By comparison with unhappy marriages, or by comparison with all other possibilities? The second view, proposed by the economist John Maynard Keynes (1921), is that the figure of one-half comes from a logical analysis of the notion of a fair coin. Again this view applies nicely to gambling, but less well to everyday life. A more radical alternative, but one whose antecedents can be traced to early work on probability by Pierre de Laplace (1749–1827), is that of *Bayesian* statisticians. Bayesians take a judgement about the probability of an event to represent the degree of belief of an 'ideal' person, whose beliefs are perfectly consistent, that the event will occur. These degrees of belief may, indeed, be completely subjective, as long as they obey certain rules (the axioms of probability theory; see below). With fair coins and dice, degree of belief should be based on logical analysis, and, more generally, beliefs are usually based, at least in part, on objective evidence. The subjective view of probability is not incompatible with this fact, and to some extent the term 'subjective' is misleading. Bayesians differ from adherents of the other two views in two mains ways. First, they are likely to accept Laplace's *principle of indifference*. This principle states that, when there is no evidence about the relative likelihoods of two events, they should be taken as equiprobable. Second, they are likely to make greater use of Bayes' theorem (see §9.3.2 below). Bayes' theorem requires judgements about the probabilities of hypotheses *before data that tests between them has been collected*. It is often impossible to assign such probabilities on the basis of relative frequency or logical analysis. However, it is always possible to believe in a hypothesis to a greater or lesser extent.

Adherents of all three views agree about the fundamental mathematical properties of probabilities.

1   A probability is a number in the range 0 (impossibility) to 1 (certainty).
2   The sum of the probabilities of all the possible events in a given situation is 1. For example, the probability of a fair coin coming down heads plus the probability of it coming down tails is (one-half + one-half =) 1. As a special case, the probability of an event not happening is one minus the probability of it happening.
3   For mutually exclusive events in the same situation (the throw of a die coming up 6 and the same throw coming up 5, for example), the probability of one or other event is the sum of the probabilities of the events. In this example the probability of a 5 or a 6 is one-sixth plus one-sixth (= one-third), for a fair die.
4   To find the probability of two independent events both happening (the throw of one die coming up 6 and the throw of a second die coming up 6, for example), the probabilities of the two events have to be multiplied together (in this example, one-sixth times one-sixth = one in thirty six).
5   The probability of one event (A) happening given that another (B) has happened (called the *conditional probability* of A given B) is the

probability of both happening divided by the probability of B happening:

$$p(A|B) = \frac{p(AandB)}{p(B)}$$

For example, the probability of a fair die showing an even number, given that it shows a number less than four, is the probability of it showing a number that is both even and less than four (i.e., 2, with probability one-sixth) divided by the probability of a number less than four (i.e., 1, 2 or 3 with probability one-half), which comes to one-third, because one out of the three numbers less than four is even.

Although people make informal judgements of likelihood, and about what might and might not happen, it is far from clear that their judgements conform to these principles. For example, they might judge two events to be independent, yet their estimate of the likelihood of both happening might be quite different from the result of multiplying their estimates of the individual events happening. If they make inferences based on such judgements, those inferences cannot be modelled using probability theory.

The *personal* (Bayesian) view of probability, as it is known, is widely accepted in economics, and hence in psychological research on probabilistic reasoning and decision making that derives from ideas in economics. However, it has been argued that in its original version (Savage, 1954) it is not radical enough (Shafer, 1976, 1986; Shafer and Tversky, 1985). Shafer argues that it is a mistake to take probabilities (even interpreted as degrees of belief) as basic elements in judgements and decisions. Probability judgements are constructed from evidence, which is more fundamental (and more readily available to intuition), and 'on the process of exploring that evidence' (Shafer and Tversky, 1985: p. 337). Events can be assigned different probabilities, depending on what evidence is used in assessing their likelihood, and on how it is used. Furthermore, Shafer argues that Savage was wrong in assuming that judgements of probability can always be separated from judgements of value – questions about the probabilities people assign to events cannot be fully disentangled from questions about people's preferences. Shafer's arguments have implications for normative theories of decision making discussed in the next chapter.

Ironically, however, as Gigerenzer (1993; Gigerenzer and Murray, 1987) has pointed out, the personal view of probability has virtually no place in the inferential (hypothesis testing) techniques taught to psychologists in research methods and statistics courses. These techniques are based almost entirely on the frequentist views of Fisher, and of Neyman and Pearson. Since the frequentist approach does not allow probabilities to be assigned to unique events, Gigerenzer argues that some of the experimental results that are taken to indicate failures of probabilistic reasoning need to be reinterpreted. They refer to situations (such as the occupations of unique individuals; see §9.2.4a below) to which probabilities cannot be attached on the frequentist view.

9.2   Judgements of Probability

Psychological research on probability necessarily focuses on people's estimates of probabilities. Since these estimates cannot always be based on observation of long-term frequencies, or on logical analysis, this work is broadly consistent with the personal view. Likelihood estimates are useful to the extent that they are accurate reflections of the way the world is. Yet they may be mistaken. More importantly, we can ask whether, when people make and combine judgements of likelihood, they adhere to the axioms of probability theory. If they do not, and if the real world is well modelled by probability theory, errors in reasoning will ensue.

9.2.1   Simple estimates of probability

A fundamental question in psychological research on probability is: how good are people at estimating probabilities from the evidence around them? Given a simple task – watching someone drawing balls out of an urn one at a time and replacing them – people are fairly accurate at estimating the proportions of balls of different colours (Peterson and Beach, 1967; Estes, 1976; Hintzmann, 1976). There is, however, a tendency to overestimate very small proportions. A further finding in these 'urn' studies provides additional evidence of accurate frequency estimation. If the task is changed so that the subject has to guess the colour of the next ball, the guesses are usually apportioned in the same ratio as the balls. In a sense this *probability matching* is odd, since it does not give the highest expected number of correct guesses. The strategy that does is to choose the most common colour every time. Fischhoff (1988) suggests that the attraction of probability matching is that it seems to be a strategy that could produce the right answer every time, whereas choosing the most common colour does not. In fact both could, by chance, be right for each ball drawn in an experiment.

Although probability judgements are accurate in artificial situations, such as the urn task, they are easily upset with more meaningful material. For example, Kahneman and Tversky (1973) asked people to listen to a list of 39 names (either 19 famous women and 20 fairly well-known men or 19 famous men and 20 fairly well-known women). People tended to judge, incorrectly, that there were more people of the 'famous' sex than of the 'fairly well-known' sex. When probability (or frequency) estimates rely on something other than mere 'counting', biases affect people's ability to make reliable judgements. We will discuss the *availability heuristic* that Kahneman and Tversky use to explain their result below.

A more straightforward bias in frequency estimates is found when subjects make judgements about a wider range of frequencies. In such experiments more meaningful materials are again used, because they provide a simple way to introduce extreme frequencies. With such materials, low frequencies are overestimated and high frequencies underestimated. This result was obtained, for example, by Lichtenstein, Slovic, Fischhoff, Layman and Combs (1978) when subjects had to judge the frequencies of causes of death. The subjects were, nevertheless, reasonably accurate in estimating the relative frequencies of different causes of death.

9.2.2   Overconfidence

Probability estimates also break down in a systematic way when people judge how well they have performed. They are *overconfident* about their judgements (except for very easy tasks on which they tend to be slightly underconfident). One technique (Fischhoff, Slovic and Lichtenstein, 1977) is to give people simple, two choice, questions ('is absinthe a drink or a precious stone?') and to have them rate their confidence about each answer. The number of correct answers to questions for which their confidence was between, say, 90 per cent and 100 per cent can then be computed. Typically the proportion is 80 per cent or less. Furthermore, overconfidence increases with the difficulty of the questions. Confidence judgements are said to be *incorrectly calibrated*. This incorrect cali-bration can sometimes be corrected with intense training, especially when feedback is clear and relatively immediate. For example, Murphy and Winkler (1984) showed that expert weather forecasters were almost perfectly calibrated in their estimates of the likelihood of rain. However, studies of other experts (e.g., clinical psychologists and lawyers) show that intense training does not automatically protect against overconfidence, though it does tend to produce more accurate calibration (see Griffin and Tversky, 1992).

Gigerenzer, Hoffrage and Kleinbölting (1991) propose a theory of *probabilistic mental models* to explain overconfidence on general knowledge problems. Probabilistic mental models are used to solve problems by inference 'using probabilistic information from a natural environment' when those problems cannot be solved directly by *local mental models*, that is 'by memory and elementary logical operations' (Gigerenzer et al., 1991: p. 507). Because a proportion of general knowledge questions have a 'trick' element to them (and those questions will be difficult, if the trick is disguised), probabilistic or indirect methods often generate wrong answers. For example, Liverpool is on the west coast of the UK and Edinburgh is on the east, yet Edinburgh is the more westerly of the two cities. An indirect attempt to answer the question 'which is more westerly, Liverpool or Edinburgh?' will produce a wrong answer but a reasonably high confidence rating. Gigerenzer et al. predicted that, with a different type of question, overconfidence should be eliminated. They chose pairs of German cities at random from all the cities with more than 100,000 inhabitants, and asked people to judge which in each pair had more inhabitants. Such questions can be answered indirectly, for example, by considering whether each city is a regional capital or whether it has a football team in the main football league. However, there are no trick questions. Overconfidence was greatly reduced for city questions compared with standard general knowledge questions. A further finding was that, with both sets of questions, subjects were highly accurate in judging how many questions they had answered correctly overall. Gigerenzer et al. explain this result by assuming that the confidence judgements about individual questions and judgements of long-run success in question-answering are made using different probabilistic mental models. In the first case models related to the specific questions are used. In the second, models of the subjects' own question-answering abilities, including, for the general knowledge items, the well-known fact that some of the questions will be trick questions.

Griffin and Tversky (1992) have shown, however, that eliminating the 'trick' element in questions does not by itself eliminate overconfidence. They asked subjects to compare randomly chosen pairs of US states on measures of population, education and voting habits. Population estimates were good, but those on the other two measures were poor. Estimates on all three measures, but in particular on education, showed overconfidence. Griffin and Tversky explain these results by assuming that people give more credence than they should to the prima facie *strength* of evidence and not enough to its *quality*. For example, for their education measure (high-school graduation rate) Griffin and Tversky predicted high overconfidence because their subjects were well aware of factors such as number of famous universities in a state, but they did not realize that there is little relation between the number of such universities and high-school graduation rate – the measure they were trying to judge. There might be strong evidence that a state has a good education system, but that evidence is poor evidence about achievements in its high schools. Griffin and Tversky also point out that part, if not all, of Gigerenzer et al.'s finding can be attributed to the fact that the general knowledge questions were harder than the city questions, so more overconfidence would be expected on that basis alone.

9.2.3 Hindsight bias

'It's obvious with hindsight' is a common observation. And, indeed, it is one that has been confirmed by psychologists. For example, subjects can be asked to make a retrospective judgement of the probability of the outcome of an event after they have been told the outcome – they are asked what they would have predicted if they had not known the outcome. Under these circumstances, they are strongly influenced by the actual outcome. This *hindsight bias* was demonstrated by Fischhoff (1977), using general knowledge questions. Some subjects were told the answers to the questions and others were not. The second group had to generate answers themselves, and assign probabilities to them. Those subjects who were told the answers claimed they would have assigned higher probabilities to the answers than the ones who had to produce the answers themselves.

9.2.4 Kahneman and Tversky's heuristics

When subjects make probabilistic judgements about everyday situations they often make gross errors. To explain these errors, and intuitive statistical judgements in general, Tversky and Kahneman (e.g., 1974) proposed that people use heuristic methods for assessing the probabilities of events or of properties that objects might have. These heuristic methods produce direct estimates of probability or frequency, so it is appropriate to discuss them as methods of assessing probabilities. However, in problems that people solve using these heuristic methods there are often statistical *inferences* that people 'should' be making from information that is given to them. So, heuristics bypass inferences as well as generating probabilities. Tversky and Kahneman (1974) described three heuristics: *representativeness, availability* and *anchoring and adjustment*.

9.2.4.a Representativeness

According to the representativeness heuristic, a person, thing or event will be judged to be a member of a class whose stereotypical members it closely resembles, regardless of other information, such as the relative sizes of all the classes of which it might be a member. So, when people are given a description of someone, and asked whether they are an engineer or a lawyer, they base their judgement on whether the description is typical of what they think lawyers and engineers are like. In applying the representativeness heuristic people, therefore, bypass the correct procedure, which takes into account the so-called *prior odds* of any person chosen at random being a lawyer or an engineer (the *base rate* or relative frequency of those occupations in the relevant population).

The representativeness heuristic can lead to more serious errors of judgement, as the following problem illustrates (Tversky and Kahneman, 1982b):

> Linda is 31 years old, single, outspoken, and very bright. She majored in philosophy. As a student, she was deeply concerned with issues of discrimination and social justice, and also participated in anti-nuclear demonstrations. Which of the following statements about Linda is more probable? (1) She is a bank teller. (2) She is a bank teller who is active in the feminist movement.

Many undergraduates favoured the second statement, including about half of those who had followed a statistics course. However, since every bank teller who is active in the feminist movement is also a bank teller, the first statement must be at least as probable as the second. On the reasonable assumption that some bank tellers are not active in the feminist movement, the first statement is *more probable*. Kahneman and Tversky call the error of selecting the second statement the *conjunction fallacy*, since people fail to recognize that everything that is both A *and* B must also be A. The fallacy can be explained on the assumption that people's judgements are based on the representativeness heuristic. Linda is more representative of members of the feminist movement than she is of bank tellers. She is, therefore, more representative of bank tellers active in that movement than of bank tellers in general. If people judge the likelihood of a person's belonging to a class by whether they seem typical of that class, as the representativeness heuristic claims, they will judge Linda more likely to be a bank teller active in the feminist movement than a bank teller, despite the logical impossibility of this state of affairs.

Considerations of representativeness can also explain the so-called *gambler's fallacy*, and other misconceptions of chance. According to the gambler's fallacy, a run of losses 'must be' followed by a run of wins to 'even things up', or to accord with the 'law of averages' (in other words, to make the current sequence of wins and losses more representative of the longer-term pattern). This argument is fallacious because, no matter how long a run of heads a fair coin has produced, for example, the probability of a head on the next toss remains one-half. However, if people are asked to judge which of the following sequences is more likely in the tosses of a fair coin:

HTHTTH or HHHHHH

they almost always pick the first. Both are equally probable. Each is just one of 64 sequences of heads and tails in six tosses of a fair coin. This fact should not be confused with the fact that only one of these 64 sequences has six heads, whereas 20 of them have three heads and three tails. Each one of those 20 has the same probability as the run of six heads, namely 1 in 64. Similarly, in a sequence of births, Girl Boy Girl Boy Boy Girl is no more likely than Girl Girl Girl Girl Girl Girl, though three boys and three girls (in any order) is more likely than six girls.

Tversky and Kahneman (1982b) distinguish between judgements *by* representativeness, such as those made about Linda, and judgements *of* representativeness, in which small samples are taken to be representative of the population from which they are drawn, ignoring the random fluctuations found in such samples. The two uses of representativeness are logically independent, but people apparently use representativeness in both types of circumstance.

9.2.4.b   *Availability*

Kahneman and Tversky's second heuristic is availability. According to this heuristic the probability of an event, or of an item having a property, is judged by the ease with which instances can be brought to mind – their availability from memory. Availability tends, for example, to make people overestimate the frequency of highly publicized, but comparatively rare, events. Thus, judgements of the probability of dying in an air crash tend to be grossly overestimated.

A number of experimental results have also been explained in terms of availability. For example, Kahneman and Tversky's (1973; see also Tversky and Kahneman, 1973) results on judging the numbers of men's and women's names in a list (see above) can be explained by appeal to the availability heuristic. Better known names come back to mind more easily when the subjects were asked to make their judgements – they are more available. In another experiment subjects were asked whether they thought there were more (English) words beginning with a certain letter or with that letter in third position. People almost always judge that there are more words beginning with the letter rather than words with the letter in third place, even when the reverse is the case, as it is for R and for K. It is much easier to think of words from the letters they begin with – words beginning with R are more available than those with R in third place.

9.2.4.c Anchoring and adjustment

The third, and least well documented, of Kahneman and Tversky's heuristics is anchoring and adjustment. The idea underlying this heuristic is that people often make estimates, of probabilities among other things, by taking an initial value, or anchor, and adjusting it. The anchor 'may be suggested by the formulation of the problem, or it may be the result of a partial computation' (Tversky and Kahneman, 1974). The anchor affects the final judgement because the adjustments are insufficient. Anchoring and adjustment can best be illustrated by a non-probabilistic example. High-school students were asked to estimate, in five seconds, the values of the following products:

$$1 \times 2 \times 3 \times 4 \times 5 \times 6 \times 7 \times 8$$
$$8 \times 7 \times 6 \times 5 \times 4 \times 3 \times 2 \times 1$$

The mean estimates were 512 and 2,250, while the correct answer is 40,320. Tversky and Kahneman assume that these estimates, made too quickly for the students to perform a complete calculation, were usually based on an extrapolation from a partial computation made on the first part of the series of numbers. Insufficient adjustment explains why underestimates were obtained for both series. The different estimates for the two series are explained by the fact that, in typical left to right working, the anchor was larger for the second series.

The effect of an anchor on statistical judgements was demonstrated by asking people to estimate such quantities as the percentage of African nations in the United Nations. Different groups of subjects were given arbitrarily chosen numbers of 10 per cent and 65 per cent as a starting point. They were asked to say whether these numbers were over- or underestimates and to go on to give what they thought was the proper estimate. The mean estimates for these two groups were 25 per cent and 45 per cent.

9.3   Some Difficult Statistical Concepts

In the following sections we discuss some concepts from statistical theory with which people have problems, and which specify inferences that people often fail to draw. Where appropriate we will show how Kahneman and Tversky's heuristics can explain the mistakes that people make.

9.3.1   Regression to the mean

Regression towards the mean is a phenomenon that is both counter-intuitive and comparatively difficult to explain. Indeed, many professional psychologists have problems understanding it, though there is evidence that people who have taken courses in statistics can apply the principle to everyday situations (see chapter 15). It is most straight-forwardly illustrated using the kind of data that led to its discovery. Francis Galton, the nineteenth-century polymath and half-cousin of Charles Darwin, investigated the way both physical and psychological characteristics are inherited. He noticed what at first appeared to be a puzzling fact about his data. Taking height as an example, he found that tall parents tended to have children who were tall, but not quite so tall as them, and that short parents tended to have children who were short, but not quite so short as them. At first he sought an empirical explanation of this fact, but he was puzzled, because it seemed to suggest that differences in height in the population would gradually disappear, an idea for which there is no empirical support. However, Galton was also a capable statistician, and was able to demonstrate not only that the phenomenon is a statistical one, but also that it is perfectly compatible with the amount of variability in people's heights remaining the same from one generation to the next.

Regression to the mean is not limited to inherited characteristics, but is a much wider phenomenon. It is found whenever two measurements reflect, imperfectly, some underlying ability or quality. For example, height is determined to some extent, but not entirely, by genetic factors, and since parents and children share genes, one sees regression to the mean when the two measurements are parents' height and child's height. Regression to the mean is also found when a single person takes a test twice. So, for example, children who do exceptionally well on a spelling test one week are likely to do not quite so well in a similar test the next week, whereas children who do very badly are likely to do rather better. Scores on a spelling test are not a perfect reflection of spelling ability. Only where a measure is perfectly accurate, or effectively so, will there be no regression towards the mean. Tall people are not found to be shorter when their height is measured for a second time.

In the test-retest case, regression towards the mean is often described by saying that, if an above average person takes a test twice, they are likely to do worse on the second test than on the first. In some people's minds this suggestion puts the whole idea of psychological testing into doubt. In fact, this description is highly misleading. Regression, as introductory statistics courses explain, is about predicting one thing from another. Galton was effectively predicting the height of children from the height of their parents, and in test-retest one predicts a person's score on the retest from their score on the first test. If someone has done very well on the first test, the best bet is that they will do less well the second time. But it is equally true that, if what you find out about first is a person's score on the second test, your best bet about their score on the first test is that it would be *closer* to the mean. Similarly, given a very tall child, the best bet is that its parents are tall, but not quite so tall. Regression to the mean occurs only when predicting one measurement or test score from another. The best bet about scores by the same person on test and retest before either result is known is that they will be the same.

How can that be? The reasons are complicated, and can be explained properly only by a detailed mathematical argument. However, a rough indication of that argument can be given. First, we assume that if the same person was given the same test over and over again their score wouldn't be exactly the same each time, but would vary (ignoring improvement with practice). Given certain reasonable assumptions, the best bet about what a person will score on any particular administration of the test is their average score. So, if a person is going to take a test twice, we predict that each time their most likely score is their average score. However, things are different if we already know that a person has got a high score on a first test – no prediction is necessary, we have the score. Since different people have different average scores, and people don't always score their average, someone who has, say, 45 out of 50 in a spelling test may have a true average of 45 and be scoring their average, but they may have a true average of 43 and be scoring above average, or they may have a true average of 47 and be scoring below average. Assuming that 45 is above the average for all people taking the test, there will be more people with a true average of 43 than 45 and more with a true average of 45 than 47. So, although the best bet about what any particular person scores is their average score, a person who has actually scored 45 is more likely to be a person with a real average of 43 who by chance exceeds this score than a person with a true average of 45 scoring their average. To predict a score on the second test we are forced back on the strategy of assuming that the person will score their average, so our prediction is that the person who scored 45 first time round will score 43 second time round. Exactly the same argument can be made for a person who scored 45 on the *second* test. Our best bet would be that they scored 43 on the first test!!

Before leaving regression to the mean, we should answer Galton's problem. Why are differences in, for example, spelling test scores not obliterated over time (which of course they are not!)? The reason stems from a corollary of what we have just been saying. Although people who score 45 on the first test tend to drift down on the second test, a few drift up (we are talking about statistical tendencies). Similarly, some of those who scored 43 will drift up. Because more people have a true average of 43 than 45, the small proportion of 43s drifting up counterbalances the large proportion of 45s drifting down. Given the assumptions about variation both in individuals and in the population that Galton was able to make, he showed that these two kinds of drift cancel each other out, and the overall variability in the population remains the same.

Tversky and Kahneman (1974) suggest that regression towards the mean is difficult to understand because it produces results that conflict with representativeness. In the test-retest case, for example, the first result suggests that the person is, say, outstandingly good at spelling. The (regressed) retest result is less representative of outstanding spellers. Tversky and Kahneman further argue that the failure to understand regression to the mean has at least one pernicious effect – overestimation of the effect of punishment and underestimation of the effect of reward. A very poor performance, which is likely to be punished, will, by chance alone, typically be followed by a better one, making the punishment seem effective, whereas a very good (rewarded) performance is likely to be followed by a poorer one.

9.3.2   Bayes' theorem

Bayes' theorem is often the most difficult part of probability theory taught on undergraduate statistics courses for psychology students. It is highly unpopular, which suggests that the ideas underlying it are not intuitively obvious. Nevertheless those ideas are comparatively straight-forward. Suppose there is a fact to be explained, and there are two or more possible explanations of that fact. These explanations will usually be derived from (either scientific or everyday) hypotheses about how the world works. For example, the fact might be a symptom exhibited by a patient in a hospital, and the explanations of the symptom might be possible diagnoses of the patient's illness. Bayes's theorem gives us a way of calculating the probability of the explanations being true, given that the fact is true, from two other sets of information.

1 The probabilities of those explanations before the fact was known: in the case of diagnoses, these probabilities indicate how common the different illnesses that can give rise to the symptom are. These probabilities are referred to as the *prior odds* of the hypotheses or the *base rates* of, for example, illness.
2 For each hypothesis, the probability of the fact being true given that the hypothesis is true: for diagnoses, these probabilities indicate how likely the symptom is given that a patient definitely has the disease. These probabilities are conditional probabilities of the kind described on pp. 155–6.

In the case of diagnoses, both sets of probabilities can be estimated from medical records.

For interest, we will state Bayes' theorem for the simple case where there are just two hypotheses, H_0, the one we are primarily interested in, and H_1, the alternative. The mathematical details are not important, but it is important that the final result depends on both the conditional probabilities and the base rates.

$$P(H_0 \,|E) = \frac{P(E|H_0).P(H_0)}{P(E|H_0).P(H_0) + P(E|H_1).P(H_1)}$$

In this formula, $P(H_0|E)$ is the probability of hypothesis H_0 given the evidence (fact) E; $P(E|H_0)$ is the probability of the evidence given H_0; and $P(H_0)$ is the probability of H_0 being true independent of evidence E. $P(H_0)$ does *not* mean the probability of H_0 independent of any evid-ence. $P(H_0)$ means the probability of H_0 before the evidence E has been considered. So repeated application of Bayes' theorem as new evidence comes in allows a continued updating of the assessment of the probabil-ity of a hypothesis.

In many everyday situations people fail to realize the importance of

$P(H_0)$ and $P(H_1)$ in assessing the relevance of evidence to the truth of hypotheses, despite the intuition that one needs better evidence for an implausible hypothesis than for a plausible one. Kahneman and Tversky (1973) argue that use of the representativeness heuristic often results in failure to take account of these probabilities, which are usually known as the *prior odds* for or against a hypothesis (or of the corresponding *base rate* frequencies). In one study subjects were asked to decide whether an individual was an engineer or a lawyer, given that the individual had been selected at random either from a group of 70 engineers and 30 lawyers or from a group of 30 engineers and 70 lawyers. There were three conditions in the experiment. In one, a description of the individual fitted the stereotype for either a lawyer or an engineer. In the second, the description was neutral, and in the third no description was provided. Or in the third condition did the frequency of the two types of individual in the group influence subjects' judgements. In the first condition, the judgements reflected representativeness judgements, regardless of the constitution of the group. The second condition usually elicited the judgement that the individual was just as likely to be an engineer as a lawyer. Thus, unless prior odds are the only relevant information, subjects bypass the correct procedure and use the representativeness heuristic as the basis of their judgement.

9.3.3   Diagnosticity

Bayes' theorem refers to situations in which there are at least two hypotheses – in its general form it allows for more. And much of the best science pits one hypothesis against another. To choose between hypotheses, *diagnostic* evidence is needed – evidence that is more likely given one hypothesis than the other. In determining the diagnosticity of evidence, base rates have to be taken into account. There may be more patients with chest infections who cough than patients with lung cancer who cough, but that may be because there are more patients with chest infections overall. The number of patients with the disease who do not cough has to be taken into account in deciding whether coughing is a useful symptom in *distinguishing* the two diseases.

To obtain diagnostic information, it is, therefore, necessary to ask questions than can, at least potentially, produce it. A further complication is that it is not only questions that vary in their diagnosticity. Different answers to the same question do as well (Slowiaczek, Klayman, Sherman and Skov, 1992). Slowiaczek et al. argue that people are more sensitive to *question diagnosticity* than to *answer diagnosticity*. Their subjects had to imagine meeting an inhabitant of the planet Vuma who is either a Glom or a Fizo, and to select one question to try to find out which it is. They preferred to ask as question that 90 per cent of Gloms will answer positively and 50 per cent of Fizos, rather than one that 70 per cent of Gloms will answer positively and 50 per cent of Fizos. This preference is understandable, since the first question gives a better chance of distinguishing between Gloms and Fizos. However, the subjects' confidence that the creature was a Glom given a 'yes' answer to the first question was 68 per cent, and their confidence the creature was a Fizo given a 'no' answer was 70 per cent. Bayes's theorem shows that the respective *probabilities* are 64 per cent and 83 per cent – the 'no' answer has a higher diagnosticity. This insensitivity to differential answer diagnosticity can lead people to retain an incorrect hypothesis, particularly if, as in this case, the 'yes' answer is less diagnostic. This problem is exacerbated by the fact that people select questions that they think will have 'yes' answers. Slowiaczek et al. argue that if people regard diagnosticity as a property of questions, rather than as a property of answers, they are behaving in a *non-Bayesian* way.

The idea that people tend to retain an initial (and in the real world often favoured) hypothesis, together with the idea that people try to confirm rather than disconfirm hypotheses, has also been used to explain the phenomenon of *pseudodiagnosticity* (Doherty, Mynatt, Tweney and Schiavo, 1979; Beyth-Marom and Fischhoff, 1983). Imagine that someone is trying to decide between buying a Ford and a Toyota and that their principal considerations are fuel economy and comfort. If they know that 90 per cent of Ford owners consider their cars economical on fuel, which of the following three pieces of information is most useful to them?

1 Information about how comfortable Ford owners find their cars.
2 Information about how economical on fuel Toyoto owners find their cars.
3 Information about how comfortable Toyota owners find their cars.

Most subjects chose (1), though this choice is not so popular if the figure of 90 per cent is reduced to 50 per cent. If nine out of ten Ford owners are happy with fuel economy, Fords seem like good cars! But Toyotas might be even better than Fords on fuel economy, so although the 90 per cent seems to be providing diagnostic information, it is not. The information is only *pseudodiagnostic*. If only one other piece of information is allowed, (2) is the only one that, in conjunction with the original information, is diagnostic. Nevertheless, it is not clear that, by choosing (1), people are really expecting to find out that Fords are comfortable, too, and hence attempting to confirm the hypothesis that Fords are good cars. If they are satisfied with the 90 per cent rating that Fords get on fuel economy, information about the comfort of Fords may be more useful in helping them decide, either positively or negatively, whether to buy a Ford. The choice of (1) may better be explained in terms of Klayman and Ha's (1987) notion of a positive test strategy (see chapter 8), rather than in terms of confirmation bias.

9.3.4   Sample size – the law of large numbers

Statistics books are full of often puzzling jargon about populations and samples. The basic idea is a simple one: knowledge about giraffes, say, is not based on all the giraffes that ever were, but only a small number of them. Nevertheless, on inductive grounds (see chapter 7), we can assume other giraffes to be like the ones that have been studied, and we can draw general conclusions about giraffes on that basis. Statistical theory tell us how accurate our conclusions about giraffes will be, given the size of the sample that has been studied. Some of its results are surprising. There are not, of course, any surprises about such facts as giraffes having one head. But about more detailed facts, such as the average length of a giraffe's neck, or the average number of spots on a giraffe, there may be. Some important ideas are:

1   In most cases the size of the population (i.e., the total number of giraffes) is irrelevant. The accuracy of our estimates depends only on the number of giraffes on which we have made measurements – the more the better ('the law of large numbers').
2   In a case like the length of the giraffe's neck, the best estimate is the average of the measurements made, but the more measurements, the more accurate the estimate.
3   [the converse of (2)] If we take different samples of, say, ten giraffes, and find the average number of spots in each sample, we will probably get different results each time, and the smaller the size of the samples we take, the more variable the results will be.

These ideas do not represent formal rules of inference, but consequences of the ideas behind statistical theory. Some of Kahneman and Tversky's results demonstrate the difficulty that people have in making use of these facts about sample size. For example, Kahneman and Tversky (1972) gave people the following problem:

A certain town is served by two hospitals. In the larger hospital about 45 babies are born each day and in the smaller hospital about 15 babies are born each day. As you know, about 50 per cent of all babies are boys. However, the exact percentage varies from day to day. Sometimes it may be higher than 50 per cent sometimes lower. For a period of one year, each hospital recorded the days on which more than 60 per cent of the babies born were boys. Which hospital do you think recorded more such days?

Most undergraduate subjects thought that the number of such days would be about the same in the two hospitals. Of the remainder, about equal numbers chose each of the two hospitals. The correct answer, as is obvious from the above principles, is that the smaller hospital will record more such days, because its 15 babies a day is a smaller sample, and the proportion of male babies in small samples is more variable. It will, of course, also record more days with over 60 per cent female babies. These proportions can be thought of as a series of estimates of the (roughly constant) proportion of male births in the population as a whole. Tversky and Kahneman (1974) argue that this result, like the one in which prior odds were ignored, can be explained by assuming that subjects use the representativeness heuristic, rather than making correct statistical inferences.

Kahneman and Tversky (1972) report a similar failure to take account of sample size in a statistically more complex question.

Imagine an urn filled with balls, of which two-thirds are of one colour and one-third of another. One individual has drawn five balls from the urn, and found that four were red and one was white. Another individual has drawn twenty balls and found that twelve were red and eight were white. Which of the two individuals should feel more confident that the urn contains two-thirds red balls and one-third white balls, rather than the opposite? What odds should each individual give?

Probability theory shows that the odds are 8:1 for the first individual and 16:1 for the second. Although the first sample has a higher proportion of red balls than the second, this fact is overridden by its smallness, and hence the relatively high chance that it does not accurately reflect the composition of the population from which it is drawn. Nevertheless, most statistically naive subjects thought that the first sample provided better evidence that the urn contained more red balls. Again Tversky and Kahneman (1974) maintain that representativeness is at work. The smaller sample is more representative of samples that might be drawn from an urn with two-thirds red balls.

Tversky and Kahneman (1971) argue that people, including research psychologists, follow what they call the 'law of small numbers'. That is to say, they take small samples to provide more accurate information about populations than they in fact do (i.e., to be more representative of populations than they are; see §9.2.4a above). For example, in the hospital problem, they expect the sample of babies born on a particular day in the small hospital to reflect the proportions in the general population of births more closely than it does. Similarly, people underestimate the likelihood of, say, a run of six heads in the tosses of a fair coin. They expect each small 'sample' of tosses to contain about half heads and half tails. Among research psychologists Tversky and Kahneman found a tendency to overestimate the likelihood of replicating a result based on a small sample, again indicating a failure to realize that the small sample has quite a good chance of not being representative of the population.

People do not wholly ignore sample size in their reasoning. For example, Evans and Dusoir's (1977) subjects realized that the small hospital is more likely to have a day on which all the babies are boys. In another set of studies, Nisbett, Krantz, Jepson and Kunda (1983; Fong, Krantz and Nisbett, 1986) gave subjects information about a sample of people from an unknown tribe, animals from an unknown species, or lumps of an unknown mineral. They were asked what proportion of the corresponding population they thought had that property. In some cases, such as a metal conducting electricity, subjects generalized to the whole population on the basis of one sample. General knowledge tells us that bits of the same metal do not vary in whether they conduct electricity. However, with other properties, such as members of a tribe being obese, estimates of the proportion of the tribe that were obese increased as the number in the sample (all of whom were obese) increased. Where a property is seen as variable – in most countries some people are obese and some are not – the propensity to generalize is (correctly) tempered by sample size. However, Nisbett et al. (1983) found that this caution was not always evident in social judgements. People tend to make strong generalizations, even for social characteristics that are highly variable.

9.3.5 Correlation

Statistics textbooks warn students not to confuse correlation and cause. Causal relations usually produce correlations, but not every correlation reflects a causal relation. But before the question of how correlations are interpreted arises, there is the prior question of how they are detected.

Jennings, Amabile and Ross (1982) asked subjects to judge the relation between sets of pairs of numbers on a scale from −100 to 100. No interpretation for the numbers was given. The variability in the judgements was high, indicating that the task was difficult, but there was a clear trend in the means – strong relations led to higher ratings. Comparing the ratings with one objective measure of the relation – the standard parametric correlation coefficient (r), Jennings et al. found that the mean judgements could be approximately described by the following equation:

$$judgement = 100(1 - \sqrt{1 - r^2})$$

One consequence of this formula is that people find it easier to distinguish a strong relation from a moderate one (as measured by r, a correlation of 0.9 from one of 0.5, say) than they find it to distinguish between a moderate relation and a weak one (0.5 vs. 0.1, say).

As with other types of reasoning, reasoning about relations between variables is strongly influenced by real-world knowledge. A second consequence of Jennings et al.'s formula is that *data-based* judgements of high correlations are comparatively difficult to elicit. However, when people are asked to estimate the degree of relatedness between verbally specified variables, for example, students' self-ratings of intellectualism and students' self-ratings of ambitiousness, high estimates are common. This second part of Jennings et al.'s study shows that people often expect to perceive correlations, and that their expectations are based on how they think the world ought to be. Indeed, even when they are presented with data that falsify this assumption, they may still perceive a correlation.

One kind of study provides evidence for what is known as *illusory correlation*. Chapman and Chapman (1967) presented subjects with clinical profiles of hypothetical psychiatric patients and figures of people allegedly drawn by them (in the well-known clinical test 'draw a person'). This test is known to be useless as a diagnostic tool, but an erroneous folklore surrounds it, suggesting, for example, that people who are suspicious of others (as in paranoia) draw faces with atypical eyes. The data presented to the subjects did not, objectively, show a relation between suspiciousness and atypical eyes and, indeed, in some studies the correlation was negative. However, the folklore of clinical diagnosis overrode the evidence, even when the subjects did not specifically know about the draw-a-person test! Chapman and Chapman suggest that these results help to explain why, despite being discredited, tests such as draw-a-person and the Rorschach ink-blot test continue to be used by clinicians. Tversky and Kahneman (1974) suggest that the phenomenon of illusory correlation can be explained by the availability heuristic. Although Chapman and Chapman's subjects did not know about the draw-a-person test, they knew that suspiciousness is readily expressed in the eyes, for example, by failure to make direct eye contact. The availability of this everyday folklore is, according to Tversky and Kahneman, what accounts for the illusory correlation.

A related phenomenon is the *illusion of control* (Jenkins and Ward, 1965). Subjects are asked to press one of two buttons to make a 'score', as opposed to a 'no score', light come on. The probability with which the two buttons caused one light or the other to come on was varied. Subjects' responses were governed primarily by the frequency with which the 'score' light came on, regardless of whether the two buttons had different probabilities of making the lights come on. However, if the probabilities are the same, the subjects' choice of button has no effect on which light comes on and, hence, the subjects have no control over the display. Alloy and Abramson (1979) found that (somewhat) depressed college students were less susceptible to the illusion of control, giving a new twist to the idea of a 'sadder but wiser' person. A further finding is that subjects' perception of the effect of their action depends on the outcome following the action almost immediately. Although there is no reason why there should not be a delay between a cause and effect, the perception of causation, and hence correlation, is less pronounced if there is a delay (Shanks and Dickinson, 1991).

Summary

Much of our reasoning is based on uncertain information, though there is reason to believe that people find it difficult to use such information properly. Uncertain information can be modelled using probabilities, though there are different interpretations of the notion of probability, and different ideas about how probability theory should be applied. In psychological research on statistical reasoning and decision making, the Bayesian or subjective view of probability is the most widely accepted.

In simple judgements of probability, people fare quite well on abstract problems, but can be distracted by extraneous factors when the problems have meaningful content. A particular case of this type of error is overconfidence, which is found in many judgements of one's own performance. Hindsight bias is another factor that can distort judgements of probability.

Kahneman and Tversky suggested three heuristics that people might apply in making probabilistic judgements: representativeness, availability, and anchoring and adjustment. A judgement using representativeness will assign a person or event to a class of which they seem typical, regardless of other factors that may affect the likelihood of their belonging to that class. Availability leads to judgements of probability based on how readily instances come to mind. Anchoring and adjustment claims that people do not revise their initial ideas as much as they ought to. The assumption that people use such heuristics can explain their mistakes on a wide range of problems devised by Kahneman and Tversky, and in particular the tendency to ignore base rate probabilities.

Kahneman and Tversky argue that representativeness explains why regression towards the mean is hard to understand. Regression to the mean is one of a number of statistical ideas that ordinary people have difficulty in understanding. Others include Bayes's theorem, diagnosticity, and the effect of sample size. Correlation is also a difficult concept, one that it is important to distinguish from cause. However, people have difficulty in detecting correlations or, more particularly, detecting their absence. This problem leads to the perception of illusory correlations that fit with preconceptions and to the illusion of control.

Further Reading

Gigerenzer, G. and Murray, D. J. (1987). *Cognition as Intuitive Statistics.* Hillsdale, NJ: Lawrence Erlbaum Associates.

Kahneman, D., Slovic, P. and Tversky, A. (eds) (1982). *Judgement under Uncertainty: Heuristics and Biases.* Cambridge: Cambridge University Press.

10

Decision Making

Common sense tells us that people's decisions depend both on their beliefs and on their desires. Some philosophers have been sceptical about common-sense psychological theories (e.g., Stich, 1983). Decision theorists, however, have, for the most part, accepted the common-sense analysis of decision making, and have, furthermore, assumed that beliefs and desires can be completely disentangled from one another (though see Shafer, 1986, for a dissenting view). Decision making is, therefore, a more complex process than judging probabilities. Indeed, it typically requires a combination of the probability judgements associated with our beliefs and information about our preferences. Whether someone takes an umbrella when they go out depends both on whether they think it will rain, and whether they want to avoid getting wet. Indeed, probability theory was originally developed for analysing games of chance and for assessing insurance risks. In both cases, judgements of probability inform decisions with outcomes people really care about – outcomes of financial gain and financial loss.

Some decisions do not depend on probability judgements, and the rational thing to do is to choose the more favourable alternative (which might be to do nothing). Other things being equal, would you rather be given $10 or $100? Obviously, $100. However, many decisions do involve probabilities, and they can be divided into those that involve *risks*, and those that involve *uncertainties* (Luce and Raiffa, 1957). *Decision making under risk* means that the probabilities of the outcomes are known, although the actual outcome cannot be predicted. Bets on the throw of a fair die come into this category, since the probability of each outcome is one-sixth. *Decision making under uncertainty* means that the probabilities of the outcomes are unknown. In most everyday decisions the outcomes are uncertain, at least to the extent that their probabilities cannot be quantified as precisely as the probability of a fair die coming up six. Decision making under uncertainty is more complicated than decision making under risk, because each outcome has to have not just a probability, but a probability distribution associated with it. Much of the discussion in this chapter is couched in terms of decision making under risk. However, our conclusions extend to decision making under uncertainty, since it is usually assumed that choices are made using best bets about uncertain probabilities.

In the previous chapter we showed that people are poor at handling statistical information. This fact must be taken into account when studying decision making under risk and under uncertainty. However, the fact that people misjudge probabilities does not mean that their decisions need be otherwise incorrect or irrational. A probability judged by availability or representativeness can be used in a rational decision procedure. However, estimates of likelihood produced by heuristics may not satisfy the axioms of probability theory.

10.1   Maximizing Subjective Expected Utility

A *normative* theory is provided by logic for deductive reasoning and by probability theory for statistical reasoning. Psychology provides a *description* of how people actually reason. In the decision-making literature a further distinction has been drawn between normative and *prescriptive* interpretations of a theory (e.g., Bell, Raiffa and Tversky, 1988). Any theory that can be formalized (typically, in decision theory, using the axiomatic method; see chapter 4) provides a set of norms, as opposed to a description of how people actually make decisions. A further question is what real people should be told to do in order to satisfy their goals (what should be *prescribed* to them). Whether they should be told anything other than to follow the norms of a normative theory, once that theory has been correctly formulated, is an open question. In this section we consider the most important normative theory for decision making.

When a decision is to be made, there are, by definition, several possible courses of action. Each course of action leads to one or more possible outcomes. Some of these outcomes will be preferred to others, and some will be more likely than others. Unfortunately, the preferred outcomes are not necessarily the most probable ones! If a decision maker can judge the likelihood of each outcome (following each course of action), and attach a value to that outcome, he or she will be in a position to make a rational choice between the courses of action. In early work on games of chance and on insurance (by the eighteenth-century Swiss mathematician Daniel Bernoulli, 1700–82) the values of the outcomes were measured in cash terms: the player loses $10.00 with a high probability or wins $200.00 with a low probability; the insurer pays out nothing with a high probability and a large amount of money (depending on the insured risk) with a low probability. The expected value of a course of action is found by multiplying the value of each outcome by its probability, and adding up the results. Since, in these examples, each course of action has an expected monetary value, the one with the highest value can be chosen. In this way, decision makers can *maximize* the *expected values* of their decisions.

Comparing monetary values of outcomes is straightforward, but it may not always be useful in the analysis of decision making. There are two related complications in linking outcomes to monetary values. First, outcomes cannot always be readily converted into cash values, so that different outcomes may at first seem incommensurable. Is a $500 vacation preferable to $500 cash? Organizers of competitions often have to offer both these alternatives, since some people prefer one, some the other. Some people would prefer $400 to $500 vacation. Some would prefer much less cash to the vacation. Even if the alternatives can be valued on the same scale (e.g., cash value), there is no guarantee that one person will prefer the more valuable, or that different people will have the same preferences. The subjective value of an outcome to a particular person may not be the same as its objective value (if it has one), but depends on their tastes, and on what they already have (it is much better to win a car if you do not already have one, want one, and can afford to run one, for example, than if one or more of these conditions does not hold).

The second complication is that, even if outcomes have clear monetary values, the same amount of money may have different values to different people, or even to the same person under different circumstances. Losing a house and all its contents in a fire would be financially devastating to most families if they were not insured. But a large insurance company will not suffer a comparably crippling loss if it has to pay out $200,000, as long as it does not have to do so too often. $100 may be very useful to a poor family, but if they win a large prize in a lottery, it does not make much difference whether it is $100,000 or $100,100. Bernoulli is supposed to have realized that the value of an outcome to a person cannot be equated with cash value when one of his cousins brought to his attention what has become known as the *St Petersburg paradox*, because it was first described in the journal of that city's academy of sciences. How much would you pay to be allowed one play of the following gamble?

> Someone throws a fair coin as many times as they need to until it comes down heads. You get $1 if it comes down heads first throw, $2 if it comes down heads second throw, $4 third throw, $8 fourth throw, and so on.

Clearly, you always win something, but, less obviously, the expected value of this gamble is infinite:

$$\frac{1}{2}.1 + \frac{1}{4}.2 + \frac{1}{8}.4 + \frac{1}{16}.8 + \ldots = \frac{1}{2} + \frac{1}{2} + \frac{1}{2} + \frac{1}{2} + \ldots = \infty$$

However, people will pay only a small amount of money (usually less than $10) to be allowed to play it. Bernoulli therefore suggested that what was important was not the cash (or objective) value of an outcome but its subjective value, which he called *moral expectation*. However, although it may have convinced Bernoulli, the St Petersburg paradox is not as compelling an argument for the notion of a subjective value as much simpler observations, such as the fact that $10 is worth more to a beggar than to a millionaire. For one thing, people do not realize that the expected value of the St Petersburg gamble is infinite.

From Bernoulli to the middle of the twentieth century most work in decision making was carried out in economics. In a market economy, it was assumed that people would make decisions that would maximize the value of their expected gains (or, if they are in trouble, minimize their expected losses). In economics what a commodity is worth (to a particular person), which, as we have just seen, cannot be equated with its cash value, is referred to as its *utility* (to that person). An economist can assume that markets set the comparative value of commodities, so the main complication is that the value of additional amounts of money to a person depends on how much they have already got. In technical terms, money follows a law of *diminishing marginal utility*. The marginal (or extra) utility of a fixed cash sum gets smaller as the sum to which it is added gets bigger. This idea explains why people are averse to risk when they stand to make financial gains. Most people would rather have $900 for certain than a 90 per cent chance of having $1,000. The expected value of each of these gains is the same ($900). However, the decreased marginal utility of the $100 difference between $900 and $1,000 means that that $100 is not (usually) worth as much to someone as each of the first nine $100s. So the 1 in 10 chance of losing those $900 will not be offset by the 9 in 10 chance of gaining a further $100. The qualification 'usually' is required because, if someone desperately wants something that costs $1,000 and sees no other way of getting the final $100, they may prefer the 9 in 10 chance of $1,000. Asking people to choose directly between options is just one way of trying to measure utilities so that, for example, the exact relation between money and utility (for a given person in a given context) can be established.

Much of twentieth-century economics is based on the assumption that, when making decisions, people will act rationally by attempting to maximize their *expected utility* (EU), and decision theory attempts to establish the conditions (expressed as a set of axioms) under which a person can always act so as to maximize his or her expected utility. Von Neumann and Morgenstern's (1944) expected utility theory, set out in their book *Games and the Theory of Economy Behavior*, analyses decisions as gambles, and assumes that the probabilities of the outcomes are already specified. Savage's (1954) *subjective expected utility* (SEU) theory shows how probabilities can be constructed from preferences, and therefore allows the probabilities as well as the utilities to be subjective (as defined in the previous chapter). The formulations are different, but the following ideas are common to them (see Baron, 1985: pp. 59–61).

1   Preferences are *well ordered*. For any two possible outcomes, A and B, either A is preferred to B, or B to A, or the decision maker is indifferent in the sense of not caring which transpires.
2   Preferences are transitive, so that if A is preferred to B, and B is preferred to C, A is preferred to C.
3   If someone is indifferent between A and B, they are indifferent between any gambles that differ *only* in that one has outcome A where the other has outcome B (with the same probability).
4   If someone prefers A to B, then if there are two gambles that differ only in that one has outcome A where the other has outcome B, that person should prefer the first gamble. This axiom is a version of the 'sure thing' principle.
5   No alternative is infinitely better than any other. More formally, if someone prefers A to B, and B to C, there must be some some probabilistic mixture of A and C, such that they are indifferent between B and that mixture.

These axioms are all intuitively plausible, or can be made so. Some people initially reject (5), claiming, for example, that there is no way that they would risk dying for 10 cents. They might, however, cross a busy street to buy something for 40 cents rather than 50 cents, and there is a small but real probability of being killed when crossing a street. The axioms provide a *foundation* for the principle of maximizing EU or SEU. As von Neumann and Morgenstern showed, if someone adheres to the axioms, they can assign utilities to outcomes in such a way that they can maximize their expected utility in any decision they make.

If everything, including money, can be assigned a utility, not only every person but also every thing has its price (though not necessarily a cash price, since the utility of money might reach an asymptote that is below that for some other good, such as freedom from pain). Some people find the idea that everything has a price unattractive, or even repulsive. It is, nevertheless, an assumption of the SEU theory that people have well-ordered preferences. However, as Shafer (1986) emphasizes, when people's preferences are measured empirically, they are not stable, but vary according to how the options are presented. Savage thought that such inconsistencies should be eliminated by revising one's preferences. However, Shafer suggests that, if there is no single scale (utility) on which all possible outcomes can be evaluated, we should not simply conclude that people's decisions are irrational because they do not follow the standard normative model. Perhaps the normative model is incorrect.

Shafer's own suggestion is that we should view choices as based on *arguments*, not predefined preferences. Arguments are used to *construct* choices on the fly, and they are suggested by how options are presented. Hence, choices are not stable, because they do not reflect built-in preferences, and because different ways of presenting options suggest different arguments for or against different choices. On reflection, it is hard to deny Shafer's claim. People have not necessarily assigned values even to things to which they are deeply committed – what, for example, is the value of a degree in psychology, for which most readers of this book will be studying? Shafer suggests that Savage erred because he failed to distinguish between indecision (in the sense of not having decided between two options, perhaps because they have not even been considered) and indifference. Someone might be indifferent between two brands of toothpaste, in the sense of not caring which they use, but genuinely undecided about whether to have children. Savage tried to make all cases of indecision into cases of indifference.

10.1.1   Multi-attribute utility theory

In simple cases, people know the utilities of outcomes, or can easily compute them. Indeed, some methods of assessing utilities are based on *direct scaling*, in which people are asked to assign numerical values directly to stated outcomes. In applying utility theory to real-world problems – in the profession known as *decision analysis* – it is often more illuminating to suppose that the value of the outcomes is determined by a number of separately identifiable factors. To give an everyday example, when a person is buying a new house, a number of attributes of the alternatives on offer, such as price, location, availability and material state, are likely to be relevant. Furthermore, it is often easier to compare different houses on each attribute separately, rather than trying to make a global evaluation of which is best. This much is common sense. However, if the different attributes make *independent* contributions to the overall decision, a simple extension of the unidimensional utility theory can be used that will guarantee to produce optimal decisions. This extension is called *multi-attribute utility theory* (MAUT; see, e.g., Keeney and Raiffa, 1976), and later versions of the theory can cope with non-independent attributes. If a problem is analysed using MAUT, the utility for each option on each attribute must first be assessed. This assessment can be carried out using any of the methods used to establish overall utilities. The utilities for the different attributes must be measured on comparable scales, not because each attribute will be equally important in making the decision, but because the *relative weights* of the different attributes must be established. There are several ways of determining these weights. The most satisfactory, from a theoretical point of view, uses a technique called conjoint measurement (Luce and Tukey, 1964), which guarantees independent attributes. The simplest, which assumes the dimensions are independent, is to ask directly about trade-offs between pairs of attributes. If the attributes are independent, only one such judgement is needed for each pair of attributes. Once the relative importance of each attribute is fixed, an overall utility for each alternative can be calculated. It is the weighted sum of its utilities on each attribute.

It is plausible that people make some complex decisions by considering different attributes of the alternatives among which they are choosing. MAUT analysis also shows how different goals lead to different choices among the same set of alternatives, and why some goals lead to more similar choices than others. For example, many of the same considerations would apply to choosing a house for oneself, or for one's son or daughter, but different considerations would be appropriate for choosing a house to illustrate an article on Victorian England. MAUT (even in its simplest form) does not assume that attributes are objectively independent – there may, for example, be a relation (in the real world) between the location of a house and its price. However, if this relation does not affect the decision maker's use of the attributes, a simple MAUT analysis is appropriate. MAUT adds to utility theory a detailed account of how utilities can be computed. However, it does not alter the predictions of SEU theory about which sets of choices are consistent, so it does not save that theory either from Shafer's criticisms or from the empirical results discussed below. Furthermore, its primary application has been to decisions that, although they are complex, are risk-less, in the sense that once the decision is made, the outcome is certain.

10.2 Psychological Research on Decision Making

In psychology, the study of decision making has been undertaken largely by mathematical psychologists, who borrowed directly from von Neumann and Morgenstern (1944) and Savage (1954). We saw in chapters 5 and 6 how psychologists investigate, and try to explain, departures in human thinking from the norms of logic. Similarly, in the study of decision making, psychologists took the (normative) idea of trying to maximize SEU, and asked whether people actually follow this principle, and the axioms that underlie it. In particular, the axioms have clear implications for relations between certain sets of choices (most obviously in the case of the transitivity axiom). So it is possible to ask whether the actual choices that people make are consistent with the axioms. In general, the deviations in behaviour from utility theory are more readily apparent, and less obviously identifiable as errors, than deviations from the norms of logic.

To keep matters simple, psychologists often ask people to make decisions between gambles or between outcomes that can be readily compared in monetary terms. They assume that people have a desire (or can empathize for the purposes of the experiment with a desire) to make money, and that, roughly speaking, the more the better. Part of the reason for studying such decisions is that it is relatively simple to construct variants of a problem that can be used in controlled experiments. for example, it is often possible to produce versions of a problem that should produce the same choices according to SEU theory, but which differ in some way, such as focus of attention.

10.2.1   Transitivity of preferences

The computations demanded by MAUT can be complex and time-consuming, even though they are usually applied only to decisions that do not involve uncertainty, or even risk. In everyday life, it is unlikely that these computations are carried out because of limitations on human processing capacity. Furthermore, it would be irrational to carry them out for decisions where it is unlikely that that there will be much to choose between the alternatives. It is not worth expending much mental effort on a trivial decision. The question therefore arises as to whether people follow utility theory even when they make riskless decisions.

Empirical evidence suggests that they do not. Tversky (1969) showed that one of the basic predictions of SEU theory – transitivity of preferences – does not always hold. Transitivity of preferences means that if A is preferred to B and B to C, A should be preferred to C. Tversky presented subjects with information about the intelligence, emotional stability and social facility of five putative candidates for a college place. The candidates, labelled A to E, increased slightly in intelligence, but decreased in their scores on the emotional and social dimensions. For the comparisons AB, BC, CD, DE the first candidate was preferred. However, in the AE comparison, E was preferred, because the large difference in intelligence was seen as important, and as outweighing the differences on the other dimensions. Tversky suggested that people tend to underweigh, or even ignore, small differences. Small differences should not, of course, be given much weight, but they should be given some.

10.2.1.a   Non-compensatory models

In a MAUT analysis the weakness of one alternative (a house or a candidate for a college place, for example) on one attribute can be traded off against, or *compensated for* by, a strength on another. In an attempt to explain intransitivity of preferences, among other things, non-compensatory models of decision making have been suggested. For example, a conjunctive model sets cut-offs for each attribute, and if an alternative falls below any of these cut-offs, it is rejected. A disjunctive model, on the other hand, looks for excellence in any one attribute.

Tversky (1972) proposed a non-compensatory theory of multi-attribute decision making, *elimination by aspects*, which requires much simpler computations that those of MAUT. In elimination by aspects, the decision maker first selects one attribute on which the alternatives differ. This first attribute should be, in some sense, the most important one, though the model assumes a probabilistic component to the selection process. All alternatives that are not satisfactory on this attribute are eliminated from consideration. This process requires the identification of a range or ranges of values on this attribute that are satisfactory. Another attribute is then selected and further alternatives are eliminated. The process continues until only one alternative remains. Elimination by aspects is an intuitively attractive method of making decisions, and it will generally impose fewer demands on memory than the computation of utilities for multi-attribute stimuli. However, the process has certain properties that make it 'undesirable' for making decisions, and prevent it from being a serious contender for a normative theory. In particular, there is no guarantee that what, from a broader perspective, might be a very good choice will be eliminated at an early stage. More generally, the final choice may be affected by the order in which the attributes are considered.

Other researchers have observed more radical departures from the decision-making procedures suggested by MAUT. The phenomenon of *single-mindedness* is well known in the everyday world. One kind of single-mindedness can be thought of as focusing on a single attribute to the exclusion of others – in other words, from a reluctance to engage in trade-offs between different attributes. For example, Gardiner and Edwards (1975) found that, in making decisions about possible developments on the California coast, some people focused almost entirely on the environmental impact of the developments, whereas others focused on economic advantages. Only when the subjects were forced to engage in a multi-attribute analysis, and to give some weight to the attributes that had initially been ignored, did the judgements of the two groups come closer.

Non-compensatory models raise, in an acute form, the question of *how* decisions are made. There is conspicuously little research on the on-line processes of decision making. An exception is the work of Payne (1976; Payne, Bettman and Johnson, 1988). Payne (1976) presented information about attributes of apartments, such as rent, distance from work, and size, in boxes on an information board (a computer screen in later work), and subjects had to decide which apartment they preferred. Each piece of information was initially 'hidden', and had to be requested by the subject (using the computer's mouse in the computerized version). With small numbers of apartments and attributes subjects tend to request all the information, as though they were using a compensatory (utility-based) procedure. With more complex decisions, they tried to find ways of eliminating alternatives, for example, on the basis of one unacceptable attribute (high rent, for instance), in a non-compensatory manner.

10.2.1.b   *Bounded rationality and satisficing*

Part of the appeal of elimination by aspects is the relatively simple mental operations which it suggests underlie decision making. This idea is related to Herbert Simon's (1955) notion of *bounded rationality*. Simon argued that among the constraints on a theory of rational decision making should be the limitations on the information processing capacity of the human mind. One decision-making technique proposed by Simon (1978), within the bounded rationality framework, is *satisficing*. A satisficer recognizes that making the best decision is a time-consuming process, and that the difference between a satisfactory decision and the best one (defined by SEU theory) will probably not justify the effort of computing utilities. In satisficing, a criterion is set for a satisfactory decision and the first alternative that meets that criterion is accepted. This criterion may be complex, and involve multiple attributes. Satisficing is a simpler procedure than computing and comparing utilities, since the decision maker has simply to compare alternatives with the criterion as they are encountered. Like elimination by aspects, satisficing does not always produce the same results for the same decision, and it does not guarantee transitivity of preferences. In satisficing the decision will depend on the order in which the alternatives are encountered, which may or may not be under the decision maker's control. A further problem, which can be solved only by obtaining more knowledge of the range of alternatives available, is that too low a criterion can result in poor decisions.

10.2.2   Violations of invariance

Elimination by aspects and satisficing are techniques that might plausibly be used for complex decisions. Both procedures, unlike a full analysis of utilities, can result in different decisions among the same options, even when the decision maker's goals are the same – they violate a principle of *invariance* (same options, same outcome) that follows from SEU theory. Invariance should apply to both the way the outcomes are described (descriptive invariance) and the way the choice is made (procedural or response mode invariance).

10.2.2.a Framing: violations of descriptive invariance
The effect of how the options are presented, which potentially violates descriptive invariance, is known as *framing*. Tversky and Kahneman (1981) present examples of two different framing effects. In the first subjects had to choose between two programmes for tackling an unusual disease, Asian flu. There were two versions of the task, a 'make gains' and a 'prevent losses' version, which were equivalent according to utility theory. In the 'gains' version, the choice is between programmes that either:

(a) definitely save 200 people, or
(b) save 600 people with a one-third chance, and 0 people with a two-thirds chance.

In the 'losses' version the choice is between:

(a) having 400 people die for certain, and
(b) having a one-third probability that no one will die, and a two-thirds probability that 600 people will.

In the 'gains' version (a) is preferred to (b). This result accords with the standard finding of risk aversion for gains, whereas in the 'losses' version (b) is preferred to (a) – risk seeking for losses. Effectively the choice is the same in both cases:

(a) 200 alive, 400 dead for certain
(b) one in three chance of 600 alive and 0 dead, two in three chance of 0 alive and 600 dead.

There is no way of constructing a utility function that can justify the choice of (a) over (b) in the 'gains' version and (b) over (a) in the 'losses' version.

In Tversky and Kahneman's second problem, a person goes to buy goods in a store for $140, and is told that one of the items is $5 cheaper in another branch of the same store, twenty minutes' drive away. People were more likely to elect to make the twenty-minute drive if the $5 saving was on an item costing $15 dollars than if it was on an item costing $125, even though the overall outcome was the same in each case – a $5 dollar saving on total expenses, in return for a twenty-minute drive. In a similar problem, fewer people said they would replace a $10 theatre ticket, if they arrived at the theatre and found they had lost it, than said they would still buy a $10 ticket if they arrived and found they had lost a $10 bill. In each case, the overall financial loss is the same. In both these problems people's reactions to financial gains or losses depend on the function to which the money was assigned. Kahneman and Tversky (1984) refer to this phenomenon as *topical accounting*. Thus, in the store problem, a $5 saving on $15 seems better than a $5 saving on $125, because of the law of diminishing marginal utility. If you are going to spend $120 you might as well spend $125, but $15 rather than $10 is a different matter. However, different decisions result only if the accounting is for individual items (or 'topics'). If the accounts were not kept separate, the decision to save $5 would not depend on which item was discounted. So, the way a problem is framed affects the choices people make in a way it should not if people maximize their expected utility.

The idea of accounting also explains everyday sales techniques. Thaler (1985) distinguishes between *integrating* and *segregating* (as in topical accounting) gains and losses. A salesman who wants to be successful should try to integrate the losses that the buyer will incur, since a small loss is readily absorbed into a bigger one. Gains, on the other hand, should be segregated, so that each stands on its own. Thus, additional features (gains to the buyer) on a car should be introduced one by one and their benefits described in detail, but their cost (loss to the buyer) should be hidden in the overall purchase price. A buyer who would not pay $200 to have a rear wiper fitted to a car after buying it may be persuaded to pay that much, given that they are already paying out several thousand dollars for a new car.

10.2.2.b   *Response mode effects*

In the classic study of response mode effects, Lichtenstein and Slovic (1971) showed a *preference reversal* between pairs of bets depending on how subjects made their choice. Subjects were presented with pairs of bets such as:

Bet 1   99 per cent chance of winning $4, 1 per cent chance of losing $1 (expected value $3.95)

Bet 2   33 per cent chance of winning $16.00, 67 per cent chance of losing 2.00 (expected value $3.94)

In each case the first bet offered a higher probability of winning, the second bet the possibility of a larger win. Many subjects chose the first bet over the second in a straight choice, but offered more money to play the second bet than the first. In a later study Lichtenstein and Slovic (1973) set up a gambling game in the Four Queens Casino, Las Vegas, and found that real gamblers showed a similar preference reversal when they were playing for real stakes.

A preference reversal for a different type of decision is reported by Tversky, Sattath and Slovic (1988). Subjects had to choose between two alternatives (e.g., candidates for a job) each rated on two dimensions (e.g., technical knowledge and human relations). Decisions were made either by direct choice (e.g., between a candidate rated 86 out of 100 for technical knowledge and 76 for human relations, and one rated 78 and 91) or by a 'matching' technique. For matching, one of the four scores was missing and had to be filled in to make the candidates equally attractive. Tversky et al. propose that, when people choose directly between alternatives, they focus on the attribute that is most important to the choice in question (e.g., their subjects were told that technical knowledge was more important in selecting a candidate for the job). Matching, however, forces them to consider the other attribute and, hence, to give it more weight. Neither weighting is necessarily better, though when confronted with their inconsistent decisions the subjects (who were surprised by their inconsistency) tended to revise their judgements towards those made by direct choice.

10.2.3 The independence principle and the sure thing principle

The third and fourth of the axioms we presented above embody the idea that outcomes which are common to the choices open to a decision maker should not affect the decision. This idea is known as the independence principle, and is closely related to the sure thing principle, a version of which is embodied in the fourth axiom. An alternative rendering of the sure thing principle – roughly that used by Savage to justify the independence principle – states that, if A is preferred to B in every possible context, it should be preferred when the context is not specified.

10.2.3.a The Allais paradox

One of the earliest critics of SEU theory was the French economist Maurice Allais (1953), who devised sets of gambles which for many people do not satisfy the independence principle. For example, most people will not give up a sure $1,000 for a small possibility of winning $5,000 and a smaller possibility of getting nothing (still getting $1,000 most of the time). They will, however, exchange a small probability of winning $1,000 for a slightly smaller probability of winning $5,000.

Table 10.1　The Allais paradox

	1% of the time	5% of the time	94% of the time
1(a)	$1,000	$1,000	$1,000
1(b)	$0	$5,000	$1,000
2(a)	$1,000	$1,000	$0
2(b)	$0	$5,000	$0

More precisely, the so-called *Allais paradox* arises for the gambles shown below, in which most people prefer 1(a) to 1(b), but 2(b) to 2(a).

Choice 1	(a)	$1,000	for certain
	(b)	$1,000	with probability .94
		$5,000	with probability .05
		$0	with probability .01
Choice 2	(a)	$1,000	with probability .06
		$0	with probability .94
	(b)	$5,000	with probability .05
		$0	with probability .95

The paradoxical nature of these preferences may not be immediately apparent, but it is brought out by showing the outcomes in a different way, as in table 10.1. Table 10.1 shows, in each gamble, that 94 per cent of the time the outcome will be the same, no matter whether (a) or (b) is chosen. For choice 1 this outcome is $1,000 and for choice 2 it is $0. For either choice, these cases should not affect the decision between (a) and (b), according to the independence principle. The other 6 per cent of the time the options are identical for choice 1 and choice 2. Which is preferred, (a) or (b), depends on the decision maker's utility function, but the choice should be the same in both cases. However, as we saw, people tend to prefer 1(a), but 2(b). Savage agreed that his first reaction was to have these preferences, but argued that thinking the choices through more carefully made him change his mind. However, Slovic and Tversky (1974) found that university subjects could not be so easily convinced.

10.2.3.b　The Ellsberg paradox – preference for risk over uncertainty

Ellsberg (1961) gave subjects the option of picking risky choices or uncertain choices, and found that risky choices were preferred to uncer-

Table 10.2 Choice between risk and uncertainty

	Red	Black	Yellow
1(a)	$30	$0	$0
1(b)	$0	$30	$0
2(a)	$30	$0	$30
2(b)	$0	$30	$30

tain ones, and that this preference could also lead to violations of the independence principle. In Ellsberg's experiments a ball is to be drawn from an urn containing ninety balls. Thirty of these balls are red. The rest are either black or yellow, but the exact proportions of black and yellow balls is not known. Subjects prefer winning $30 if a red ball is drawn to winning $30 if a black ball is drawn (with nothing for a yellow ball). The probability of a red ball is 1 in 3, the probability of a black ball is somewhere between 0 and 2 in 3 (i.e., it is uncertain). With no other information, the expected value of the two choices is the same, $10. However, people prefer black over red, if yellow also wins $30. In this second case black or yellow wins with probability 2 in 3, whatever the proportion of yellows and blacks, whereas red or yellow wins with a probability of between 1 in 3 and 1. Table 10.2 shows that the choice between red and black is the same in the two cases and, according to the axioms of SEU, it should not be influenced by the outcome for yellow, which is constant for each of the two choices.

10.2.3.c The sure thing principle

Savage (1954) considered a businessman trying to decide whether to buy a particular property. He knows there is a presidential election soon, but reasons that if he knew the Republican would win he should buy, and that if he knew the Democrat would win he should buy. He concludes that he should buy, even though he cannot predict the result of the election. The businessman is using a version of the sure thing principle, and Savage, himself, felt that 'no other extralogical principle governing decision . . . finds such ready acceptance' (1954: p. 21). However, Tversky and Shafir (1992a) have shown that people do not always follow the sure thing principle in their decision making. For example, subjects were asked to imagine they had taken an important exam. They were asked if they would take the opportunity of a cheap vacation in Hawaii. Some were told they knew they had passed, some that they had failed, and some did not know the result. However, while the majority of both those who had passed and those who had failed chose to take the vacation, only 32 per cent of those who did not know the result chose it. Tversky and Shafir argue that this failure to adhere to the sure thing principle is explained partly by the fact that the reasons for taking the vacation are different in the two cases (a reward for passing, or a consolation for failing). However, Tversky and Shafir further showed, in a more abstract version of the problem, that if the same subject was given the two specific versions first and asked to make a decision in each case, and then asked to make a decision in the case where the (equivalent of) the exam result was not known, they *did* adhere to the sure thing principle.

10.2.3.d   Regularity

Another consequence of utility theory is the *regularity* principle. Informally, this principle states that, if an additional alternative is added to a set of choices, none of the original members of the set should become *more* popular than it was before. However, adding choices can increase the *conflict* in the decision maker's mind, and make the status quo a more favoured alternative. More precisely, it can lead to the decision being deferred. This idea is illustrated in study by Tversky and Shafir (1992b). They offered to pay students $1.50 to complete a questionnaire, but when they had finished they asked the subjects if they would rather take an alternative to the money. Some subjects were offered a metal pen. Others were offered the metal pen or two cheaper plastic pens. Each alternative was worth about $2.00. Only a quarter of the students kept the money (the status quo) when there was one alternative, but over half kept it when there were two. This outcome conflicts with the regularity principle described above, since the overall popularity of the original payment increased when an additional alternative was added.

10.2.4   Descriptive theories of decision making

Elimination by aspects and satisficing are descriptive theories of decision making that apply primarily to complex, but riskless, decisions. In this section we consider two descriptive theories, prospect theory and regret theory, that are intended to be broader in scope.

10.2.4.a   Prospect theory

One framework in which the Allais paradox, framing effects, and a number of other problematic aspects of real decision making can be explained is Kahneman and Tversky's (1979) *prospect theory*. Prospect theory is a modification of SEU theory that differs from it in two main ways. First, Kahneman and Tversky proposed that people assess gains and losses relative to *reference points*, rather than by their absolute values. The status quo is a common reference point, but other reference points can be created by the way a decision is framed. Gains (from the reference point) follow the law of diminishing marginal value. Losses show a similar effect – a loss of $2,000 is considered less than twice as serious as a loss of $1,000. However, according to the *value function* of prospect theory, a loss has a greater (negative) value than the positive value of a gain of the same (nominal) size. This aspect of the theory is based on, among other things, the fact that most people do not accept fair bets (with expected value $0).

The form of the value function, which relates monetary gains to subjective values, also explains *risk aversion* with respect to gains and *risk seeking* with respect to losses. In laboratory studies, risk aversion for gains is well established. Its extent depends on how sharply the marginal value of money diminishes. The more rapidly it falls off, the more risk averse the person is. In real life many risks are seen as having positive (excitement) value in themselves. This applies not only to dangerous sports, but also to gambling. However, in these cases there are losses as well as gains to be taken into consideration, and, for losses, people are *risk seeking* rather than risk averse (though the fact that they buy insurance is difficult to explain in terms of risk seeking!). This phenomenon is the mirror image of risk aversion for gains and again depends on diminishing effects at the margins – an extra loss of $100 on top of a $100,000 loss seems less serious than a $100 loss on top of a $10 loss. So, where people prefer a sure gain of $900 to a 90 per cent chance of $1,000, they prefer a 90 per cent chance of losing $1,000 to a sure loss of $900. The reason is that the *prospect* of an extra $100 loss on top of $900 is less than a ninth as bad as losing the first $900.

Although risk aversion for gains and risk seeking for losses arise from the same basic mechanism, the operation of these two tendencies can give rise to paradoxical choices – choices that cannot be reconciled with the idea that people always try to maximize expected utility – in decision problems where the losses and gains are complementary. The paradox in the Asian flu problem (see §10.2.2.a above), which we described as a framing effect, can be explained by prospect theory. The reference point in the gains version of this problem is 600 people dead if nothing is done. The lives saved are, therefore, seen as gains, and the choice is one of risk aversion. In the losses version the reference point is the current situation in which no one has died. From this reference point, the deaths are losses, resulting in a risk seeking choice.

The second major difference between prospect theory and utility theory is that according to prospect theory probabilities are distorted, even when they are presented numerically. Low probabilities are slightly over-weighted and higher probabilities are underweighted. Probabilities of 0 and 1 are, however, treated veridically. Thus, certainty (probability of 1) behaves in a peculiar way compared with slightly lower probabilities, which are underweighted. This idea helps to explain the Allais paradox, since only one of the choices (1) has a certain option.

10.2.4.b   *Regret theory*

A different approach to explaining apparent deviations from utility theory is based on the emotions that are anticipated when the result of making a particular decision becomes known. This approach has been referred to as *regret theory* (Bell, 1982, 1985; Loomes and Sugden, 1982). In regret theory, deviations from SEU theory may only be apparent, be-cause, as Baron (1988) points out, SEU calculations can take antici-pated emotions into account. However, a rational approach to decision making might be to try to overcome these emotions, so that we can better fulfil our goals.

Regret theory identifies four emotions that might be anticipated when a decision is made: regret, rejoicing, disappointment and elation. Regret and rejoicing arise from considering what would have happened if a different choice had been made, given that the world turned out the way it did. To return to an earlier example, if it actually rains, a person is likely to regret not bringing an umbrella or to 'rejoice' that they have brought one. Disappointment and elation arise from considering differ-ent ways the world might have turned out, given a particular choice on the decision maker's part. If a person decides to take a picnic, they will be disappointed if it rains, and elated if it is sunny. Anticipated emo-tions are not enough in themselves to explain departures from SEU theory. Regret theory also assumes that the amount of anticipated emotion does not accurately reflect the difference between the outcomes, but that small differences are underweighted or ignored, and large differences are overweighted. When outcomes are presented in monetary terms, as they are in the Allais paradox, choices can seem inconsistent if anticipated emotions are not taken into account.

10.2.5   Decisions by two or more people

Some of the decisions we have discussed have been decisions *about* other people – whether to offer them a job, for example – but they have not depended directly on the decisions taken *by* other people. Sometimes,

Table 10.3 Prisoner's dilemma

		Prisoner A	
		Confesses	*Does not confess*
Prisoner B	Confesses	A – 5 years B – 5 years	A – 10 years B – free
	Does not confess	A – free B – 10 years	A – 1 year B – 1 year

however, we have to make decisions whose outcomes depend on what other people, over whom we may have no influence, may decide. In analysing such decisions, the notions of probability, outcome and utility remain crucial. Indeed, the *conflicts of interest* that arise in multi-person decisions can be analysed using a mathematical theory called *game theory* (von Neumann and Morgenstern, 1944), which is closely related to SEU theory. However, complications arise in analysing two-person decisions that are not found in one-person decisions. In game theory, outcomes are defined in terms of combinations of choices made by the different parties, and each outcome is assigned a utility, again for each of the parties to the decision – what is good for one person may be bad for another.

Much of the psychological research inspired by game theory is addressed to social psychological questions about bargaining, and about cooperation and defection. We will not discuss this research in detail here. An important tool in the psychological study of multi-person decisions is the *prisoner's dilemma*. Two prisoners, jointly accused of a crime, for which there is insufficient evidence to charge them, are separately invited to confess. If one confesses, but not the other, the one who confesses will be allowed to turn state evidence and go free, while the other will be given the maximum sentence for the crime. If both confess, they will be given reduced, but still substantial, sentences. If neither confesses, they will both receive light sentences for a minor offence for which the evidence is already in. The dilemma is illustrated in table 10.3, with sentences of one, five and ten years as examples. The dilemma arises for the prisoners, because when each examines the outcomes shown in table 10.3, they see that, whatever the other chooses, confessing is the preferred alternative. So, prisoner A can argue: (i) if B confesses, confessing gives five years in prison as opposed to ten; (ii) if B does not confess, confessing gives freedom as opposed to one year in prison. Both prisoners might convince themselves to confess by this argument, but then they will both get five years in prison, as opposed to one each if neither confesses. Much of the experimental work on the prisoner's dilemma, from Rapoport and Chammah (1965) on, has investigated the circumstances under which people cooperate, and those in which they defect. Interestingly, the strategy that produces the best results in the long run (as determined by playing strategies against each other on a computer) is tit for tat, which starts off by cooperating, and then responds the same way that its 'opponent' responded last time. Thus, tit for tat rewards past cooperation and punishes past defection. The success of tit for tat has profound implications for theories of how cooperative behaviour might have evolved by natural selection (Axelrod, 1984).

Some results with the prisoner's dilemma parallel those found with single-person decisions. For example, Shafir and Tversky (1992) have shown that, in a single play of the prisoner's dilemma, almost every subject who has been told of the other player's strategy will choose to defect. However, when players do not know that strategy, a significant proportion cooperate. Like the failure to decide on a vacation when the result of an exam is unknown (see §10.2.3.c above), this pattern of choices violates the sure thing principle.

10.3 Predicting Decisions by Multiple Regression

The deviations from the predictions of SEU theory that we have presented so far have been systematic. There can also be unsystematic deviations that can be explained only in terms of 'noise' in the decision-making process. If someone uses a multi-attribute analysis to choose between houses, their estimates of the utility of the location of a house will vary from occasion to occasion, even when there is no new information to influence their judgement. Variations in this and other components of the decision will affect the overall utilities assigned to the choices, and may even result in a change in which house is favoured.

In the house buying example, a person is trying to make a single decision among a set of alternatives. Since it is an important decision, they must take precautions to overcome unreliability in their judgements. This kind of unreliability has been studied in a different but related type of judgement, in which a single person (usually an expert) makes repeated judgements about different individuals, each with many attributes that are relevant to the decision. The point is not to choose between the individuals, but to select, for each individual, a course of action. Typical examples are diagnosis and choice of care regimes for medical patients, and selection of applicants for places at college. Such decisions, to some extent, can be objectively checked after they have been made. A medical diagnosis may or may not turn out to be correct; a suggested programme of care may or may not be effective; the achievement of students can be assessed after they have been admitted to college. If we also know the data on which the decision was based – the relevant information about the patients or applicants – we can apply the statistical technique of *multiple regression* (or a related technique) to derive an equation for predicting, say, the final exam scores of students from the data used to select them.

Multiple regression equations are generally better at making such predictions than the *clinical intuition* of people who are trained to make them (Meehl, 1954). Dawes (1971), for example, showed that a multiple regression equation based on previous achievement was a better predictor of how well graduate students (at the University of Oregon) were later rated by their supervisors than were the judgements of people who had selected them. Part of the explanation of this phenomenon is that the equation abstracts away from the random variability (caused, for example, by boredom or inattention) in the behaviour of decision makers, and focuses on the factors that really count in making the decisions. Another reason (Dawes, 1979) is that expert decision makers are better at determining what information is relevant to a decision, and at obtaining it, than they are at integrating that information. So, although the equation makes better predictions, it does not replace experts. Dawes (1979) has also shown that equations other than those produced by multiple regression analysis can make better predictions than experts – for example, equations in which only a few important variables are included, or in which all the variables are given equal weights (unlike in multiple regression or MAUT), possibly with different signs, or equations that model the expert's predictions (rather than the actual outcomes).

On the basis of his investigations, Dawes suggests that interviews are not only a waste of time in selecting candidates for jobs or college places, they are a hindrance to good decision making, because information gained in interviews is used instead of more reliable information from other sources. However, people are reluctant to let formulas replace human judgement, a problem that is exacerbated by the overconfidence of human judges about how well they are making decisions. A half-hour interview produces a wealth of information, much of which is apparently relevant to the decision about whether to hire a candidate or offer them a place in college. Despite numerous demonstrations that the strength of a 'clinical intuition' bears little relation to its soundness, that much decision making is poor, and that equations can do better, the resistance to their use has proved hard to overcome.

Summary

Decision making requires the combination of beliefs, which may be expressed in terms of probabilities, and desires. Risky decisions are ones in which the probabilities of the outcomes are known. Decisions under uncertainty are those in which those probabilities are not known. The best-known normative theory of decision making, SEU theory, claims that a rational decision is one that maximizes the decision maker's subjective expected utility. However, an influential critique by Shafer suggests that this theory is flawed because it confuses indecision and indifference, and assumes that beliefs and desires can always be completely separated. Multi-attribute utility theory attempts to explain how the utility of individual outcomes might be determined. It has been applied primarily to riskless decisions.

In psychological research people's decisions have been shown not to follow the principles of SEU theory. In particular, preferences are not always transitive, so that if A is preferred to B, and B to C, A will not necessarily be preferred to C. Two alternative accounts of decision making that can accommodate intransitive preferences are Tversky's elimination by aspects and Simon's satisficing. Other phenomena that are difficult to account for in standard utility theory include the effect of the way a problem is framed on the decisions people make, and the effect of the way their judgements are elicited. Finally, violations of the independence principle, as exemplified in the Allais and Ellsberg paradoxes, and in violations of the sure thing principle, are inconsistent with utility theory. Kahneman and Tversky's prospect theory and regret theory are two alternative attempts to modify SEU theory to make it compatible with the psychological evidence.

The outcome of some decisions depends on what someone else decides. Such cases where there is a potential conflict of interest can be analysed using an extension of EU theory called game theory. A particularly important problem in studying two-person decisions is the prisoners' dilemma.

People's decisions are influenced by factors beyond their control that are effectively random. More consistent and better decisions can be made by using multiple regression models of experts, which eliminate this noise from the decision-making process. More controversially, in some domains even very simple equations can make better predictions than experts. For example, overconfidence in the ability to judge people's ability in interviews means that much better predictions about, for instance, the future success of graduate students can be made by other means.

Further Reading

Dawes, R. M. (1971). A case study of graduate admissions: application of three principles of human decision making. *American Psychologist*, 26, pp. 180–8.

Payne, J. W., Bettman, J. R. and Johnson, E. J. (1992). Behavioral decision research: a constructive processing perspective. In M. R. Rosenzweig and L. W. Porter (eds), *Annual Review of Psychology* (vol. 43, pp. 87–131). Palo Alto, CA: Annual Reviews Inc.

Shafir, E. (1993). Intuitions about rationality and cognition. In K. I. Manktelow and D. E. Over (eds), *Rationality: Psychological and Philosophical Perspectives* (pp. 260–83). London: Routledge.

11
Problem Solving

The Gestalt psychologist Duncker (1945) pinpointed the essence of problem solving when he wrote:

> A problem arises when a living organism has a goal, but does not know how this goal is to be reached.

In information processing terms, this idea implies that a problem has three crucial elements:

1 a starting state
2 a goal state
3 a set of processes (usually called *operators*) that can transform one state into another.

The starting state is the state of the 'world' that poses the problem. *World* is in quotes because in many problems – those in puzzle books, for example – the world of the problem is a fictional one, created for the purpose of setting a puzzle. The goal state is another state of the world in which the problem is solved. Or, rather, there is usually a collection of states each of which has the property that it solves the puzzle. In chess, for example, the starting state is the board at the beginning of the game and the goal (for either player) is any one of a number of positions in which they check-mate their opponent, or in which their opponent resigns. The processes are things that can be done to the world in an attempt to move from the starting state to a goal state – in chess, the moves allowed by the rules of the game.

From a psychological point of view, the problems that are easiest to study, and to theorize about, are ones in which the starting state, the goal state and the processes can be clearly specified. Most of the puzzle-book puzzles, mathematics and physics problems, and games on which psychological research has been carried out have this property. However, many everyday problems do not. People's ability to solve these problems is, therefore, at once more interesting and more difficult to study. Any one of the three elements of a problem may be poorly specified. Someone may feel unhappy, but not be sure what is causing the problem; they may know they have a problem, but not be clear what a solution to the problem would look like; and they may not know what they can do to get from where they are to where they want to be. However, a 'problem' in which all three elements are unclear is in danger of degenerating into a vague sense of unease!

Psychological research on problem solving has traditionally been divided into research on puzzles (non-adversary problems) and research on game playing (adversary problems). However, the importance of this distinction lies not so much in the methods used in the research, but in the fact that most research on puzzles has been carried out with novices – expert puzzle-book puzzle solvers are a comparatively rare breed – whereas much of the work on game playing has investigated the way that experts play games such as chess, and how their play differs from that of novices. Since about 1980 this divide has been broken in research on such topics as physics and mathematics problems and problems of medical diagnosis. This work has focused, on the one hand, on individuals tackling problems on their own but, on the other hand, on the use of domain-specific knowledge, and on differences between experts and novices. We will discuss game playing, and expertise in general, in the next chapter. In this chapter, we will consider the relation between problem solving and other kinds of thinking, and present the main tools that psychologists believe people use to solve problems, including the use of analogy.

11.1 Problem Solving and Other Kinds of Thinking

For reasons that are largely historical, problem solving and reasoning have been treated as distinct research topics. Part of the explanation is that behaviourists, though they eschewed many aspects of the study of thinking, were for the most part happy to study the processes of trial and error that, according to Thorndike, enabled cats to escape from puzzle boxes. Much of the Gestalt psychologists' work on thinking also focused on how people solve problems, though their motivation was different from that of the behaviourists. Gestalt psychologists were interested in the processes that led to the sudden feeling of insight which is often experienced in solving puzzles, but which is less common in, for example, deductive reasoning. Finally, an important line of research on thinking in artificial intelligence, beginning with Newell, Shaw and Simon (e.g., 1963), was strongly influenced by an interest in, and a desire to model, the ability to play games such as chess. Game playing has more in common with solving puzzle-book problems than with solving syllogisms, for example. However, a more analytic approach shows that both deductive and inductive processes are often required to solve problems and, indeed, another of Newell, Shaw and Simon's (1957) projects investigated proofs of theorems in propositional calculus as an example of problem solving. So problem solving as a research area is defined (at least implicitly) by a research tradition, and it can be difficult to draw a clear line between research on problem solving and research on other aspects of thinking and reasoning.

Many of the problems studied in the problem-solving literature can be formulated as deductive reasoning problems, in the broad sense of deductive reasoning described in chapter 4. The solution to such problems does not depend only on the meanings of the logical constants *not, and, or, if . . . then, if and only if*. However, if the definitions and other information given in the problem are encoded in predicate calculus formulas, the solution can be derived using deductive methods – though people may use other techniques to solve such problems. The missionaries and cannibals problem (see §11.2.1 below) is a typical problem of this kind. Other problems fall under the broadest definition of inductive reasoning – the expansion of knowledge in the face of uncertainty (see chapter 7). In particular, analogical problem solving is regarded as a kind of inductive reasoning in Holland, Holyoak, Nisbett and Thagard's (1986) book *Induction*.

We have suggested that many kinds of problem solving can be conceptualized as other kinds of thinking – some as deductive reasoning, others as inductive, for example. A diametrically opposed view attempts to assimilate other kinds of thinking and, in more ambitious recent versions, other aspects of cognition as well, to problem solving. This approach stems primarily from the work of Newell and Simon and their colleagues (see especially Newell and Simon, 1972). In their earliest work, Newell and Simon studied theorem proving in the propositional calculus (the Logic Theory Machine – Newell, Shaw and Simon, 1957) and chess playing (Newell, Shaw and Simon, 1963). Both theorem proving and chess playing can be thought of as types of problem solving, though theorem proving in propositional calculus sounds suspiciously like deductive reasoning! One of the most important ideas to emerge from this research was that of a *heuristic* procedure for solving problems, which has a good chance of finding a solution quickly, but which is not guaranteed to find one even if one exists. Heuristics are contrasted with *algorithmic* methods, which will always find a solution, if there is one, but which may be very slow.

Ideas from the Logic Theory Machine and the chess playing programs were incorporated into the General Problem Solver (see §11.2.1 below). This program attempted to generalize from the earlier programs and to establish the (heuristic) method of means-end analysis as a general method for solving problems. The ideas underlying this program were highly influential, even though the performance of working versions was not particularly impressive.

A further important development (Newell and Simon, 1972) was the realization that heuristics could be expressed in a uniform way as sets of *if... then* rules (if certain conditions hold, then perform a certain action – with the notion of action interpreted in a broad sense). Such rules are known as *productions,* and a problem-solver or *production system* can, therefore, be built from a set of productions, together with a *conflict-resolution strategy* for deciding what to do when the conditions for more than one production are satisfied. Conflict resolution strategies are needed because the actions of different productions may be incompatible. Many different strategies are possible. One widely used component of such strategies is that a production with more specific conditions is preferred to one with less specific conditions.

In using production systems as a psychological model, Newell and Simon proposed that the productions themselves are stored in long-term memory as part of knowledge about the world. Their use is *triggered* by the contents of short-term memory, which are determined largely by the current focus of attention. A production is triggered when its conditions – the *if* part of the rule – are fulfilled, so limitations on short-term memory impose constraints both on how complex the conditions of an individual production can be, and on how many productions can be triggered at once. A further assumption is that the contents of short-term memory are open to conscious inspection. This assumption guides the use and interpretation of so-called *think-aloud protocols,* collected by asking people to 'say what is in their mind' as they solve problems. Such protocols have assumed an important role in research on thinking and reasoning within the production system framework.

Although production systems were originally developed to explain how people solve problems, they have been used more generally in both artificial intelligence and psychology. Indeed, they can be regarded as a programming language that is specially appropriate to the modelling of thinking, reasoning and related abilities. An example of the use of production systems to model psychological abilities that are not traditionally regarded as forms of thinking and reasoning is Mitch Marcus's (1980) syntactic parser, PARSIFAL. Productions are also widely used in expert systems (see next chapter). More generally, many cognitive processes other than problem solving can be characterized as search processes – problem solving is thought of as a search through a space of possible solutions for an actual solution (see §11.2.1 below for more details). For example, syntactic analysis is the search for an analysis of the current sentence in the space of possible analyses for sentences. Search techniques originally developed for problem-solving applications in AI have subsequently been used in the simulation of a range of other cognitive abilities, both in production systems and in programs using other techniques.

The general applicability of production systems suggests that Newell and Simon's views provide the basis for a general theory of the *cognitive architecture* of the human mind – a *unified theory of cognition*. The first substantial proposal for such a unified theory was John Anderson's (1983) ACT* (act-star, ACT = Adaptive Control of Thought), which adds a database of factual information, in the form of a semantic network, to the working memory, and the set of productions in long-term memory, of a standard production system. Newell himself (1990; Laird, Newell and Rosenbloom, 1987) has proposed an alternative architecture called SOAR (State, Operator, And Result). In SOAR, unlike ACT*, there is no distinction between procedural and factual memory – all of long-term memory is a production system. However, SOAR recognizes that there is more to cognition than productions being triggered by conditions in short-term memory. In particular, the short-term working memory of SOAR is not just a place where information that can trigger productions resides. It contains a hierarchy of goals, to which SOAR can add, and among which it can select candidates for immediate attention. All triggered productions are copied into working memory, so there is no conflict resolution in the standard sense. When a goal is selected, a corresponding *problem space* is created. Every attempt to satisfy a goal requires a search, in the corresponding problem space, for a sequence of operations that gets from the starting state to a goal state (see §11.2.1 below for a fuller account of this kind of search). Newell contends that the problem space is a fundamental category of cognition.

SOAR also contains a learning mechanism, *chunking*, that is *impasse-driven*. When the current problem space does not contain sufficient information to allow its goal to be fulfilled, SOAR automatically creates a new subgoal (and its associated problem space) to resolve this (local) impasse. Examples of how impasses arise are: there are no operators that can be applied; there is no basis for choosing one operator over another; there is an apparently relevant operator, but it is not clear how to apply it. If SOAR succeeds in removing an impasse, it adds a new chunk of information, in the form of a production, to its long-term memory. This chunk encodes directly the information about what action SOAR should take if it is in a similar situation in future. Detailed information about how this chunk is created is not saved, since the sub-space in which the impasse was resolved disappears when the resolution occurs.

Laird et al. (1987) give an example of chunking in the eight puzzle.

2	6	5
4		7
3	1	8

In trying to solving this puzzle, the problem solver is often faced with a choice between, for example, moving one number up or moving a different number to the right. For example, in the configuration above, the six can move down, the one up, the four to the right, or the seven to the left. Initially, SOAR may have no reason for choosing one of these moves over any of the other. Hence, it has reached an impasse, and sets up the subgoal of resolving it. If it follows the moves through, it may be able to show that one of them is preferred. It can then create, by chunking, a production that says: *if* the board configuration has such-and-such properties, *then* make such-and-such a move. The details of how the decision was originally made need not be stored. However, as this example shows, learning is possible only if there are productions that solve the problem. SOAR thus provides an account both of problem solving (or, more generally, cognitive abilities) and of how those abilities are learned. Newell claims that the two are intimately related, so that if we have an account of how some behaviour is carried out we have, from SOAR, an account of how it is learned. Furthermore, SOAR's method of learning, together with assumptions about the order in which goals in the hierarchy in working memory are worked on, can be used to generate detailed predictions, which can be tested experimentally.

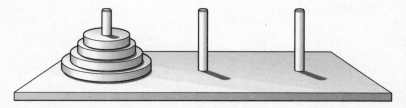

Figure 11.1 The tower of Hanoi

11.2 Puzzles and Other 'Knowledge-Lean' Non-Adversary Problems

We turn now to research on particular types of problem, and we will begin this section with some examples of puzzles that have been studied by psychologists. We start with puzzles in which the starting state, goal state and operators are well defined, and end with some where they are less well defined.

1 Eight Puzzle: eight movable numbers in a 3 × 3 matrix. Move them so that they are set out as illustrated below (or in some other specified configuration).

1	2	3
8		4
7	6	5

2 Missionaries and Cannibals: transport three missionaries and three cannibals across a river, using a boat that can carry only two people, and that needs at least one person to get it across the river. There must never be more cannibals than missionaries on either bank, or the missionaries will get eaten.

3 Jug Problems: example – three jugs, A, B and C, can hold 8, 5 and 3 litres, respectively. A is initially full, B and C empty. Find a sequence of pourings that leaves 4l in A and 4l in B.

4 Tower of Hanoi (see figure 11.1): three vertical pegs with two (or more) discs of increasing size piled on one peg. Transfer all the discs to the third peg, moving only one disc at a time, and never placing a larger disc on top of a smaller one.

5 Cryptarithmetic Problems: example

> DONALD
> + GERALD
> = ROBERT

    Given D = 5 and that each letter stands for a different number between 0 and 9, find the numbers that make the sum correct.

6 Cord around the earth problem: a cord is wrapped around the equator so that it lies on the surface all the way around. It is then made one metre longer. If it is now the same distance above the earth's surface all the way around, how far above the surface is it?

7 A patient has an inoperable tumour. The tumour can be destroyed by radiation. Although weak radiation will not harm normal flesh, radiation strong enough to destroy the tumour will. How would you treat the patient?

8 How can you construct four equilateral triangles out of six matches so that each side of each triangle is equal in length to a match?

9 Estimate how much it cost the Prince Regent (later George IV of England) to build Brighton Pavilion (an ornate summer palace, built 1811).

11.2.1 State-action representations

In puzzle-book problems, the starting state and the goal state are usually described explicitly. In some problems the exact form of the available operators (the actions that can be performed) is given explicitly, too, though they may have to be inferred. So the first step in trying to solve such a problem might be to decide what moves are possible or, at least, to decide what is the best way to describe them. Once this has been done, the problem solver can think about the problem, and more importantly about ways of finding a solution to it, in the following way. At any moment, the world is in a particular state, and there are a number of ways in which the state of the world can be altered. A state of the world can be represented in a mental model of the relevant part of the world, and the actions (or operators) can be represented as (methods of making) transitions from one state of the world to another. In a particular state of the world only some actions may be possible. For example, in the missionaries and cannibals problem the boat can hold either one or two people on any trip. However, if it is on one bank, and there is only one person on that bank, a journey with two passengers is not possible as the next move. Nevertheless, at each point where an action has to be selected, there is usually more than one option. The problem solver has to find a sequence of actions that leads from the starting state to one of the goal states – to choose the right action at each choice point. The complete set of choices can be set out in a diagram called a *state-action tree*, in which the possible states of the world are represented together with the actions that lead from one state to another.

Such trees are usually drawn upside down, with the starting state, as the root of the tree, at the top. Below the starting state are the states that can be reached by the application of one of the operators ('in one move'). Below each of those are the states that can be reached in a further move, and so on. Figure 11.2 shows the first three levels of a state-action tree for the missionaries and cannibals problem. State-action trees rapidly become very large. For example, if there were three choices at each point, there would be three states on the line below the starting state and nine on the second. By the tenth line there would be nearly 20,000 states, and on the twentieth approaching 1,200 million! The missionaries and cannibals problem can be solved in eleven moves (requiring a twelve-level state-action tree; see figure 11.3). In chess, where the number of possibilities for each move is usually larger, and the number of moves in a game greater, the figures are even more astronomical. Searching state-action trees is an example of what is known as a *computationally intractable problem*. In the state-action scheme, a natural way of measuring the difficulty of a problem is by the number of steps needed to solve it. Searching the corresponding trees is computationally intractable because, as the difficulty of the problem (number of steps) increases, the number of states in the tree increases at an unmanageable rate. In this case it increases exponentially.

People obviously do not solve problems by constructing state-action trees and looking for solutions in them. They could neither represent enough distinct states (in chess hugely more than there are neurons, or even atoms, in the brain), nor search through them to find a solution. However, problem solvers may well think in state-action terms – the state-action scheme is both a natural one and an appealing one. And even if a complete tree cannot be constructed, people may still have to search for solutions to problems. Introspection suggests that solutions to problems can be 'hard to find' – a metaphor based on the idea of search. Furthermore, research on problem solving, in both psychology and artificial intelligence, has given a prominent place to the notion of search. However, the extent to which people use search procedures, and whether they conduct their searches in (parts of) a state-action tree, are

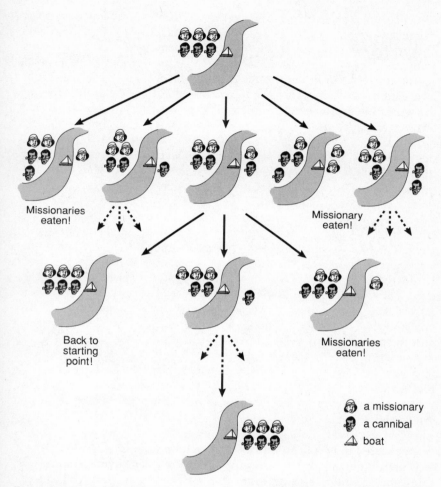

Figure 11.2 State-action representation of the missionaries and cannibals problem

questions that must be answered by empirical research, since there are other ways of thinking about problems.

If problem solvers think about problems in state-action terms, how do they set about finding solutions? One possibility is to attempt a systematic search. For some problems this option is a realistic one – those that have small state-action trees – but we have already shown that for many problems it is not. Systematic searches can either proceed *depth first* or *breadth first*. In a depth-first search, one sequence of moves

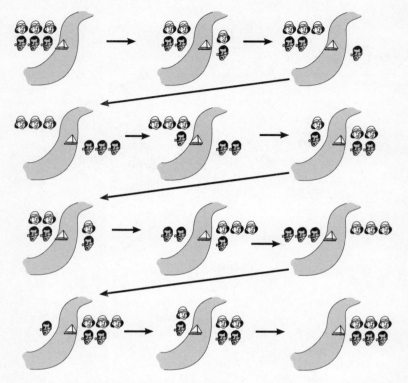

Figure 11.3   Solution to the missionaries and cannibals problem (key as in figure 11.2)

is considered until a solution is found or until a point is reached where no further move can be made. For many problems this procedure is problematic, since some branches through the tree never end. If depth-first search is used in a computer program, it is usually necessary to set an arbitrary bound on the number of moves considered in each sequence. In breadth-first search, every possibility at each level of the tree is inspected before moving on to the next level. Given the way that the number of possibilities increases, the time taken by breadth-first search is prohibitive, except for problems that can be solved in relatively few moves.

There are many ways of generalizing depth-first and breadth-first searches, and of making them more efficient. However, neither of these two basic schemes provides a plausible account of how people attempt to solve any but the simplest of problems. When people are faced with a choice of things to do, as they are at each point in their attempts to find a solution to a problem, they use *heuristic*, rule-of-thumb, methods to select what they hope is the best action. Many of the heuristic methods proposed in AI and psychology reflect a well-known fact about how people try to solve problems. Given the current state of the world, and knowledge about the goal state, people like to perform the action that gets them closest to the goal state. If they are to choose such an action, they must have a way of measuring the 'distance' between one state and another. For almost any problem, it will be possible to devise a reasonable method of measuring this distance. Indeed, there may be several plausible measures, which may lead to different choices of move. More importantly, there is no general method of measuring the distance between states that is suitable for all types of problem. *Domain-specific knowledge* must be used.

The most direct embodiment of the idea that one should always head, as directly as possible, for the goal state is found in the search procedure known as *hill-climbing*. Hill-climbing is a modification of depth-first search in which a single path is followed through either to a solution or to a dead end, or for a set number of moves. At each point the move that gets nearest to the goal is chosen. For many problems, hill-climbing does not work, because there is no route from starting state to goal state in which every move gets nearer the solution. For example, in missionaries and cannibals, if distance from the solution is measured by the number of people on the far bank, it is necessary to shift away from the solution on several of the moves in the sequence that solves the problem (see figure 11.3). Furthermore, hill-climbing may lead a problem solver to a state which is not a goal state, but from which no move gets closer to the goal state. Such a state is called a *local maximum*, and, if hill-climbing is to be generally applicable, it must have a way of escaping from such local maxima. One possibility for some problems is to make a random move to a different state.

A related method of solving problems is the *means-end analysis* used in Newell and Simon's (1963) General Problem Solver (GPS). Although it bears some similarities to hill-climbing, GPS's method of using differences between the current state and the goal state is more complex, and incorporates techniques related to problem reduction (see §11.2.2 below). GPS can recognize a series of differences between the current state and the goal state, and decide which one to work on – the one it considers most difficult to remove and which, if removed, would reduce the distance from the goal state by the largest amount. Furthermore, GPS is not deterred if it cannot remove that difference immediately. If there is an impediment to removing the difference, GPS will try to remove the impediment, rather than simply moving on to a different difference. GPS also uses a more sophisticated method of deciding when to abandon the current path than a simple depth bound. Intuitively, it tries to ensure that the new problems it sets itself are easier than the one it is trying to solve.

Means-end analysis is one of a number of *weak methods* for solving problems identified by Newell and Simon (1972). Others include working forwards (from the initial state), working backwards (from the goal state), and generating solutions (more or less at random) and testing them to see if they work (generate and test). Weak methods are so called because they do not use specific information about the problem domain, but only procedures that can be applied generally. If there are methods that are specific to the type of problem, they are likely to be more effective in solving it ('stronger').

Although weak methods are heuristic methods, and would not take so long to solve a problem as a complete breadth-first search, they have to examine many possibilities. Indeed, they can only solve comparatively simple problems in a reasonable amount of time. For this reason, although GPS solved problems in a number of domains, its success was limited, and it was soon set aside by much of the AI community.

11.2.2   Goal-reduction representations

Given a problem in which the starting state, goal state and operators are all well specified, a state-action analysis is always possible. So any problem that is well specified, or which can be converted into a well-specified problem, can be analysed using the state-action method. However, thinking about a problem in state-action terms is not necessarily the best way of thinking about it. A different technique, called *problem-* or *goal-reduction*, uses the method of 'divide and conquer' to reduce one large problem to several smaller ones. These problems are then further subdivided until the subproblems can be solved directly by the operators available.

Not every problem can be usefully divided into simpler problems, but when a problem can be so divided, the problem-reduction method usually produces a more elegant solution than the state-action method. This is true, for example, with the Tower of Hanoi (figure 11.1). A state-action analysis produces a sequence of movements of single discs that solves the problem. Of itself, it identifies no structure in that sequence, though someone using the method might see structure. The problem-reduction method is more insightful, and analyses the problem

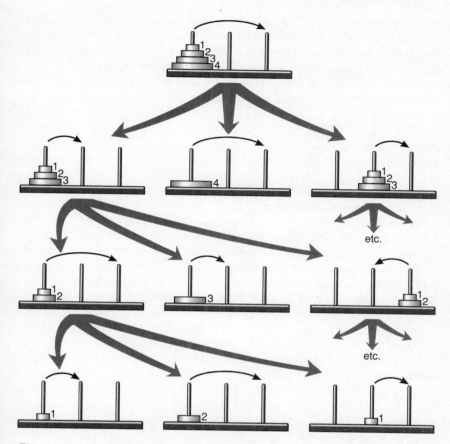

Figure 11.4 Problem-reduction representation of the tower of Hanoi

as shown in figure 11.4. The overall goal is to solve, say, a four-disc version of the problem. The four-disc version can be divided into two three-disc problems, and a (trivial) one-disc problem. To solve the four-disc problem, one has move the top three discs onto the second peg (first three-disc problem), move the largest disc onto the third peg, where it is to form the base of the new pile (one-disc problem), and then move the pile of three discs from the second peg to the third, onto the largest disc (second three-disc problem). Each three-disc problem can be divided into two two-disc problems and a one-disc problem, and each two-disc problem can be divided into three one-disc problems. Since one-disc problems are trivial, the only remaining worry is, for each problem, to decide onto which of the two possible pegs to move the smallest disc on the first move. There is a simple general solution to this problem: if you are moving an odd number of discs, move the first one onto the peg where you want the pile to end up, otherwise move it onto the other one. With a real Tower of Hanoi, you can readily convince yourself that this is a good way of thinking about how to solve this problem.

11.2.3   AND/OR trees

At first sight the state-action and problem-reduction methods of representing problems seem different and, perhaps, incompatible, even though both can be represented in tree diagrams. The state-action method leads to trees in which different sequences of moves are represented, such as the one shown in figure 11.2, whereas the problem-reduction method leads to trees in which the division of the problem into subproblems is represented, as in figure 11.4. These trees have different interpretations. In a state-action tree, each path through the tree represents a different way of trying to solve the problem. In a problem-reduction tree, there is a division of the problem into parts, each of which has to be solved. They are not alternatives as in the state-action tree. However, the state-action and problem-reduction methods can be combined into a single method that includes both (i) the idea that a problem can be broken down into subproblems, and (ii) the idea that there may be alternative ways of solving each subproblem. In the resulting tree representation, each branching point must be labelled either as an AND (problem-reduction) branching, or as an OR (state-action) branching. If there are two subproblems under an AND branching, both the first *and* the second must be solved to solve the problem as a whole. If there are two alternatives under an OR branching, either one *or* the other must be done. Such a tree is called an *AND/OR tree*. State-action and problem-reduction trees are special cases of AND/OR trees, ones without any ANDs, and ones without any ORs, respectively.

Empirical research on how naive subjects solve puzzles suggests that, although puzzles such as missionaries and cannibals are typically conceived in state-action terms, people's ability to look ahead through the search tree is severely limited. Indeed, one detailed mathematical model of how people solve such puzzles (Jeffries, Polson, Razran and Atwood, 1977) suggests that only the states reachable in one move are considered. The model also proposes that people hold (partial) information in long-term memory about states in which they have been, and that they use this information to avoid repeatedly looping through sets of states. With problems that have a straightforward goal-reduction analysis, such as the Tower of Hanoi, there is some indirect evidence that people will impose this analysis on the problem, perhaps after a period of thinking about it in state-action terms (e.g., Egan and Greeno, 1974).

11.3 Analogical Problem Solving

An alternative to searching for sequences of operators that solve a problem is to use the solution of a different problem as a pattern for the solution to the current one. We have already mentioned, for example, in chapter 8, the use of a solution to a previous problem of a similar type. And in the next chapter we will consider, further, the way that such domain-specific knowledge can be used to solve a problem. As we will see, experts are better at seeing the right parallels between problems in the same domain – those based on underlying principles rather than surface features.

Using a problem from a different domain as a pattern for solving a new problem requires the establishment of a mapping between the two domains – usually referred to as the source (or base) domain and the target domain. There have been many claims about the importance and ubiquity of such *analogical mappings*, both in everyday thinking and in high-level scientific thinking (in cognitive psychology the analogy between the mind and computer software is particularly important, for example). However, it has been relatively difficult to induce subjects in psychological experiments to make use of analogies to help them solve problems.

A favourite problem in the study of analogical reasoning is the 'inoperable tumour' problem, originally introduced by Duncker (1945) (number 7 in the list at the beginning of §11.2). One plausible solution to the problem is to direct several weak beams of the rays towards the tumour, so that only at the tumour itself is the combined effect strong enough to destroy tissue. An analogue to this problem was devised by Gick and Holyoak (1980). A general is trying to capture a fortress that can be approached by several roads. The roads are mined in such a way that if the general's whole army marches down one road, the mines will be detonated, but a smaller group of marching soldiers will not detonate the mines. The general, therefore, sends small groups of soldiers down each of the roads, and coordinates their movements so that they all arrive at the fortress together. Gick and Holyoak showed that subjects who were instructed to use this analogy to solve the tumour problem were able to do so. However, simply presenting the story about the general, with no instructions to use it in solving the tumour problem, produced a much lower success rate and, indeed, no evidence of better performance than when the story about the general was not presented at all.

In a later study Gick and Holyoak (1983) showed that analogical transfer was possible without explicit instructions to use an analogy. However, it was facilitated by the use of two different stories containing solutions to analogous problems, and by an explicit statement of the general principle underlying the solution. For the general/tumour problems an appropriate statement would be: if you need a large force to accomplish some purpose, but are prevented from applying such a force directly, many smaller forces applied from different directions may work just as well.

The spontaneous use of analogies is also helped by a greater *surface similarity* between the source and target domains. Keane (1987) showed that a story about destroying a brain tumour was more likely to help subjects to solve a problem about destroying a stomach tumour than the story about the general. However, the brain tumour and stomach tumour stories are not really from different domains. Holyoak and Koh (1987) showed that recognizing an analogy was easier if there were both surface and structural similarities between the problems. However, structural similarities were more important for generating the solution once the relevance of the problem in the source domain had been recognized. In this study the analogue to the tumour problem was provided by different versions of a 'lightbulb' story, in which filaments inside a special bulb had to be either fused with laser beams or separated by ultrasound, both of which would break the glass at high intensities. Laser beams are more similar than ultrasound waves, at the surface level, to the x-rays of the tumour problem. Structural similarity was manipulated by comparing a 'standard' version of the story to one in which only low intensity lasers/ultrasound sources were available.

Holyoak explains his findings within the 'framework for induction' proposed by Holland et al. (1986). On the broad definition of induction (see chapter 7) given by those authors, use of analogy is a species of induction. In this framework, the effect of surface similarity arises at a stage of spreading activation, which follows the encoding of the problem in the target domain. Holyoak (e.g., 1985) has contrasted this view with the *structure-mapping* hypothesis of Gentner (1983, 1989). The distinction is sometimes portrayed as between a pragmatically based theory of analogy and a syntactically based one. However, this characterization is incorrect (see Johnson-Laird, 1989), since structure mapping is guided by the meaning of the relations, not just their form. Gentner's view is that the drawing of analogies involves finding structural similarities between the source and target domains. Objects in the two domains should be put into correspondence as far as possible (e.g., fortress: tumour), but the properties of those objects can be ignored. In mapping relations between domains, a principle of *systematicity* applies. Not all relations can be mapped from the source domain to the target domain. In selecting a mapping, interlinked sets of relations are preferred, and isolated relations are dropped. Higher order relations are used to determine which simple relations form systems.

Like Holyoak, Gentner stresses the importance of structural similarity in analogical problem solving, though this emphasis is inevitable, given the meaning of 'analogy'. Gentner has little to say about the effects of surface similarity, since, unlike the PI (processes of induction) theory of Holland et al., her theory is not concerned primarily with how an appropriate source domain is found (though see Gentner, 1989: p. 215ff.). An important aspect of Gentner's work is the idea that a well-established structure in the source domain can be imposed, sometimes with misleading results, on a less well-understood target domain. For example, Gentner and Gentner (1983) showed that analogies for understanding electricity based on water flowing in pipes and on people teeming through turnstiles produced different results when subjects had to reason about the operation of electric circuits. The effects of combining batteries in different ways were best understood on the water analogy. Separate batteries could be modelled by separate sources of water pressure, whereas the crowd analogy provides no satisfactory equivalent for batteries. Combinations of resistors were best understood on the turnstile analogy, in which the turnstiles themselves correspond to the resistors. The constricted pipes of the water flow analogy do not model the properties of resistors so well.

Summary

Problems arise when people do not see immediately how to get from where they are (their starting state) to where they want to be (their goal state). In well-specified problems, the starting state, the goal state, and the methods available for getting from one to the other are clearly defined. Such problems are easy to study empirically, and have been the focus of psychological work on problem solving. Newell and Simon developed the notion of heuristic, or rule-of-thumb, methods for solving problems, and invented production systems – collections of *if . . . then* rules – to model them. Newell and others have claimed that such an approach can be developed into a unified theory of cognition.

Puzzle-book problems can be analysed using state-action representations or, more usefully, if the problem can be divided into subproblems, goal-reduction representations. A state-action representation depicts states of the problem world, and ways of moving between them. For all but the simplest problems, such representations quickly become extremely large. A psychological account of problem solving based around such representations must propose ways of restricting the parts of the representation that are considered. Such problem-solving techniques typically make use of heuristic methods.

The use of analogy in problem solving provides an alternative to techniques such as those described by Newell and Simon. However, the spontaneous use of analogies is rare. Gentner stresses the importance of mapping structures from one domain to another in analogy formation. Holyoak claims that a more pragmatically oriented view is required.

Further Reading

Keane, M. T. (1988). *Analogical Problem Solving*. Chichester, West Sussex: Ellis Horwood.

Newell, A. (1990). *Unified Theories of Cognition: The 1987 William James Lectures*. Cambridge, MA: Harvard University Press.

Newell, A. and Simon, H. A. (1972). *Human Problem Solving*. Englewood Cliffs, NJ: Prentice-Hall [the classical presentation, but not for the faint-hearted].

12

Game Playing and Expertise

In the previous chapter we considered the solving of so-called knowledge-lean problems. We introduced the ideas of state-action representations, problem reduction, and the use of analogy. In this chapter we consider the application of the state-action method to games such as chess. This technique has been used, in a relatively pure form, by computer chess programs. However, unlike naive experimental subjects solving puzzle-book problems, human chess players draw on a pool of knowledge about the game, which constitutes their chess-playing expertise. They may think about chess moves in terms of states and actions, but their choice of which actions to consider is strongly guided by their knowledge.

In the second part of the chapter, we discuss expertise in detail. We describe psychological research on expert problem solving, and we present research that has sought to build computer systems that replace or augment human expertise. We conclude by considering how expertise develops, and what we can learn about expertise from the existence of idiot savants.

12.1 Game Playing as Problem Solving

A puzzle-book puzzle is set by a puzzle-setter. But the setter cannot intervene when the solver is tackling the puzzle. In games such as noughts and crosses (tic-tac-toe), draughts (checkers) and chess, the situation is different. Players take turns and, in deciding what moves to make, each player has to take account of the likely response of his or her opponent.

The overall goal of each player in a game of noughts and crosses, draughts or chess is to win the game. However, even in a game of noughts and crosses, which cannot last more than nine turns, players do not always look ahead through the sequences of possible moves to find one that will lead to a win. Or, rather, once a person is able to do so, they no longer find the game interesting. In chess it is impossible to examine all the possibilities. It is estimated that there are 10^{120}. 'Locally', the problem to be solved by a chess player is: which move shall I make now? To make a rational decision, players must be able to evaluate the positions that can be reached in one move. But how? There is no obvious way of measuring the difference between an immediately reachable position and a winning position, as would be required by, say, the hill-climbing procedure described in the last chapter. Chess positions must, therefore, be evaluated in some other way, by what is called in artificial intelligence a *static evaluation function*.

Chess players do have methods for evaluating positions. A prime consideration in such evaluations is the number and type of the pieces that each player has. But other factors, such as which pieces have relative freedom of movement, which are vulnerable, which parts of the board are controlled, and where the pawns are located are also important. A human chess player at the master or grandmaster level will typically think through a relatively small number of developments of the game and, assuming a rational opponent, will try to force play to the one that seems most favourable. To decide on the current move, the choices are assessed not in terms of the position they create immediately, but in terms of the position to which they will eventually lead. However, most moves are not followed up. They are assumed to be less valued that those that are.

It should now be apparent how chess playing can be analysed using the state-action method described in the last chapter. The states are board positions, and the actions are legal chess moves. The choice of move depends on which leads to the best position at a later stage in the game. The simplest method, conceptually, of mechanizing this process is to consider all possible developments for a fixed number of moves. We will describe how to do so below, since the general principles are of interest and can be refined. However, the technique is problematic for two main reasons. First, without a very powerful computer – which the top computer chess programmers have – it is not possible to look far enough ahead for the technique to produce really high-class play. Even chess players as bad as the present authors know that short-sightedness does not make for good chess. Supercomputers can play grandmaster level chess by following up each possibility for five moves on each side (ten plies). Second, human chess players neither follow up every possibility, nor follow up possibilities for fixed numbers of moves. They follow developments through to so-called quiet positions, at which they hope to make a further in-depth assessment of the way they want the game to go. The 'brute force' methods of the current computer chess champions are of only restricted and indirect use in understanding how people play chess.

The technique for mechanically choosing a move in a game of chess is known as *minimaxing*. Chess is a *zero-sum game* (von Neumann and Morgenstern, 1944; see also chapter 10), since what is good for one player is bad (in equal measure) for the other. The sum of the benefits of a move to the two players is zero. In the state-action representation of chess, the alternate layers correspond to moves by white and black. If a program views the game from white's perspective, on its moves it will try to maximize its benefit. It must assume, however, that black will play rationally and, on its moves, try to maximize its own benefit. Since chess is a zero-sum game, anything that maximizes black's benefit minimizes white's. When white picks a move, it must therefore ensure that it MINImizes the MAXimum loss that black can inflict upon it – hence minimax.

When human chess players follow a development through, they assume that their opponents will make the best moves available to them. Hence, the procedure of evaluating current moves in terms of the positions to which they lead already incorporates the idea of minimaxing. In a computer system, all the positions that can be reached in a fixed number of moves are evaluated using the static evaluation function. The values are then 'backed-up' the tree, assuming that, at alternative levels, each player chooses the best move for him or her. The backed-up values of the positions that can be reached in one move – which are, in general, different from the values the static evaluation function would assign them directly – are used to choose between those moves. This procedure is illustrated in figure 12.1.

As with the depth-first and breadth-first search strategies for solving non-adversary problems (see previous chapter), there are ways of making minimaxing more efficient. The most important is *alpha-beta pruning*. The idea of 'pruning' develops the tree metaphor. Alpha-beta pruning allows some possible developments to be ignored, on the basis of ones that have already been evaluated. For example, imagine that you have evaluated the first of your possible moves as having a backed-up value of +4. You then start considering the second possible move and you find out that the first sequence you consider gives it a value of only +2. You can then ignore all the other possible developments

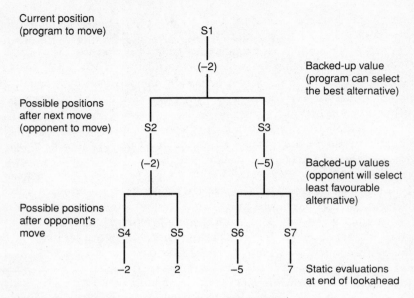

Figure 12.1 Backing-up values for minimaxing in game playing

because, whatever values they have, your opponent can ensure your gain is at most +2 (by forcing the game to follow the development you have already considered). So, whatever the result of the other developments of the second move, the first move, which you can guarantee will lead to a gain of 4, should be chosen over the second.

Up to the mid-1980s (almost) pure brute-force techniques produced the most successful chess-playing machines (especially HITECH and CRAY BLITZ). More recently, DEEP THOUGHT (Hsu, Anantharaman, Campbell and Nowatzyk, 1990) has combined two developments to make a yet more powerful chess-playing computer. First, it runs not on a general-purpose computer, but on specially built hardware. Second, although it examines more positions per second than HITECH and CRAY BLITZ, its search through the tree is selective. In particular, it uses a technique called *singular extension* to explore certain parts of the tree to a greater depth. If the backed-up value of a position depends strongly on one possible development (e.g., on white's move there is one highly favourable option and the rest are all poor), that option is examined further, since so much depends on it. When there are a number of approximately equally favourable options no such selective search is carried out.

There is another use to which massive computer power can be put in analysing chess problems, which illustrates some limitations on human thinking about chess (see Michie, 1987). Chess players study previously played games, and some specialize in analysing specific parts of the game – in particular the end-game. In an end-game, each player has only a few pieces, and the number of possible moves is more manageable than in the mid-game. However, it is possible for the players to 'go round in circles' in the end-game, a fact that motivated the so-called fifty-move rule: if fifty moves occur without any substantial change, such as castling, capture or pawn movement, the game is drawn. With a high-powered computer it has been possible to analyse exhaustively all possible developments in some end-games that human end-game experts had not previously mastered (see also chapter 7).

Such analyses have overturned received wisdom in a number of cases. For example, the King and Rook vs. King and Knight end-game was thought, in general, to be a draw. However, computer analysis showed that the King and Rook can win from about half of the possible starting positions (of which there are well over one million), with the longest win taking 27 moves. The leading end-game scholar A. J. Roycroft, with partial knowledge of the computer analysis, was able to acquire a working mastery of this end-game. Analysis of a more complicated end-game (King and two Bishops vs. King and Knight) led to further surprising results. It had been claimed in the middle of the last century, and repeated as received wisdom, that the King and Knight could force a draw if they could reach the so-called Kling and Horwitz position. Thompson (1986) showed, by exhaustive computer analysis, that the King and two Bishops could win from all but a very few of the approximately 200 million starting positions in this end-game. The first surprise was that the King and Bishops could win from the Kling and Horwitz position. The second was that for some other positions the win took more than fifty moves. Such analyses have forced the World Chess Federation to change the fifty-move rule (see Michie, 1987, for further discussion).

12.2 Expertise

The principle of division of labour applies to thinking as well as to manual work. And as with manual work part of the reason for the division of labour is that in any society, but more particularly in modern 'developed' societies, there are many different mental tasks, each of which need be carried out only by a relatively small number of people.

Indeed, there are many parallels between mental skills and other skills – those that are predominantly manual and those that have an important manual component. For example, to reach a high degree of proficiency can take a long time – mental skills, like manual skills, can take many years to develop. And cultivating any kind of skill can be regarded as a challenge. In societies where people have leisure time, leisure activities requiring both manual and mental skills are commonplace. In this section we consider what can be learned about the nature of thinking and reasoning from the study of expertise.

The study of expertise has a somewhat complex history. Commenting on trends in AI research, Goldstein and Papert (1977) noted the shift to the knowledge-based paradigm that took place in the decade from 1966 to 1976. The shift was away from the search-based paradigm described in chapter 11, and its associated weak methods. It led to the rejection of general purpose systems, such as GPS, and towards specialized domain-specific problem-solving systems – the expert systems described below. These systems do not eschew completely the notion of search, but they so limit the search space that simple search techniques suffice. The main programming effort goes into encoding the domain-specific knowledge in a usable form. One of the principal influences on AI research was the publication in English of de Groot's (1965) study of chess playing (originally published in Dutch in 1946). This work was taken up almost immediately by Newell and Simon, but its impact in psychology more generally was considerably delayed. Edward Feigenbaum (see 1989), a student of Simon's, realised that AI programs with the domain-specific knowledge on which expertise was based might carry out commercially or intellectually useful tasks. His Heuristic Programming Project at Stanford University led to the expert systems DENDRAL and MYCIN, described below, and was primarily responsible for the trend identified by Goldstein and Papert. Because commercial considerations have been less important in psychology, the shift from the study of search-based problem solving to the study of knowledge-based problem solving has not been as dramatic as in AI. Nevertheless, knowledge-based problem solving has attracted considerable attention.

12.2.1 Psychological research on knowledge-based problem solving

If certain kinds of problem solving are knowledge-based, having the right knowledge is crucial. However, people who are good at problem solving of this kind do not simply have additional factual knowledge. One way to find out what differentiates them from people who do not have the requisite knowledge is to compare *experts* and *novices* in the same domain. Research of this kind was initially inspired by the work of de Groot (1965), who compared strong and less strong chess players. This work was also important in assessing the contribution of computer chess programs to our knowledge of human chess skill (see §12.1 above). An advantage of studying chess is that there is an internationally agreed rating scale on which any chess player's ability can be measured. On this scale beginners typically have scores of between about 600 and 1,100, and tournament players between 1,200 and 1,900. International masters have scores of around 2,400 upwards and grandmasters around 2,500 upwards. The highest ratings for human chess players are around 2,900. The computer chess program DEEP THOUGHT was rated 2,552 in 1990.

An important question for de Groot was the number of possible developments of the game considered by players at different levels. As we saw above, computer chess programs may consider hundreds of thousands of developments. De Groot found that human chess players consider only a few. From a psychological point of view, aside from any detailed knowledge of chess play, this finding is not surprising, given our knowledge about limitations on short-term memory. More surprising, perhaps, was de Groot's finding that excellent players (at the grandmaster level) do not follow up any more moves than good tournament players. They do, however, follow up better moves (as rated by other players), and they assess moves more quickly.

Another topic studied by de Groot was short-term memory for chess positions. Players were shown board positions briefly and then asked to reconstruct them from memory. Better players did so more accurately. In a more systematic study, Chase and Simon (1973) showed that highly skilled and less skilled players performed equally poorly in remembering the positions of similar numbers of pieces when the configuration did not make sense as part of a chess game. This finding led Chase and Simon to propose that the difference between chess players of different levels was in the amount of information stored in long-term memory – in the form of board positions. They further proposed that moves are chosen on the basis of similarities between the current board position and positions stored in memory, and that searching ahead through possible developments is relatively unimportant. Chase and Simon suggested that a grandmaster might have 50,000 'chunks' of information in long-term memory, each encoding a significant grouping of pieces. This idea is consistent with the fact that expertise in chess is attained in large part by studying the games of other players, and by developing a repertoire of tactics that can be brought into play, given a particular board position. It also helps to explain why, as Chase and Simon suggested, the attainment of grandmaster status requires about ten years of dedicated practice.

Chase and Simon's evidence for what Holding (1985) calls the *recognition-association* method of selecting moves is indirect. The 'chunking' skills used to encode briefly presented board positions may not be the same as those to select moves. Holding, therefore, suggested that differences in the ability to search through possible developments had not been ruled out, and he presented some indirect evidence for its importance. Furthermore, a number of studies have shown that, when more time is allowed for the analysis of random board positions, or when different tasks are used, expert–novice differences re-emerge (e.g., Holding and Reynolds, 1982; Saariluoma, 1985). Nevertheless, even if search is used in chess play, it is hard to produce direct evidence that differences in ability to search determine chess skill, and Charness (1989) presents an interesting case study of a player whose rating rose, over nine years, from 1,570 to 2,423 without any measurable increase in his search abilities.

Experts know more than novices, but they do not simply have more information stored in long-term memory. Their knowledge is organized differently from that of novices, and it enables them to encode new information more efficiently. Research by Jill Larkin and others on textbook physics problem solving illustrates these ideas. Larkin (1979) showed that, when physics students tried to solve problems, potentially relevant equations tended to come to mind one at a time, whereas professional physicists retrieved equations in related groups. More importantly, Larkin (1983) showed that novices' representations of a problem were *naive*, drawing on everyday concepts instead of the specialized concepts of physics that experts used in representing the problems. Indeed, the naive representations were often inappropriate, and failed to lead to a solution to the problem. Naive representations are often based on superficial aspects of a problem. Chi, Feltovich and Glaser (1981) showed that, when asked to sort problems into groups, novices relied on such superficial features as whether the problem was about an inclined plane, whereas experts classified the problems according to the physical principles that were relevant to their solution.

The Italian psychologist Paolo Bozzi (1958, 1959), in work that anticipated the naive physics research described above, showed that naive physical theories affected the perceived naturalness of the motion of pendulums and of blocks sliding down inclined planes. For example,

Bozzi's subjects found it natural that a pendulum with a wide swing should oscillate considerably more slowly than one with a narrow swing. This result is in line with naive theories of pendular motion and, indeed, the first correct analysis of the motion of compound pendulums, by Galileo, was criticized by other physicists because it did not accord with how they thought they saw pendulums moving. In reality the increase in the time taken for one swing is only slightly increased by the width of the swing. Bozzi's work was originally published in Italian, and has only recently become well known in the English-speaking world (for an account in English, see Pittenger and Runeson, 1990).

Apart from differences in their knowledge, it has also been suggested that experts and novices use different methods in trying to solve physics problems. Larkin, McDermott, Simon and Simon (1980) suggested that experts try to work forwards from the information given to the answer, whereas novices try to work backwards from the answer. However, Priest and Lindsay (1992), in a more extensive study, have cast doubt on this idea, showing that both experts and novices prefer working forwards. The main difference that they found between the groups was in the ability to produce a high-level plan before attempting a solution. This idea is consistent with research on expert–novice differences in computer programming, which suggests that a major difference lies in the level at which the two kinds of programmers plan (e.g., Soloway and Ehrlich, 1984).

12.2.2 Expert systems

Partly because experts are expensive to train, and because each one has to undergo the same protracted training regime, attempts have been made to embody human expertise in computer programs. Computers themselves are now cheap, but, more importantly, once an expert computer program has been developed, it can easily and cheaply be duplicated. Such *expert systems* are important in themselves, and are already marketed to some effect. We, however, will be interested primarily in how the development of expert systems contributes to the study of human expertise. At the most general level, many expert systems are intended to embody (and sometimes improve on) human expertise. Thus, they are models of human experts, and can provide information about the knowledge those experts use. Furthermore, in so far as expert systems outperform human experts, they can suggest what knowledge human experts do not use, or use inefficiently. To construct an expert system, knowledge must be elicited from human experts. The problems that arise in this elicitation process provide information about how expert knowledge is encoded in the human mind. For example, experts cannot write down all the knowledge they have, or say how they use it. If they were able to, new experts would be easier to train.

Since expert systems take the form of computer programs, they have been developed primarily within artificial intelligence. Work on the earliest expert systems began in the mid-1960s, and came to fruition about fifteen years later. However, despite the proliferation of expert systems since the late 1970s, the principles of expert systems are best illustrated from these early, and highly successful, efforts. The first two important systems were intended primarily for use by researchers and, like many subsequent expert systems, do not replace human experts but help them to work more efficiently. MACSYMA is a program that can be used by mathematicians for a variety of purposes, such as simplifying complex expressions and performing symbolic integration. Although it has been widely used, it is less famous than the other early expert system, DENDRAL (Lindsay, Buchanan, Feigenbaum and Lederberg, 1980), which works out the structure of complex organic molecules, given data from a machine called a mass spectrograph. A mass spectrograph breaks up complex molecules and 'weighs' the pieces. Given the weights of the atoms (mainly carbon, hydrogen and oxygen) that make up organic molecules, it is possible to make inferences about the composition of the fragments produced when the molecule is broken. From information about how such fragments fit together, and what changes they undergo when they are detached from a complex structure, the complex structure itself can be deduced. Many papers have been published in chemistry journals reporting results obtained with the help of DENDRAL.

Much of the power of DENDRAL comes from the completeness of its knowledge about possible structures. The mathematical proofs of this completeness are largely the work of Joshua Lederberg, the Nobel Prize-winning chemist who contributed to the project. The way DENDRAL uses its knowledge ensures that, unlike human experts, it does not overlook possible, but statistically improbable, structures. The ability to 'remember' these unlikely structures is one of the main reasons why expert systems are useful for supplementing human expertise, even when they cannot replace it. However, it also means that such systems do not reason in the same way as human experts, and it makes it harder for them to produce comprehensible accounts of how they make particular decisions. Such accounts are crucial if someone with a lower level of expertise is to assess whether the decision made by an expert system is correct.

Perhaps the best-known application of expert systems is medical diagnosis. Again, the earliest system, MYCIN (Shortliffe, 1976), is both the best known and one of the most impressive. MYCIN, like DENDRAL, was developed at Stanford University, and the two systems have some similarities. MYCIN diagnoses and suggests treatment for bacterial diseases. Although many bacterial infections are not particularly serious, those that MYCIN deals with are. They require early treatment – before a culture has been developed – with powerful drugs that should not be given in too large doses or in combination with other similar drugs. MYCIN reasons backwards from its currently hypothesized diagnosis to discover what information it needs to check that dignosis. Its knowledge is stored in a large set of about 500 productions, the *if ... then* rules described in the previous chapter. Each rule has a *certainty factor* associated with it. This certainty factor reflects the fact that a given piece of information (a symptom or a test result) is not certainly, but only probabilistically, associated with one or more diagnoses. The treatment of uncertain information is an increasingly important issue in the design of expert systems. Despite MYCIN's success, its approach to uncertainty is regarded as at best an approximation to a properly justified method. Other systems use techniques from probability theory, such as *Bayesian inference* (familiar to psychologists from Bayes' theorem; see chapter 9), or a more sophisticated mathematical approach called Dempster–Shafer theory. We have already seen (chapter 9) that people are poor at handling statistical information, particularly in a quantitative way. Human experts are no exception, and much of the statistical information encoded into expert systems, such as those used in medical diagnosis, comes from professionally processed survey data.

As we have already said, there are now large numbers of expert systems, including a significant number whose success can be measured in financial terms. Rather than describing more of these systems, we will consider some of the psychologically important aspects of expert system design. In particular we will consider four design principles described by Davis (1984). Expert systems use large amounts of domain-specific knowledge. MYCIN's database of several hundred productions is relatively modest in comparison with expert systems that followed it. However, although modern expert systems incorporate large amounts of knowledge, that knowledge remains domain specific and, more importantly, computationally tractable. Unlike everyday reasoning, expert reasoning of the kind modelled in expert systems cannot depend on just any piece of knowledge about the world. Davis's first two principles are about the domain-specific knowledge. The first is that this knowledge should be represented in a uniform way. The second is that it should be kept separate from the processes that manipulate it – usually referred to as the *inference engine*. It is easy to add new pieces of information to an expert system designed according to these principles, which presumably reflect a desirable characteristic of how a human expert's knowledge might be stored. Indeed, if all of the knowledge is stripped out of an expert system, the remaining inference engine can be used as the basis of another expert system. An expert system with no knowledge in its called a *shell*. E-MYCIN (E for empty), a stripped-down version of MYCIN, has been used as the basis for other medical diagnosis systems. Davis's third principle is that the inference engine should be simple. One way of achieving this aim is to program an expert system as a production system, though by no means all expert systems are production systems. Production systems capture well the 'if this, then that' nature of diagnosis, in particular. Finally, to guard against error, expert systems should use as much information as possible in coming to their decisions, even if some of it appears to be redundant. Given the serious consequence of error in many decisions made by experts, human experts should also operate in this way.

Eliciting information from human experts is difficult and can be frustrating. Is there any way that expert systems can learn to become experts for themselves? In general, expert systems are not expected to learn inference rules. However, Tom Mitchell (Buchanan and Mitchell, 1978) has written a program, meta-DENDRAL, that learns rules for the DENDRAL system, both in its original version and in a version that interprets data from nuclear magnetic resonance (NMR) rather than the mass spectrograph. Mitchell's program uses induction techniques of the kind described in chapter 7. Some of the interpretation rules it has discovered have been considered important enough to merit publication.

Many expert systems, particularly those whose inference rules are not known to be completely accurate, need to generate explanations of how they have arrived at their decisions. In principle, a system such as MYCIN can explain a decision by citing the rules it has used in coming to that decision. However, such explanations are not readily understood by human experts, let alone by less skilled people. Part of the job of the program TEIRESIAS (Davis, 1982) is to generate comprehensible explanations of MYCIN's behaviour. Its more important function, however, is to automate the transfer of knowledge from human experts to an expert system. TEIRESIAS allows an expert to interact with an expert system designed in a similar way to MYCIN, but which is only partly constructed, or otherwise incomplete. By observing the errors of the system – both errors of diagnosis and errors in judging what information is useful in making a diagnosis – the human expert is encouraged to verbalize the knowledge he or she has, but which is not present in the system. This technique of focusing on particular cases is more effective in eliciting information from human experts than asking them less focused questions about what they know. Once TEIRESIAS identifies an error, it has to explain to the human expert how the expert system made its decision, so that the human expert can determine why the program went wrong. Hence TEIRESIAS's ability to generate explanations and its job of transferring knowledge from human to machine are intimately related.

An unresolved problem about expert systems is whether their reasoning should follow the complex processes that apparently underlie that of human experts. As we saw in chapter 10, the judgements of human experts (e.g., in medical diagnosis) are often surpassed by using multiple regression equations that combine factors identified as important by human experts, but in a very simple way. As Camerer and Johnson (1991) have pointed out, the implications of this fact for expert system design have yet to be considered by the AI community.

Expert systems tend to rely entirely on domain-specific knowledge. Human experts can, however, draw on general knowledge when solving problems in their domain of expertise. Lenat and Guha (1990) have suggested that expert systems might work better, particularly when faced with a new kind of situation, or incorrect input, if they had access to a large pool of everyday knowledge. In addition, such expert systems could dispense with simplifying assumptions about, for example, space, time and causality, if knowledge about these matters were encoded in the database of everyday knowledge. In their Cyc project, Lenat and Guha aim to encode about one million everyday facts in such a way that they could be readily available to an expert system. This task is a formidable one, requiring difficult decisions about knowledge representation (see Garnham, 1988, chapter 2), inference mechanisms, and making sure that finding one fact among a million does not take forever.

12.2.3 Becoming an expert

The 'ten-year rule' suggests that about ten years of sustained practice is necessary to achieve world-class performance at a recognized skill. While this idea is not inconsistent with the existence of innate abilities for chess, or music, or any other skill, it suggests that having such an ability is, by itself, far from sufficient for skilled performance. Furthermore, as Howe (1990) points out, many reports of the feats of child prodigies are likely to be exaggerated, or to omit details of early training, thus creating the impression that the prodigious performance appeared 'from nowhere'. Howe argues that people such as H. G. Wells and Bernard Shaw have, for personal reasons, exaggerated the poverty of their early years. Properly documented cases of child prodigies, for example the nineteenth-century British philosopher John Stuart Mill, almost always reveal parental encouragement, and sometimes extreme pressure, to do well.

Howe argues that, in addition to parental pressure, temperamental differences may go some way to explaining the acquisition of expertise. Those children who are prepared to stick at the tasks that they or their parents set them are those that are most likely to succeed. For example, Sosniak (1990) found that highly successful concert pianists were not recognized as outstanding until a relatively late stage in their childhood, and only after they started devoting unusually large amounts of time to practising. As very young pianists, it was their 'devotion to duty' (and that of their parents), not their musical ability, that was unusual. The overwhelming importance of practice in skill acquisition has also been stressed in Ericsson's influential account (e.g., 1990). Furthermore, since practice is specific to a particular skill, its effects do not transfer to other abilities. Hence, a highly skilled pianist will not necessarily be skilled in other areas, not even on other musical instruments. Howe argues that the separability of skills is further emphasized by the existence of so-called *idiots savants*. He also suggests a motivational explanation for the fact that moderate levels of different skills often go together. For example, a child who is good at mathematics in school is likely to be good at English, too. On this view, there is no need to postulate an intrinsic link between the two abilities, such as general intelligence.

12.2.4   Idiots savants

Occasionally an individual is found whose general level of mental functioning is extremely low (the term *idiot* was formerly defined as indicating an IQ of less than 25 or a mental age in adulthood of less than two), but who has one highly developed ability. Such people have been called idiots savants, though savant, by itself, is becoming more popular (see Howe, 1989, for a detailed account). Examples of the skills shown by savants are mathematical skills (particularly working out days of the week to go with dates), musical ability (generally exhibited in the playing of a particular instrument) and drawing. The ability of a savant results in levels of performance well above average. Indeed, although there are idiosyncratic aspects of the skill of savants, they can often be compared with experts. In most cases, rote memorization can be ruled out, though savants often show remarkable memory abilities – in playing from memory pieces of music that they have just heard, for example. However, many savant calendar calculators can work over a range of dates that is too large for memorization to be plausible (see Howe and Smith, 1988), and the talents of savant musicians depend on knowledge of the conventions of tonal composition (see Sloboda, 1991: p. 159). It must be remembered, however, that although savants may, for example, be highly skilled at producing notes on a piano, the range of their interpretive skills is not comparable with that of a concert pianist. Similarly, a savant artist may have high reproductive drawing skills, but is unlikely to express complex ideas through abstract art. Many savants are classified as autistic, and the existence of autistic savants appears to have contributed to a somewhat distorted view of the abilities of autistic children. Most such children are mentally retarded, with no special abilities.

The abilities of idiots savants underline the selective nature of expertise. However, they raise further questions. A normal intelligent adult might be trained as an expert in a number of fields. But could a savant date calculator have become a savant artist instead? Or do savants suggest the existence of abilities that are separate from general intelligence and which, for some unknown reason, happen to be highly developed in certain people with otherwise severe mental retardation? Savancy tends to be found in abilities (mathematics, music, art) in which folklore is most prone to recognize inborn talents, though the reasons why there are no savant surgeons, for example, are obvious. The 'practice' hypothesis plays down the importance of innate abilities for skill acquisition in people with normal levels of intelligence. If there are no innate abilities, savants must have some sort of 'mental island' in which one ability can develop. However, there is no clear evidence either for or against this hypothesis. A savant's abilities almost always become apparent before any encouragement has been given, but why a particular talent develops (piano playing as opposed to calendar calculating, for example) is not known.

Another vexed question is how much practice a savant must put in to reach a certain level of ability. Indeed, in what sense do idiot savants 'practice' at all? For a long time this question was not addressed sensibly, but it has recently become clear that savants do spend a great deal of time exercising their talents, and have high intrinsic motivation to do so (see, e.g., Sloboda, 1991: pp. 158–60). Indeed, they have fewer distractions than normal people and may, therefore, be able to bypass the ten-year rule. In this respect, the talents of savants and of other skilled performers are similar.

Summary

Games, such as chess, can be analysed using the state-action representations introduced in the previous chapter. An additional complication is that players alternate in their moves. Human chess players work through a small number of possible developments of the game, but chess-playing programs use the power of modern computers to make a more thorough, but less 'intelligent', search of possible upcoming positions. Computers have also been used to analyse chess end-games and have produced results that end-game experts had previously been able to prove.

Experts solve problems in particular domains effectively, but they are often expensive to employ. They draw on a large store of domain-specific knowledge acquired over many years of training, and an ability to appreciate the important, but perhaps hidden, aspects of problems. Expert systems are computer programs that attempt to mimic the abilities of experts. Expert systems have shown excellent performance, particularly in mathematics (MACSYMA), analysis of complex molecules (DENDRAL) and medical diagnosis (MYCIN). However, such programs have taken many years to perfect, and the lessons learned in developing them cannot readily be transferred to other domains. The construction of expert systems might be simpler if each could have access to a large body of everyday knowledge.

Expertise rarely develops without extended practice and encouragement, and the evidence for natural talents is scanty. Idiots savants also devote a great deal of time to their talents, and their existence underlines the selective nature of expertise.

Further Reading

de Groot, A. D. (1965). *Thought and Choice in Chess*. The Hague; Mouton.
Ericsson, K. A. and Smith, J. (eds) (1991). *Toward a General Theory of Expertise: Prospects and Limits*. Cambridge: Cambridge University Press.
Garnham, A. (1988). *Artificial Intelligence: An Introduction*. London: Routledge & Kegan Paul [chapter 7].

Howe, M. J. A. (1989). *Fragments of Genius: The Strange Feats of Idiots Savants*. London: Routledge.

Hsu, F-h., Anantharaman, T., Campbell, M. and Nowatzyk, A. (1990). A grandmaster chess machine. *Scientific American*, 263, 4, pp. 18–24.

13

Creativity

Cognitive scientists, with their focus on what happens in the minds of individuals, are often accused of ignoring social aspects of the phenomena they study. Such criticisms are sometimes based on a misunderstanding of the aims of cognitive science, but in other cases there are genuine problems, which cognitive scientists would do well to acknowledge.

The study of *creativity* is one area in which social considerations impinge on the cognitive scientist's concerns. The reason is that whether a solution to a problem is a creative one, or how creative it is, depends not only on the mental processes of the individual who produces the solution, but also on contextual factors, some of which have little or no direct effect on the thought processes of the problem solver. So, of two identical, or at least very similar, solutions to a problem – ex hypothesi the result of similar mental processes – one may be highly creative and the other hardly creative at all. For this reason alone, it is plausible to argue that the mental processes underlying creative thought are not essentially different from those underlying other kinds of thinking. Furthermore, once a creative solution to one problem has been found, it can be used as a model for solutions to other, similar, problems. These solutions will not be considered as creative as the one on which they were modelled. Creative solutions to problems seem, therefore, to be ones that are difficult to find in particular circumstances, not because they require unusual thought processes, but for some other reason. They may require the synthesis of a large amount of material, and hence something akin to expertise, or they may depend on connecting bodies of knowledge that previously appear unconnected.

These considerations, among others, have suggested that the study of creativity starts from four major foci (e.g., Mooney, 1963; Stein, 1969). The first three foci are creative *people*, the creative *process* and the *products* of creativity. The fourth 'p' is variously identified, either passively, as creative *places* (environments), or more actively as *persuasive* powers of creative people. The latter view (e.g., Simonton, 1984) is based on the observation that, once creative ideas are accepted, they have a profound influence on other people's lives, and that the main way they become accepted is by their creator persuading other people of their importance.

Before discussing these four ways of studying creativity, we will mention another general issue. Talk of creative *solutions* to *problems* is more obviously applicable in mathematics and science than in the arts and humanities. However, this appearance is misleading, and perhaps reflects the fact that Western society has been too greatly influenced by the romantic notion of creativity in the arts – of artists simply expressing themselves. Probably the majority of art objects are produced to fulfil certain goals. Many are commissioned, and their functions (for a piece of decorative art, perhaps simply what it is to 'decorate') are specified by the person or body commissioning them. The artist's problem is how to satisfy the goals set by the commission, together with the constraints set by the particular art form. The principal difference between the arts and the sciences lies not in their notions of creativity, but in those of cumulative knowledge and progress. There may be other differences between creativity in the arts and in the sciences. Indeed, it is an empirical question, which psychologists might address, whether there are essential differences between create processes in these two realms. However, *some* of the apparent differences are only apparent.

13.1   Approaches to the Study of Creativity

The four foci from which research on creativity starts (the four *p*'s) suggest different empirical approaches to the study of creativity. The first two approaches we will consider – the psychometric approach and the (auto)biographical approach – have as their starting point a focus on creative people. To the extent that the psychometric approach also attempts to *predict* creative achievement, it must also identify the products of creativity. The biographical approach almost inevitably considers the products of creativity, the environments in which they arose, and how persuasive their creators were in getting them recognized. In a broad sense, the biographical approach also describes the creative process. However, only the information processing approach considers in detail the mental processes that contribute to creativity.

13.1.1   The psychometric approach

One of the crucial questions about creativity is: what makes a person (in a particular environment) creative – what distinguishes people who produce creative solutions to problems from people who do not? This question is not readily studied within the information processing framework that has informed most of our discussion in chapters 4 to 7. As we saw in the previous chapter, a similar question can be asked about expertise – what distinguishes experts from novices? In that case an answer in information processing terms was appropriate. There *is* a close connection between creativity and expertise, but when we ask why one person is creative and another not, we generally assume that both have the relevant training. Creativity almost always depends on the sort of familiarity with a subject area that constitutes expertise. However, much of the thinking of experts, though it is beyond the powers of the untrained, is not creative in the sense in which we are using that term.

One type of psychometric study of creativity – one that was particularly, important in the 1950s and the early 1960s – tried to answer systematically the question of what creative people are like, in the sense of what other personal characteristics they have. Although there is room for the question 'what are creative people like?' in the study of creativity, this kind of psychometric analysis does not address the questions that are most important in the context of this book: how do creative people think, and how do their thought process differ from those of other people? What they do is to sketch out a stereotype of a moderately creative individual. We will, therefore, summarize their findings only briefly.

In these studies the products of creativity are important only indirectly in that they are used to identify creative individuals, to whom a batch of psychometric tests can then be administered. For example, Roe (1952) examined North American scientists who were deemed creative by their peers. She found that the typical scientist was the first-born son of WASP (white Anglo-Saxon Protestant) parents, who had been isolated at school, married late, and worked long hours – often seven days a week, with little time off. He was intelligent, and introverted but self-sufficient. There were minor differences among the groups of physical, biological and social scientists, with the social scientists being more extrovert, more aggressive and more prone to get divorced. Much the same profile emerged from Cattell and Drevdahl's (1955) study of scientists, and from Drevdahl and Cattell's (1958) consideration of artists and writers. Not surprisingly, the artists were found to be more sensitive, and to have more inner tension, than the scientists.

Subsequent research has suggested a wide variety of cognitive characteristics, personality traits and motivational qualities that are common among creative people (see Tardif and Sternberg, 1988: pp. 433–7). One of the most important cognitive characteristics that distinguishes highly creative from other highly intelligent people is the ability to find appropriate problems (Getzels and Csikszentmihalyi, 1976). The ability to defer judgement on possible solutions is also important (MacKinnon, 1962). Personal traits that are common among creative people include a desire for originality, failure to conform to social pressure (one aspect of Roe's self-sufficiency) and tolerance of ambiguity (during the often lengthy period before a new idea reaches its final form). Sternberg (1988) argues that creative thinkers are distinguished by their form of *mental self-government*. They prefer a legislative (rule creating), rather than an executive (rule following) or judicial (rule assessing) style. Since the manner of directing one's intelligence is as important as the intelligence itself in determining creative ability, high IQ is not itself sufficient for creativity. However, since the legislative style of mental self-government is defined, at least in part, in terms of the desire to create, Sternberg's claims are dangerously close to being circular. On the motivational side, deep commitment is almost always essential, not least because it is needed to acquire sufficient domain-specific knowledge.

The studies described so far aimed to produce a psychometric profile of creative people. A more obvious goal for psychometricians would be to produce a test of creative potential, and, indeed, many of them have tried to do so. Inevitably, the production of tests of creativity has been closely bound up with questions about the difference between intelligence, as measured by IQ tests, and creativity. Psychometric profiles show that creative people tend to have high IQs, but not all people with high IQs are creative. What differentiates those that are from those that are not? Can a psychometric test be devised to distinguish the two groups? Much of the impetus for research into these questions, which was carried out mainly in the United States, was provided by the Russians' launching of the first satellite, Sputnik. The Americans wondered if they had lost this first 'space race' because they were failing to discover their best (i.e., most creative) minds and to direct them into appropriate research.

One hypothesis about the difference between IQ and creativity derives from the work of Guilford, whose 1950 presidential address to the American Psychological Association is widely cited as the starting point for modern work on creativity. In the context of his general theory of the intellect, Guilford (e.g., 1956, 1967, 1986) distinguished between *convergent* and *divergent* productions. In convergent thinking, which is the kind of thinking needed to answer most items in IQ tests, the thinker is expected to converge on the correct or best answer to a problem. Divergent thinking, on the other hand, can lead to many possible solutions to the same problem. It requires both originality and flexibility. Guilford's evidence for divergent thinking was only partly empirical, though both Guilford himself and subsequent researchers (e.g., Hudson, 1966) have shown that divergent thinking can be reasonably easily identified. However, its relation to creativity and other types of achievement have been harder to establish. If divergent thinking *is* important, that fact has far-reaching consequences for social issues, such as education policy. Those who championed divergent thinking argued against rote learning and the use of IQ tests in schools, for example.

Many attempts to create psychometric tests of creativity sprang directly or indirectly from Guilford's ideas. However, the results of this work have been disappointing. It is relatively easy to produce creativity tests with face validity – tests that appear to measure divergent or creative thinking. A simple example is the 'uses of a brick' test, in which people are asked to write down as many uses as they can think of for an ordinary building brick. Divergent thinkers would be expected to think up more, and more unusual, uses than convergent thinkers. However, when such tests are assessed in terms of their construct validity – whether they really measured creativity – the results are mixed. The early tests tended to fall into two classes. Either scores on these tests did not correlate with independent assessments of creativity, such as peer reports or amount and quality of work produced, or they did so only because they correlated strongly with IQ tests, which, as we have already mentioned, are weakly related to creativity. Later tests produced somewhat better results, but predictive success remains comparatively modest.

Early work on creativity tests by Getzels and Jackson (1962) showed that groups of bright adolescents could be found who scored relatively high on IQ tests and relatively low on tests such as Guilford's uses of a brick, or vice versa. The two groups did not differ in scholastic achievement. However, not only did Getzels and Jackson fail to validate their 'creativity tests', they also failed to show that either IQ or 'creativity' predicted scholastic achievement, because they did not check the performance of individuals who scored high or low on both tests. Subsequent work with similar tests, in particular the Torrance Tests of Creative Thinking (TTCT; Torrance, 1966), has shown that tests can be produced that correlate moderately well later measures of creative achievement, with some correlations in the range 0.4 to 0.6 (see Torrance, 1988, for a summary). A different type of test, the Symbol Equivalence Test (see Barron, 1988), has also been validated in studies of creative people from a wide range of professions. In this test people have to produce metaphors ('symbolically equivalent images') for images described to them verbally (e.g., 'leaves being blown in the wind'). Responses are scored for both acceptability and originality (defined in terms of how many other people produce the response).

13.1.2 Biographical and autobiographical approaches

A more interesting, if less tractable, approach to the question of what creative people are like is via biography and, more particularly, autobiography (we will use the term 'biography' to cover both). One important difference between the biographical and the psychometric approaches is that biographical material is most readily available for people whose creative ability is highly developed. Psychometric studies, particularly those that aim to produce tests of creativity, need to include a large number of people, and are forced to focus on those who are only relatively creative. The biographical literature, insofar as one can interpret it, given its age, suggests that IQ and creativity are not closely related. What it certainly shows is that creativity and ordinary scholastic achievement are not linked. Creative people often fail to be inspired by traditional schooling, and only shine once they are able to use their imagination for their own purposes. Einstein, for example, was late in learning to read, and had only a moderate school record. Ramanujan, the Indian mathematician, was so absorbed in mathematics that he failed examinations in most of his other college subjects. This conclusion is consistent with a finding from the psychometric approach to human abilities. Above what Hudson refers to as 'a surprisingly low level' (1987: p. 171), IQ and achievement of any kind are not related. For this reason alone, it is not surprising that creativity tests that correlate highly with IQ are impossible to validate.

The starting point for a biography is the life of a creative person. The biography provides information about that person in a less systematically, but usually more interesting, form than a psychometric study. It also provides information about environments that are conducive to creativity, about the products of creativity, and, in an unsystematic way, of some of the thought processes of its subject. Such accounts have to be interpreted carefully. Even in an autobiography they are either introspective or retrospective or both. They may be partly or wholly distorted to produce a particular impression, and, even if the writer is aware of the importance of unconscious processes, they can only be described indirectly. A telling analysis of distortion in autobiographical accounts of creativity is given by Perkins (1981, chapter 1). He compares two very different descriptions of the writing of a poem. The first is Samuel Taylor Coleridge's well-known account of how 'Kubla Kahn' ('In Xanadu did Kubla Kahn a stately pleasure dome decree . . .') came to him in a dream, and of how his writing down of it was fatally interrupted by a man on business from Porlock. The second is Edgar Allan Poe's analytic account of how he composed 'The Raven'. Perkins shows how independent evidence, which has subsequently come to light, shows that Coleridge's poem was not entirely the result of inspiration from a source beyond his control, and that Poe was not so free from non-analytic influences as he claimed. Despite such problems, the study of biography has led to some useful ideas about creativity. In particular, Wallas (1926) suggested a four-stage account of creative thinking, based largely on his study of autobiographical material.

According to Wallas (1926) the four stages of creative thinking are *preparation, incubation, inspiration* and *verification*. In the preparation stage, which may be prolonged, particularly in cases of profound creativity, the requisite background information is absorbed. Attempts to solve the problem may be frustrating and appear fruitless. In the incubation stage the problem is set aside, for whatever reason. It is not consciously thought about, and the problem solver typically engages in some unrelated activity. Wallas attempted to determine the best activity for this period and decided it was mental rest, together with light physical exercise. He thought that reading was inadvisable. Inspiration is when the solution first presents itself. It may come in a flash of insight but, more often, the thinker has an intimation that a solution is about to emerge. Wallas believed that creative thinkers should try to develop a sensitivity to this intimation, and avoid distractions until the inspiration came. Finally, the solution must be verified, to see that it works. This idea can be illustrated with the example of a mathematical proof. A mathematician may, at the point of inspiration, have the idea that will solve the problem, but in the verification stage he or she must develop the detailed proof, based on this idea, and show that it does indeed solve the problem. In formulating his ideas about incubation and inspiration, Wallas was particularly influenced by the autobiographical writings of the German physiologist and physicist Hermann von Helmholtz (1821–94) and the French mathematician Henri Poincaré (1854–1912). Helmholtz described the way 'happy ideas come unexpectedly, without effort, like an inspiration' and Poincaré wrote of two mathematical discoveries in which the solution came 'with the same characteristics of conciseness, suddenness and immediate certainty' (Wallas, 1926: pp. 79–80). Poincaré was convinced that unconscious mental activity, similar to conscious problem solving, took place in the incubation period that preceded insight, and other mathematicians have agreed with him. A particularly clear statement of his idea is found in the writings of G. H. Hardy, in a review of *The Psychology of Invention in the Mathematical Field* by the mathematician Jacques Hadamard (1949). Hardy is widely regarded as the most important British mathematician of the first half of the twentieth century. Hadamard is best known for his proof of the prime number theory, an important result in number theory, which provides a general formula for estimating the number of prime numbers in the first n numbers. (Although prime numbers are not scattered uniformly among other numbers, the formula becomes more and more accurate for larger and larger numbers.) Hardy wrote:

> unconscious activity often plays a decisive part in discovery; that periods of ineffective effort are often followed, after intervals of rest or distraction, by moments of sudden illumination; that these flashes of inspiration are explicable only as the result of activities of which the agent has been unaware – the evidence for all this seems overwhelming. (1979: p. 835)

The above description of Wallas's stage theory might suggest that the stages are separate, with one following another. This interpretation is not supported by the biographical data, and was not intended by Wallas, who noted that not only can two stages overlap, but that an earlier stage may be revisited during the solution of a particular problem. This interpretation of the stage theory makes it descriptively more adequate, but it detracts from its predictive power, rendering it difficult, for example, to form any clear prediction about the time course of a particular piece of creative thinking.

Although Wallas's four-stage theory was based primarily on his study of biographical material, there is a small amount of experimental evidence for the different stages of the creative process. In two studies by Patrick (1935, 1937) subjects were asked either to produce a poem in response to a painting, or a painting in response to a poem. While they were carrying out their task they were asked to think out loud, and their thoughts were noted down. In each case some of the subjects were skilled in the response medium and others were not. Patrick claims that the results of her studies are in broad agreement with Wallas's theory, though the evidence is indirect. *Thought changes*, which tended to occur towards the beginning of the session, were taken to indicate preparation. The first time that the form of the solution emerged was identified with inspiration, and subsequent revisions of the form with verification. Given the nature of the studies, and the comparatively small amount of time allowed to each subject, incubation was somewhat harder to detect, though ideas were often suggested, set aside, and taken up again later. In a subsequent interview, most of the expert subjects indicated that the setting aside of problems was part of their normal working practice. However, the setting aside of a problem is only one aspect of what Wallas meant by incubation. Patrick's studies provided no evidence for unconscious mental activity during the period in which a problem was set aside. One final, and interesting, aspect of the data was that, except in the quality of their output, there were no differences between the skilled and unskilled groups of subjects.

The weakest part of Patrick's experimental evidence was for Wallas's second stage – incubation. Not only was there little time for incubation in these studies, there was no setting aside of the problem, as described by Helmholtz, Poincaré and Wallas. A later study (Murray and Denny, 1969) attempted to provide clearer experimental evidence for this stage. In this study subjects were initially divided into two groups, high and low problem-solving ability, on the basis of a 'uses of objects' test. All the subjects were then given twenty minutes to work on a more difficult problem, devised by Gestalt psychologists, about transferring metal balls to a distant container. Half of the subjects worked solidly for twenty minutes on the problem; the other half spent five minutes on an unrelated task after the first five minutes on the experimental problem. The five minutes on the unrelated task was intended to model the incubation period. The low ability subjects, but not those of high ability, were helped by this opportunity for 'incubation'. If anything, the high ability subjects were hindered. In order to explain this result, Murray and Denny suggested that incubation is only useful for problems that a person finds hard. For the high ability subjects, for whom the experimental problem proved comparatively simple, the distractor task was just that – a distraction from a job that they were working on steadily. Murray and Denny's explanation of their results is intuitively plausible. The biographical accounts that led Wallas to formulate his concept of incubation describe people solving problems that they find difficult.

Nevertheless, more so than in many psychological studies, the gap between the experimental task and the phenomenon of interest seems particularly wide in these studies of incubation. Furthermore, the studies that have been carried out appear incapable of answering the question: what happens during the period of incubation?

Perkins (1981: p. 50ff.) points out that autobiographical claims about the usefulness of setting problems aside cannot necessarily be taken at face value. In most cases, there is no way of telling how quickly the autobiographer would have solved the problem if it had not been set aside – hence the importance of experimental studies such as that of Murray and Denny. Furthermore, Perkins notes that the occurrence of incubation may be exaggerated. People may think about problems that are important to them at odd moments, when they are ostensibly working on something different. Such problems have not really been set aside. In addition, even if incubation does occur, which is a reasonable assumption given the many autobiographical accounts, its mere existence must be distinguished from claims about the mechanism by which it produces its effect. Is there really unconscious problem solving – complex combinations and recombinations of ideas, as Poincaré suggested – or merely 'physical refreshment, fruitful forgetting, losing commitment to an ineffective approach, and noticing clues in the environment' (Perkins, 1981: p. 57)? Perkins's suggestions are more parsimonious that the notion of unconscious problem solving, and they should not be dismissed without strong evidence.

The notion of combination and recombination is important in the study of creativity regardless of whether such processes happen in incubation. Many authors have emphasized that creative thought processes bring together elements that were previously unconnected in the thinker's mind, though whether in a way that is qualitatively or merely quantitatively different from what happens in more mundane kinds of problem solving is a moot question. Mednick's (1962) notion of *remote association* sees a connection between creativity and the linking of individual ideas. Koestler (1964) holds that it is previously unrelated 'frames of reference' that must be brought together.

However, as Perkins (1981), among others, has pointed out, creative solutions to problems almost inevitably bring together ideas that were previously unrelated. Any *explanation* of creative processes has to do more than simply say that unrelated ideas have been united. There are at least two main problems with associative theories. The first is that they do not provide an account of the mechanism that combines the unrelated ideas to form a creative solution to a problem. Association itself can only juxtapose the ideas. It is not powerful enough do the work assigned to it. Koestler, for example, implies that there may be many mechanisms at work, without attempting to describe them.

The second problem is related to the first. Not every association between remote ideas or remote frameworks leads to creative solutions to new problems. People have enormous numbers of ideas in their minds, and there are even more possible combinations of these ideas. How can associative theories explain which combinations lead to creative solutions to problems? Not only is it implausible that all combinations are tried, it is almost certainly impossible in any practical sense. In any case, there are strong constraints both on how ideas can usefully be recombined, and on which combinations are likely to be fruitful. In solving a mathematics problem, for example, one cannot go against firmly established mathematical results. Indeed, many of the constraints on creative solutions to problems are specific to the domain in which the creative person is working. Hence the importance of expertise for problem solving. Furthermore, in many cases we cannot state precisely what these constraints are. What, for example, distinguishes a good novel from a bad one? However, adhering to constraints is at least partly what differentiates the creative from the unsuccessful or the merely eccentric. Anyone can bring together ideas that have never been juxtaposed before, but most such combinations will be worthless. This idea underlies a common definition of creativity – that it leads to products that are both *novel* and *valuable*. On this view one kind of lack of success arises from the recognition, at the verification stage, that a new juxtaposition of ideas is worthless, while one form of eccentricity would be failing to recognize its worthlessness.

The vast number of possible outcomes of associative processes underlines the importance of verification in the creative process. Indeed, many people who consider themselves 'unrecognized geniuses' have not properly determined whether their ideas work. Nevertheless, individuals are occasionally found who are highly creative, yet who do not properly verify their results. One example is the Indian mathematician Ramanujan, of whom J. E. Littlewood (1953: p. 88), the English mathematician and colleague of Hardy, wrote 'the clear cut idea of what is *meant* by proof . . . he perhaps did not possess at all'. Many of Ramanujan's theorems, which were for the most part correct, took other mathematicians a great deal of time to prove. However, Ramanujan's methods must be interpreted carefully, for two reasons. First, he certainly engaged in activities designed to satisfy himself that his theorems were true, though he was never able to impart his methods to other mathematicians. Second, much of what, in the history of mathematics, has passed for mathematical proof has turned out to be wanting in certain respects.

Indeed, Ramanujan's champion Hardy was largely responsible for introducing rigorous proofs into British mathematics, and his work followed that of European mathematicians only a few decades earlier.

The discussion so far shows that Wallas's four-stage theory is useful in thinking about creativity, However, it is not without its critics. Perkins, for example, (1981: pp. 184–5) suggests that Wallas's account is strongly biased by the particular biographical accounts on which he relied. For example, in addition to delaying its publication for fear about its reception, Charles Darwin took a long time to formulate his theory of the origin of species. In a detailed study of Darwin, Gruber (1981) stresses the cumulative nature of Darwin's achievements. He also claims that Darwin's own most famous insight – his realization on reading Malthus's *Essay on the Principle of Population* that natural selection could act positively to favour certain characteristics as well as negatively to eliminate unfavoured characteristics – gained most of its importance in retrospect, and is not singled out in Darwin's notebooks from other insights that proved ultimately less important. Perkins suggests that Getzels and Csikszentmihalyi's (1976) notion of problem finding, mentioned above, is a more likely candidate for a universal characteristic of creative endeavours. Getzels and Csikszentmihalyi asked art students to select objects for a still-life picture, and then to execute that picture. Students who spent more time handling and selecting the material, both before and after starting to paint, and who chose more unusual objects, produced pictures that were judged more highly. Furthermore, those students had achieved greater professional success seven years later. Creativity, therefore, emerges when the possibilities are not narrowed down too much too soon. This idea is related to the notion of tolerance of ambiguity, which emerged from the psychometric approach to creativity, discussed above.

13.1.3 Environments for creativity

Some environments encourage creative thinking – particularly those in which individuals see themselves as self-motivated rather than working to fulfil externally set goals (Amabile, 1983). However, there is another sense in which environment is important to creativity. As we mentioned at the beginning of this chapter, environmental factors are important in defining what counts as creative. Although we will consider, in the next section, the cognitive processes that underlie creative achievement, a purely cognitive account of creativity is not possible, since the status of a product as creative, or otherwise, depends on the environment in which it was created. Csikszentmihalyi (1988) argues that three main forces shape creative achievement: the creative individual, a social field that determines which new ideas are worth retaining, and a stable cultural domain that can preserve ideas selected by the field. And as Csikszentmihalyi reminds us with examples from the history of art, ideas about what is (or, rather, was) creative can be revised long after the artist is dead. Botticelli's late fifteenth-century paintings have been more highly valued since their reassessment by Ruskin and other mid-nineteenth-century art critics. Csikszentmihalyi likens the work of the social field to that of natural selection in the theory of evolution. This idea explains why the behaviour that Getzels and Csikszentmihalyi call problem finding is important. Probem finding produces more, and more extreme, variations from current norms for the field to operate on.

Perkins (1988) has also suggested an account of creativity based on the analogy with evolution. Perkins's notions of generation, selection and preservation map readily onto Csikszentmihalyi's notions of creative persons, who generate ideas, the social field, which selects ideas, and the social domain, which allows them to be preserved. Both Perkins and Csikszentmihalyi recognize that the evolution of ideas proceeds differently from the evolution of animals and plants. Both refer to Richard Dawkins's (1976) concept of a *meme* as a unit of cultural evolution, though memes are not restricted to creative ideas and they are supposed, to some extent, to have a life of their own (see also Dennett, 1991).

13.1.4   Creative processes

The predominant contemporary view of the cognitive processes underlying creativity is that they do not differ in kind from those in other kinds of thinking (e.g., Perkins, 1981; Weisberg, 1988). A more specific version of this claim is that Newell and Simon's (1972) account of problem solving (see chapter 11) can be used to analyse the cognitive aspects of creativity. Simon himself suggested this idea in the 1960s (e.g., Simon, 1966). However, as we saw in chapter 12, later accounts of problem solving emphasize the role of memory and of domain-specific knowledge. These ideas are incorporated in a suite of computer programs, written by Simon and his colleagues (Langley, Simon, Bradshaw and Zytkow, 1987), that model scientific creativity. The programs are collectively known as BACON (after Sir Francis Bacon; see chapter 7). The main BACON program derives quantitative laws, such as laws of planetary motion, by numerical induction from raw data, using mathematical constraints on what would count as a plausible scientific law. Other programs in the suite model qualitative reasoning. For example, the program DALTON, which models the thinking of the chemist John Dalton (1766–1844), assumes an early version of the atomic theory of matter, and works out structures for molecules, based on information about chemical reactions. To understand creativity, it is essential to model the cognitive processes that lead to creative products. However, as we have already argued, it is unlikely that the nature of these processes is constitutive of creativity.

Johnson-Laird (1988) takes a somewhat different view of these cognitive processes from Simon, though he also focuses on what happens in the minds of individuals. Although Johnson-Laird allows that social factors are important in creativity, for example, in defining constraints on a genre in the arts, he argues that their effects must be mediated by the mind of the individual creator. Thus, whereas Csikszentmihalyi emphasizes the difference between a picture by Rembrandt and a forged copy of it, Johnson-Laird stresses that two independent (and usually roughly contemporary) discoveries of the same thing (e.g., Newton's and Leibniz's discovery of calculus) can both count as creative. The dispute is partly one about what psychologists, or cognitive scientists, can legitimately study when they investigate creativity. Since what it creative is determined partly by what happens in minds other than the creator's, and often in ways that cannot possibly impinge on the creator's thought processes, a purely cognitive approach, while essential, cannot distinguish the creative from the non-creative.

Is it possible to say anything about the mental processes that underlie creativity from a cognitive viewpoint? We will consider two attempts, those of Johnson-Laird (1988) and of Boden (1990).

13.1.4.a *Johnson-Laird's working definition of creativity*
Johnson-Laird suggests the following working definition of creativity:

1 The results of a creative process must be new, at least for the creative person, though they are produced from existing elements.
2 The results must not be produced by recall from memory, rote computation or any other simple deterministic process.
3 The results must satisfy a set of criteria.

Johnson-Laird (1993) further suggests that creativity should be distinguished from induction (see chapter 7). According to Johnson-Laird, an induction increases the semantic information in the premises on which it is based. A creative solution to a problem overlaps in semantic information with the premises from which it is derived.

Johnson-Laird claims that it is possible to remain agnostic about the source of non-determinism in creative thinking. One possibility is that creative processes appear non-deterministic at the level of analysis appropriate to a theory of creativity merely because of our ignorance of what causes people to make the choices they do. Another is that the human mind has a facility for making genuinely arbitrary choices. A third, rather far-fetched, possibility is that the non-determinism arises from quantum-level processes (an idea first suggested by the English physicist Arthur Eddington, 1882–1944, and recently revisited by Roger Penrose, 1989).

On the assumption that a computational account of creativity is possible, Johnson-Laird considers the kinds of algorithm that might underlie creative processes. Like Perkins and Csikszentmihalyi he draws on ideas from evolutionary theory, and suggests that there are three possible classes of algorithm: neo-Darwinian, neo-Lamarckian, and mixed. A neo-Darwinian algorithm combines old elements in a random way, thus introducing the element of indeterminism. The results of the combinations are then subjected to a selection process in which only the viable (or promising) combinations are retained. As in natural selection, many iterations of this procedure may be needed before a combination that is really creative emerges. In a neo-Lamarckian algorithm, the initial stage in which old elements are combined is not random, but is subject to appropriate constraints. If several viable combinations emerge, there may be a random process of selection among them at a second stage to introduce an element of indeterminism. If the constraints at the first stage are strong enough, no iteration is required. A mixed algorithm combines neo-Darwinian and neo-Lamarckian aspects.

Johnson-Laird has analysed two aspects of jazz improvization within this framework: the creation of chord sequences, and the creation of bass lines. Chord sequences are not constructed during a live performance, but are composed and developed in rehearsals, often over a lengthy period of time. They may be written down in a standard notation, and explicitly discussed. Jazz musicians typically have conscious knowledge of the chord sequences they use. Johnson-Laird has shown that, contrary to the intuitions of jazz musicologists, chord sequences require comparatively complex descriptions, using grammars of the kind that are needed to analyse the sentences of natural languages, such as English. If jazz musicians did attempt to create new sequences as they played, they would place a high computational load on their working memories.

Bass lines, on the other hand, which are improvised, can be produced using machinery that embodies only very simple grammars. Indeed, Johnson-Laird has written programs that generate reasonably acceptable bass lines using the simplest kind of grammar (regular grammar) that is capable of generating indefinitely many different sequences from a finite set of elements. The procedures used by Johnson-Laird make no use of working memory, but rely wholly on grammatical 'rules' stored in long-term memory. This is just as well, as they have to be run in real time during a performance. The fact that working memory is not used suggests that jazz musicians would have no conscious access to the processes they use to construct bass lines (see chapter 1). Jazz musicians do talk a great deal about how they improvise. However, their comments do not, according to Johnson-Laird, indicate they have access to the processes that underlie their ability. Furthermore, just as speakers of natural languages have no conscious access to the processes used in producing and comprehending utterances of the languages they know, jazz musicians do not know how they improvise bass lines.

Thus, the two aspects of creativity in jazz improvisation studied by Johnson-Laird have different properties. The 'off-line' process of constructing chord sequences depends on a mixed algorithm, in which weak constraints allow a large number of possible sequences. The possibilities then have to be narrowed down by neo-Darwinian processes. The 'on-line' process of constructing bass lines uses a neo-Lamarckian algorithm, in which the 'grammatical' rules allow just a few choices of note at each point, among which an arbitrary decision is made immediately. Both algorithms incorporate constraints: on what makes an acceptable chord sequence or bass line. Jazz musicians absorb such constraints from their musical experience. Johnson-Laird's programs show how such constraints can be modelled and satisfied in the production of creative outputs.

Johnson-Laird's work on jazz focuses on *creativity within a genre*, but the grammars and selection algorithms provide no account of what makes one chord sequence or bass line better than another. What the grammars provide is a description of the rules that jazz musicians know, either implicitly in the case of bass lines, or probably explicitly in the case of chord sequences, when they are able to improvise a certain type of jazz. In other words, Johnson-Laird's account is really an account of jazz musicians' expertise – what they have to know if they are to have the possibility of being creative. Perhaps that is all that cognitive psychology can provide, since, as we have already argued, other factors determine what actually counts as creative.

13.1.4.b   *Boden's impossibility theory*

Boden (1990) suggests that an idea is creative (for a particular person) if that person *could not* have had that idea before. It is historically creative if no one could have had the idea before. The 'could not' is defined in terms of what the person's mental representations and processes allow. So creativity always requires some mental restructuring. This restructing can take various forms, but it must be defined in computational terms. For example, a creative solution to a problem might require a complete restructuring of the problem space, or the devising of a new technique (a heuristic) for directing the search for the solution to a particular part of the space. Like Johnson-Laird, Boden stresses the role of constraints in distinguishing creativity from eccentricity and other less useful types of novelty. She also recognizes the role of chance in creativity. On Boden's view, some of the constraints on what counts as creative are provided by usurped ideas and methods of solving problems. In science, with its accumulation of knowledge, new ideas have to explain many of the same facts as old ones. In the arts, a new style of painting, for example, gains much of its point from its contrast with preceding styles. Furthermore, it is only possible to tell that someone could not have had a particular thought before, given an account of the sort of thoughts they could have. Something cannot be recognized as creative, on this view, except by people who know about previous ways of doing things. Creativity can only be assessed in a historical context.

Despite her claims to the contrary, Boden's account applies more obviously to creativity in the sciences than to creativity in the arts. On Boden's view, the creation of a new genre would be the most creative thing an artist could do, since it requires the most radical restructuring. However, this idea does not accord with the facts. For example, as Truscott (1966) shows, the origins of the symphony are lost in history, and probably depend on a series of innovations by composers who are now forgotten. What we prize in symphonic music is not the original development of the symphonic form, but what was achieved within that form by Haydn, Mozart, Beethoven, Schubert, Brahms, Bruckner, Mahler and the rest. Although each of these composers made important formal innovations, those innovations are not necessarily what we value most, or regard as most creative, in their music. Similarly, the creativity of the impressionist painters lies not so much in their invention of a technique, but in the use to which they put it. Works of art should not just be novel, they should appeal to us. In science, matters are different. The restructuring of concepts of space, time and gravity that constitute Einstein's general theory of relativity *is* the crucial creative step, always provided that the theory survives its verification. Science does not have the equivalent of artistic genres, within which the earliest work cannot necessarily assume pride of place.

Summary

Cognitive scientists focus on processes in the minds of individuals. However, a full account of creative thinking may have to make reference to social factors, some of which may not impinge on the mind of the creative individual. Psychologists have taken many approaches to the study of creativity. Psychometricians have administered batches of established psychometric tests to creative people, in an attempt to discover what they are like. They have also tried to devise tests of creativity, and in particular of the *divergent* type of thinking originally identified by Guilford as important for creativity.

Another approach focuses on biographic and, more especially, autobiographic accounts of creativity. Using such material, Wallas identified four stages in the creative process: preparation, incubation, inspiration and verification. These stages can, to some extent, be reproduced in the laboratory, though the proper interpretation of the incubation stage is controversial. There is, however, no reliable evidence that unconscious problem solving takes place in this stage.

The environment in which ideas are put forward and assessed also determines whether they are regarded as creative, or how creative they are taken to be. Csikszentmihalyi and Perkins have both used analogies based on Darwin's theory of natural selection in their account of how ideas are determined to be creative.

Johnson-Laird, in his account of creative *processes*, also uses evolutionary ideas to explain how creative ideas are put together in an individual's mind. He has applied these ideas, in different ways, to the composition of both chord sequences and bass lines in jazz. Boden has suggested that creativity depends on having ideas that could not be had before, given the available mental machinery.

Further Reading

Boden, M. A. (1990). *The Creative Mind: Myths and Mechanisms*. London: Weidenfeld & Nicolson.

Johnson-Laird, P. N. (1993). *Human and Machine Thinking*. Hillsdale, NJ: Lawrence Erlbaum Associates, chapter 3.

Perkins, D. N. (1981). *The Mind's Best Work*. Cambridge, MA: Harvard University Press.

Sternberg, R. J. (ed.) (1988). *The Nature of Creativity: Contemporary Psychological Perspectives*. Cambridge: Cambridge University Press.

14

Everyday Reasoning

In previous chapters we have presented ideas about thinking that are derived primarily from experimental work in laboratory settings. As we have emphasized, this work focuses on well-defined problems. Partly for this reason, its relevance to understanding reasoning in everyday life has been questioned – many everyday problems are not well defined. In this chapter we discuss two kinds of research on more naturalistic reasoning. First, we look at people's ability to reason about problems in the real world, but ones that they personally are unlikely to have to solve – such as how to reduce the level of unemployment or whether to subsidize ballet. Second, we describe how people solve practical problems in their everyday lives, primarily arithmetical problems that arise in the course of their work.

14.1 Everyday Reasoning and Formal Reasoning

Reasoning has great practical significance – in everyday life we draw numerous conclusions, and make numerous decisions, about matters both trivial and important. For example, many aspects of everyday reasoning (and scientific reasoning) are based on induction (see chapter 7) which, as we have seen, is by no means infallible. A major disaster that occurred, at least in part, through faulty inductions was the capsize of the roll-on roll-off car ferry the Herald of Free Enterprise, just outside the Belgian port of Zeebrugge, in 1987. One hundred and eighty-eight people were drowned. This disaster, like many, did not have a single cause. There were many contributory factors, such as the ship leaving harbour in a rush, and having too much ballast on board, which made it low in the water. However, the accident would probably have been avoided if the bow doors had been shut, because they would have largely prevented the water from entering the ship. At the time the ship left Zeebrugge, the assistant bosun, whose job it was to close the bow doors, was asleep and he had not closed them. The captain of the ship, the chief officer and the bosun all made the plausible (inductive) assumption that the bow doors were shut, because in their past experience the doors had been shut under such circumstances. The bosun, in fact, admitted noticing that they were open, but it was not his job to close them so he assumed (again inductively) that the assistant bosun would do so, with terrible consequences.

Most everyday reasoning is different, at least in some respects, from the sorts of reasoning we have discussed in the preceding chapters. Galotti (1989) distinguishes between *formal reasoning*, in which all the information needed (though not necessarily all of the information actually used) is set out explicitly, so that the problem is well defined, and *informal reasoning*, in which the problem is ill defined, at least to some degree. On this view, formal reasoning includes analogical problem solving (see chapter 11), three-term series problems (see chapter 5) and syllogisms (see chapter 6). Informal reasoning includes planning, evaluating arguments and choosing between options.

We have seen in the preceding chapters that, when people act as subjects in reasoning experiments, they often make errors on apparently simple problems. These errors are typically most serious when the problems are purely formal, and it is often assumed that, although people perform poorly on formal reasoning tasks, they manage better in 'everyday' reasoning. This assumption can be based either on the observation that most people 'get by' in the real world or, more generally, on the inference that evolution has fitted people (and other animals) to solve the kinds of problems with which their normal environment presents them. However, neither version of this argument is compelling. People may 'get by' despite their mistakes. Indeed, if people in general are poor reasoners, making errors may be the norm. And modern Western culture bears little resemblance to the environment in which people evolved. Informationally, for example, it is more complex.

Since few psychologists regard the study of reasoning in the laboratory as an end in itself, but rather as a useful way of studying reasoning in a controlled environment, the question arises as to how formal and everyday reasoning skills are linked. There are, of course, parallels that obtain simply because both are species of reasoning. For example, in both formal and informal arguments, reasoners should take care to avoid contradictory premises, avoid fallacies and draw reasonable conclusions. Formal deductive reasoning offers a framework within which informal reasoning can be characterized, and indeed Aristotle's intention in developing the theory of the syllogism was to formalize everyday arguments (see chapter 4). However, many recent authors have stressed the differences between formal and everyday reasoning.

Galotti (1989) presents three possible views of the relation between formal and everyday reasoning. The first is that all or most of everyday reasoning is formal reasoning in disguise: syllogisms, for example, can appear implicitly, or even explicitly, in prose. On this view, everyday reasoning will typically be *more difficult* than formal reasoning. It requires extra work: the premises have to be generated and evaluated, and any emotional or belief biases attached to premises or conclusions have to be overcome. If this view is correct, training in formal reasoning ought to improve reasoning generally (it typically does not). A second view is that formal and everyday reasoning share some processes, but that formal reasoning is harder because it requires an objective, analytic stance, which ignores everyday knowledge and biases and which must hold to a standard of logical necessity, rather than being guided by what is pragmatically feasible. The third view is that the two sorts of reasoning make use of different processes, and have little in common. One proponent of this third view is Perkins (1985). He argues that there are a number of important differences between formal and informal reasoning. If he is right, skill in formal reasoning tasks need not be related to reasoning skills more generally, and training in formal reasoning would not necessarily improve everyday reasoning skills.

Perkins identifies three main differences between formal and everyday reasoning, though he takes a narrow view of formal reasoning on which, for example, probabilities have no place. First, in formal reasoning, the premises are given, and cannot be modified, added to or discarded. In informal reasoning, the premises can be revised or supplemented as further relevant information is presented, or comes to mind. Second, a formal reasoning problem leads to a single conclusion. Counter-arguments, which Perkins refers to as *other-side arguments*, are irrelevant. Only from inconsistent premises can deductive arguments lead to opposing conclusions. If the premises of a deductive argument are true, and the reasoning is valid, the conclusion must be true (see chapter 4). Informal reasoning, by contrast, has a 'double-sided' nature. There may be numerous probabilistic arguments on each side of a case. Inferences may be unreliable, and they cannot easily be generalized. Third, according to Perkins, formal reasoning typically comprises 'long chains' of deductive steps, like mathematical proofs. Good informal reasoning, on the other hand, comprises many short lines of argument, usually with several on each side of a case. Because many of the links in an informal argument do not support their conclusions with certainty, an informal argument with many steps would lend only weak support to its conclusion. However, probabilistic or uncertain reasoning can be formalized (see chapters 9 and 12). This formalization is most straightforward when numerical values can be assigned to the probabilities. In such cases, different probabilities can be integrated to produce a single (probabilistic) conclusion, as in Tversky and Kahneman's (1982a) taxi problem:

> 85 per cent of the taxis in a particular city are green and the rest are blue. A witness identifies a cab involved in an accident as blue. Under tests the witness correctly identifies both blue and green cabs on 80 per cent of occasions. What is the probability that the cab was in fact blue?

The fact that most of the taxis in the city are green makes it likely that the colour of the taxi was green. The fact that a comparatively reliable witness describes the cab as blue is evidence for the alternative conclusion that it is blue. Bayes' theorem (see chapter 9) suggests, perhaps counterintuitively, that the probability of the cab being blue is only 0.41. Everyday arguments differ from this formal argument not because they are probabilistic, but because there is no definitive way of assigning probabilities, and hence no way of combining pieces of evidence on different sides of the argument. More generally, given Perkins's characterization of formal reasoning, it is unclear that people ever engage in it.

Perkins's idea that multiple arguments are needed indicates that individual arguments in everyday reasoning are not usually compelling. Hence, an important aspect of such arguments is their *strength*. As we described in chapter 7, Osherson and his colleagues (Osherson et al., 1990) have discovered some of the factors that make one type of everyday argument strong (arguments such as: cows have spleens, so horses have spleens). In an earlier paper, Osherson et al. (1986) classified a wider range of arguments, but were unable to find a general account of what makes an argument strong. A similar classification has been developed by Allan Collins (see Collins and Michalski, 1989, for a recent formalization of these ideas). Types of argument identified by Collins and Michalski include: deduction, analogy, induction, generalization and abduction. These authors, therefore, see some overlap between formal and everyday reasoning. However, they assign probability factors to arguments, so that, for example, a deductively invalid argument may lend some support to its conclusion. Like Osherson et al., Collins and Michalski are unable to provide a detailed account of what makes an argument strong. Nevertheless, their scheme has been applied with some success to a collection of decision-making protocols from subjects who acted as jurors in simulated trials (Pennington and Hastie, 1993). Although the types of argument in the Collins and Michalski scheme can be thought of as rules of inference, Pennington and Hastie follow Collins and Michalski in suggesting that jurors construct mental models of the incidents about which they have to make decisions, and that the inference rules are tools for building and fleshing out the models. Hence, they claim to reconcile rule-based and model-based methods of reasoning (see chapter 5).

Comparatively little empirical work on everyday reasoning has been carried out. One explanation for this is that, in contrast to formal reasoning, there is no well-defined methodology. Another is that it is difficult for an experimenter to be sure how subjects will interpret a problem – they can apply world knowledge and personal biases in an uncontrolled manner. In addition, there is often no 'correct' answer to a practical reasoning problem, so standard techniques of assessing subjects' performance, such as number of problems correctly solved, cannot be used. Nevertheless, the topic is increasingly regarded as important, and a number of theories about how people reason in their everyday lives have been developed, for example, the theory of Collins and Michalski mentioned above.

Much of the work on everyday reasoning has focused on problems people solve in their working lives (see, e.g., Scribner, 1986; Wagner and Sternberg, 1986). We will discuss this work later in this chapter. First, however, we will consider research on informal reasoning that has only indirect links with practical action. In particular we will describe work by Perkins (e.g., 1989; Perkins, Farady and Bushey, 1991) and by Kuhn (1991). This research assesses people's ability to develop convincing arguments about everyday issues. Billig (1987) points out that this aspect of thinking has been neglected. In his view this neglect is disastrous, because much of our thinking takes the form of arguments with ourselves! Perkins characterizes everyday reasoning as *situation modelling*, and explains errors in such reasoning as resulting from situation models that are biased or incomplete (or both). Although the notion of a situation model has similarities with that of a mental model, in Perkins' view everyday reasoning contrasts with formal reasoning because issues of bias and completeness do not arise in a formal context. By completeness, Perkins means consideration of all possible arguments about an issue. Bias means considering mainly (or only) arguments on one side of the case. In practice, completeness is defined relatively, by determining the number of arguments produced by a subject who is prompted. Indeed, it is not clear that there is any limit to the number of arguments that can be made about any issue.

A valid formal argument is not incomplete or biased. It is a proof, and other strands of argument will not strengthen its case. However, the work discussed in previous chapters (see especially chapters 5, 6 and 8) suggests that Perkins has either overstated the differences between formal and everyday reasoning or underestimated the difficulty with which people can engage in purely formal reasoning.

14.2   The Study of Informal Arguments

Perkins has assessed subjects' informal reasoning extensively (see Perkins, Farady and Bushey, 1991, for an overview). Subjects in his experiments were given questions of general social and political significance to think about, for example: Would providing more money for state schools significantly improve the quality of teaching and learning? A three-part experimental procedure was used. First, subjects were asked to make an immediate decision, and to rate their confidence in their judgement, their interest in the issue and the amount of time they had devoted to it previously. Second, they were asked to think about the issue more carefully, to come to a considered opinion, if they could, and to give their reasons for that opinion. The third phase was more structured. The subjects' reasoning was guided by an experimenter, who prompted them to consider all the relevant aspects of the situation, to look for arguments for both answers to the question, and to evaluate these arguments objectively. The aim of this third phase was to see whether subjects could develop and add to their initial arguments with appropriate *scaffolding* (a sort of Socratic guidance).

The completeness and bias of the arguments was assessed by counting the number of 'my-side' and 'other-side' arguments ('my-side' arguments are those that support subjects' initial judgements). Over a wide range of studies, Perkins and his colleagues found that people performed poorly: 'situation modeling marred by incompleteness and bias is the norm rather than the exception' (Perkins, Farady and Bushey, 1991: p. 90). Even college students and graduate students consistently produced sparse, one-sided arguments – at least three-quarters of the identified weaknesses indicated bias or incompleteness. Unguided reasoning, in the second phase of the experiments, was poorer than the scaffolded reasoning of the third phase. For example, when subjects were prompted, they could produce at least six arguments on each side. However, even graduate students, when left to their own devices, produced on average only 3.3 arguments in favour of a position and 1.3 objections. There was little improvement with increasing amounts of formal education. Nor did out-of-school experience provide much help. Adults who had been out of school for several years performed similarly to school subjects of the same educational level. The general conclusion from these studies was that not only is everyday reasoning not very good, but it does not improve much with education, maturation or life experience.

Perkins (1989) identified three main types of errors in everyday reasoning: formal errors, such as affirming the consequent (see chapter 5); 'informal' fallacies, such as arguing *ad hominem* or *begging the question*; and errors in situation modelling. A more detailed analysis of his experimental data suggested 18 categories of mistake, which accounted for 90 per cent of subjects' failings. The majority of the categories reflected deficiencies in situation models. The most common was 'contrary consequent', in which the subject fails to notice that a different argument from the same premises leads to a contrary conclusion. For example, someone might reason that if 'the draft' (army service) were compulsory, the army would be strengthened, and the country's influence on world events increased. They would, however, be ignoring a line of reasoning that leads to the opposite conclusion: that people would resent being drafted, and would not serve well in the army, so that the army, though larger, would be of poor quality, and not stronger.

In general, the faulty reasoning uncovered by Perkins was not fallacious, in the formal sense. Rather, it was best characterized as under-elaboration of situation models. Nevertheless, some errors of logic were found. Subjects sometimes produce non sequiturs or contradictions, arguing, for example, that the US could not obtain more influence via the draft because it already has great influence. Baron (1988) points out that everyday reasoning is not usually deductive, but relies on sets of plausible arguments. He argues that the informal fallacies should not, therefore, be regarded as errors of reasoning. For example, an argument from authority is not deductively valid, but an authority on a particular subject has a better chance of being right about that subject than a layperson. So, the opinions of authorities should be given credence. Baron suggests that so-called fallacious arguments are best characterized as *overweighting* of evidence, and not as the use of irrelevant evidence, as traditional characterizations suggest. The conclusion of an everyday argument cannot usually be established with absolute certainty from the premises *alone*. Good everyday arguments use relevant, but not necessarily decisive, evidence. Poor arguments are not necessarily poor because they are illogical, but because they ignore some relevant possibility or piece of evidence.

So, do people in everyday life approach important decisions in a biased manner, never see the true 'vexedness' of the problems, and make hasty decisions on the basis of simplistic situation models? The answer seems to be 'no', or at least 'not necessarily'. If someone perceives an issue as personally important, and recognizes that a decision may be difficult, they develop a more elaborate situation model than those typically produced for thinking about social issues in laboratory studies. Ironically, our view of reasoning can be distorted by studying *everyday* reasoning in the laboratory, just as it can be by the use of standard laboratory tasks. Nevertheless, Perkins, Farady and Bushey (1991) found that the ability to argue about personal and social issues correlated, suggesting that similar underlying reasoning mechanisms were being engaged.

Perkins and his colleagues also examined the effects of knowledge and general intelligence. They took the judgements of the amount of time previously spent thinking about an issue as an index of knowledge about it, and found no evidence of a relation between quality of situation modelling and familiarity with an issue. By contrast, IQ did relate to how well elaborated the situation models were, especially for students. However, the relation between IQ and number of arguments was stronger for my-side than for other-side arguments. Subjects with higher IQs use their intelligence to elaborate the case for their own point of view, rather than to explore issues more impartially. Galotti (1989), who reviews a wider range of studies, concludes that skill in everyday reasoning correlates only slightly, if at all, with IQ.

The work of Kuhn (1991) corroborates and extends that of Perkins. In particular, she studied in more detail the effect of *expertise* on everyday reasoning skill. Kuhn used what she called urban social problems, such as 'what causes unemployment?'. Although these problems are acknowledged by experts to be highly complex, they tended to invoke more simplistic causal reasoning than the problems used by Perkins. The subjects were asked to justify and defend their reasoning, and provide evidence for their conclusions. Kuhn's subjects were highly confident in offering causal explanations, though they 'knew' the answer only in the naive sense of never having thought about the alternatives. This suggestion that subjects take a particular viewpoint for granted is substantiated by the small numbers who suggested alternative accounts: only 33 per cent for all three topics used in the studies, and 8 per cent for none. Similarly only 34 per cent consistently generated counter-arguments, either to their own theories, to alternatives, or both, and 9 per cent never did. Furthermore, counter-evidence to my-side arguments was particularly sparse in the protocols. Only 14 per cent of subjects consistently considered it, and 21 per cent never did. Not surprisingly, subjects were also poor at weighing the evidence on the two sides of an argument to produce a reasoned decision. Thus, Kuhn's data provides clear evidence for the my-side bias and for a 'makes-sense' epistemology (or theory of knowledge), according to which people accept ideas for which they have arguments that make sense to them without considering alternatives.

Kuhn considered what skills her subjects would need if they were to assess whether a particular viewpoint was tenable relative to alternative positions. She argues that this kind of reasoning requires the reasoner's own theory to become an object of thought. The ability to reflect on one's own thoughts is a *metacognitive* skill, and Kuhn argues that many reasoning skills are metacognitive. She believes that people have an implicit command of such skills, but that they may need to make this command explicit if they are to apply them appropriately. One of Kuhn's most interesting suggestions is that thinking skills might be developed by 'externalizing' one's reasoning in argumentation with others.

To assess the effect of expertise on everyday reasoning, Kuhn selected groups of people who could be expected to be experts on each of the three topics she used. Like Perkins, she found that detailed knowledge of a topic does not necessarily improve thinking in that domain. For example, the performance of experienced teachers was variable, but they were no better at thinking about reasons for school failure than about the other topics. However, philosophers were better than all other groups. They showed perfect performance in the generation of germane evidence, alternative theories, counter-arguments and rebuttals. They also showed a good appreciation of the complexity of the issues.

Kuhn attempted to relate strategies in informal reasoning to those exhibited in formal reasoning. She sees links between the one-sided nature of her subjects' argumentation and the confirmation bias shown, for example, in Wason's selection task (see chapter 8), in which subjects typically select only the cards that are consistent with their hypothesis. Belief bias effects in syllogistic reasoning are also thought to occur when subjects are biased by their own initial beliefs in evaluating conclusions and seeking contrary evidence (see chapter 6). Kuhn further relates her findings to the phenomenon of overconfidence in judgement and decision making – subjects are typically more confident about their answers to general knowledge questions than is warranted by their actual performance (see chapter 9). Kuhn's subjects were similarly overconfident in their evaluation of evidence and in their certainty about the correctness of their causal theories. Kuhn does not believe that that the same mechanisms underlie formal and informal reasoning, but rather that the two sorts of reasoning have cognitive strategies in common.

Johnson-Laird and Anderson (1988; see Johnson-Laird and Byrne, 1991: p. 205) investigated people's ability to draw alternative conclusions from the same premises, using a different technique from Perkins and Kuhn. They gave their subjects problems such as:

> The old man was bitten by a poisonous snake. There was no known antidote available.

The subjects were questioned as to what they thought followed from the statements, and were then asked for further possible conclusions. Like Perkins, Johnson-Laird and Anderson found that subjects were all too ready to endorse a single conclusion, and that there was a strong consensus among subjects about what that conclusion should be: that, in the example above, the man died. One interesting aspect of their study, however, was that subjects who were told that a conclusion was 'possible but not, in fact, true' generated more alternatives than subjects told that it was 'possible, and may well have been the case', even though both groups were pressed to generate further conclusions. Johnson-Laird and Anderson interpret these findings as showing that subjects engage in an active process of constructive search, and do not simply retrieve responses from memory. They suggest that reasoning in these situations has much in common with analogy: subjects generate relevant information by being reminded of similar situations. However, this idea does not explain *how* the premises lead to the recovery of relevant ideas: current theories of analogy are not powerful enough to explain how relevant ideas can be constructed, rather than simply recovered from existing knowledge (see Johnson-Laird, 1989).

14.3   Theoretical Perspectives on Everyday Reasoning

14.3.1   Everyday reasoning and everyday errors

One possible source of a theory of everyday reasoning, and in particular of its shortcomings, is a general theory of human errors, such as that of Norman (1988) or Reason (1990). Indeed, these authors have suggested that their ideas apply to reasoning. However, their theories focus primarily on *slips*, such as pressing the wrong button, and *lapses*, such as getting upstairs but forgetting what you meant to do when you got there. Both Norman and Reason analyse the kinds of mistake (in reasoning and in other spheres) that lead to major disasters, such as nuclear power plant emergencies and plane crashes. Reason, for example, considers a variety of cognitive sources of error, such as attending to psychologically salient, rather than logically important, features (as in matching bias in the Wason selection task; see chapter 8), confirmation bias (see chapter 8), overconfidence (see chapter 9), illusory correlation (see chapter 9) and processing limitations. However, he also considers factors such as the design of machinery.

Norman (1988) also invokes a tendency to explain away anomalies. As he points out, novel situations can look misleadingly like familiar ones. For example, if a car's exhaust is slightly loose, and rattles from time to time, a rattling noise from under that car may cause no great concern. The loose exhaust *explains* the rattle, and makes it unlikely that the car's owner will look for an alternative explanation. There might, however, be something else wrong with the car which needs urgent attention. Failure to consider this possibility could prove fatal. Like Reason, Norman shows how poor design can cause errors, and he also considers social factors. There are, for example, strong pressures not to shut down a nuclear power plant unnecessarily (a mistake of this sort might cost someone their job). Similarly, if a pilot decides against flying a passenger airliner because the weather looks bad, the passengers will probably be angry, and the airline will lose money. If the pilot risks flying, it is unlikely that there will be an accident. So, the social pressures to take the risk may be overwhelming.

Norman emphasizes the role of design in everyday errors. Poorly designed objects – VCRs are a good example – are difficult to use. This observation suggests that part of people's knowledge about how objects work is located in the objects themselves, and not in the mind of the user. More generally, people can use *external* aids to their thinking. And, although the use of diaries and other aides-memoires is an everyday experience, cognitive psychology has not paid much attention to the externalization of thought. Norman and others have developed these ideas into a theory of *situated action*. Vera and Simon (1993) argue that situated action can be explained straightforwardly in standard theories of cognition (but see the replies in the special issue of *Cognitive Science* on situated action, vol. 17, no. 1).

One aspect of the externalization of thought that has received some attention is the use of diagrams. Larkin and Simon (1987) argue that, even when they carry the same information as descriptions in words, diagrams may make recognizing patterns easier, may support certain inferences more directly and may make the search for a problem's solution (see chapter 11) simpler. Since drawing diagrams on paper is easier than trying to construct them in the mind, using external aids can considerably help thinking. John Anderson's geometry tutor (see next chapter) uses diagrams to teach students geometry proofs, and Barwise and Etchemendy's (1992) Hyperproof program uses diagrams to teach logic. And, although Barwise and Etchemendy found that diagrams were of little help for disjunctive reasoning, Bauer and Johnson-Laird (1993, and see chapter 5 above) found that circuit-like diagrams could help with difficult disjunctions.

14.3.2   Perkins's theory of shortcomings in everyday reasoning

Perkins (1989) explains everyday reasoning errors by postulating two main shortcomings: *metacognitive shortfall* and *confirmation bias*. The first leads to errors because people lack knowledge about effective reasoning strategies. Perkins suggests various contributory factors: failure to realize how badly biased a situation model is; failure to realize how easy it is to extend a model; and failure to reconsider a conclusion in the light of further information. As we mentioned above, the importance of metacognitive skills in reasoning was also pointed out by Kuhn. The second shortcoming, 'confirmation bias', is related to the phenomenon of the same name in hypothesis testing (see chapter 8). In everyday reasoning, Perkins equates confirmation bias with a preference for constructing and maintaining simple, one-sided pictures. Perkins argues that such a bias arises for two main reasons. The first is ego defence: people do not want to examine their deep-rooted beliefs too closely. The second is a natural tendency to minimize cognitive load. Weighing up conflicting arguments, and coming to a single conclusion, requires substantial cognitive effort.

Perkins, Farady and Bushey (1991) suggest, therefore, that people use simple rules of thumb to decide whether a conclusion is acceptable. They are satisfied with inadequate situation models if those models are coherent, and congruent with their own prior beliefs. If a model 'makes sense', there is no need to think further. This way of reasoning is quick and easy, and adequate for many purposes. As Perkins et al. say: 'a makes-sense epistemology keeps people pretty happy with their beliefs and adequately functional most of the time' (1991: p. 99). However, the makes-sense epistemologist has difficulties with the messy, but important, problems that beset people from time to time, to which there is no obvious solution that fits with their existing beliefs and biases. In such situations, Perkins argues, a *critical epistemology* is needed. A critical epistemologist uses metacognitive knowledge to counteract ego defence and the problems of cognitive load, and builds more complete situation models. Perkins (1989) stresses that it is not being intelligent *per se* that allows someone to become a critical epistemologist. It is having the relevant metacognitive skills.

14.3.3 A mental models theory of everyday reasoning

The theory of mental models is intended as a general theory of inference, and should, therefore, provide an account of everyday reasoning. Johnson-Laird and Byrne (1991) outline such an account, which is, in some ways, similar to that of Perkins. In particular, mental models have much in common with Perkins's situation models. However, Johnson-Laird and Byrne emphasize similarities between everyday reasoning, formal reasoning, and those other cognitive skills that have been accounted for within the mental models theory. Thus, they propose that, like deductive reasoning, everyday reasoning should be characterized not in terms of inference rules, but in terms of the construction of plausible models and the search for alternatives to them.

One unanswered question, which is particularly pressing in the case of everyday reasoning, is how relevant information from long-term memory is brought to bear on the current problem. If, for example, someone were asked to defend the claim that 'The Government should subsidize ballet' (an example from Johnson-Laird and Byrne, 1991), they might suggest that, 'without a subsidy, ballet would be too expensive for all but the very rich'. Johnson-Laird and Byrne suggest that bringing relevant information to mind is similar to *abductive* reasoning (see chapter 7), and that a theory based on formal rules of inference cannot explain it. The semantic information in the model of the (explicit) information from which reasoning starts must make contact with the relevant facts in memory (see Gentner, 1989). However, the details of this process remain to be elucidated, and some researchers have doubted whether an account within the mental models framework (or indeed any non-connectionist framework) is possible (Oaksford and Chater, 1991; but see Garnham, 1993, for a riposte; see also chapter 4 above). Johnson-Laird and Byrne also suggest that there should be a close connection between theories of everyday reasoning and theories of reasoning from uncertain or probabilistic information (see chapter 9). Indeed, as we saw above, Perkins lays particular emphasis on the probabilistic nature of everyday arguments. As Johnson-Laird and Byrne point out, Tversky and Kahneman (1973: p. 229) described probabilistic reasoning in terms that are reminiscent of mental models theory:

> In thinking of such events we often construct *scenarios*, i.e., stories that lead from the present situation to the target event. The plausibility of the scenarios that come to mind, or the difficulty of producing them, then serve as a clue to the likelihood of the event. If no reasonable scenario comes to mind, the event is deemed impossible or highly unlikely. If many scenarios come to mind, or if the one scenario that is constructed is particularly compelling, the event in question appears probable.

Johnson-Laird (in press, b) has also suggested a mental models account of the strength of everyday arguments in terms of the proportion of possible states of affairs consistent with the premises in which the conclusion is true. To explain how people estimate this proportion, Johnson-Laird appeals to the heuristic processes of probability estimation described by Kahneman and Tversky (see chapter 9).

Johnson-Laird and Byrne further contrast a view of this kind with one that uses the complex formal apparatus of *fuzzy set theory*. They argue that the use of (a mental analogue of) this complex apparatus would very likely make everyday reasoning more difficult than formal reasoning. They claim, however, that the opposite is the case.

14.4   Solving Practical Problems in Everyday Life

So far, we have discussed one particular type of everyday reasoning: arguing for and against general propositions. In this section, we will consider how people solve practical problems in real life, and how their everyday abilities relate to the way they solve more formal problems (as discussed in chapter 11).

Much of this research investigates how people solve problems when they do not know, or for some reason do not use, standard methods. Rogoff (1984) suggests that children's problem solving is different in and out of school, and this observation has been confirmed in studies of Brazilian children who sell goods in street markets (Carraher, Carraher and Schliemann, 1985). These children have to add up prices, and calculate how much change should be given, without pencil and paper. They have to work out bargains, and to compete with one another for trade. Carraher et al. found that, although the children had little formal schooling, they solved complex arithmetical problems accurately, and performed better when working as street vendors than on analogous tasks, using the same numbers and operations, in a more formal setting. They also performed better than non-vendors with comparable education. What was interesting was the way the children solved the problems. They relied on invented procedures, rather than those they would have learned in school. For example, a child who was asked for the price of ten coconuts at 35 cruzeiros each did not use the 'add 0' method of multiplying by 10, as she had undoubtedly been taught in school. She worked out the cost of three (105), added the cost of a further three twice (315), then added a further 35 (350). In almost all cases, the children used different strategies in the street and in the formal situations. In the street they usually used what the authors term *convenient groups* for their additions, and attempts to use school-taught procedures usually *interfered* with, rather than helped, their problem-solving.

Lave and his colleagues (Lave, Murtaugh and de la Rocha, 1984; Lave, 1988) also investigated arithmetical problem solving in a naturalistic setting, as compared with more formal tests. The subjects were either given verbal problems, and asked to imagine that they were in a food store making decisions between products, or they were actually sent to a food store, and had to describe their thoughts as they made real decisions. A typical problem was: 'Which is the best buy for sunflower seeds: package A, which costs 30 cents for 3 oz., or package B, which costs 44 cents for 4 oz.?' The difference between shoppers' arithmetic in the food store and on analogous problems in a paper-and-pencil task was remarkable. The subjects scored 98 per cent correct on the problems in the food store, but only 59 per cent correct in the formal setting.

Once again, what was interesting was the range of strategies used. When comparing prices of different brands with different amounts per pack, people only occasionally used the school-taught method of working out the price-per-unit for each brand. In the food store, they used two other strategies. In one, the *difference* strategy, they compared the difference in quantity with the difference in price, and assessed whether the one justified the other. When using the second, *ratio* strategy, they assessed whether the ratio of the prices was greater or less than the ratio of the quantities. For example, a 10 oz. tin of peanuts for 90 cents is clearly a better buy than a 4 oz. tin for 45 cents, because the larger tin is twice the price, but contains more than twice as many peanuts. Only rarely (5 per cent of the time) did the shoppers in the food store work out unit prices. In both contexts, however, the subjects were flexible in their strategies, and tended to choose one that fitted the problem. Their reluctance to use the unit price strategy in the food store perhaps reflects the fact that they usually resorted to it only when the other strategies would not work. Furthermore, it can be difficult to work out and compare unit prices without pencil and paper. In fact, some people simply gave up when faced with the prospect of having to use unit prices! These data show that people are inventive and adaptive in their problem-solving strategies. Furthermore, in a naturalistic setting, shoppers made little use of the school-taught strategy, even though they knew about it, if some less demanding strategy would enable them to reach a decision.

Scribner (1984) investigated a range of practical problem-solving techniques used by workers in a milk-processing plant. Her aim was to develop a functional view of practical thinking, and she compared the problem-solving techniques of various groups in the plant, and from outside. As in the two studies discussed above, she found that practical thinking was adaptive and inventive. The workers did not follow school-based methods of arithmetic, but invented more efficient ways of solving problems. For example, Scribner found that the *preloaders* (workers who prepared orders for the next day's delivery) used a wide range of strategies, and they did additional mental work if it saved physical work. If, for example, an order required a case of chocolate milk, minus six quarts, they would not immediately select a full case and remove six quarts from it. They would, rather, look for part-filled cases, and work out which to add to, or subtract from. According to Scribner, such strategies *always* produced the least physical effort solution. Scribner found that the preloaders were better at producing optimal solutions than clerks from the same plant, or a group of students. The students, in particular, were less flexible in their problem solving. Interestingly, the preloaders often avoided overt arithmetical computations, and worked 'directly' from what they could see. For example, one preloader stated:

> I walked over and I visualized. I knew the case I was looking at had ten out of it, and I only wanted eight, so I just added two to it. . . . I don't never count when I'm making the order. I do it visual, a visual thing, you know. (Scribner, 1984: p. 26)

Thus, visual inspection often provided the necessary information, with little or no overt use of arithmetic. Skilled product assemblers know the numbers of containers in a variety of configurations, and use that information in arriving at their solutions. Scribner relates this knowledge about products to expertise in chess. She suggests that skilled product assemblers learn the value of configurations of containers in much the same way that master chess players know many configurations of pieces, which enables them to assess complete board positions very readily (de Groot, 1965; Chase and Simon, 1973; see also chapter 12).

Scribner also investigated the calculations of delivery drivers, who were responsible for computing the total value of each order. Pricing of orders can, in principle, be straightforwardly achieved by multiplying the number of units by the unit price for each type of item in the order, and adding up the results. However, she found that the drivers often deviated from this method. Again, they were flexible in their techniques. In general, they solved multiplication problems by addition and subtraction, and many of their solutions were based on both case and unit prices. This strategy, too, seemed to be an effort-saving one, but in this case the saving of effort was mental rather than physical. For example, one driver worked out the cost of twelve gallons of punch, at 84 cents per gallon, as follows:

> All right, you got twelve, now it's eighty-four a gallon, so ten gallons would be eight forty. So I take the eight forty and two gallons would be one sixty-eight. That's two times eighty-four. So it's ten and two is twelve. Ten-o-eight.

Even on novel problems (with new products), all but one of the drivers were flexible, and all of the control group of students were inflexible. They used a unit-price strategy throughout.

Scribner's comment on her findings is that practical thinking is 'goal-directed and varies adaptively with the changing properties of problems and changing conditions in the task environment . . . practical thinking contrasts with the kind of academic thinking exemplified in the use of a single algorithm to solve all problems of a given type' (1986: p. 39). Practical thinking becomes adaptive in the interests of *economy of effort*.

A general conclusion from these studies of practical arithmetic is that, when presented with problems, people are inventive – they make up new strategies that differ from those of school arithmetic. These strategies are tailored to particular problems and, not only do they produce accurate results, they often minimize the amount of effort expended by the problem solver. Furthermore, people are more flexible in real life than in the laboratory. These findings indicate the need to be cautious in drawing conclusions about ordinary thinking from the results of laboratory studies of how people solve contrived problems. Some researchers take a more pessimistic view. Mayer, for example, suggests that the implication of the studies we have just reviewed is that 'sterile laboratory studies of how people solve puzzles and abstract problems may tell us only about problem solving within laboratory contexts, whereas research on thinking within real situations may tell us more about genuine human problem solving' (1992: p. 507). Although this view is unduly negative, if we are to learn anything from laboratory studies, we need a clear account of the undoubtedly indirect way that the results of those studies relate to the processes of ordinary thinking.

The contrasting results of studies of real-life problem solving and everyday reasoning in the laboratory (by Perkins and Kuhn) further emphasize the need for caution in interpreting laboratory studies of any kind. When people are actively engaged in a task, and when they can make real savings of effort, they do better than when they are, effectively, trying to play an intellectual game.

Summary

Everyday reasoning often appears different from the formal reasoning we have discussed in previous chapters. There are, however, various views about how the two are related. Perkins argues that the two are fundamentally different. He stresses, in particular, the importance of arguments for and against a case in informal reasoning. On his account everyday reasoning is based on the construction of situation models and their use to generate arguments and counter-arguments. Situation models are similar to mental models, and attempts have also been made to account for everyday reasoning within the mental models framework. The mental models theory, however, emphasizes commonalities between everyday and formal reasoning. General theories of everyday errors provide a further source of ideas about everyday reasoning.

In experimental work, Perkins, and also Kuhn, found that reasoning about general issues was typically incomplete and error prone. Surprisingly, expertise in a domain did not improve informal reasoning in that domain. Perkins identified metacognitive shortfall and confirmation bias as the two main contributory factors to shortcomings in everyday reasoning.

Studies of people solving problems – very often arithmetical problems – that they encounter in their working lives have shown that they use different methods from those taught in schools, and that they perform better using their own methods. People readily invent their own methods of solving such problems, and attempt to reduce the amount of effort they must expend in doing so.

Further Reading

Carraher, T. N., Carraher, D. W. and Schliemann, A. D. (1985). Mathematics in the streets and in schools. *British Journal of Developmental Psychology*, 3, pp. 21–9.

Kuhn, D. (1991). *The Skills of Argument*. Cambridge: Cambridge University Press.

Norman, D. A. (1988). *The Design of Everyday Things*. New York: Doubleday.

Perkins, D. N., Farady, M. and Bushey, B. (1991). Everyday reasoning and the roots of intelligence. In J. F. Voss, D. N. Perkins and J. W. Segal (eds), *Informal Reasoning and Education* (pp. 83–105). Hillsdale, NJ: Lawrence Erlbaum Associates; Ann Arbor: University of Michigan Press.

Reason, J. (1990). *Human Error*. Cambridge: Cambridge University Press.

15

Teaching Thinking Skills

In this chapter we consider whether it is possible to teach thinking skills that are useful in everyday life, rather than in the laboratory. We focus first on the general question of how thinking might be taught, and discuss whether people apply in their everyday lives what they learn in higher education courses about certain types of reasoning. We then describe programmes that are specifically designed to teach thinking skills, and assess their effectiveness. Finally, we consider whether teaching people to use techniques such as brainstorming can increase the number of creative ideas they produce.

15.1 How Should Thinking Be Taught?

In the previous chapter we saw that people devise inventive and efficient ways of solving problems, even when they receive no explicit training. Indeed they often ignore potentially relevant methods of, for example, solving arithmetical problems, which they have been taught in school. However, although people are good at developing problem-solving methods, at least in some domains, they could still benefit from being taught how to think. There may, for example, be domains in which people are not good at spontaneously generating methods of solving problems. Or, with tuition, people might develop general problem-solving methods, rather than the specific ones that they generate in everyday life. However, if thinking skills can be developed, the appropriate methods of tuition may well be different from those typically employed in formal education, since the problem-solving methods that people favour in their everyday lives differ from those taught in schools.

With such ideas in mind, much time and effort has been devoted to developing methods of teaching thinking, partly for humanitarian reasons, and partly because of anticipated financial gain. In this chapter we review some of this work and some attempts to assess its success. Our treatment will, necessarily, be selective, because many programmes to improve thinking have been devised, and because so much has been written about their success, or otherwise. We cannot describe and assess them all; we can only attempt to give a feeling for the types of scheme that have been proposed.

Despite the apparent failure of formal education to prepare people for practical problems, teaching students to think is often viewed as one of the key features of education, as Baron (1988) and others have pointed out. Indeed, Dewey, in his influential book *How We Think* (1933), argued that the point of education was to teach children to think reflectively and critically. His ideas were a crucial factor in the development of the now-dominant *progressive education* school of thought, with its stress on understanding and critical thinking, rather than on rote learning and blind acceptance.

Perhaps the most important question that people who wish to teach thinking skills must confront is whether thinking should be taught as a general skill, independent of particular subject matter, or whether appropriate ways of thinking in a particular domain should be taught alongside the relevant subject matter. Obviously, thinking skills that are not domain specific, and can be used in a wide range of situations, would be the most useful ones. However, it may that there are no skills of this kind, or that they are difficult to teach, or that the only general skills that can be taught are less effective than more specific ones. If the teaching of thinking skills is to be useful, the skills that are taught must transfer to some extent. The question is whether there are skills that generalize beyond a particular domain of thought and which can usefully be taught independently of any particular subject matter.

Baron (1988) claims that psychological research on thinking and reasoning, as described in the preceding chapters, suggests that there are *general heuristics* that could help people avoid some of the biases and errors that have been identified. The most general of these heuristics would be such things as: 'Look for evidence against the first idea you think of', and 'Consider alternative possibilities'. It should be clear to the reader of this book that some of the common errors in formal and everyday reasoning could be avoided by following advice of this kind.

These heuristics could, therefore, be effective in improving reasoning. For example, they could help to avoid belief bias effects (see chapter 6), or errors that arise from relying on information that is highly available in memory (see chapter 9). However, as Baron points out, it is no good teaching the use of such heuristics by rote or drill. It is necessary to show why the heuristics are important, and they can *be* important only for people who are *motivated* to think well, and who have a clear idea of what 'thinking well' entails.

According to Baron, successful teaching of thinking must also provide standards by which particular examples of thinking can be judged, beliefs about what good thinking is and why it is important, and, as we have already said, the motivation to think well. Standards, like heuristics, should not simply be presented as something to be learned, but the advantages of adhering to them should be demonstrated by example. The relevant beliefs include beliefs about thinking itself, and beliefs about one's ability to think. Holding certain beliefs about thinking can affect one's ability to think, either for better or for worse. Baron identifies several unhelpful beliefs of which people should be disabused. Examples include: 'changing one's mind is a sign of weakness', 'making a quick decision is a sign of strength or wisdom', and 'being open to alternatives leads to confusion and despair'. Examples of helpful beliefs, which should be inculcated, include: 'good thinkers are open to new possibilities and to evidence against possibilities that they favour' and 'there is nothing wrong with being undecided or uncertain for a while' (1988: p. 464). A second point about beliefs is that, if someone believes that the effectiveness of their own thinking can be improved, the quality of their thinking probably *will* improve, particularly if they are guided in the appropriate way. Problem-solving ability, for example, can be influenced by past successes and failures.

The motivation to think well must come from the goals a person wishes to achieve. Baron argues that students must *want* to make good decisions, even if they go against their own or others' thinking. He also claims that it should be possible to show how clear thinking will serve goals that people already have. Other more general goals will also encourage good thinking – for example, curiosity (especially the search for evidence) and desire for competence. Baron suggests that 'cultures that encourage rational thinking are those that value questioning, inquiry, the satisfaction of curiousity, and intellectual challenge' (1988: pp. 466–7).

Baron's heuristics, standards, beliefs and goals are all general, and, if he were right, the teaching of thinking skills could be domain independent, and it should be comparatively straightforward. Unfortunately, although his claims are eminently sensible, he provides little or no evidence that the teaching methods he outlines would be successful. Furthermore, there is reason to believe that the general skills he describes would be difficult to teach, because it is considerably easier to find evidence for the development of specific thinking skills than for general ones. Transfer, in particular, is mainly specific: skills learned in one domain usually transfer only within that domain. For example, in a review of several major thinking-skills programmes. Bransford, Arbitman-Smith, Stein and Vye (1985) failed to find convincing evidence for 'the idea of developing general skills that permit transfer to a wide variety of domains . . . there was no strong evidence that students . . . improved in tasks that were dissimilar to those already explicitly practiced.'

15.1.1   Transfer

There are three interrelated questions about transfer. The first is whether skills transfer across domains: from thinking about mathematics to thinking about politics, for example. The second is whether skills transfer across settings, and in particular whether they transfer from the classroom to everyday life. The third is whether, or to what extent, transfer is spontaneous. Richard Nisbett and his colleagues have considered the specific question of how ideas taught in tertiary education courses transfer to thinking about everyday problems. For example, Nisbett, Fong, Lehman and Cheng (1987) examined the effects of different university courses on students' statistical, logical and methodological reasoning. Statistical reasoning ability was examined by asking the students to explain why, for example, 'a traveling saleswoman is typically disappointed on repeat visits to a restaurant where she experienced a truly outstanding meal on her first visit' (Nisbett et al., 1987: p. 629). Such happenings could be explained either in non-statistical terms or statistical ones. The most plausible statistical explanation is based on the principle of regression towards the mean discussed in chapter 9. An explanation based on this principle, from Nisbett et al.'s data, is: 'very few restaurants have only excellent meals, odds are she was just lucky first time'. Nisbett et al. assessed logical reasoning using conditional reasoning problems, such as Wason's selection task (see chapter 8), and what they called *methodological* reasoning by presenting fallacious 'everyday' arguments for comment. These arguments were typically one-sided, in Perkins's sense (see chapter 14).

For statistical reasoning, Nisbett et al. found that courses in psychology produced the biggest improvements in performance, and that the same was true for methodological reasoning. The latter was also improved by medical training, but not by either law or chemistry. Disappointingly, logical reasoning was not improved by either formal or informal logic. It did improve with two years' postgraduate training in law, medicine or psychology. Again chemistry courses provided no benefit. Nisbett et al. emphasize that the transfer of skills was to problems not directly relevant to the disciplines taught formally. Psychology, for example, is not particularly concerned with disappointment about restaurants. Nisbett et al. also relate the kinds of thinking fostered in psychology, medicine and law to the kinds of improvements they found in statistical, logical and methodological reasoning. However, while the study undoubtedly demonstrates effects that are specific to the courses followed, it is difficult to agree, for example, that statistical reasoning is not important to lawyers. Whether their training fails to emphasize that kind of reasoning is another matter.

15.1.2   Can general thinking skills be taught?

Although Nisbett et al. demonstrated transfer of reasoning skills, the kinds of thinking they investigated were not as general as those discussed by Baron, which he calls *open-minded thinking*. Later studies, however, suggest that open-minded thinking can also be improved by training. In particular, Perkins, Farady and Bushey (1991) attempted to assess whether quality of thinking can be improved by teaching general strategies. They examined students' performance, in the type of everyday reasoning tasks described in the previous chapter, before and after they had taken one of four courses: a high-school debate class; the first year of a liberal arts programme, noted for its efforts to improve general reasoning skills; a semester at a graduate school of education, in which one of the main courses encouraged exploratory reasoning; and first year at law school. They found that only the first two produced improvements in reasoning. Furthermore, even these courses produced only modest improvements, which were restricted to increasing the number of my-side arguments.

In another study, an attempt was made to improve reasoning in the experimental setting itself by the use of metacognitive prompts, a method that Perkins et al. call *scaffolding* (see also §14.2). The subjects were allowed to reason for themselves until they could think of nothing else to say. At that point the experimenter prompted them in a general way. If, for example, a subject produced arguments on only one side of a case, the experimenter suggested that they consider whether someone might take the opposite point of view. The prompts were intended to induce subjects to explore further the issue they had been thinking about. With this help, they improved dramatically, in terms of both completeness and overcoming bias. My-side arguments doubled while, more encouragingly, eight times as many other-side arguments were produced.

Perkins et al. argued that the subjects could have generated the experimenters' prompts on their own: they should be able to 'scaffold themselves', and thereby improve their own reasoning. This idea was tested by designing a sixteen-hour course for high-school students. The course emphasized the need to search thoroughly for arguments on both sides of the case. In the classes, the students analysed arguments in essays, wrote short arguments, and learned strategies to facilitate skilled situation modelling. Before and after the course, the students' reasoning ability was tested using the methods and materials described in the previous chapter. The main effect of the course was to reduce bias. The number of my-side arguments remained constant, but the number of other-side arguments doubled. The rated quality of the arguments also increased. Because the course increased other-side arguments preferentially, and not general thoroughness, it can be thought of as increasing open-mindedness. It therefore contrasts with the debating and liberal arts courses, mentioned above, which increased only the number of my-side arguments. A crucial question, which Perkins et al. do not claim to have answered, is whether such training can have lasting effects, or effects that transfer beyond the instructional context.

15.1.3 Intelligent tutoring systems

A different approach to understanding how thinking might be taught has emerged from the development of computer programs to teach problem-solving skills. Such *intelligent tutoring systems* are intended to emulate a good human tutor, who will impart general thinking skills in addition to techniques specific to a particular subject matter. Such tutors are easiest to develop for subjects such as mathematics and computer programming, in which problems have model solutions. Anderson, Boyle, Farrell and Reiser (1987) have developed programs to teach students geometry proofs and programming in LISP, a programming language widely used in artificial intelligence. These tutoring systems draw on the general principles of Anderson's ACT* theory of cognition (see Anderson, 1983; also chapter 11 above).

Geometry and programming problems are typically tackled using the problem reduction technique described in chapter 11, and one aim of these tutoring systems is to make students more aware of the structured sets of goals and subgoals that they have to solve. Anderson et al. claim that the need to make subgoals explicit is often neglected in standard instruction. The programs embody a number of other principles, such as promoting an abstract understanding of the knowledge needed for problem solving, minimizing working memory load and providing feedback. Anderson et al. describe a partial assessment of these tutoring systems, though primarily for the LISP tutor. This program produced as good learning as a human tutor, as measured by the time taken to solve problems, and significantly better learning than working alone with an instruction manual. However, the data did not show which aspects of the tutoring system contributed to their effectiveness. A later assessment of the LISP tutor (Anderson, 1990) was based on its use for teaching a course at Carnegie-Mellon University. Students who used the tutor did better that those who did not. Although the tutor itself is highly structured, Anderson found that the bits of information about LISP (individual productions in the tutor; see chapter 11) were learned independently. Each was initially acquired in one lesson, and was then strengthened as it was put to further use.

15.2   Thinking Skills Programmes

The studies described in the first part of this chapter are small-scale, experimental investigations. In this section, we will consider broadly based programmes that aim to teach thinking skills. There has been an interest in teaching thinking for hundreds of years, and many programmes were developed in the earlier part of this century, including brainstorming and synectics, which are intended to promote creative thinking and are described later in this chapter. A number of new programmes have emerged in the last twenty years (for an extended discussion, see Nickerson, Perkins and Smith, 1985). We will discuss three of them below. These programmes for the most part emphasize the component skills of thinking, rather than thinking in general, and, in practice, their advocates have been satisfied with specific, rather than general, transfer of skills, though in unguarded moments some have made rash claims about the generality of transfer.

These training programmes need not be thought of as attempts to improve intelligence, though they sometimes are. Indeed, the design and use of such programmes require no assumptions about the modifiability of intelligence. Even if intelligence is not modifiable, training could improve performance on intellectually demanding tasks, by helping people to use the intelligence that they have more effectively. Questions about the nature of intelligence – what it is, whether it is modifiable – are not directly relevant to the question of whether thinking can be taught, and we will not consider them here. The primary issue is whether people can be taught to think more critically and creatively.

Despite the long history of attempts to teach thinking, the systematic development and assessment of realistic courses that have some chance of success is still at an exploratory and experimental stage. In particular, no single approach has emerged as the best. In this section, we will focus on three widely known projects. Many more are discussed by Nickerson et al. (1985), though even their coverage is exhausting rather than exhaustive. Nickerson et al. identify five broad approaches to the teaching of thinking skills, though they are not mutually exclusive:

1 *Cognitive operations approaches*, which attempt to identify, from a cognitive point of view, the component skills that contribute to thinking, and to train people in the use of those skills.
2 *Heuristics-oriented approaches*, which emphasize general methods of problem solving, as described by expert problem solvers, or by people trying to program computers to solve problems.
3 *Formal thinking approaches*, which claim that people need training in what Piaget called formal operational thinking (see chapter 16), and attempt to teach it, primarily as part of conventional subject-matter courses.
4 *Symbolic facility approaches*, which focus specifically on symbol-manipulation skills.
5 *Thinking-about-thinking approaches*, which attempt to improve thinking by getting people to think about the nature of thought.

In fact, almost all programmes include an element of 'thinking about thinking'. They recognize, as this chapter and the previous one have emphasized, that many thinking skills are *metacognitive*. The third and fourth of Nickerson et al.'s categories are highly specialized, and we will comment here only on the first two, noting, however, that many programmes both train simple operations and teach general heuristics.

Cognitive operations approaches to the teaching of thinking emphasize simple processes, such as comparing and classifying, which they assume to be basic in some sense. Heuristics-oriented approaches aim to teach specific heuristics, strategies and problem-solving techniques. They are based on an influential theoretical analysis of problem solving (that of

Newell and Simon; see chapter 11), and view skill in thinking as, at least in part, a matter of 'know how'. However, their emphasis on general rather than specific know how is rather dated (see chapter 12). Heuristic-based approaches aim to teach students how to break a complex task into small steps that they are able to perform readily. However, as the term heuristic suggests, these methods are unlikely to guarantee a solution, but will only be good bets. The small steps are typically too complex to be regarded as 'basic cognitive operations', though in principle they could be that simple. Furthermore, heuristics-based approaches place little emphasis on training students how to perform the small steps. Cognitive operations approaches, by contrast, focus not on methods of breaking problems down, but on training the component operations. The two methods are, therefore, to some extent complementary.

15.2.1   Feuerstein's Instrumental Enrichment

The first programme we will consider is a highly influential one, which focuses strongly on training simple cognitive operations: the *Instrumental Enrichment* programme of Reuven Feuerstein (see, e.g., 1980). The programme was originally developed for special education students in Israel. Feuerstein noted that many of these students had parents who did not explain, discuss or interpret events with their children. The programme attempts to compensate for this shortfall in *mediated learning experiences* by getting the children to work *with* adults to solve problems. Special education students obtain low scores on standard tests, and Feuerstein assumes that this poor performance arises from their relative lack of mediated learning. He also assumes, however, that the resulting deficits can be overcome by appropriate training.

Feuerstein describes the goal of Instrumental Enrichment as follows: 'to sensitize the individual so that he will be able to register, elaborate, and become modified by direct exposure to life events and experiences in such a way that learning and the efficient handling and use of incoming stimuli are increasingly facilitated' (1980: p. 384). It is difficult to make much of this general statement. However, the programme has a number of more concrete subgoals, including the imparting of certain basic concepts and vocabulary needed for skilled thought. In addition, Feuerstein stresses the importance of establishing an intrinsic motivation to think well: students must not simply learn skills in order to pass the course.

Instrumental Enrichment also encourages students to think about their own thinking, and in particular its successes and failures. They are taught to think of themselves as people who produce solutions to problems, not as passive learners of problem-solving methods. The emphasis is on *metalearning habits*, and learning how to learn.

The programme takes three to five years to complete, with several classes per week. It comprises a large number of exercises, on topics not directly linked to subject matter found elsewhere in the school curriculum. The students work individually on a problem at the beginning of a lesson, before the teacher initiates a discussion of their problem-solving activities. Students are given a wide range of problems, and have to compare the ways that they and other students attempt to solve them. This thinking about their thinking is a major vehicle for the mediated learning that Feuerstein regards as so important. The teacher brings the students' attention to the cognitive processes they use in carrying out the exercises.

Not surprisingly, Feuerstein's own attempts to evaluate Instrumental Enrichment have proved positive. For example, Feuerstein, Miller, Hoffman, Rand, Mintzker and Jensen (1981) showed lasting effects, as measured by IQ tests administered two years after completion of the programme. There was also evidence that the programme enabled individuals to learn better on their own. However, the interpretation of this study is problematic, because the authors were not able to provide a detailed comparison of teaching quality in the Instrumental Enrichment and control groups. Nevertheless, other, better controlled, studies (Arbitman-Smith, Haywood and Bransford, 1984) have also shown benefits, including some domain-independent transfer. Thus, although the programme is time-consuming, it does seem effective in producing transferable improvements in thinking skills.

The success of Instrumental Enrichment is success in practice, and does not show that the analysis of thinking on which it is based is correct, or that Feuerstein's identification of the components of thinking is correct. Furthermore, as Nickerson et al. point out, even if its decompositional approach is basically correct, a programme that focuses strongly on simple cognitive operations neglects the question of how complex cognitive acts are built up out of simpler ones. They might, therefore, be more appropriate for weaker students than for stronger ones, because the more able students will probably already be skilled in the simple operations that these courses train. Indeed, in Feuerstein et al.'s (1981) evaluation, students who were weaker initially showed the biggest gains in IQ. Nickerson et al. also suggest that part of the success of cognitive operations approaches may be explained by the diversity of the tasks on which they require students to practise and in their regimes of frequent testing, both of which are related only indirectly to their fundamental philosophy.

15.2.2   The Venezuela project

An even more ambitious project was undertaken in Venezuela, with the aim of improving the intellectual performance of the entire population! A Ministry for the Development of Human Intelligence was set up in 1979, headed by Luis Machado. This new ministry initiated a number of educational programmes. In particular, in collaboration with consultants from Harvard University and Bolt, Beranek and Newman Inc., in the USA, a thinking skills programme for schoolchildren in their early teens was developed. This programme – originally called Project Intelligence, but subsequently renamed Odyssey – was intended to develop reasoning and creative thinking skills through dialogue and discovery. Odyssey does not stress basic cognitive operations as strongly as Instrumental Enrichment, and it places more emphasis on teaching problem-solving strategies that might be described as heuristics. Its lessons cover various aspects of thinking, including problem solving, decision making, verbal reasoning and inventive thinking. In one assessment of the programme (see Chance, 1986), students who had received Odyssey training for a year performed twice as well as controls on problems that were similar to those given during training, but only slightly better on problems that were different from those on which they had been trained. These results point, once again, to the problems of attaining transfer of skills. Other initiatives in Venezuela have used both Instrumental Enrichment and CoRT (see §15.2.3 below).

15.2.3   De Bono's CoRT

In this section we consider a programme that Nickerson et al. describe as heuristics oriented. The CoRT (Cognitive Research Trust) programme is based on the ideas of Edward de Bono, who is probably best known for his concept of lateral thinking. Not surprisingly, therefore, it lays particular emphasis on inventive, creative or divergent thinking. De Bono has, however, written more generally about teaching thinking skills (see, e.g., 1976), and the CoRT programme represents his most extensive effort to apply his ideas. This programme can be used both with schoolchildren (it has been used in schools in many countries) and with adults (e.g., in attempting improve the thinking of business people). According to de Bono, the programme 'deals with the perceptual area of thinking' (1983: p. 117), and not, for example, with problem solving in the narrow sense (see chapter 11) or deductive reasoning (see chapters 5 and 6). De Bono believes that thinking is a skill and, more particularly, that perceptual thinking is a skill of perceiving patterns. He believes that this skill can be enhanced by the various thinking *tools* introduced in his programme. The tools, however, need to be used skilfully themselves, and to this end CoRT emphasizes extended practice with the tools on subject matter that has little intrinsic interest. This procedure is intended to facilitate transfer of learning by making the use of the tools automatic, and by avoiding any connection between the tools and particular subject matter. The tools fall into six groups. They are introduced individually or in pairs in a series of lessons, with ten lessons in each group. The six groups are:

1 *Breadth* of thought about a problem, with particular emphasis on ways of thinking about a situation that might otherwise be neglected
2 *Organization*, and in particular the ability to focus attention on a problem
3 *Interaction*: the adequacy of evidence and arguments, in particular when two or more people may have different views on a subject
4 *Creativity*: the generation and, to a lesser extent, the evaluation of ideas; this section includes lateral thinking
5 *Information and feeling*: affective factors in thinking
6 *Action*: a general framework for tackling problems, into which the tools in the other five sections can be incorporated.

  Each lesson is designed to teach a specific skill for representing or analysing practical problems. De Bono gives many of these skills mnemonics, so that they can readily be brought to mind. For example, CAF stands for 'considering all factors'. It is intended to encourage students to think carefully about problems and list all the factors that might be relevant to their solution. PMI stands for 'plus-minus-interesting', and suggests that students should deliberately examine ideas for their good, bad or interesting points, instead of immediately accepting or rejecting them. Each lesson starts with the teacher describing the operation to be learned. The students then work on practice problems in groups, spending only a short time on each problem. They then discuss their solutions, and the usefulness of the thinking tool, with the teacher. After further group discussion about the principles of the tool, they may be given written work to complete in their own time, for example as homework, if the programme is being used in a school.

Although the CoRT programme has been promoted since the early 1970s, there is still no thoroughgoing objective assessment of its efficacy. Nickerson et al. (1985) discuss the results of a few small-scale studies, and conclude that, although many of the studies have limitations, the findings in general are favourable. There is clear evidence of transfer of the skills in the course to tasks similar to those used in training. There is, however, only anecdotal evidence that CoRT improves general problem-solving skills. Another relatively secure finding is that CoRT training leads people to generate substantially more ideas about how to solve problems, and to take a more balanced approach to individual problems. Thus, CoRT produces similar results to the programme devised by Perkins et al. (1991) and described above. Nickerson et al. conclude that 'the CoRT operations can be seen as simple practical tactics that may help individuals to think sensibly about non-technical things and, also, help them to come to perceive themselves as thinkers. Within its scope, it seems to us that CoRT is likely to have beneficial effects' (1985: p. 220). Nevertheless, the lack transfer is disappointing, though perhaps not surprising, given current thinking about the domain-specificity of much problem solving (see chapter 12).

15.3   Can Thinking Be Taught?

No 'magic' method for teaching people to think has been discovered. Furthermore, those methods that have met with success require extensive training and a substantial amount of practice on the part of the students. Indeed, what Instrumental Enrichment, Odyssey and CoRT have in common is practice on a wide range of simple problems, with group discussions in which the teacher encourages the students to learn from how they, and other students, try to solve problems. One might say that so much is simply good educational practice. More generally, attempts to teach people to think leave the impression that learning to think is a long and time-consuming process – rather like learning any complex skill, in fact (see chapter 12).

Although no single method or programme has emerged as *the* way to teach thinking, many do seem to be effective. In particular, there can be broad and lasting gains with populations of low initial ability. However, even if we can be reasonably sure that thinking skills can be taught, further research must determine the most effective method or methods, and the way they should be geared to particular objectives or populations. What is desperately needed is an understanding of why the methods that work are successful. Regrettably, as the analogous study of learning to read shows, such questions can be frustratingly difficult to answer. It may be, as with learning to read, that the skill and commitment of the teacher are all important. Most learning to think programmes are taught by people who have a vested interest in their success.

Again, as with other skills, much of the research on teaching thinking suggests that the transfer of newly acquired expertise is limited. It is difficult to teach global skills that improve general thinking ability. Nevertheless, the idea that such skills should be teachable, as set out, for example, by Baron, remains plausible. It is reasonable to hope that effective methods for them, and for inculcating cognitive styles that are conducive to good thinking, will eventually be developed. In particular, the training of metacognitive skills – the ability to reflect on, and monitor, one's own cognitive processes – is a good candidate for a programme that could improve thinking of all kinds. However, since it is relatively easy to characterize these skills, it is not clear why attempts to teach them have met with such limited success.

15.4   Increasing the Flow of Creative Ideas

So far in this chapter we have been concerned primarily with everyday thinking. However, creative thinking is not only important (see chapter 13), but potentially lucrative. In business, for example, an idea for a new product can give a company an advantage over its competitors. Creativity is a valuable, yet comparatively rare, asset. The question therefore arises as to whether people can be taught or trained to be more creative, and in this section we will consider methods of trying to promote creativity.

Academic research on creativity began in earnest in the 1950s, and was given a boost by the aftermath of Sputnik. However, industrial organizations, particularly in the USA, had been attempting to find methods of increasing the flow of creative ideas since at least the 1930s. The most widely researched method of trying to make people more creative is *brainstorming*. Research on the efficacy of brainstorming is instructive, not only because it has produced directly applicable results, but because it shows how the unsupported (or not systematically supported) intuitions of a practically oriented layman were sometimes right and sometimes wrong.

The practically oriented layman was the American businessman Alex Osborn, who invented the technique of brainstorming, and described it in a book called *Applied Imagination* (1953). Brainstorming assumes that there is a reasonably well-defined problem to be solved, and aims to encourage the production of possible solutions to the problem. Once the solutions have been produced, they must be evaluated in the normal way. Osborn's assumption is that by increasing the number of proposed solutions, brainstorming will allow the emergence of ultimately useful solutions that would otherwise not have been found. It is by no means obvious that it will. The additional solutions might all be poorer than the ones that naturally come to mind.

Osborn believed that people do not mention possible solutions that they are, perhaps for spurious reasons, unhappy about. Brainstormers are, therefore, told to produce as many solutions as possible, deferring judgement on their viability. In addition to producing a steady flow of ideas, brainstormers are also encouraged to search, again uncritically, for variations on, or connections between, suggested solutions. Brainstorming, thus, tries to foster some of the factors contributing to creativity that we identified in chapter 13.

Brainstorming was originally developed as a group technique, and the stereotype of a brainstorming session is one in which a group of people try to hammer out a solution to a problem together. However, brainstorming can be carried out by individuals, and some of the most interesting psychological research has addressed the question of whether brainstorming works best in groups, as Osborn originally thought, or when people work alone. This work is, of course, predicated on the assumption that brainstorming is an effective technique. Evidence for its efficacy was provided by Meadow, Parnes and Reese (1959) and Parnes and Meadow (1963), who report an increase in the number of high-quality ideas generated under brainstorming instructions, for groups and for individuals respectively.

The first study suggesting that individual brainstorming is better than brainstorming in groups was carried out by Taylor, Berry and Block (1958). They compared individuals and people working in groups of four on three problems: stimulating tourism, coping with a temporarily increased school population, and working out the consequence of people having two thumbs per hand. This result was replicated even for people who were more accustomed to working in groups (Dunnette, Campbell and Jaastad, 1963), and it was later shown that the disadvantage of working in groups increased as the size of the group increased (Bouchard and Hare, 1970). The usual explanation of the group disadvantage is that groups are dominated by a small number of individuals, and the non-dominant members of the group do not express all of their ideas.

Brainstorming encourages the bringing together of different ideas. A different approach, *synectics* (Gordon, 1961), more explicitly directs its users to juxtapose apparently unconnected elements of the problem domain, in particular by using analogies and metaphors. This idea is related to associative accounts of creativity mentioned in chapter 13 (e.g., Mednick, 1962; Koestler, 1964). Synectics also contains 'offbeat' ideas, such as the suggestion that the problem solver should try to identify personally with elements of a problem (the so-called *personal analogy*). Nevertheless, it is a technique that has been widely used in the US business community, although it has not been subjected to the detailed evaluation applied to brainstorming. Most of the evidence for its efficacy is anecdotal.

In Britain, the notion of *lateral thinking* as a way for generating solutions to difficult, or apparently difficult, problems was made popular by de Bono (e.g., 1968). Lateral thinking emphasizes not the number of creative ideas for solving problems, but the rejection of standard methods applied by rote to problems for which they are inappropriate. Applying a standard method is called *vertical thinking*. Lateral thinking requires the taking of fresh perspectives on a problem, and in de Bono's examples these perspectives are often visual or visuo-spatial. For example, in the well-known problem of making four equilateral triangles from six matches, the 'vertical solution' is to try to solve the problem by arranging the matches in two dimensions on a flat surface. Lateral thinking might suggest the possibility of a three-dimensional structure, which is, in fact, the correct solution (the six matches form the sides of a tetrahedron). Whether lateral thinking can increase the flow of creative ideas has not been systematically assessed. De Bono himself moved on to devise a more general programme for teaching thinking skills (the CoRT programme, described above), not just creative thinking.

Summary

Teaching people how to think has long been recognized as an important educational goal. However, there is a largely unresolved debate about whether domain-general thinking skills can be taught, or whether thinking must be taught along with particular subject matter. Baron has identified a series of general heuristics, standards, beliefs and goals that characterize good, or *open-minded*, thinking. However, it remains to be seen whether they can be taught effectively.

A major problem in teaching thinking is that transfer of skills, both to other domains and out of the classroom, is often limited. Nisbett and his colleagues have shown some transfer to real-world problems of statistical and methodological skills as taught in undergraduate and postgraduate courses. However, they failed to find any transfer of teaching in logic. Perkins found some transfer of more general thinking skills, and devised a training programme to enhance it.

Many programmes have attempted to teach thinking skills systematically, and often commercially. Feuerstein's Instrumental Enrichment programme attempts to teach the component simple cognitive operations required for good thinking. There is some evidence of success for the programme, particularly with students of low initial ability. However, how it works, or whether its analysis of thinking is correct, are questions that its practical success fails to answer. A similarly complex programme, used throughout Venezuela, has also met with some success. De Bono's CoRT programme emphasizes heuristic problem-solving techniques rather than the breakdown of thinking into small components. Again success has been claimed, though a full-scale evaluation is still needed.

Attempts to increase the number of creative ideas that people produce include brainstorming, synectics and lateral thinking. There is some evidence that brainstorming can be useful, but, contrary to original suggestions, it seems to work best when individuals brainstorm on their own. The other methods have not been systematically evaluated.

Further Reading

de Bono, E. (1968). *The Five-Day Course in Thinking*. London: Allen Lane.
Nickerson, R. S., Perkins, D. N. and Smith, E. E. (1985). *The Teaching of Thinking*. Hillsdale, NJ: Lawrence Erlbaum Associates.
Osborn, A. F. (1953). *Applied Imagination*. New York: Scribners.

16

The Development of Thinking: Piagetian and Information-Processing Approaches

In this and the following chapter we consider how the skills discussed in the preceding chapters develop throughout childhood. We begin here by introducing the two major perspectives on the development of thinking – the Piagetian and the information-processing approaches – and describe in detail how they account for various aspects of the development of thinking. In the next chapter we discuss research that has not been so strongly influenced by the Piagetian vs. information processing debate. This research focuses on scientific and everyday thinking about the world, including hypothesis testing and mathematical reasoning.

16.1 Two Major Perspectives on the Development of Thinking

There are two main theoretical perspectives on the development of thinking: Piagetian and information-processing. The perspectives are not entirely incompatible. Indeed, in a later section we will see that attempts have been made to reconcile them. Both approaches try to identify the limitations on the cognitive capacity of children at different ages, and try to explain how later, more advanced ways of understanding the world grow out of earlier ones. Both try to identify concepts that children of different ages do, or do not, understand, and both emphasize the impact of existing ways of understanding on the ability to acquire new ones. Nevertheless, there are important differences between the approaches. First, the information-processing approach emphasizes the need to understand *how* change occurs, including changes in *what* information can be represented and *which* processes can be carried out. Second, most information-processing theorists regard cognitive development as a *continuous* process. They see no qualitative difference between the thinking of adults and the thinking of children. They propose that development occurs through the *quantitative* expansion of knowledge structures and of memory efficiency. This contrasts with the Piagetian approach, in which development is seen as *discontinuous*, with a series of *qualitatively* different stages, each with its own set of cognitive structures. On the information-processing view cognitive development is like the construction of a building out of bricks, whereas according to the stage approach it is more like the dramatic metamorphosis of caterpillar to chrysalis, and chrysalis to butterfly. Third, the methods of investigation used by Piagetians and information-processing psychologists differ. Piaget relied on observations (mainly of his own children) and on children's explanations of how they solve problems. He kept detailed observations of his three children, which provided the basis for several books (e.g., Piaget, 1951, 1952, 1954). So, although his data are, at least to some extent, naturalistic, they lack experimental rigour. Information-processing theorists, by contrast, make use of controlled experiments to obtain a fine-grained analysis of performance on particular tasks, and an understanding of how the child's cognitive system operates at each stage. Fourth, the mechanisms by which growth in understanding is said to occur differ considerably – these mechanisms will be discussed in more detail below. The concept of stages of development is not entirely incompatible with an information-processing approach. Indeed, *neo-Piagetian* theorists try to reconcile the two traditions, although they conceptualize the stages in a different way.

16.2   Piagetian Theory

Piaget's interest in child development grew out of his interests in biology and a branch of philosophy called *epistemology* – the study of the origins and evolution of knowledge. Piaget added enormously to our understanding of children's development, and promoted the idea that development should be conceptualized as a series of stages. He made three assumptions about the stages through which children pass. First, the stages are *qualitatively* different. Second, the transition from one stage to the next is abrupt. Third – the *concurrence assumption* – at a given stage of development, children use the same ways of thinking about the world in a wide range of cognitive tasks. Piaget claimed that children's understanding is limited by the stage of intellectual development they have reached, and that they cannot be taught to think and function at higher levels until they have passed through the lower ones. In this section, we will briefly outline the stages proposed by Piaget (more detailed accounts are available elsewhere, e.g., Siegler, 1991, chapter 2; Case, 1985, chapter 2), and then show how Piaget would describe development in particular areas of thinking, using his stage theory.

The first stage, the *sensorimotor*, has six sub-stages. The need for subdivisions makes sense when one considers the intellectual changes that take place between birth and two years, the range covered by this first stage. We will not consider the details of these six sub-levels, but only the general development that takes place over the stage as a whole. Children's physical interactions with objects provide the basis for development in this stage. At birth, the child's responses are simple reflexes: it will suck on a nipple, grasp a finger, blink at a light, and so on. However, infants gradually modify their responses to make them more adaptive, and they begin to anticipate the effects of their actions on the environment. If an action produces an interesting effect, they repeat it. By the fifth sensorimotor sub-stage (at about one year), simple repetition may be replaced by repetition with variation, either in the action itself (an object may be hit harder, or with a clenched fist instead of a palm), or in the object to which it is directed (the child may hit something else in the same way). Such behaviour is seen as indicating that the child has goals, and is no longer responding merely by reflex. By the end of the sensorimotor period, the beginnings of representational thought are present.

A major development in the *preoperational* period is the ability to think about objects in their absence. This ability emerges with the development of representational skills: language, imagery and drawing. However, Piaget argued that children in this stage, which runs roughly from two to six or seven years, can use these representational skills only to view things from their own perspective. To use his term, they are *egocentric*. Preoperational children often focus on only one aspect of a problem, and cannot represent transformations of information, only static states. One example of their limitations can be seen in the *three mountains* task (Piaget and Inhelder, 1956). A four-year-old sitting in front of a model of three mountains is able to select a picture of the view they can see. The same child, however, will be unable to envisage what someone looking at the mountains from a different direction will see. It cannot, for example, mentally rotate the scene to overcome its egocentrism.

Children in the *concrete operational* period have overcome these basic limitations. They can take other points of view, take into account more than one perspective, and represent transformations as well as static situations. These skills are explained by a newly developed ability to manipulate mentally or *operate on* their representations of the world. However, they are still unable to consider all logically possible outcomes, and do not grasp abstract concepts. The operations they perform represent transformations of concrete objects and situations.

In the period of *formal operations*, children are able to reason on the basis of theoretical possibilities as well as concrete realities. Thus, they are able to entertain, and think about, hypothetical situations. Piaget drew a parallel between children's reasoning in this stage, and that of scientists, who are able to devise experiments from theoretical considerations and interpret them within a logical framework. Formal operations can be viewed as operations on operations. At this stage, for instance, children are capable of thinking about their own thinking – their thoughts themselves become objects of thought. In other words, they have acquired *metacognitive* skills.

In Piaget's theory, change occurs via three main processes: *assimilation, accommodation,* and *equilibration.* Assimilation is the representation of experiences using the current level of understanding. Such assimilation often leads children to mistaken conclusions. So preoperational children, who cannot understand the effects of transformations, mistakenly conclude that there is more juice in a tall thin glass than there was when the same juice was in a short wide glass. These mistaken conclusions conflict with other aspects of the child's world – a fair parent does not think it unjust for one child to have the tall thin glass, for example. Eventually, children become aware of these conflicts. They no longer assimilate experiences to their current way of thinking. Instead, their way of thinking has to *accommodate* to experiences they can no longer make sense of, or in which they can no longer ignore the conflicts. Equilibration is the mechanism by which assimilation and accommodation interact. Children start off in a state of equilibrium. Then, if they have an experience which cannot be assimilated within their current cognitive structures, they may become aware of the shortcomings of those structures, and accommodate them to suit. In this way, they reach a more advanced state of equilibrium.

16.2.1 The development of thinking within Piaget's stages

In this section, we will consider how Piaget's ideas can be applied to the development of some aspects of thinking and reasoning in children. Our aims are to illustrate how children of different ages think, and to outline Piaget's views on aspects of development which we will later reconsider from a different perspective.

One concept that Piaget explored extensively is *conservation* (see §17. 2.1 for a detailed discussion of conservation of number). During the sensorimotor period, infants acquire a simple form of conservation, the conservation of existence, which Piaget called *object permanence*. Piaget observed that very young infants do not search for hidden objects, and claimed that they fail to understand that objects still exist when they cannot see them. This understanding develops gradually through the six stages of the sensorimotor period. By Stage 4 (about eight to twelve months), infants do search for objects that have disappeared, indicating that they believe the objects continue to exist, but it is not until eighteen to twenty-four months (Stage 6) that they can solve complex problems about the location of objects, such as those in which there is an *invisible displacement* – when the object is hidden under a cover, and the covered object is then moved to another location. At this stage, too, children form simple understandings of classes and relations. Their understanding of relations develops from their sensorimotor activities, as they gradually learn the causal relations between their activities and the consequences of them. In the final stage of the sensorimotor period, children are capable of symbolic representation. They understand that symbols (e.g., words) represent things, and they can think about things, and name them, even in their absence.

In the preoperational period, children are increasingly able to represent their thoughts and ideas in language and mental images. However, they cannot solve conservation and class inclusion problems. In conservation tasks, they fail to realize, for example, that, although spreading out a row of objects will make them take up more space, it will not increase the *number* of objects (conservation of number). Similarly, they fail to understand that pouring liquid from a short wide glass to a tall thin one leaves unchanged the *amount* of liquid (conservation of volume). In one example of a *class inclusion* problem, children are presented with eight flowers, six red and two yellow, and are asked, 'Are there more red flowers or more flowers?'. Before age seven or eight, children claim that there are more red flowers. Piaget attributed these errors to children's inability to consider more than one dimension of an object, or more than one way of classifying it, at a time, and to their tendency to focus on salient perceptual cues rather than transformations. In the class inclusion problem, children find it difficult to keep in mind that a particular flower belongs simultaneously to a subset (red flowers) and its superset (flowers). They reinterpret the question, and compare red flowers with yellow ones. In the conservation problems, they are misled by appearances. They only consider one aspect (e.g., height of water), and do not realize that the particular perspective they have adopted may be misleading. They do not appreciate that, when the superficial appearance of something changes, relatively complex underlying measures, such as number or volume, may be conserved in the transformation. Although children's understanding grows considerably during the preoperational period, their ability to take account of all the *relevant* features of a problem remains limited.

In the *concrete operational* period, according to Piaget, children acquire true *operations*, which permit them to solve concrete conservation and class inclusion problems. These operations allow them to represent transformations, and to understand, for example, that properties such as number, amount and weight are conserved over transformations that alter appearances. Thus, they realize that a long sparse row of counters does not have more counters in it than a short dense row with the same number of counters. In this stage they can also solve more complex classification problems that require them to attend simultaneously to two dimensions, for example, both the colour and the shape of an object.

By the stage of *formal operations* children can understand transformations of transformations. They can perform operations on their representations, and they develop the ability to reflect on their own thoughts. Children in this stage can think of possible outcomes, and can relate actual outcomes to those that are possible. They also have a sophisticated understanding of classes and relations.

16.2.2   Problems with Piaget's theory

There are two main problems with Piaget's theory. The first lies in the formulation of the theoretical ideas themselves. They are often stated in a vague or over-general way, and sometimes they are not even testable.

Even when they are testable, they are not always supported by the evidence. For example, a central feature of Piagetian theory is that reasoning in many different tasks will show characteristics of the stage a child is in. However, there are complications that the theory has no satisfactory way of explaining. For example, conservation of number, class inclusion and seriation are all concepts that are supposed to develop at the concrete operational level. However, conservation of number develops much earlier (about six years) than does conservation of weight (about ten years).

The second problem is that the theory is often grounded in, or supported by, dubious empirical evidence. As we mentioned above, Piaget's claims about children's abilities are based primarily on informal observational studies, which emphasize children's ability to explain what they are doing verbally, and in which suitable experimental controls are often missing. Piaget tends to focus on things that children cannot do at particular stages of development. By contrast, subsequent work, using more rigorous experimental techniques, has shown that children can be induced to solve problems that Piaget claimed they could not solve. These experiments show that young children are more competent than Piaget allowed. For one reason or another, children often have conceptual understanding that they are not able to explain to someone using Piaget's methods. A common technique in recent experimental work is to reduce sources of difficulty that are not central to the problem itself, for example, by decreasing the amount to be remembered, making the instructions simpler and clearer, and eliminating misleading cues (see, e.g., Donaldson, 1978, for an overview of these issues).

16.3 Information-Processing Theories of Development

Information-processing theories of the development of children's reasoning can be seen either as an alternative to, or an extension of, Piaget's theory, depending on one's perspective. The objectives of an information-processing theory are to give a precise account of the representations and processes used by the child when he or she reasons, and to show how developmental changes in reasoning ability can be explained by changes in the cognitive system. Information-processing accounts, thus, attempt to explain *why* changes occur. Rather than focusing on *stages*, the information-processing approach tries to specify what information children attend to, what representations and processes they use, and how memory limitations might constrain the use of those representations and processes. The ultimate aim is to produce explicit and testable theories of cognitive functions and their development. In the first part of this section, to give the reader a feel for this work, we will outline two theories of cognitive development in the information-processing tradition. We will then consider children's performance on verbal reasoning problems (deductive inferences), and how their development might be modelled in information-processing terms.

No single information-processing theory is as comprehensive as Piaget's, but each provides more detail about a particular aspect of development. Some theorists – the *neo-Piagetians*, whose ideas we will consider in the next section – have tried to modify Piagetian theory to incorporate information-processing considerations. Others have reinvestigated some of Piaget's findings, using concepts and methods from the information-processing approach. Siegler's *Rule Assessment* methodology (1976) is an example of the second of these approaches. We will outline it here as an example of how performance on Piagetian tasks can be studied from an information-processing perspective. Siegler views cognitive development as the acquisition of increasingly complex rules for solving problems. His hypotheses about the rules are derived, at least in part, from Piaget's findings. The basic idea of his theory is that, as children's reasoning develops, they encode aspects of problems that they previously ignored. This encoding heightens their ability to learn from experience, and leads to the development of more advanced rules. The methodology, which allows the assessment of what rules children are using, requires the creation of sets of problems for which the different rules produce different answers.

One problem to which Siegler has applied this methodology is the *balance beam problem*. In this problem, the child is shown a balance beam with equally spaced pegs, and has to decide whether or not the apparatus will balance when a number of equal weights are placed on one (and only one) of the pegs on each side of the fulcrum. Siegler formulated four rules that children might use in trying to solve these problems (see figure 16.1):

Rule 1:   Take account of the total weight on each side only, and ignore the distance of the weights from the fulcrum. Children using this rule will perform correctly when the weights are equal and equidistant from the fulcrum, or if the weights are different and equidistant (as will children using the other rules). They will also perform fortuitously correctly when their simplistic rule happens to make the same prediction as a more

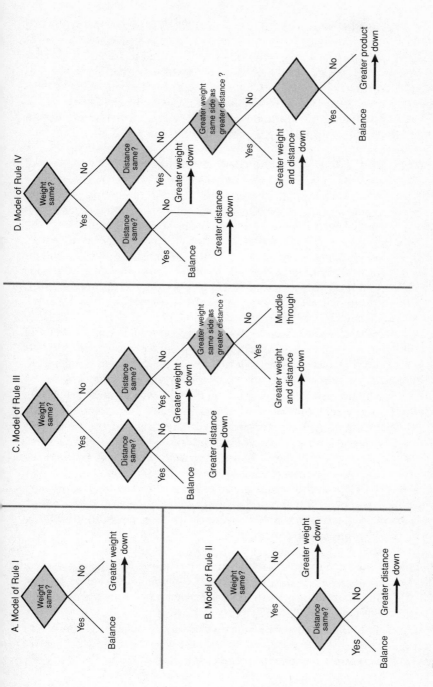

Figure 16.1 Models of rules for performing the balance beam task (from R. S. Siegler (1983). Information processing approaches to cognitive development. In W. Kessen, ed., *Handbook of Child Psychology*, vol. 1. New York: Wiley, p. 160.)

complex (correct) rule (in so-called *conflict-weight* problems; see figure 16.2).

Rule 2:   As for Rule 1, except that, when the weights are equal, predict that the side on which the weights are further from the fulcrum will go down. Children using this second rule will perform better on problems where the weights are the same on both sides, but those on one side are further from the fulcrum (children using Rule 1 will say the beam will balance in such cases).

Rule 3:   With this rule, children realize that they should always take account of both weight *and* distance. If both are equal, they predict balance. If one is equal and the other not, they base their judgements on the unequal dimension. If both are unequal, then they will only be right if both dimensions independently favour the same side. Otherwise, they will guess. Interestingly, Siegler found that seventeen-year-old subjects (most of whom used this rule) were *worse* than five-year-olds on certain sorts of problems. When weight and distance conflict, and the correct answer is that the side with more weight will go down (conflict-weight problems: see figure 16.2), the older children made more errors. The five-year-olds (most of whom were using Rule 1, which ignores distance and simply predicts that the heavier side will go down) were correct 89 per cent of the time. The seventeen-year-olds, by contrast, who knew that they *should* be attending to both weight and distance in these sorts of problems, but did not know how to combine the information, were correct only 51 per cent of the time. This striking finding – that older children performed considerably *worse* than younger ones – is readily explained by Siegler's approach, and provides strong support for his analysis.

Rule 4:   If weight and distance are in conflict, then the *torques* (weight × distance) for each side should be calculated and compared. This rule is the correct one, and is the only rule that will give the right answer in all cases.

According to Siegler, most five-year-olds use Rule 1. By nine years, most children are using Rule 2, and thirteen to seventeen-year-olds tend to use Rule 3. Very few of his subjects used Rule 4, even in the oldest age group.

Siegler has applied his Rule Assessment approach to a number of Piagetian tasks, with similar results. In each case he proposes a set of rules of increasing complexity, where complexity is indicated by the

Problem – type	Rule			
	I	II	III	IV
Balance 	100	100	100	100
Weight 	100	100	100	100
Distance 	0 (Should say 'Balance')	100	100	100
Conflict – weight 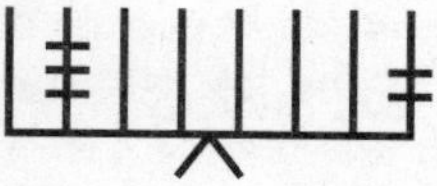	100	100	33 (Chance responding)	100
Conflict – distance 	0 (Should say 'Right down')	0 (Should say 'Right down')	33 (Chance responding)	100
Conflict – balance 	0 (Should say 'Right down')	0 (Should say 'Right down')	33 (Chance responding)	100

Figure 16.2   Problems used to assess understanding of the balance beam (from R. S. Siegler (1983). Information processing approaches to cognitive development. In W. Kessen, ed., *Handbook of Child Psychology*, vol. 1. New York: Wiley, p. 160.)

number of decisions, or pieces of information to be interrelated, to solve a problem. The increase in the complexity of the rules that children use fits with the idea that cognitive development is restricted by processing limitations. It is well established that attentional resources are limited, for example, and Hitch and Baddeley (1976) propose a working memory of limited capacity. Information-processing theorists argue that processing resources increase with age and, as they do so, more complex forms of reasoning and problem solving become possible. Below a certain memory capacity, children may find it difficult or impossible to solve problems, or acquire concepts, beyond a certain level of complexity. Their working memory will not allow them to attend simultaneously to all the relevant pieces of information, and to interrelate them.

An increase in working memory capacity might occur in one of two ways, either through an increase in total processing space, or by a decrease in the space used for operations performed in working memory. In the latter case *available* space increases, even if the *total* capacity remains constant. There is, in fact, evidence that the *size* of working memory does not change with age. What might change is either the speed with which information can be processed (sometimes called *operational efficiency*), or the child's knowledge in a certain domain (expertise). An example of how knowledge influences memory is the finding that ten-year-old chess players are better than adult non-players at recalling the positions of pieces on a chess board (Chi, 1978). Presumably, they can use their knowledge of the game, and of likely configurations of pieces, to aid their memory in a way that the adult non-players cannot (see also chapter 12). The standard account of this phenomenon is in terms of the *chunking* of information (Miller, 1956), so that it can be stored more efficiently in short-term memory.

Development is more than just the acquisition of knowledge in various domains. Changes in the way knowledge is used also take place. The information-processing view of the mechanisms by which development occurs is different from that of Piagetians. It focuses on four mechanisms: *automatization, encoding, generalization,* and *strategy construction.* The first of these, automatization, refers to the way mental processes become more and more automatic with practice, so that they gradually take up fewer resources. For example, a young child learning to read may labour over the letters in a word, and take some time to sound it out. A skilled reader, however, will recognize words apparently effortlessly, usually with no conscious realization of any mental effort. The second process, encoding, refers to the aspects of a situation that receive attention. Young children typically focus on one aspect of a problem, perhaps the wrong one or an irrelevant one, whereas skilled problem solvers are better able to select all the relevant information. The third mechanism, the ability to make generalizations from evidence, is one aspect of inductive reasoning (see chapter 7). After repeated exposure to situations of a particular kind, perhaps electrical toys that do not work because they do not have batteries, children will make the generalization (in our experience over-generalization!) that toys of a certain kind need batteries to make them work. The fourth mechanism, strategy construction, is self-explanatory. Children develop more sophisticated strategies for solving problems and testing hypotheses. In general, the more carefully thought-out their strategies, the more effective thinking and problem solving will be.

A further question is: what causes change? Why do processes become automated? How do children come to encode more aspects of a problem? How do they know when to generalize? What makes them develop new strategies? Indeed, Siegler (1993) argues that psychologists' obsession with differences among children of different ages has diverted attention from the question of *how* change occurs. He suggests a new way of conceptualizing the development of thinking, which is consistent with what is known about children's thinking and more helpful for understanding the process of change. He assumes that, from an early age, children have a variety of strategies available, and that some of these strategies become more dominant, some less dominant, with development. New strategies might develop too, but at any age one strategy is likely to be dominant. Development is through competition among alternative ways of thinking about things. Siegler has developed a new methodology (the *microgenetic* method) to study change. This methodology will be illustrated in the next chapter, when we discuss the development of mathematical reasoning.

16.3.1 The 'neo-Piagetian' approach

As we mentioned earlier, attempts have been made to reconcile Piaget's stage theory with an information-processing approach. Pascual-Leone (1970), for example, has tried to integrate the idea of growth in working memory (which he calls *M-space*) with a Piagetian stage theory. Similarly, Case (1985) has developed a stage theory which views development as the acquisition of increasingly complex cognitive structures. Case argues for four stages, which are based on Piaget's, but his theory also incorporates information-processing principles. Case characterizes these stages by the types of mental representations and mental operations that are available to the child. Briefly, his stages are as follows (their relation to Piaget's stages should be obvious):

1 *Sensorimotor operations*: At this stage, children's representations are based on their sensory input. Their actions are physical movements.
2 *Representational operations*: At this stage, children's representations include more durable (though concrete) internal images, and their actions include the use of representations to produce new representations.
3 *Logical operations*: At this stage, children also represent more abstract stimuli, and their actions include actions on their representations: they can perform simple transformations on them. In other words, they become capable of some kinds of logical thought and reasoning.
4 *Formal operations*: This stage is closely related to the third, in that children represent stimuli abstractly, but they are capable of performing more complex transformations on their representations.

Some examples (from Siegler, 1991) will clarify the sorts of thinking that are possible at the four stages. At the sensorimotor stage, the child might see a frightening face (sensory representation) and run out of the room (physical action). At the representational operations stage, the child might see the same face, but produce a mental image of it (internal representation), and use this image to draw a picture of the face when it is no longer present (representational action). A logical operation might occur if a child realizes that two of his friends dislike one another (abstract representation), and tells them that they would have more fun together if they were all friends (simple transformation). Finally, at the formal operations stage, the child might realize that such simplistic attempts at fostering friendship rarely work (abstract representation), and that bringing all three of them into a situation where they could work towards some common need or cause might be a better way to foster friendship.

Like Siegler, Case proposes that children develop by acquiring more complex strategies (which he calls *executive control structures*). He also suggests that the acquisition of these more sophisticated strategies is limited by the child's experience in particular domains, and by working memory capacity. Case's view is that development occurs through the interaction of age-invariant activities (such as exploration and problem solving) and general factors that do vary with age (in particular, memory capacity). He distinguishes two components of working memory, which he terms *operating space* and *short-term memory space*. He believes that the absolute size of working memory does not increase, but that, as a child develops, less space is devoted to basic operations. As these operations become more automatic, the demands on operating space are reduced, and there is a concomitant increase in available capacity. The same problem will invoke one strategy in a four-year-old and another in a six-year-old because the older child has more available capacity to integrate his or her experiences.

A study by Noelting (1976) illustrates how working memory might limit problem solving. Noelting asked children which of two mixtures would taste more strongly of orange, when they knew how many cups of water and of orange squash had been tipped into each. He showed that increased sophistication in reasoning goes hand-in-hand with an increase in the number of steps required to reach a solution and, correspondingly, the number of items that need to be held in working memory. The four strategies are shown in figure 16.3. The strategies can be summarized as follows:

Strategy 1: Children from about three to four and a half years base their judgement on the presence or absence of orange juice. If a jug gets some juice then it will taste of orange. These children take no account of the *relative* quantities of juice and water and, hence, can only guess if *both* jugs have some orange juice. Noelting proposes that this strategy requires two steps, and that only one piece of information needs to be held in working memory – whether or not the first jug has juice in it.

Strategy 2: Between about four and a half and six years, children base their judgements on the number of cups of *juice* in each jug, and disregard the amount of water. Hence, if one jug has more juice, but a smaller *proportion* of juice, they will get the answer wrong. In Noelting's conceptualization, this strategy requires three steps and a maximum of two items in memory (the number of cups of juice in each of the jugs).

Strategy 3: Around seven to eight years children begin to use a third strategy. They consider the relative amounts of juice and water in the two jugs. If one jug gets more juice than water, and the other does not, they say the one with more juice will taste more strongly of orange. If both jugs have more juice than water, or neither does, they guess. This strategy has seven steps, and a maximum of three items in working memory (whether the first jug has more juice than

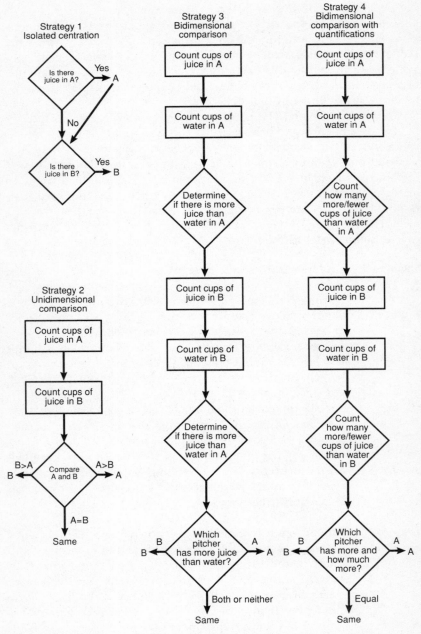

Figure 16.3   Four strategies for solving juice mixture problems (from R. E. Mayer (1983). *Thinking, Problem Solving, Cognition*. New York: Freeman, p. 285.)

water, the number of cups of juice in the second jug, and the number of cups of water in that jug).

Strategy 4: At nine to ten years, children start to make a more sophisticated comparison of the relative amounts of juice and water in the two jugs. However, they assess strength by *subtracting* the numbers of cups of juice from cups of water (or vice-versa), a strategy that fails in some cases, because they should be calculating *ratios* rather than differences. For this strategy, there are again seven steps, but a maximum of four items in working memory.

Although this theory is plausible, this kind of account faces the problem that it is hard, or sometimes impossible, to obtain *independent* evidence about what strategy a child is using, and hence what demands a task puts on that child's working memory (see Flavell, 1978). The theory, therefore, faces the danger of circularity. Certain problems are found to be difficult for the children, and the difficulty is explained by high working memory demands. But how do we know that there are high working memory demands? Because the problems are difficult! A theorist may, therefore, be biased towards suggesting strategies with more or fewer processing components, according to how hard the task is known to be.

16.3.2 Deductive reasoning within the information-processing framework

In the study of children's deductive reasoning, there are two opposing theoretical views, which correspond roughly to the Piagetian (mental logic) and information-processing approaches. Gellatly (1989; p. 233) caricatures the difference between them as 'whether logic is descriptive of thinking processes or merely prescriptive of what is considered to be sound reasoning'. The mental logic approach posits rules of inference in the mind that closely resemble formal inference rules, though it admits the influence of processing limitations. Piaget saw the development of reasoning as the acquisition of logics of increasing complexity, culminating at the stage of formal operations in the propositional calculus (see chapter 4)! So, abstract deductive reasoning is possible only at the fourth of the Piagetian stages. The information-processing account, by contrast, argues that deductive reasoning is mediated by a developing information-processing system, in the same way as other forms of cognition (see Johnson-Laird, 1983).

The information-processing approach to deductive reasoning is not as well worked out as for the balance beam and juice problems (the most detailed account is probably that of Trabasso, 1977), but it is easy to see how its principles might be applied. The goal of the information-processing approach is to discover *how* problems are solved. In its account of deductive reasoning it therefore focuses on memory and language skills, and on the ability to *form and manipulate representations of the premises*, rather than on formal rules of inference. *Transitive inference* is the most frequently studied reasoning skill in children, and we will use it to illustrate how the information-processing approach can be applied to children's deductive reasoning. A typical example of a transitive inference problem is:

A is longer than B
B is longer than C
Is A longer than C?

Children, especially younger ones, are not usually given purely verbal versions of transitive inference problems. They are shown (parts of) the objects corresponding to A, B and C. A common method is to use sticks of different lengths, with the sticks partly hidden, so that the children cannot see the relation between the lengths of A and C. They are then told about the relations between the lengths of some pairs of sticks, and required to make inferences about other pairs. Piaget argued that transitive inferences about length require concrete operations, and that children could not make them until the age of about seven or eight. Until then, they do not understand that 'longer' and 'shorter' are *relative* terms. Once they reach this stage, and are able to bear in mind that B can be both relatively large (compared with C) and relatively small (compared with A), they can work out the relation between A and C using B as an intermediary.

Many studies have challenged Piaget's claim about the age at which children can make these deductions. The earliest and most famous is by Bryant and Trabasso (1971), who used five sticks to avoid the potential problem of *labelling* (or *end effects*). In a version with only three sticks the crucial A and C sticks lie at either end of the series, and are only ever referred to as being 'longer' and 'shorter', respectively. Therefore, children could base their answer on these labels ('A is longer', 'C is shorter'), and could be correct 100 per cent of the time without making a proper transitive inference. In a five-stick version, the middle three sticks (B, C and D) can equally often be labelled 'longer' and 'shorter', and children cannot judge the length of B with respect to D by a labelling strategy.

In the training phase of their study, Bryant and Trabasso showed children pairs of coloured sticks, adjacent to one another in the series, but whose actual length was hidden. They were told, for example, that A is longer than B, E is shorter than D, C is longer than D, and C is shorter than B. This information supports the series A > B > C > D > E. Each child was then shown the training pairs, asked which was longer, and then told whether they were right or wrong. Once the child had thoroughly learned the training pairs, they entered the test phase where they were quizzed on all ten possible pairs. The crucial comparison was between the B and D sticks, because their relative length can be judged only with respect to the C stick. With sufficient training on the initial pairs, even four-year-olds could get the answer right. Bryant and Trabasso concluded that young children's traditional failure on these problems is not one of understanding transitivity, but one of memory. So long as they can remember the initial information about the relative lengths of pairs of sticks, they can make the transitive inference.

There has been some debate about the interpretation of Bryant and Trabasso's findings. Breslow (1981) claimed that the results could be explained in terms of what he called *sequential contiguity*. He argued that children do generate a linear order of stick lengths during training, *but not by making transitive inferences*. They derive a set of contiguity relations: which sticks 'go with' which other sticks. Thus, they can derive a linear ordering from the end sticks – the only ones which are consistently labelled 'long' and 'short' – from these contiguity relations. Furthermore, Piagetians argue that because Bryant and Trabasso asked their subjects only for judgements about relative length, and not justifications of these judgements, their findings do not challenge Piaget's account.

As this riposte indicates, part of what is at stake is how much emphasis should be placed on verbal explanations in assessing children's cognitive skills. Children of four cannot necessarily verbalize their understanding of a concept – young children are notoriously bad at explaining how they know something. Thayer and Collyer (1978) provide a thorough review of the research in this area, and try to account for the disagreement between Piagetian and information-processing theorists in terms of the methods they used. They suggest that Piagetians, who claim that transitivity is not attained until about eight years, have identified the age at which the principle is spontaneously applied over a range of situations:

Piagetian methods of diagnosis exclude those younger children for whom transitivity is evocable, given appropriate environmental conditions, but not yet spontaneously utilised in the absence of special conditions. . . . Transitive inference may become available to the young child by age 4 or 5 under optimal conditions of training, feedback, and so forth; however, there is some reason to judge that the principle is not fully developed until age 8 or 9 when it can function reliably with minimal environmental support across many varied situations.

A problem in this debate is that, since their investigations spring from different theoretical assumptions about cognitive development, Piagetians and information-processing theorists are asking different sorts of question. Piagetians focus on whether the child has really acquired the concept under investigation, and whether it really understands 'logical necessity' (that if A is longer than B and B is longer than C, then A *must* be longer than C, given that length is a transitive relation). Information-processing psychologists ask about the processes and strategies underlying the child's ability to give the correct answers on tasks designed to assess inference skills. Another way of looking at this distinction is by considering the difference between drawing an inference (which Bryant and Trabasso's children did), and understanding *why* that inference is valid, which is a metacognitive skill (and which Piaget wanted his children to demonstrate). The distinction is highlighted by research on transitive inference in animals. McGonigle and Chalmers (1977) demonstrated that, under conditions similar to those used by Bryant and Trabasso, non-human primates (squirrel monkeys) show transitive choice patterns. Subsequently, rats (von Ferson, Wynne, Delius and Stadden, 1991) and pigeons (Davis, 1992) have also been shown to 'draw transitive inferences'. However, since animals cannot talk, it is hard to see what would count as evidence for their understanding why transitive inferences are valid. One cannot do much more than show that they can perform transitive inference tasks. However, the important issue is not which is the *right* approach, but *which is more likely to produce interesting insights into development*.

Let us return to the role of memory in deductive reasoning. Children sometimes make incorrect inferences, even when they can recall the premise information, so inability to recall the premises cannot be the only reason for children's failure (e.g., Smedslund, 1977, cited in Russell, 1981). Furthermore, Russell (1981) found that young children who make *incorrect* inferences often justify their conclusions by citing the correct premises! Trabasso (1977) argues that a distinction must be made between rote learning of premises and understanding them. In his experiments, he tried to ensure that children *understood* the contrastive relations by training them on both a premise and its converse, for example, 'A is longer than B', and 'B is shorter than A'.

Once again, working memory might provide the key to understanding children's difficulties. In order to make inferences, children have to *represent and integrate* the information in the premises, not just recall them. Oakhill (1984) showed that aspects of a deductive reasoning problem that decreased processing load increased the chance of reaching the correct solution. Processing load was reduced in two ways: by decreasing the linguistic complexity of the problems, and by giving the children memory cards so that they could represent some of the relations described in the premises. Both forms of processing load reduction helped. Information-processing theories of deductive inference have had little to say about *how* children develop the relevant reasoning skills. The idea from Case and Siegler that children's cognitive development is related to a corresponding development in working memory is a fruitful one, and it would be useful to analyse deductive reasoning in the same detail as the balance beam and juice problems.

16.4   The Development of Problem Solving

We have already discussed the development of specific problem-solving abilities (e.g., for the balance beam problem). In this section we will consider problem solving more generally and, in particular, the kinds of strategy that children use. Siegler (1991) stresses the importance of *encoding* in problem solving. Children often fail to encode crucial features of a problem, or fail to encode them efficiently, perhaps because they do not know which features to attend to, or do not understand their importance. Siegler suggests that encoding is closely related to the building of *mental models* (see chapters 5, 6 and 11). The mental model of the problem must accurately represent the structure of the problem itself. However, an adequate mental model should represent not just the components of a problem, and the relations between them, but also the possible moves that can be made in attempting to solve the problem (see also chapter 11). A good mental model should help problem solving by ruling out some moves and suggesting others. Hence, the adequacy or otherwise of a mental model could influence problem solving in a number of ways. In particular, some of the components and the relations between them might be omitted or misrepresented, or the possible moves might be inadequately represented. The developing ability to form mental

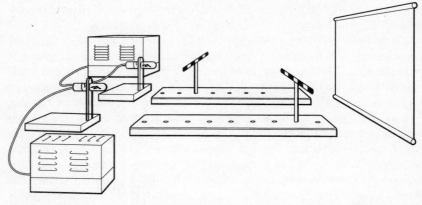

Figure 16.4 Projection of shadows apparatus used by Siegler (1981): turning on the point light sources led to different-size shadows on the screen, with the shadows' sizes depending on the length of the T-shaped bars and their distances from the light sources and the screen

models of problems is a major factor in the development of problem-solving skills.

We saw, earlier in this chapter, how children's ability to solve balance beam problems can be characterized using Siegler's rule assessment approach. Increasing skill in solving these problems can be attributed to the developing ability to attend to *both* of the relevant dimensions (weight and distance from fulcrum) and to combine them appropriately. The rules that the children use vary in complexity and in how many of the relevant dimensions they take into account. Siegler has demonstrated that children approach a variety of other problems in similar ways. For example, Siegler (1981) showed a similar sequence of stages on a problem about projection of shadows. The children were asked to predict which of two bars (located between a light source and a screen) would cast the larger shadow when the light sources were turned on (see figure 16.4). Both the size of the bars and their distance from the screen could be varied. The youngest children (five-year-olds) typically based their judgements on the size of the bars, and said that the larger bar would make the bigger shadow. At the next level, eight- and nine-year-old children also relied on size except that, when the bars were the same size, they were able to take distance into account. Twelve- to thirteen-year-olds knew that they should take both sources of information into account, but did not know the correct way to combine them. Indeed, few subjects, whatever their age, knew the proportionality rule that would ensure a correct solution for all of the problems. The parallels with the developmental stages in solving the balance beam problem discussed earlier should be clear. Siegler cites many other studies that have found similar sequences of rules for a wide variety of problem types: problems about happiness and fairness, about causal reasoning and about concept formation.

A central feature of young (four- to six-year-old) children's problem solving is that they focus their attention on only one dimension of a problem, even when two or more dimensions are relevant. Older children realize the importance of considering other dimensions. They do not, however, always know how to combine the information from different dimensions, though they gradually develop more sophisticated strategies for doing so. It is not that young children are *incapable* of attending to more than one dimension, but that they have a strong bias to attend to one dimension only, perhaps because of the limitations on their working memories. Other evidence suggests that they would find it hard to attend to, and integrate, different sources of information because of processing limitations (see, e.g., the work on deductive reasoning, described in §16.3.2 above).

16.4.1 Planning in problem solving

Planning is often an important aspect of problem solving. For example, a child who is trying to decide which particular material will be useful for part of a construction he or she is building will do well to consider exactly what is needed (does the material need to be rigid or flexible, opaque or transparent, for example?) and how the materials available might satisfy those needs. The child who plans in this way, rather than trying things out on a trial-and-error basis, will save time and avoid frustration, and will likely produce a more effective model. However, planning has costs as well as benefits. Although it can save on mistakes and unnecessary effort, planning itself takes time and might be cognitively demanding. Good planning must strike a balance between procrastination and hasty action. As we mentioned above, the mental model of a problem can be used to consider possible moves and operations. In other words, it can be used in the planning of a solution.

One form of planning that is widely applicable is means-ends analysis (see chapter 11). In means-end analysis the goal is compared with the present situation, and an attempt is made to reduce the difference between them in a series of recursive steps. The rudiments of means-end analysis can be seen in infants as young as four to eight months (Willats, 1984; Case, 1985). The development of means-ends analysis is dependent on children's ability to keep subgoals in mind and to persist in pursuing longer-term goals.

Such changes are evident in developmental differences in children's approaches to the Tower of Hanoi problem (see chapter 11). In order to solve this problem successfully, with the minimum number of moves, a considerable amount of planning is needed. Klahr and Robinson (1981) gave pre-school children a simplified version of the problem. Earlier studies had shown that even five- and six-year-olds find a two-disc (three-move) problem difficult. However, as Klahr and Robinson point out, this finding is inconsistent with the observation that, in everyday life, children of this age can find solutions to problems that require many more moves. One possible reason for this discrepancy, they hypothesize, is that children often make mistakes because they forget, or choose to disregard, constraints, such as that larger discs may not be placed on top of smaller ones. In their modified version of the Tower of Hanoi, Klahr and Robinson used nests of inverted cans on posts, with the constraint that smaller cans must not be placed on top of larger ones. If the child forgot the constraint, or attempted to violate it, they were rapidly reminded, since the smaller can fell off the larger one! In addition, the problem was presented in the context of a story about monkeys, to make it more appealing. The cans were presented as mummy, daddy and baby monkey, who could jump from tree to tree (post to post). The child had to tell the experimenter how to move his or her can so that they were in the same configuration as the child's, with all moves subject to the constraint mentioned above.

After some practice, the child simply had to *tell* the experimenter a sequence of moves, without the experimenter moving the cans. Despite the fact that this task was probably more difficult than actually moving cans, Klahr and Robinson found that most four-year-olds could provide the optimal solution to two-move problems, whereas five- and six-year-olds were good on four-move problems, and over 50 per cent of the six-year-olds could solve six-move problems. They hypothesized that the problem for the younger children was that they were less able to create an internal representation of the problem on which to try out procedures. While there was evidence that all of the children divided their overall goal into a number of subgoals, the younger children made many illegal moves, and often lost track of their objectives. The older children were better able to establish and execute subgoals to work towards their final goal, and looked further ahead when planning their moves.

16.4.2   Children's use of analogy in problem solving

According to Piaget, analogies both of the kind found in IQ tests (horse is to foal, as sheep is to ?), and those derived from one problem and applied to another (see chapter 11), require formal operations, and are therefore not systematically mastered by children until they reach their teens. An opposing view (e.g., Goswami, 1992) is that the difficulty young children have in solving or using analogies can be explained by their lack of knowledge about the domain from which the analogy is drawn or the domain to which it is applied. Since analogies are usually based on relational information, it is knowledge about relations in those domains that is particularly important.

Goswami and Brown (1989) showed that even three-year-olds could solve analogies based on causal relations, such as cutting and melting, with which they were familiar. For example, given pictures of chocolate and melted chocolate as the basis for an analogy, and a picture of a snowman, the children selected a picture of a melted snowman to complete the analogy. The alternatives included the wrong change to the same object (dirty snowman), the wrong object changed in the right way (melted crayon), a physically similar object (scarecrow) and an associate (sled). These results clearly support the knowledge-based view of the development of analogical reasoning, and suggest that previous results should be explained by the fact that the analogies children had to solve drew on knowledge which they did not have.

Summary

There are two main perspectives on the development of thinking, the Piagetian and the information processing. Piaget regards cognitive development as comprising four qualitatively different stages: sensorimotor, preoperational, concrete operational and formal operational. The processes of assimilation, accommodation and equilibration determine change both within and between stages. Tasks, such as conservation, illuminate children's thinking, and its shortcomings, at various ages.

Information-processing theories tend to see development as more continuous. They focus of the role of, for example, increasing memory capacity in the development of cognitive skills, and on the mechanisms of automatization, encoding, generalization and strategy construction. Siegler has proposed that children use an expanding set of rules to solve problems such as the balance beam problem, and has attempted to determine, empirically, what those rules are.

Neo-Piagetians, such as Pascual-Leone and Case, have attempted to combine the Piagetian and the information-processing approaches. They have proposed stage theories, like Piaget, but have incorporated considerations, such as the development of working memory, from the information-processing approach.

Piaget claims that many abilities develop comparatively late. For example, he regards deductive reasoning, and also analogical reasoning, as characteristic of the stage of formal operations. However, more experimentally oriented techniques suggest that such abilities, and in particular transitive inference and the use of analogy, develop sooner. Anti-Piagetians argue that Piaget may have been misled because he did not concern himself with questions such as how well children remember the premises of transitive inferences, and how familiar they are with the domain from which the analogy is drawn.

Memory limitations may also explain young children's relatively poor performance in problem-solving experiments. Memory is important both in considering simultaneously several aspects of a problem and in planning ahead towards a solution.

Further Reading

Boden, M. A. (1979). *Piaget*. London: Fontana.
Case, R. (1985). *Intellectual Development: Birth to Adulthood*. Orlando, FA: Academic Press.
Siegler, R. S. (ed.) (1978). *Children's Thinking: What Develops?* Hillsdale, NJ: Lawrence Erlbaum Associates.
Siegler, R. S. (1991). *Children's Thinking* (2nd edn). Englewood Cliffs, NJ: Prentice-Hall.

17

The Development of Thinking: Scientific and Conceptual Thought

In the previous chapter we introduced the Piagetian and information-processing approaches to the development of thinking. We also described how these approaches explain developmental changes in deductive reasoning and problem solving. In this chapter we turn to research on other topics in the development of thinking – research that has not been so intimately linked with the dispute between Piagetians and adherents of the information-processing approach. This work centres on the topics of how children conceptualize the world, and how they work out whether their ideas are correct. In particular, we discuss hypothesis testing, scientific thinking, mathematical reasoning, children's conceptual development and children's ideas about other people's minds.

17.1 Hypothesis Testing and Induction

Young babies are able to entertain simple hypotheses about causes. They make predictions about series of events, and show surprise when things do not turn out as they had expected. Even at four or five months, babies use *contiguity* (occurrence close in time and space) to infer that events are related. They look longer when they see an object start moving without any collision, or when an object does not start moving until half a second after a collision (Leslie, 1982). In other words, they *expect* that a collision will cause movement, and are surprised when it does not, or when the expected movement is delayed. Similarly, Spelke (1991) has shown that between four and six months infants begin to appreciate the principles of gravity. They infer that falling objects, when hidden from view, continue falling to a surface. By three or four years, children can use the order of events to infer which event caused another, at least in some situations. If they are shown three events in the order A, B, C, and then asked 'What made B happen?' they will be more likely to choose A, which preceded B, than C, which followed it (Bullock and Gelman, 1979). By five, their understanding is stable, and they consistently say that the earlier event is the cause.

Young children are also able to perform well on versions of the Wason selection task (see chapter 8) that adults find easy. They are, of course, very bad on the standard version that even 85 per cent of college students fail to solve correctly. Vittorio Girotto, Paul Light and their colleagues showed that, with deontic rules (which have to do with permissions and obligations) and very familiar content, for example,

If you sit in the front of a car then you must wear a seat belt.

80 per cent of ten-year olds correctly selected the cards corresponding to possible violations of the rule (representing someone sitting in the front of a car, or someone without a seat belt). In a simplified version of the selection task, 70 per cent of seven-year olds succeeded with deontic rules (see Girotto and Light, 1992, for a summary). From a Piagetian perspective, the selection requires formal operational skills, and should not be solved until the early teens. However, as we saw in chapter 8, even adults do not solve the selection task using formal, domain-independent reasoning rules.

In more complex domains, the analogy of the 'child as scientist' has been used to characterize the way children make sense of the world. Children, like scientists, are supposed to explore the environment, and construct and test models to help them understand it. However, Kuhn (1989) has shown that this metaphor can be misleading, because the thinking of children, and of adults in their everyday lives, differs from that of trained scientists, even when it is guided by *lay theories*. The most influential proponents of the concept of 'child as scientist' are people who study the development of scientific understanding and conceptual change (e.g., Carey, 1985, see §17.3.2 below).

Children have a variety of naive, and often incorrect, ideas about how the world works, and they may have multiple, mutually incompatible conceptions of the same phenomenon, which they use in different contexts. These 'mental models' allow them them to explain how and why things happen, and to predict when they will happen. Despite their inadequacies, these lay conceptions are remarkably resistant to change. The development of scientific reasoning can, therefore, be seen as the construction, the refinement and to some extent the integration of a series of models of particular domains. People who espouse this view argue that there is no evidence for changes in the child's 'cognitive machinery', but that development can be accounted for in terms of conceptual change (see also Keil, 1984). However, others (e.g., Kuhn, Amsel and O'Loughlin, 1988; Schauble, 1990) have suggested that the *processes* of 'scientific' thinking are significantly different in children, lay adults and scientists. Such theorists accept the findings of Carey and others on 'developing knowledge structures', but they also look for strategy changes. A clear example of this approach can be found in the work of Kuhn described below (for a more detailed review, see Kuhn, 1989).

17.1.1 The nature of children's scientific reasoning

Before considering *why* children's scientific reasoning might go wrong, we will look at the kinds of error that children make. Kuhn, Amsel and O'Loughlin (1988), in one of their studies, told children that the sort of cake people ate (chocolate or carrot) affected whether they caught colds. The children were then introduced to two story characters: one of whom thought that children who ate *chocolate* cake were likely to catch colds, and the other who thought those who ate *carrot* cake were. They then saw evidence, graphically depicting covariation or non-covariation between eating different types of cake and susceptibility to colds. This evidence indicated which people ate chocolate cake, and which ate carrot cake, and whether they caught colds. The children were either asked to explain how the evidence showed that eating a particular type of cake made a difference, or they were asked to say which type of cake led to colds. They were also asked which story character's hypothesis was correct. Children performed poorly on all tasks. When asked to assess the evidence, they either ignored it, and insisted it was consistent with their prior theory, or they used the evidence to construct a new theory, but failed to understand that this new theory contradicted a previous one they had held. Kuhn et al. concluded that, before about eleven or twelve children have little insight into how hypotheses are supported or contradicted by evidence and, even when they get older, their understanding is often labile. Indeed, Kuhn (1989) argues that young children do not differentiate between theory and evidence.

Other experiments on children's scientific reasoning, using a variety of tasks (e.g., Dunbar and Klahr, 1989; Schauble, 1990), have shown that children often confound variables when trying to assess which one is causally effective and make little effort to manipulate variables systematically. For instance, Schauble (1990) gave ten- and eleven-year-olds the task of trying to determine what factors affected how fast a car would travel. She did so by allowing the children to experiment over a period of several weeks with a microcomputer racetrack, where the cars had different features, such as colour, engine capacity, and presence or absence of tail fin. She found that the children were poor at designing and interpreting experiments: only 22 per cent of their experiments could be classed as valid tests, and only 38 per cent of the judgements they made, based on their experimental findings, were valid. In part, the children performed poorly because they did not know what they needed to know if they were to come to a valid conclusion. Not a single child recorded covariation data, which is essential for inferences about which factors are causally related to speed. Some recorded the cars' features without outcomes, others the outcomes without features. Most wrote down nothing at all, preferring to rely on their memory of the variables and outcomes over the eight weeks of the experiment.

Like adults, the children in Schauble's experiment used what Klayman and Ha (1987) call a positive test strategy (see chapter 8). They spent more time testing variables they believed would influence speed (such as engine size) as opposed to the ones they believed would have no effect (such as colour). Indeed, the children showed a confirmation bias – a special case of the positive test strategy. They spent most of their time trying to construct fast cars, and hence trying to confirm their hypotheses about features associated with high speed, rather than trying to work out the relation between features and speed more systematically. However, despite their poor strategies, most of the subjects eventually discovered simple effects through their experiments, though those with more efficient procedures discovered them faster. The ability to produce high-level plans, and to make useful comparisons and valid judgements from those comparisons, all increased markedly over the course of the experiment, though only two of the twenty-two subjects discovered that engine size and tailfin had interactive effects. Given the inadequacy of their experiments, and their inability to record the results and interpret them, it is surprising that the children made any progress at all. Their main strategy was to make substantial use in their road tests of one or a few cars whose performance they were familiar with (*prototypical* cars, in Schauble's terminology). The performance of these cars was used to predict and interpret the speeds of other cars, depending on whether those cars were considered similar to or different from the prototypical car(s).

Dunbar and Klahr (1989) showed eight- to eleven-year-olds how to operate a computer-controlled robot tank by pressing command keys on a keyboard on top of it. They had to discover the function of a key they had not been taught – the repeat key – by conducting experiments. Dunbar and Klahr found that children, like adults, did not abandon a hypothesis on the basis of a single disconfirming instance. However, whereas adults tried to understand inconsistencies, children simply ig-nored them. Similar tendencies have been reported by Karmiloff-Smith and Inhelder (1974). Dunbar and Klahr characterize children as having *lax* criteria for accepting hypotheses. They appear not to realize that the results of earlier experiments must be considered when evaluating a hypothesis. Not only do children accept a hypothesis on the basis of incomplete evidence, they maintain it in the face of inconsistency.

Further work by Klahr, Fay and Dunbar (1993), using a similar robot-manipulation task, showed that both adults and children attempted to confirm rather than to disconfirm hypotheses, but that their strategy varied with the *plausibility* of the hypothesis. Hypotheses, which were always incorrect, were suggested to the subjects. All age groups (nine- and eleven-year olds and adults) responded similarly to plausible hypo-theses by attempting to confirm them. However, adults and children differed in their response to implausible hypotheses. Adults attempted to discriminate experimentally between the implausible hypothesis they were given and a plausible one of their own devising. Children, and in particular the younger group, also proposed an alternative plausible hypothesis but, instead of comparing the two hypotheses, they ignored the original implausible one, and tried to generate evidence for their own plausible hypothesis. Thus, an implausible hypothesis led to a re-duction in confirmation bias in adults, but not in the younger children.

Schauble also found that, even if a particular belief was consistently disconfirmed, children did not necessarily abandon it. It seemed to 'fade' gradually, reappearing less regularly, rather than being conclusively re-jected. This idea is consistent with models of induction that describe it as a process in which the relative strengths of rules are gradually modified (e.g., Holland, Holyoak, Nisbett and Thagard, 1986). However, other work which we will discuss below shows that children are capable of formulating and explicitly testing hypotheses at a much younger age.

17.1.2   Why is children's scientific reasoning so limited?

Two main skills are needed for effective scientific reasoning. First, children must understand the meaning of evidence and develop consistent criteria to evaluate it. Second, they must understand the relation between theory and evidence. Kuhn's main focus is on the way theories are revised in the light of new (often discrepant) evidence. Her results indicate that this process of theory revision undergoes important developmental changes. Kuhn found that not only do children have difficulty in changing their theories in the light of new evidence, but, even when theory and evidence are congruent, children do not distinguish between them. If asked to evaluate the *evidence* for a particular theory, they frequently restate the *theory*. This conflation of theory and evidence was common in eleven-year-olds, but it declined with age, and was never found in experts (Kuhn et al., 1988). The younger children had no sense of evidence 'standing apart from' a theory, and bearing on it. When theory and evidence were discrepant, the children used a variety of techniques for making them consistent: they either changed the theory (usually prior to acknowledging the discrepant evidence), or they 'adjusted' the evidence, either by ignoring it, or by using to it in a selective, distorting manner. Schauble (1990) also found that children were often reluctant to interpret evidence without first having a theory that would account for it. Furthermore, younger children were more likely to merge theory and evidence, and less likely to resolve a conflict between them, even if they were aware of it. However, college students had the same difficulties when the problems were more complex.

Kuhn (1989) argues that effective coordination of theory and evidence depends on three *metacognitive* abilities. First, children must encode and represent the evidence and the theory separately, so they can recognize relations between them. Second, they must treat the theory as an independent object of thought. Third, they must set aside their acceptance of the theory temporarily, so that the implications of the evidence for the truth or falsity of the theory can be assessed. In Piagetian terms, the metacognitive skills needed to reflect on one's cognitive processes are operations on mental operations, and hence not available until the stage of formal operations. Kuhn suggests that problems in relating evidence to theory arise because the acquisition of metacognitive skills is a gradual process. So, for example, at a certain stage of development, discrepancies between theory and evidence might be recognized, but children's metacognitive skills may not be sufficiently well developed for them to distinguish what comes from their own thoughts (the theory) and what from external sources (the evidence) – hence the frequent conflation of theory and evidence.

However, Kuhn's tasks may underestimate children's scientific reasoning abilities. As Ruffman, Perner, Olson and Doherty (1993) have noted, this idea is supported by findings on a related topic: children's *theory of mind* (see §17.4 below). The theory of mind literature indicates that, from about six years old, children have the conceptual prerequisites for understanding how evidence bears on a hypothesis. Ruffman, Olson, Ash and Keenan (1993) show that even four- and five-year-olds infer that misleading evidence will lead an onlooker to form a false belief about who took an item. Thus, Ruffman et al. (1993) argue, if children possess the metacognitive abilities to judge how evidence will affect an onlooker's beliefs at such an early age, it is odd that they cannot assess how evidence bears on a general hypothesis until eleven or later, as Kuhn et al. claim. Beliefs and hypotheses are both mental states, and understanding their origins requires metacognitive or metarepresentational abilities.

Sodian, Zaitchik and Carey (1991) showed that by six or seven children could distinguish between conclusive and inconclusive tests of a hypothesis. The children were told a story about two brothers who had different beliefs about the size of a mouse in their house: one thought it was large and the other thought it was small. They were asked which of two boxes the brothers should put out to find out how big the mouse was. Each box had food in it, but one had a large opening, and the other a small opening which was only big enough for the small mouse to fit through. Most children chose the small box, which was the only one that could provide a conclusive empirical test of the mouse's size. Furthermore, the majority of six-year-olds and almost all of the seven-year-olds showed that they understood the goal of testing a hypothesis, and that they knew that one test was conclusive while the other was inconclusive. Sodian et al. point out two reasons why Kuhn may have underestimated children's competence. First, she used problems in which children might have to overcome strong beliefs of their own. Second, she used complex tasks, in which there were several potentially causal variables, only some of which were actually causal.

Ruffman et al. (1993) have also found that younger children can understand the relation between evidence and hypothesis, given the right conditions. They used a *faked evidence* task, which is best explained by outlining one of their experiments. Ruffman et al. showed children pictures of boys who had either lost some of their teeth, or who had a full set. Some boys had eaten red food and some green, and whether they had lost teeth was completely determined by the colour of the food eaten. The children were asked which type of food caused tooth loss. Then the experimenter tampered with (faked) the evidence, so that the other colour food seemed to cause tooth loss. A character who had not witnessed this faking then arrived, and so, unlike the subjects, should have been led to a mistaken hypothesis about the colour of the food associated with lost teeth. The children were asked what conclusion this character would come to, given the evidence as it then stood. Ruffman et al. suggest that this faked evidence technique has three advantages over earlier techniques. First, it does not require complex verbal justifications. Second, the children had to consider only one type of cause: colour of food. Third, the task ensures that correct responses reflect a genuine understanding of the hypothesis–evidence distinction. To get the right answer, subjects have to realize that the story character should form a different hypothesis from their own, because he saw a different pattern of evidence. The results showed that even five-year-olds grasped the hypothesis–evidence relation.

In a second experiment, Ruffman et al. showed that by the age of six children understand that evidence need not be perfect for a hypothesis to be upheld. A third experiment tested children's understanding of prediction from hypotheses. It showed that children of six to seven understand that specific pieces of evidence can be construed as support for a general hypothesis (see chapter 7), and that general hypotheses form the basis for predictions about objects or events that are similar to those that provided the original evidence. Ruffman et al. conclude that their faked evidence task reveals earlier understanding of the evidence–hypothesis relation than asking children directly about why evidence supports a hypothesis: 'By 6 years of age children's metacognitive abilities are sufficiently developed to allow them some form of insight into hypotheses and the way they are constructed from patterns of evidence' (1993, p. 1635).

These results show that children of six or seven have a sophisticated understanding of how evidence bears on a hypothesis. However, the covariation relations used by Ruffman et al. were straightforward and the children were not required to design their *own* experiments to test hypotheses, a skill which, as Schauble has shown, is lacking in older children. Where the patterns of covariation are complex, older children, and even adults, have considerable difficulties in scientific reasoning tasks.

17.2 Mathematical Reasoning

In this section, we will consider children's ability to reason about quantity and number. The development of early mathematical reasoning is interesting, because it provides examples of imaginative problem solving. Piaget, whose ideas have been infiuential in education, claimed that children should not be taught number concepts until they are conceptually ready, and, in particular, not until they have grasped the idea of conservation of number (which we will explain shortly). Young children's facility with numbers and counting, Piaget argues, should be treated with caution. It is based on rote learning, and does not reflect real understanding of number. However, as we shall see, even pre-school children's ability to count and reason about numbers is more subtle that Piaget believed.

17.2.1 Conservation of number

In the standard conservation of number task, children are shown two rows of objects, which are set out so that each object in one row is next to one in the other row. Most pre-school children will agree that there are the same number of objects in each row. The experimenter then moves the objects in one of the rows, to make it longer or shorter. Children of six or seven will then incorrectly state that the longer row contains more objects. Older children realize that the number of objects in the transformed row is *conserved* when the row's layout is changed. According to Piaget, appreciation of conservation of number requires the conceptual apparatus of his stage of concrete operations. Therefore, it is not found before six to seven years.

Piaget's conclusions about conservation of number have been criticized in two ways. First, it has been argued that his criteria for number conservation are too stringent. As usual, Piaget asked children for verbal justifications. Second, it has been suggested that children are misled by being asked the same question twice ('Which row has more in it?'). They think that they should give a different answer the second time. In addition, many experimental demonstrations show that children can conserve number earlier than Piaget claimed. When the displacement of the second row is accidental – for example, when the objects are knocked out of place by 'naughty teddy' (McGarrigle and Donaldson, 1975) –

a higher proportion of children exhibit number conservation than on the standard task.

Gelman and her associates (Gelman, 1972; Gelman and Gallistel, 1978) have also shown that pre-school children have a better understanding of number than Piaget supposed. Using a 'magic' game, Gelman showed that children as young as three could understand that altering the layout of three objects or fewer did not change the number of objects. The children were shown plates with either two or three mice on them, and learned that the plate with three mice was the 'winner'. They were not told *why* it was the winner: it could have been because of the number of mice, or because of the length of the row of mice, for example. After this initial training, the experimenter 'magically' transformed the winning row, either by removing a mouse, or by shortening or lengthening it. Gelman found that even three- and four-year-olds based their judgements about which row was now the winner on number, rather than length. When the length of the row was changed, but the number of mice was not, they continued to choose the three-mouse row, even when it was shorter than the two-mouse row. If a mouse was removed from the three-mouse row, however, they did not know how to respond, even if the rows differed in length. From these results, Gelman concluded that even young children understand that moving the objects does not affect how many there are, whereas adding or subtracting objects does. Although her task does not depend on exactly the same abilities as the Piagetian conservation task, it demonstrates that young children have an understanding that Piaget would have thought beyond them.

17.2.2   The development of counting

Questions about children's conservation of number have engendered much debate – about how to test for it, and about when it is acquired, for example. However, at whatever age children acquire number conservation, counting is of central importance. Indeed, it has been argued that number conservation is understood earlier and is more stable than conservation of liquid, weight and mass because counting will provide a fail-safe answer (McShane, 1991).

One-to-one matching and counting are interesting in their own right, as well as for the role they play in the acquisition of conservation of number. Indeed, the development of counting has been studied extensively. We will discuss some of the main findings (for a more extensive review see McShane, 1991, chapter 6). Gelman and Gallistel (1978) identified three 'how to count' principles: the one-to-one principle, the stable-order principle and the cardinal principle. The one-to-one principle states that, in counting, number words must be paired one-to-one with the things to be counted. However, one-to-one pairing by itself is not sufficient for counting. Reciting an arbitrary series of number words in one-to-one correspondence with the items is not counting. The other two principles, which are related to basic properties of the number system *ordinality* and *cardinality*, are also important. Numbers have a standard order (1, 2, 3, etc.), and ordinality is the property of a number that allows it to represent position in a series. Gelman and Gallistel's stable-order principle states that a stable sequence of number words is necessary for counting. They emphasize that understanding this principle does not require a child to learn the actual number words, only a stable list of some kind. Letters of the alphabet would suffice, for example, though most children will learn to count using the number words of their own language. Cardinality is the property of numbers that allows them to stand for the number of items in a group. The principle of cardinality in counting is that the number of objects is the last number counted. Gelman and Gallistel claim that some children as young as two obey these three principles, though they may use idiosyncratic lists of number words. They argue that these counting principles are innate, though this view is not universally accepted. Gelman and Gallistel propose two further principles necessary for a full understanding of counting: the abstraction principle (any objects can be counted) and the order-irrelevance principle (the order in which items are counted does not matter). These principles differ from the first three in that they do not require knowledge about count words.

Counting is an important starting point for the development of arithmetical reasoning more generally, which includes understanding of ordinality and cardinality, and the processes of addition, subtraction, division and multiplication. In addition to finding early ability in conservation of number, Gelman also claims that many three- and four-year-olds understand addition and subtraction. For example, in the magic game, if children noticed that a mouse had been removed, they often looked for it. They realized that adding it back into its row would reverse the effects of taking it away. Hughes (1981; 1986, chapter 3) provides more direct evidence to support the same claim. He showed that children between three and five could do simple addition and subtraction if the numbers were small. They were 83 per cent correct on concrete problems: for example, when they knew how many blocks were in a box, and watched as blocks were taken out of or put into the box. They also scored 62 per cent correct on verbal problems, such as 'If there were three children in a sweet shop, and two went out, how many children would be left in the shop?'. More than a quarter of the children could also add and subtract when the numbers were large (five to eight). Hughes concludes that 'Most children who are approaching school age, it would seem, understand the invariance of number, and can carry out simple additions and subtractions, when the numbers involved are small. Moreover, a sizeable proportion of children have similar competence with slightly larger numbers' (1988: p. 283).

By contrast, Hughes found that the same children were poor at school arithmetic questions, such as: 'What does one and two make?' or 'How many is one and two?', getting only about 10 per cent correct. Hughes (1988) argues that such questions are part of the *formal code of arithmetic*. He calls them *context-free*, since they do not make reference to particular objects or entities, and so are not about anything specific. He suggests that this code will not be acquired through ordinary conversation, but must be formally learned. Hughes argues that it may be difficult for children to find links between this new code and their existing number knowledge. That such links do not come naturally is shown in the following conversation (from Hughes, 1988: p. 286):

> *Adult*: How many is two and one more?
> *Child*: Four.
> *Adult*: Well, how many is two lollypops and one more?
> *Child*: Three.
> *Adult*: How many is two elephants and one more?
> *Child*: Three.
> *Adult*: How many is two giraffes and one more?
> *Child*: Three.
> *Adult*: So how many is two and one more?
> *Child*: (looks adult straight in the eye) Six.

Other work by Hughes (see Hughes, 1988) shows that children between five and seven years do not realize that the arithmetical symbols they use in their workbooks can also represent quantities of objects, or operations on those quantities. Or, at least, they do not choose to use them in this way. He suggests that children often fail to understand the symbolism of written arithmetic, and in particular its relation to concrete situations. He claims that this ability to translate between different modes of representation is important for arithmetical competence. However, he has also demonstrated that even pre-school children can grasp the rudiments of arithmetical symbols if their usefulness is stressed. Children must be able to see the rationale for using them and appreciate

the purpose of translating between symbols on the one hand, and concrete objects and events on the other.

We will consider next how counting is related to learning to add and
subtract. Arithmetic procedures can be viewed as counting shortcuts,
and children often devise their own methods of solving addition and
subtraction problems. The use of such methods continues into the school
years, until children learn the number facts – addition and multiplication
tables, for example. Children will even replace a taught procedure with
one of their own devising. Groen and Parkman (1972) used a response-
time paradigm to show that children worked out the answers to addition
problems by starting with the larger number, and counting on from it
by the smaller number (e.g., for 3 + 5, they would count: 6, 7, 8). It
made no difference whether the larger or smaller number was presented
first. The use of this procedure predicts a so-called *min* model of the
response times, because the time taken to work out the answer depends
on the size of the *minimum* (or smaller) of the two numbers. Children
apparently *invent* this procedure for themselves, since it is not one they
are usually taught. Indeed, Groen and Resnick (1977) have provided
experimental evidence that children do invent it. They taught a number
of four-year-olds, who did not yet know how to add, a different method
of addition. They were taught to add 2 + 3, for example, by counting out
two blocks, then counting out three blocks, combining the sets, and
counting the total. This procedure leads to a *sum* model of response
times, since the predicted times depend on the *sum* of the numbers. Once
children had grasped the procedure, they were given a variety of addition problems. Only two of the five subjects' data were consistent with
the sum model. The data of two more were best fitted by the min
model, and the last subject changed from the sum method to the min
method during the experiment. These findings show that children must
realize that there is a *cardinal-to-count connection* (Fuson, 1982). That
is to say, they know that the number of items in a set is the number they
would reach if they counted the set out. They apply this idea to the
larger number, obviating the need to count it out.

Children also use counting in subtraction. For example, by the age of
about seven, they can work out the answer to a subtraction sum (with
positive numbers and a positive answer) by counting down from the
larger number by the smaller, or by counting up from the smaller number
to the larger (Woods, Resnick and Groen, 1975). Interestingly, children
are able to minimize the number of counting steps needed, and presumably the likelihood of error, by *choosing* either to count down or
to count up, *depending on the relative magnitudes of the number to be
subtracted and the answer they are seeking*. Thus, if the problem were
8 – 6, the child would work out the answer by counting up, 'seven,

eight', and would note that it takes two steps to get to eight from six, therefore the answer is 2. If, on the other hand, the problem were 8 − 2, they would count 'seven, six', to reach the answer 6, which is two steps down from 8. This choice between the two methods presupposes that before children do any counting they judge the magnitude of the difference between the numbers, and compare it with the magnitude of the number to be subtracted. Interviews with children and their overt use of these subtraction methods both confirm that they do make such judgements (Resnick, 1983). As with the 'min' method for addition, children are not usually taught these subtraction procedures. Furthermore, not only do they need to be competent at counting to use them, they need to be able to reason about counting. The use of these procedures, therefore, shows that children spontaneously engage in imaginative problem solving, and invent procedures to work out the answers to problems. As we pointed out earlier, learning addition and subtraction tables will eventually provide a shortcut for bypassing these counting procedures. For problems with larger numbers, the procedures would be time-consuming and error-prone.

A number of models have been proposed for the arithmetic abilities of older children (see Ashcraft, 1992, for a review). As Ashcraft points out these models emphasize 'the simple, basic facts of arithmetic, especially addition and multiplication' (1992: p. 97). We will not describe this work, since the more interesting skills of these children are based on the procedures for addition, subtraction, multiplication and division which they are explicitly taught, and which they use in problems that are more complex that the ones we discussed above. We will, however, briefly mention some work on the errors that children make when carrying out more complex calculations with pencil and paper. Brown and Burton (1978) identified systematic errors in the *procedures* that children use to add and subtract numbers, rather than in their knowledge of arithmetic facts. They compared these errors to bugs in computer programs, and wrote their own program BUGGY to help teachers diagnose the errors in the pupils' procedures. More recently, VanLehn (1990) has incorporated these ideas into a general theory of *mind bugs*, or errors in the procedures for carrying out cognitive tasks.

One bug that Brown and Burton identified in addition problems is forgetting to reset the carry to nought after each column has been added up. A pupil following this incorrect procedure will produce the answer 1,312, instead of 1,212 to the problem:

345
867 +

In the rightmost column 5 + 7 gives 12 (2 down, carry 1). In the middle column 4 + 6 + 1 carried gives 11. The 11 should be analysed as 1 down and 1 to carry. But if the child forgets to cancel the one that has already been carried, two will be carried forward into the leftmost column to give a sum of 13 instead of 12. BUGGY, which was developed particularly for the diagnosis of problems in subtraction, will take a series of errors produced by a particular pupil and attempt to find an explanation for the errors, in terms of many tens of possible faulty procedures that it knows about. Brown and Burton also hope that the use of BUGGY will sensitize teachers to the underlying problems that led to particular patterns of errors.

17.3   Conceptual Development

At the same time as children's abilities to think scientifically and math-ematically are developing, their understanding of the world is also in-creasing as their conceptual schemes become more complex. In this section we consider some of the factors that govern their conceptual development.

In chapter 2, we introduced the notion of basic level categories, such as table and chair. Basic level categories contrast with superordinates, such as furniture, and subordinates, such as armchair. Basic level cat-egories correspond to the first concepts acquired by children – they are acquired before subordinate and superordinate terms. The correlational structure of basic level categories is thought to explain, at least in part, why they are easier to learn: children expect categories to include things that mostly have the same features. Indeed, even before they are one year old, children are sensitive to correlational structure. Younger and Cohen (1983) investigated the ability of ten-month-old babies to detect correlations among attributes, using a *dishabituation* paradigm. Infants look at a stimulus less as they become familiar with it (i.e., they become habituated). However, if a stimulus they perceive to be different is then introduced, they will look longer at it (i.e., they will dishabituate). Thus, gaze duration indicates whether babies find a visual stimulus familiar or novel. Younger and Cohen showed babies schematic drawings of animals which had five possible attributes, each of which could be changed independently. Each attribute could have three possible values, for example, feathered, fluffy or horse *tail*; webbed, clubbed or hoofed *feet*. In the training phase, values of three of the attributes were always perfectly correlated and the other two varied. In the test phase, the babies saw stimuli which maintained this pattern of correlation, ones in which the correlation was destroyed, and completely novel stimuli. The ten-month-olds (but not four- and seven-month olds) dishabituated to *both* the completely novel and the uncorrelated test animals, but not to novel animals that maintained the correlation they had previously seen, demonstrating that they perceived the correlation among attributes. This work shows that, by the end of the first year, the ability to encode correlational structure is already in place.

Older children can demonstrate their classification of objects more directly by grouping, or sequential touching, for example. However, perhaps the most interesting conclusions from grouping are not about categorization, but about the strategies that children use to construct their groups. Sugarman (1982) argues that sorting objects into two groups simultaneously, rather than forming first one group and then the other, depends on the complex abilities to appreciate relations that are thought to underlie the acquisition of natural language syntax.

17.3.1   Developmental constraints on concept learning

Children learn concepts and categories in a highly systematic way. For example, although they find *thematic* relations (e.g., between a dog and its lead, or between a bird and its nest) salient, they do not form categories that include thematically related objects. Such observations have led Ellen Markman (see Markman, 1989, for a summary) to propose that children have a set of biases, predispositions and assumptions that restrict the concepts that they are willing to form and obviate the need for sophisticated hypothesis testing. Though such biases result in predictable errors in children's classification systems, for the most part they are helpful. The *assumption of taxonomic organization* leads children to interpret a new word as the label for an *object*, so that the corresponding concept is likely to be part of a taxonomy, and the related *whole-object constraint* embodies a preference to interpret a term as a label for a whole object, rather than one of its parts. In addition, as we have just seen, children prefer to form concepts at the basic level, perhaps because of the strong correlational structure. Interestingly, adults label things at this level for young children, as 'dog', rather than 'animal' or 'terrier'; 'apple', rather than 'fruit' or 'Granny Smith'.

Another constraint proposed by Markman is *mutual exclusivity*. This constraint leads children to assume that objects are not members of two different categories. A second term applied to the same object is interpreted as referring to a salient part of the object, or one of its properties.

Although the mutual exclusivity assumption is useful in vocabulary acquisition, it is, of course, incorrect. Polly is not only a parrot, she is also a bird and a pet. However, young children have well-documented problems with superordinate concepts. For example, in a standard Piagetian task, they claim that in a bunch of twelve roses and eight carnations there are more roses than flowers. The violation of mutual exclusivity makes superordinate terms difficult for children to learn, though there is an additional difficulty, because members of superordinate categories have few perceptual features in common (consider fruit, or furniture). Basic level terms are easier because the things to which they refer have the same overall shape, many common parts, and correlated attributes (wings, feathers and beaks tend to go together, for example).

Markman suggests that children initially treat superordinate terms as names for collections rather than classes. This interpretation allows them to maintain mutual exclusivity, since the labels for collections (e.g., 'forest', 'family') do not apply to members of the collection. An individual tree is not a forest, even though a forest is a group of trees. With familiar concepts, children are more likely to violate mutual exclusivity. If asked, for example, of a doll, 'Is this a toy?', even two- to four-year-olds were correct a high proportion of the time, though they made errors of the predicted sort. They would deny, for example, that a single horse was an animal, and when asked for an animal would pick up several horses. So although young children could work out class-inclusion relations for familiar categories, their errors showed a tendency to interpret superordinate category terms as names of collections. This interpretation enables children to retain their preference for labelling single objects at the basic level. When they are ready to incorporate superordinate and subordinate concepts into their conceptual scheme, they will probably be ready to understand definitions of the corresponding words and verbal explanations of how they are used. The notion of mutual exclusivity is also important in Frank Keil's (1979, 1989) work on children's most general, ontological categories.

17.3.2   How do children's concepts change over time?

We have already seen that children's conceptual schemes change as they grow older. They begin with basic level categories, and only later develop a hierarchical scheme that includes both subordinate and superordinate categories. At a more general level, Keil (1979, 1989) has identified a hierarchical organization among children's most general, ontological categories, such as that of a physical object or an event. This organization is reflected in the non-overlapping sets of properties that children will agree could sensibly be applied to things of various kinds. Physical objects have sizes and colours, for example, but not durations, whereas the reverse is true for events. Furthermore, properties that can be sensibly applied to members of a general category, such as physical objects, can be sensibly applied to members of all subsets of that category (for physical objects, such things as animals, plants and artefacts), but not to members of subsets of other categories.

Carey (1985) has investigated the development of more specific concepts (in particular, natural kinds; see chapter 2) and the role of language in that development. Carey emphasizes the importance of children's developing theories of the world in the process of conceptual change. These theories constrain the inductive inferences by which children generalize from the context in which they first encounter an example of a concept. For example, children know about the anatomy of humans and other familiar animals. They base their inferences about other animals on what they believe about humans, and on their judgements of how similar other animals are to humans.

The origin of these expectations about natural kinds is not well understood. Young children tend to group objects on the basis of perceptible features, such as colour and shape. With natural kinds (animals, for example), children might focus first on the superficial similarities between category members, and only later realize that they have other (more fundamental) attributes in common. Perhaps some level of scientific knowledge must be acquired before children can infer that categories reflect more than superficial perceptual similarities. Alternatively children may not only use correlational information to help them acquire categories, but may expect from an early age, and without any specific scientific knowledge, that the members of natural kinds have a correlational structure that is *not apparent from the perceptual properties of their members alone*. Carey (1985) argues for the latter possibility. She showed that four-year-olds distinguish between living and non-living things, and that even with similar-looking exemplars (toy animals and real animals) they do not incorrectly generalize properties of the real animal (e.g., that it breathes, eats and has babies) to the toy animal, despite the perceptual similarity.

Gelman and Markman (1986) reached a similar conclusion. They asked whether children of about four and a half generalized on the basis of an object's category, or on the basis of perceptual similarity. The children were given information about two objects (e.g., a tropical fish stays underwater to breathe, and a dolphin pops up above the water to breathe). They were then asked to infer the corresponding property of a third object, which looked like one of the first two, but which was given the same label as the other (in this example, a shark, which is a fish, but which looks more like a dolphin than a tropical fish). The children did not know the correct answers: when they were just given the test questions they performed at chance level. However, when category information and information about perceptual similarity were available, but in conflict, children answered on the basis of category information 68 per cent of the time, which was significantly greater than chance. Thus, even four-year-olds realize that natural kinds support inductive inferences. In a simplified version of this experiment, Gelman and Markman (1987) showed that three-year-olds drew more inferences based on category membership than on superficial appearance. These findings suggest that children's thinking is not influenced so much by appearance as was thought. Young children expect natural kinds to have a correlated structure which goes beyond superficial appearances. They base inductive inferences on the category to which an object belongs, even when there is a conflict with cues from appearance.

In the studies just described the children were *given* category labels, and had to make inferences about the properties of one instance based on those of another. However, children may rely more on perceptual information when they have to categorize objects for themselves. Keil (1979) found that young children used perceptual similarity more than biological properties when they were asked to classify *anomalous* objects. He asked children to classify both natural kinds and artefacts when they were given conflicting information about superficial and core properties (see chapter 2). They were told that an operation had been performed on the animal or object which changed its superficial characteristics to those of another animal or object. For example, they were told how a raccoon had had its fur shaved and dyed so that it looked like a skunk, and they were shown pictures of the raccoon before and after its transformation. The youngest children (five-year-olds) classified both natural kinds and artefacts by appearance. For the most part, they insisted that an animal that had been made to look like a skunk was a skunk, even though they had been told that it had the biological characteristics of a raccoon: it had a raccoon heart, raccoon parents and gave birth to raccoon babies. By contrast, the seven- and nine-year-olds were more often willing to concede that internal structure was important in deciding how to classify members of natural kinds. At all ages, children agreed that an artefact could be transformed into a different type of thing. For example, a coffee pot made into a bird feeder really was a bird feeder after the transformation. Although the results of this study appear to conflict with those of Gelman and Markman, they may simply show that children fall back on appearances when classification tasks become difficult. Keil's task was probably more confusing for the children than Gelman and Markman's because of the impossible animals used. Furthermore, Gelman and Markman provided the category label and asked the children decide on a feature, whereas Keil asked for a classification based on given features. An inference in the former direction is likely to be easier than one in the second.

As well as considering natural kinds in general, Carey (1985) looked specifically at the development of biological concepts and biological knowledge. She found that pre-school children organize their biological knowledge around their knowledge of humans, as prototypical living things. They infer the biological properties of other species – whether they eat, breathe, sleep, have babies, and so on – from what they believe about humans, and how similar they perceive the other species to be to humans. For example, Carey told children (and adults) that humans, or another species, have a spleen. Their judgements about whether other animals had this organ varied greatly with age. Four-year-olds projected possession of a spleen onto other animals more than onto inanimate objects *only* when they were taught that *people* have spleens. For example, they projected from people to dogs 70 per cent of the time, but from dogs to people only 18 per cent of the time. If they know that people have spleens, they will assume that other animals do, but not if they are taught that dogs or bees have spleens. In fact, four-year-olds generalize more readily from humans to bugs than from bugs to bees! Older children (ten-year-olds) and adults showed more or less symmetrical projections between humans and dogs. They generalized on the basis of how similar they perceive species to be, not by using humans as a reference point. Carey argues that this developmental change reflects a major restructuring of children's biological knowledge: by about ten the special status of humans has diminished, and children are more flexible in their thinking about other animals.

17.4 Theory of Mind

Carey's work maps out the development of children's biological knowledge. A related question can be asked about psychological knowledge. Attempts to answer this question have led to the notion of a developing *theory of mind*. This work focuses primarily on the child's understanding of other people, though the question of how they understand their own minds is an important one (see Gopnik, 1993). The most important empirical finding in this field is that below the age of about four and a half years children have difficulty in attributing false beliefs to other people. In a classic experiment (Wimmer and Perner, 1983), Maxi puts chocolate in a blue cupboard and, without telling him, his mother moves it to a green cupboard while he is out playing. Young children, who know that the chocolate has been moved, claim that Maxi will look in the green cupboard if he wants chocolate when he comes back, even though they remember that he put it in the blue cupboard. Thus, they fail to appreciate that what Maxi thinks could be different from what they think.

There are three main accounts of how children's understanding of other people develops, which attempt to explain this result and others. The first is the *simulation* theory, which has its origins in philosophy, but which has been championed in psychology by Paul Harris (e.g., 1992). This theory claims that we try to understand other people by working out how we would behave in the same situation. The other two accounts focus more strongly on the notion of a *theory* of other people's mental processes. Leslie (see, e.g., Leslie and Thaiss, 1992) argues that children have an innate understanding of minds, which is held in a special part of their own minds called the *theory of mind mechanism* and which comes into action in the second year of life, with the advent of pretend play. The alternative view (e.g., Gopnik, 1993; Perner, 1991; Wellman, 1990) is that children have to develop a theory of mind in much the same way that scientists have to develop their theories – modifying it in light of observations. Young children, however, suffer from limitations on the observations they are able to make, and on how they can integrate them with what they already know.

In the best developed version of this idea, Perner (1991) argues that, in order to understand other minds, children must develop the idea of the mind as a representational system. To do so they must have an *explicit* concept of representation. That is to say they must not only have mental representations, they must have *metarepresentations* (representations of representations). To understand Maxi's false belief that the chocolate is (still) in the blue cupboard, they must realize that his belief represents the world as Maxi thinks it is, and that that representation can differ from their own representation of how the world really is (the chocolate is in the green cupboard). Perner further links the ability to metarepresent to the ability to construct mental models not only of the here and now (which even very young children possess), but of other times and places and of hypothetical worlds (such as those of false beliefs).

Perner's account explains why the ability to succeed on the false belief task (or Sally-Ann task, as it is often called, after a version in which Maxi and his mother are replaced by characters called Sally and Ann) appears at the same time as the ability to succeed on other, apparently unrelated tasks. In particular, Flavell, Flavell and Green (1983) showed that children below four or five years had difficulty distinguishing between appearance and reality. They claimed that a piece of sponge the shape and colour of a rock looked like a sponge, rather than a rock, or that an imitation pencil made out or rubber was really a pencil. The same child sometimes made appearance-based errors and sometimes reality-based errors, depending on the object and the exact nature of the experimental task. Zaitchik (1990) found that children of a similar age failed a *false photograph* task. In this task a child sees a polaroid photograph taken of, for example, a rubber duck on a bed. The rubber duck is then put (back) into the bathtub, before the child is allowed to see the photograph. The child is then asked where the duck is, in the picture. Young children claim it shows the duck where it currently is (in the bath), rather than where it was when the photograph was taken. Both Flavell's appearance/reality task and Zaitchik's false photograph task depend on the idea of one thing standing for another. So a child who does not have a proper notion of representation will not be able to solve them. However, Leslie and Thaiss (1992) report that autistic children tend to fail the false belief task but to succeed on the false photograph task. They argue that autistic children have a specific deficit in thinking about other people's minds, and, hence, that having a theory of mind cannot depend solely on metarepresentational abilities.

Summary

Babies in their first year have some appreciation of causation and gravity. Young children of six or seven succeed on some deontic versions of the Wason selection task, though not, of course, on versions that adults find difficult. Indeed, it has been suggested (e.g., by Kuhn) that children often engage in scientific reasoning in their attempts to make sense of the world. In complex tasks, like adults, they show confirmation bias. However, they also have difficulty distinguishing between evidence and theory, a problem that has been attributed to metacognitive shortcomings. With simpler tasks, such as Ruffman et al.'s false evidence task, performance is better, and the distinction between evidence and theory is made even by five-year-olds.

Piaget argued that early counting abilities in children should not be taken as evidence for a proper understanding of number, which he believed appeared only with conservation of number. Gelman and Gallistel have shown that the ability to count is itself a complex one, requiring the use of a number of counting principles. However, learning to count does not ensure that children know about the relation between numbers and the world. Nor is it enough for them to do simple arithmetic. Further rules for addition, subtraction, multiplication and division must be learned. And as in the work on, for example, the balance beam problem, the mistakes children make indicate the kinds of rule they are using.

Strong correlations among the attributes of objects belonging to basic level categories explain why they are easy to learn. Built-in assumptions about what concepts should be like, and how they should relate to one another, explain how children acquire them. In particular, the assumption of mutual exclusivity leads children to interpret superordinate terms as names for collections. Children's understanding of natural-kind concepts develops considerably up to adolescence. Their understanding of other people's mental life changes dramatically at about four and a half years, when they are able to understand false beliefs. This observation has led to the idea of a developing theory of mind.

Further Reading

Carey, S. (1985). *Conceptual Change in Childhood*. Cambridge, MA: MIT Press/ Bradford Books.

Kuhn, D., Amsel, E. and O'Loughlin, M. (1988). *The Development of Scientific Thinking Skills*. Orlando, FA: Academic Press.

Markman, E. M. (1989). *Categorization and Naming in Children: Problems of Induction*. Cambridge, MA: MIT Press/Bradford Books.

Perner, J. (1991). *Understanding the Representational Mind*. Cambridge, MA: MIT Press/Bradford Books.

18

A Framework for the Study of Thinking

18.1 Introduction

The traditional divisions in the psychology of thinking and reasoning
are reflected in the organization of this book. We started with a historical
survey, and then discussed the principal building blocks of thought –
concepts and images – and considered the relation between language
and thinking. The middle part of the book covered three major topics
in the psychology of thinking and reasoning: deductive reasoning, inductive reasoning and problem solving, together with statistical reasoning
and decision making. Our treatment of hypothesis testing emphasized
its relation to both inductive and deductive reasoning, and we stayed
with tradition in taking the study of expertise to be part of the study
of problem solving. We followed problem solving with creative thinking, a natural progression, since creativity can be thought of as the
generation of creative solutions to problems. After considering everyday
reasoning, and attempts to teach people how to think, we finished by
discussing how our ability to think develops.

At many points our dissatisfaction with these traditional divisions
should have been apparent. There are closer relations between the
cognitive processes studied in different areas of thinking and reasoning
than the traditional divisions allow. In the minds of our readers, questions such as the following are likely to have arisen. Why is work on
decision making carried out primarily by mathematical psychologists
(and economists)? Why isn't it more closely related to work on problem

solving? Is concept formation a species of induction? Why is work on concepts and imagery often described as memory research rather than part of the study of thinking? Are there not experts in kinds of thinking other than problem solving? Is mental expertise like manual expertise? How close is the link between creativity and problem solving? Is the use of analogy a species of induction? Is deductive reasoning carried out by the same mechanism as inductive reasoning? Is all reasoning really problem solving? The list could be extended indefinitely. More importantly, puzzled readers might have wondered: can order be brought to this chaos and, if so, how?

From time to time we have mentioned attempts to introduce such order. Many of these attempts at synthesis take one type of reasoning as primary, and attempt to assimilate other types of reasoning to it. So, Holland et al. (1986) take induction to be primary, Rips (1988) chooses deduction, and Newell (1990) favours problem solving. Although this way of describing these proposals is slightly misleading, it is not a gross distortion. Holland et al. (1986, chapter 9) suggest that deductive rules, such as modus ponens, would have to be induced by standard mechanisms (they actually claim that such rules rarely are induced), and that they would have to compete with other rules for application to the current problem. A more accurate way of describing these proposals is as follows: they suggest that the theoretical ideas developed to explain inductive reasoning (or deductive reasoning, or problem solving) can form basis for a theory of reasoning of all kinds. We did not find any of these proposals satisfactory, and we certainly did not consider that any of them could provide a suitable organizing principle for a text on thinking and reasoning. Neither did we have an alternative framework that could organize the material. The traditional divisions seemed to provide the only coherent framework for presenting the material we want to present.

18.2 The Mental Models Theory

Although we have not organized this text according to a new unifying principle, we believe there is a framework in which research on thinking and reasoning will eventually be unified. In several chapters we have presented accounts of different kinds of thinking and reasoning in the mental models framework. As should have been apparent, we believe this framework is the most promising one in which research on all types of thinking and reasoning might be brought together, though we do not consider it yet well enough developed to provide the organizing principle for a textbook. In this final chapter we will say a little more about the promise of the mental models theory.

From one point of view, the mental models theory has much in common with other attempts at synthesis. It takes ideas that were originally developed in the context of explaining deductive reasoning (albeit in a very different way from Rips), and attempts to apply them to reasoning of all kinds. However, the mental models theory was never intended to be restricted to deductive reasoning. Indeed, as the subtitle of Johnson-Laird's (1983) book *Mental Models* makes clear, it is a theory of 'language, inference, and consciousness'. It is also intended to account for the relation between language and perception, discussed in detail by Miller and Johnson-Laird (1976). The starting point of the mental models theory is the question: what is thinking like? What do people do when they think, and why do they do it? In other words, the mental models theory tries to analyse thinking at the abstract level that David Marr (1982) referred to as task analysis, and that leads to what he called a computational theory.

The answer that the mental models theory gives to the question about the nature of thinking is that, when people think, they think about parts of a world – often the real world, but sometimes an imaginary world – perhaps the fictional world of a novel, or a wished-for world that they hope will be realized in the future. They represent this part of the world in a mental model that reflects its structure, and they manipulate the mental model to reflect possible changes in the part of the world they are thinking about. Mental models of familiar concrete situations are easier to work with than models of unfamiliar situations or abstract models, and problems that call for the consideration of more than one model at a time – for example, to find a conclusion that is true in each of a set of models – are hard. A mental model of the particular situation currently under consideration is structured in the same way as models both of particular situations and of types of situation stored in long-term memory. Indeed, people prefer to solve problems by retrieving models from memory, which they find easy, rather than by drawing conclusions by manipulating models in short-term working memory, which they find difficult.

We believe it is clear, in outline, how the ideas of mental models theory can be applied to the kinds of thinking that we have discussed in this book. Or, rather, we believe these ideas can explain the cognitive components of these kinds of thinking, since, at least in the case of creativity, there is a strong suggestion that considerations other than cognitive ones are operative. We have, indeed, presented mental models accounts of deductive reasoning, inductive reasoning and creativity in the appropriate chapters, and have indicated how we think that the mental models theory can be applied to problem solving. However, the detailed working out of a mental models framework in which all research on thinking and reasoning can be brought together must be left to a later date. For now, we will close by showing that the mental models theory gives a satisfying answer to the question of whether people are rational.

18.3   Are People Irrational?

We have seen many times that people have difficulty with what, analytically, are simple reasoning problems: syllogisms, Wason's three problems (the selection task, THOG problem and 2–4–6 task), statistical reasoning problems. Do they fail because they are irrational? Indeed, is it irrational to base one's reasoning on mental models? The fact that people make errors on comparatively simple reasoning problems suggests that they are irrational. However, the mental models theory embodies a view that is similar to one proposed by Herbert Simon in the mid-1950s (e.g., Simon, 1955) – that people possess *bounded* rationality. The mental processes that underlie reasoning, for example, the search for counter-examples to a putative conclusion of a piece of deductive reasoning, are basically sound ones. However, when those processes are put to use, they often fail because of other limitations on human performance, limitations on working memory capacity, for example, or on how much we can attend to, or how quickly we have to make decisions. Sometimes the only way around these limitations is to use shortcuts – heuristic methods that sometimes get the answers wrong. For example, believable conclusions are often true, so it makes sense to accept suggested believable conclusions, other things being equal. The attraction of this view of rationality is that it allows us to reconcile two indisputable aspects of human thought: our ability to construct and assess logical systems, and our difficulties in doing so. Our underlying logical capacities explain our abilities. Our cognitive limitations explain our problems.

Further Reading

Johnson-Laird, P. N. (1983). *Mental Models: Towards a Cognitive Science of Language, Inference, and Consciousness*. Cambridge: Cambridge University Press.

Johnson-Laird, P. N. (1993). *Human and Machine Thinking*. Hillsdale, NJ: Lawrence Erlbaum Associates.

Manktelow, K. I. and Over, D. E. (eds) (1993). *Rationality: Psychological and Philosophical Perspectives*. London: Routledge.

References

Allais, M. (1953). Le comportement de l'homme rationnel devant le risque: critique des posulates et axioms de l'école américaine. *Econometrica*, 21, pp. 503–46.

Alloy, L. B. and Abramson, L. Y. (1979). Judgement of contingency in depressed and nondepressed subjects: sadder but wiser? *Journal of Experimental Psychology: General*, 108, pp. 441–85.

Amabile, T. M. (1983). The *Social Psychology of Creativity*. New York: Springer.

Anderson, J. R. (1983). *The Architecture of Cognition*. Cambridge, MA: Harvard University Press.

Anderson, J. R. (1990). Analysis of student performance with the LISP tutor. In N. Frederiksen, R. Glaser, A. Lesgold and M. G. Shafto (eds), *Diagnostic Monitoring of Skill and Knowledge Acquisition* (pp. 27–50). Hillsdale, NJ: Lawrence Erlbaum Associates.

Anderson, J. R., Boyle, C. F., Farrell, R. and Reiser, B. (1987). Cognitive principles in the design of computer tutors. In P. E. Morris (ed.), *Modelling Cognition* (pp. 93–133). Chichester: John Wiley & Sons.

Arbitman-Smith, R., Haywood, H. C. and Bransford, J. D. (1984). Assessing cognitive change. In P. Brooks, R. Sperber and C. M. McCauley (eds), *Learning and Cognition in the Mentally Retarded* (pp. 433–71). Hillsdale, NJ: Lawrence Erlbaum Associates.

Armstrong, S., Gleitman, L. and Gleitman, H. (1983). What some concepts might not be. *Cognition*, 13, pp. 263–308.

Ashcraft, M. H. (1992). Cognitive arithmetic: a review of data and theory. *Cognition*, 44, pp. 75–106.

Au, T. K-F. (1983). Chinese and English counterfactuals. *Cognition*, 15, pp. 155–87.

Axelrod, R. (1984). *The Evolution of Cooperation.* New York: Basic Books.

Baron, J. (1985). *Rationality and Intelligence.* Cambridge: Cambridge University Press.

Baron, J. (1988). *Thinking and Deciding.* Cambridge: Cambridge University Press.

Barron, F. (1988). Putting creativity to work. In R. J. Sternberg (ed.), *The Nature of Creativity: Contemporary Psychological Perspectives* (pp. 76–98). Cambridge: Cambridge University Press.

Barsalou, L. (1983). Ad hoc categories. *Memory and Cognition*, 11, pp. 211–27.

Barsalou, L. (1985). Ideals, central tendency, and frequency of instantiation as determinants of graded structure in categories. *Journal of Experimental Psychology: Learning, Memory and Cognition*, 11, pp. 629–54.

Bartlett, F. C. (1932). *Remembering.* Cambridge: Cambridge University Press.

Barwise, J. and Cooper, R. (1981). Generalized quantifiers and natural language. *Linguistics and Philosophy*, 4, pp. 159–219.

Barwise, J. and Etchemendy, J. (1992). Hyperproof: logical reasoning with diagrams. In N. H. Narayanan (ed.) *AAAI Spring Symposium on Reasoning with Diagrammatic Representations* (pp. 80–4). Stanford University, California.

Bauer, M. I. and Johnson-Laird, P. N. (1993). How diagrams can improve reasoning. *Psychological Science*, 4, 372–8.

Begg, I. and Denny, J. (1969). Empirical reconciliation of atmosphere and conversion interpretations of syllogistic reasoning. *Journal of Experimental Psychology*, 81, 351–4.

Bell, D. E. (1982). Regret in decision making under uncertainty. *Operations Research*, 30, pp. 961–81.

Bell, D. E. (1985). Disappointment in decision making under uncertainty. *Operations Research*, 33, pp. 1–27.

Bell, D. E., Raiffa, H. and Tversky, A. (1988). Descriptive, normative, and prescriptive interactions in decision making. In D. E. Bell, H. Raiffa and A. Tversky (eds), *Decision Making: Descriptive, Normative, and Prescriptive Interactions* (pp. 9–30). Cambridge: Cambridge University Press.

Berlin, B. and Kay, P. (1969). *Basic Color Terms: Their Universality and Evolution.* Berkeley and Los Angeles: University of California Press.

Bernstein, B. (1971). *Classes, Codes and Control* (Vol. 1). London: Routledge & Kegan Paul.

Bernstein, B. and Henderson, D. (1969). Social class differences in the relevance of language to socialisation. *Sociology*, 3, pp. 1–20.

Beth, E. W. and Piaget, J. (1966). *Mathematical Epistemology and Psychology.* Dordrecht: Reidel.

Beyth-Marom, R. and Fischhoff, B. (1983). Diagnosticity and pseudodiagnosticity. *Journal of Personality and Social Psychology*, 45, pp. 1185–95.

Billig, M. (1987). *Arguing and Thinking: A Rhetorical Approach to Social Psychology.* Cambridge: Cambridge University Press.

Bloom, A. (1981). *The Linguistic Shaping of Thought: A Study in the Impact of Language on Thinking in China and the West.* Hillsdale, NJ: Lawrence Erlbaum Associates.

Boden, M. A. (1979). *Piaget.* London: Fontana.

Boden, M. A. (1990). *The Creative Mind: Myths and Mechanisms.* London: Weidenfeld & Nicolson.

Boole, G. (1854). *An Investigation of the Laws of Thought on which are Founded the Mathematical Theories of Logic and Probabilities.* London: Macmillan.

Boolos, G. (1984). On 'syllogistic inference'. *Cognition*, 17, pp. 151–2.

Bouchard, T. J. Jr. and Hare, M. (1970). Size, performance, and potential in brainstorming groups. *Journal of Applied Psychology*, 54, pp. 51–5.

Bozzi, P. (1958). Analisi fenomenologica del moto pendolare armonico [Phenomenological analysis of pendular harmonic motion]. *Rivista de Psicologia*, 52, pp. 281–302.

Bozzi, P. (1959). Le condizioni del movimento 'naturale' lungo i piani inclinati [The conditions for 'natural' motion along inclined planes]. *Rivista de Psicologia*, 53, pp. 337–52.

Braine, M. D. S. (1978). On the relation between the natural logic of reasoning and standard logic. *Psychological Review*, 85, pp. 1–21.

Braine, M. D. S. and Rumain, B. (1983). Logical reasoning. In J. H. Flavell and E. M. Markman (eds), *Handbook of Child Psychology* (Vol. 3, pp. 263–340). New York: John Wiley & Sons.

Braine, M. D. S., Reiser, B. J. and Rumain, B. (1984). Some empirical justification for a theory of natural propositional logic. In G. H. Bower (ed.), *The Psychology of Learning and Motivation* (Vol. 18, pp. 313–71). New York: Academic Press.

Bransford, J. D., Arbitman-Smith, R., Stein, B. S. and Vye, N. J. (1985). Improving thinking and learning skills: an analysis of three approaches. In J. W. Segal, S. F. Chipman and R. Glaser (eds), *Thinking and Learning Skills*, Volume 1: *Relating Instruction to Research* (pp. 133–206). Hillsdale, NJ: Lawrence Erlbaum Associates.

Breslow, L. (1981). Reevaluation of the literature on the development of transitive inferences. *Psychological Bulletin*, 89, pp. 325–51.

Brooks, L. (1978). Nonanalytic concept formation and memory for instances. In E. H. Rosch and B. B. Lloyd (eds), *Cognition and Categorization* (pp. 169–211). Hillsdale, NJ: Lawrence Erlbaum Associates.

Brooks, L. (1983). *On the Insufficiency of Analysis.* Unpublished manuscript, McMaster University, Hamilton, Ontario.

Brown, J. S. and Burton, R. R. (1978). Diagnostic models for procedural bugs in basic mathematical skills. *Cognitive Science*, 2, pp. 155–92.

Brown, R. and Lenneberg, E. H. (1954). A study in language and cognition. *Journal of Abnormal and Clinical Psychology*, 49, pp. 454–62.

Brunswik, E. (1956). *Perception and the Representative Design of Psychological Experiments.* Los Angeles: University of California Press.

Bryant, P. E. and Trabasso, T. (1971). Transitive inferences and memory in young children. *Nature*, 232, pp. 456–8.

Buchanan, B. G. and Mitchell, T. M. (1978). Model-directed learning of production rules. In D. A. Waterman and F. Hayes-Roth (eds), *Pattern-Directed Inference Systems* (pp. 297–312). New York: Academic Press.

Bullock, M. and Gelman, R. (1979). Preschool children's assumptions about cause and effect: temporal ordering. *Child Development*, 50, pp. 89–96.

Byrne, Richard (1979). Memory for urban geography. *Quarterly Journal of Experimental Psychology*, 31, pp. 147–54.

Byrne, Ruth M. J. (1989). Suppressing valid inferences with conditionals. *Cognition*, 31, pp. 61–83.

Camerer, C. F. and Johnson, E. J. (1991). The process-performance paradox in expert judgement: how can experts know so much and predict so badly? In K. A. Ericsson and J. Smith (eds), *Toward a General Theory of Expertise: Prospects and Limits* (pp. 195–217). Cambridge: Cambridge University Press.

Carey, S. (1985). *Conceptual Change in Childhood*. Cambridge, MA: MIT Press/ Bradford Books.

Carnap, R. (1952). Meaning postulates. *Philosophical Studies*, 3, pp. 65–73.

Carraher, T. N., Carraher, D. W. and Schliemann, A. D. (1985). Mathematics in the streets and in schools. *British Journal of Developmental Psychology*, 3, pp. 21–9.

Carroll, J. B. and Casagrande, J. B. (1958). The function of language classification in behavior. In E. E. Maccoby, T. Newcomb and E. L. Hartley (eds), *Readings in Social Psychology* (3rd edn, pp. 18–31). New York: Holt, Rinehart & Winston.

Case, R. (1985). *Intellectual Development: Birth to Adulthood*. Orlando, FA: Academic Press.

Cattell, R. B. and Drevdahl, J. E. (1955). A comparison of the personality profile (16PF) of eminent researchers with that of eminent teachers and administrators, and of the general population. *British Journal of Psychology*, 46, pp. 248–61.

Chance, P. (1986). *Thinking in the Classroom: A Survey of Programs*. New York: Teachers College Press.

Chapman, L. J. and Chapman, J. P. (1959). Atmosphere effect re-examined, *Journal of Experimental Psychology*, 58, pp. 220–6.

Chapman, L. J. and Chapman, J. P. (1967). Genesis of popular but erroneous diagnostic observations. *Journal of Abnormal Psychology*, 72, pp. 193–204.

Charness, N. (1989). Expertise in chess and bridge. In D. Klahr and K. Kotovsky (eds), *Complex Information Processing: The Impact of Herbert A. Simon* (pp. 183–208). Hillsdale, NJ: Lawrence Erlbaum Associates.

Chase, W. G. and Simon, H. A. (1973). Perception in chess. *Cognitive Psychology*, 4, pp. 55–81.

Cheng, P. W. and Holyoak, K. J. (1985). Pragmatic reasoning schemas. *Cognitive Psychology*, 17, pp. 391–416.

Cheng, P. W. and Holyoak, K. J. (1989). On the natural selection of reasoning theories. *Cognition*, 33, pp. 285–313.

Cheng, P. W., Holyoak, K. J., Nisbett, R. E. and Oliver, L. M. (1986). Pragmatic versus syntactic approaches to training deductive reasoning. *Cognitive Psychology*, 18, pp. 293–328.

Chi, M. T. H. (1978). Knowledge structures and memory development. In R.

S. Siegler (ed.), *Children's Thinking: What Develops?* (pp. 73–96). Hillsdale, NJ: Lawrence Erlbaum Associates.

Chi, M. T. H., Feltovich, P. J. and Glaser, R. (1981). Categorization and representation of physics problems by experts and novices. *Cognitive Science*, 5, pp. 121–52.

Chomsky, N. (1957). *Syntactic Structures*. The Hague: Mouton.

Chomsky, N. (1965). *Aspects of the Theory of Syntax*. Cambridge, MA: MIT Press.

Chomsky, N. (1972). *Language and Mind* (enlarged edn). New York: Harcourt, Brace Jovanovich.

Chomsky, N. (1975). *Reflections on Language*. London: Smith.

Clark, H. H. (1969). Linguistic processes in deductive reasoning. *Psychological Review*, 76, pp. 387–404.

Clark, H. H. and Chase, W. G. (1972). On the process of comparing sentences against pictures. *Cognitive Psychology*, 3, pp. 472–517.

Collins, A. M. and Loftus, E. F. (1975). A spreading-activation theory of semantic processing. *Psychological Review*, 82, pp. 407–28.

Collins, A. M. and Michalski, R. S. (1989). The logic of plausible reasoning: a core theory. *Cognitive Science*, 13, pp. 1–49.

Collins, A. M. and Quillian, M. R. (1969). Retrieval time from semantic memory. *Journal of Verbal Learning and Verbal Behavior*, 8, pp. 240–7.

Collins, A. M. and Quillian, M. R. (1972). Experiments on semantic memory and language comprehension. In L. W. Gregg (ed.), *Cognition in Learning and Memory* (pp. 117–47). New York: John Wiley & Sons.

Cosmides, L. (1989). The logic of social exchange: has natural selection shaped how humans reason. Studies with the Wason selection task. *Cognition*, 31, pp. 187–276.

Craik, K. (1943). *The Nature of Explanation*. Cambridge: Cambridge University Press.

Csikszentmihalyi, M. (1988). Society, culture, and person: a systems view of creativity. In R. J. Sternberg (ed.), *The Nature of Creativity: Contemporary Psychological Perspectives* (pp. 325–39). Cambridge: Cambridge University Press.

Davis, H. (1992). Transitive inference in rats (*Rattus norvegicus*). *Journal of Comparative Psychology*, 106, pp. 342–9.

Davis, R. (1982). TEIRESIAS: applications of meta-level knowledge. In R. Davis and D. Lenat (eds), *Knowledge-Based Systems in Artificial Intelligence* (pp. 227–490). New York: McGraw-Hill.

Davis, R. (1984). Amplifying expertise with expert systems. In P. H. Winston and K. Prendergast (eds), *The AI Business: The Commercial Uses of Artificial Intelligence* (pp. 17–40). Cambridge, MA: MIT Press.

Dawes, R. M. (1971). A case study of graduate admissions: application of three principles of human decision making. *American Psychologist*, 26, pp. 180–8.

Dawes, R. M. (1979). The robust beauty of improper linear models in decision making. *American Psychologist*, 34, pp. 571–82.

Dawkins, R. (1976). *The Selfish Gene*. Oxford: Oxford University Press.

de Bono, E. (1968). *The Five-Day Course in Thinking*. London: Allen Lane.

de Bono, E. (1976). *Teaching Thinking*. London: Temple Smith.

de Bono, E. (1983). The Cognitive Research Trust (CoRT) thinking program. In W. Maxwell (ed.), *Thinking: The Expanding Frontier* (pp. 115–27). Philadelphia: Franklin Institute Press.

de Groot, A. D. (1965/1946). *Thought and Choice in Chess*. The Hague: Mouton [orig. pubd in Dutch in 1946].

de Jong, G. (1988). An introduction to explanation-based learning. In H. E. Shrobe (ed.), *Exploring Artificial Intelligence: Survey Talks from the National Conferences on Artificial Intelligence* (pp. 45–81). San Mateo, CA: Morgan Kaufmann.

Dennett, D. C. (1991). *Consciousness Explained*. London: Allen Lane.

Dewey, J. (1933). *How We Think: A Restatement of the Relation of Reflective Thinking to the Educative Process*. Boston: Heath.

Dietterich, T. G. and Michalski, R. (1981). Inductive learning of structural descriptions: evaluation criteria and comparative review of selected methods. *Artificial Intelligence*, 16, pp. 157–294.

Dillard, J. L. (1972). *Black English*. New York: Random House.

Doherty, M. E., Mynatt, C. R., Tweney, R. D. and Schiavo, M. D. (1979). Pseudodiagnosticity. *Acta Psychologia*, 43, pp. 111–21.

Donaldson, M. (1978). *Children's Minds*. London: Fontana.

Drevdahl, J. E. and Cattell, R. B. (1958). Personality and creativity in artists and writers. *Journal of Clinical Psychology*, 14, pp. 107–11.

Dunbar, K. and Klahr, D. (1989). Developmental differences in scientific discovery processes. In D. Klahr and K. Kotovsky (eds), *Complex Information Processing: The Impact of Herbert A. Simon* (pp. 109–43). Hillsdale, NJ: Lawrence Erlbaum Associates.

Duncker, K. (1945/1935). On problem solving. *Psychological Monographs*, 58 (Whole number 270), pp. 1–113 [orig. pubd in German in 1935].

Dunnette, M. D., Campbell, J. and Jaastad, K. (1963). The effects of group participation on brainstorming effectiveness for two industrial samples. *Journal of Applied Psychology*, 47, pp. 10–37.

Egan, D. W. and Greeno, J. G. (1974). Theories of rule induction: knowledge acquired in concept learning, serial pattern learning, and problem solving. In L. W. Gregg (ed.), *Knowledge and Cognition* (pp. 43–104). New York: John Wiley & Sons.

Ehrlich, K. and Johnson-Laird, P. N. (1982). Spatial descriptions and referential continuity. *Journal of Verbal Learning and Verbal Behavior*, 21, pp. 296–306.

Ellsberg, D. (1961). Risk, uncertainty, and the Savage axioms. *Quarterly Journal of Economics*, 75, pp. 643–69.

Erickson, J. R. (1974). A set analysis theory of behavior in formal syllogistic reasoning tasks. In R. L. Solso (ed.), *Theories in Cognitive Psychology* (pp. 305–29). Hillsdale, NJ: Lawrence Erlbaum Associates.

Ericsson, K. A. (1990). Theoretical issues in the study of exceptional performance.

In K. Gilhooly, M. Keane, R. Logie and G. Erdos (eds), *Lines of Thinking: Reflections on the Psychology of Thinking* (Vol. 2, pp. 5–28). Chichester: John Wiley & Sons.

Ericsson, K. A. and Simon, H. A. (1980). Verbal reports as data. *Psychological Review*, 87, pp. 215–51.

Ericsson, K. A. and Simon, H. A. (1984). *Protocol Analysis*. Cambridge, MA: MIT Press.

Ervin-Tripp, S. (1964). An analysis of the interaction of language, topic, and listener. *American Anthropologist*, 66.

Estes, W. (1976). The cognitive side of probability learning. *Psychological Review*, 83, pp. 37–64.

Estes, W. (1986). Array models for category learning. *Cognitive Psychology*, 18, pp. 500–49.

Evans, J. St. B. T. (1982). *The Psychology of Deductive Reasoning*. London: Routledge & Kegan Paul.

Evans, J. St. B. T. (1984). Heuristic and analytic processes in reasoning. *British Journal of Psychology*, 75, pp. 457–68.

Evans, J. St. B. T. (1989). *Bias in Reasoning: Causes and Consequences*. Hove, East Sussex: Lawrence Erlbaum Associates.

Evans, J. St. B. T. and Dusoir, A. E. (1977). Proportionality and sample size as factors in statistical judgements. *Acta Psychologica*, 41, pp. 129–37.

Evans, J. St. B. T. and Lynch, J. S. (1973). Matching bias in the selection task. *British Journal of Psychology*, 64, pp. 391–7.

Evans, J. St. B. T., Barston, J. and Pollard, P. (1983). On the conflict between logic and belief in syllogistic reasoning. *Memory and Cognition*, 11, pp. 295–306.

Farah, M. J., Perronet, F., Gonon, M. A. and Giard, M. H. (1988). Electrophysiological evidence for a shared representational medium for visual images and visual percepts. *Journal of Experimental Psychology: General*, 117, pp. 248–57.

Feigenbaum, E. A. (1989). What hath Simon wrought? In D. Klahr and K. Kotovsky (eds), *Complex Information Processing: The Impact of Herbert A. Simon* (pp. 165–82). Hillsdale, NJ: Lawrence Erlbaum Associates.

Feuerstein, R. (1980). *Instrumental Enrichment: An Intervention Program for Cognitive Modifiability*. Baltimore: University Park Press.

Feuerstein, R., Miller, R., Hoffman, M. B., Rand, Y., Mintzker, Y. and Jensen, M. R. (1981). Cognitive modifiability in adolescence: cognitive structure and the effects of intervention. *Journal of Special Education*, 15, pp. 269–86.

Feyerabend, P. K. (1975). *Against Method: Outine of an Anarchistic Theory of Knowledge*. London: NLB.

Fischhoff, B. (1977). Hindsight ≠ foresight: the effect of outcome knowledge on judgement under uncertainty. *Journal of Experimental Psychology: Human Perception and Performance*, 1, pp. 288–99.

Fischhoff, B. (1988). Judgement and decision making. In R. J. Sternberg and E. E. Smith (eds), *The Psychology of Human Thought* (pp. 153–87). Cambridge: Cambridge University Press.

Fischhoff, B., Slovic, P. and Lichtenstein, S. (1977). Knowing with certainty: the appropriateness of extreme confidence. *Journal of Experimental Psychology: Human Perception and Performance*, 20, pp. 159–83.

Fisher, A. (1988). *The Logic of Real Arguments*. Cambridge: Cambridge University Press.

Flavell, J. H. (1978). Comments. In R. S. Siegler (ed.), *Children's Thinking: What Develops?* (pp. 97–105). Hillsdale, NJ: Lawrence Erlbaum Associates.

Flavell, J. H., Flavell, E. R. and Green, F. L. (1983). Development of the appearance-reality distinction. *Cognitive Psychology*, 15, pp. 95–120.

Fodor, J. A. (1975). *The Language of Thought*. New York: Crowell.

Fodor, J. A. and Pylyshyn, Z. W. (1988). Connectionism and cognitive architecture: a critical analysis. *Cognition*, 28, pp. 3–71.

Fong, G. T., Krantz, D. H. and Nisbett, R. E. (1986). The effects of statistical training on thinking about everyday problems. *Cognitive Psychology*, 18, pp. 253–92.

Frege, G. (1972/1879). Conceptual notation: a formula language of pure thought modelled upon the formula language of arithmetic. In T. W. Bynum (ed. & trans.), *Conceptual Notation and Related Articles* (pp. 101–203). Oxford: Oxford University Press [first pubd in German in 1879, Halle: L. Nerbert].

Fuson, K. C. (1982). An analysis of counting-on solution procedures in addition. In T. P. Carpenter, J. M. Moser and T. A. Romberg (eds), *Addition and Subtraction: A Cognitive Perspective* (pp. 67–81). Hillsdale, NJ: Lawrence Erlbaum Associates.

Galotti, K. M. (1989). Approaches to studying formal and everyday reasoning. *Psychological Bulletin*, 105, pp. 331–51.

Gardiner, P. C. and Edwards, W. (1975). Public values: multiattribute utility measurement for social decision making. In M. F. Kaplan and S. Schwartz (eds), *Human Judgement and Decision Processes* (pp. 1–37). New York: Academic Press.

Gardner, M. (1977). On playing New Eleusis, the game that simulates the search for truth. *Scientific American*, 237, 4, pp. 18–25.

Garnham, A. (1985). *Psycholinguistics: Central Topics*. London: Methuen.

Garnham, A. (1988). *Artificial Intelligence: An Introduction*. London: Routledge & Kegan Paul.

Garnham, A. (1993). Is logicist cognitive science possible? *Mind and Language*, 8, pp. 49–71.

Gellatly, A. R. H. (1989). Human inference. In K. Gilhooly (ed.), *Human and Machine Problem Solving* (pp. 233–64). London: Plenum Press.

Gelman, R. (1972). Logical capacity of very young children: number invariance rules. *Child Development*, 43, pp. 75–90.

Gelman, R. and Gallistel, C. R. (1978). *The Child's Understanding of Number*. Cambridge, MA: Harvard University Press.

Gelman, S. A. and Markman, E. M. (1986). Categories and induction in young children. *Cognition*, 23, pp. 183–208.

Gelman, S. A. and Markman, E. M. (1987). Young children's inductions from natural kinds: the role of categories and appearances. *Child Development*, 58, pp. 1532–40.

Gentner, D. (1983). Structure-mapping: a theoretical framework for analogy. *Cognitive Science*, 7, pp. 155–70.

Gentner, D. (1989). The mechanisms of analogical learning. In S. Vosniadou and A. Ortony (eds), *Similarity and Analogical Reasoning* (pp. 199–241). Cambridge: Cambridge University Press.

Gentner, D. and Gentner, D. R. (1983). Flowing waters and teeming crowds: mental models of electricity. In D. Gentner and A. L. Stevens (eds), *Mental Models* (pp. 99–129). Hillsdale, NJ: Lawrence Erlbaum Associates.

Getzels, J. W. and Csikszentmihalyi, M. (1976). *The Creative Vision*. New York: John Wiley & Sons.

Getzels, J. W. and Jackson, P. W. (1962). *Creativity and Intelligence*. New York: John Wiley & Sons.

Gick, M. L. and Holyoak, K. J. (1980). Analogical problem solving. *Cognitive Psychology*, 12, pp. 306–55.

Gick, M. L. and Holyoak, K. J. (1983). Schema induction and analogical transfer. *Cognitive Psychology*, 15, pp. 1–38.

Gigerenzer, G. (1993). The bounded rationality of probabilistic mental models. In K. I. Manktelow and D. E. Over (eds), *Rationality: Psychological and Philosophical Perspectives* (pp. 284–313). London: Routledge.

Gigerenzer, G. and Hug, K. (1992). Domain-specific reasoning: social contracts, cheating and perspective change. *Cognition*, 43, pp. 127–71.

Gigerenzer, G. and Murray, D. J. (1987). *Cognition as Intuitive Statistics*. Hillsdale, NJ: Lawrence Erlbaum Associates.

Gigerenzer, G., Hoffrage, U. and Kleinbölting, H. (1991). Probabilistic mental models: a Brunswikian theory of confidence. *Psychological Review*, 98, pp. 506–28,

Girotto, V. (1993). Modèles mentaux et raisonnement. In M.-F. Ehrlich, H. Tardieu and M. Cavazza (eds), *Les modèles mentaux: approche cognitive des représentations* (pp. 101–19). Paris: Masson.

Girotto, V. and Legrenzi, P. (1989). Mental representation and hypothetico-deductive reasoning: the case of the THOG problem. *Psychological Research*, 51, pp. 129–35.

Girotto, V. and Legrenzi, P. (1993). Naming the parents of the THOG: mental representation and reasoning. *Quarterly Journal of Experimental Psychology*, 46A, pp. 701–13.

Girotto, V. and Light, P. (1992). The pragmatic bases of children's reasoning. In P. Light and G. Butterworth (eds), *Context and Cognition: Ways of Learning and Knowing* (pp. 134–56). Hemel Hempstead, Hertfordshire: Harvester Wheatsheaf.

Glass, A. L. and Holyoak, K. J. (1975). Alternative conceptions of semantic memory. *Cognition*, 3, pp. 313–39.

Gluck, M. A. and Bower, G. H. (1988a). Evaluating an adaptive network model of human learning. *Journal of Memory and Language*, 27, pp. 166–95.

Gluck, M. A. and Bower, G. H. (1988b). From conditioning to category learning: an adaptive network model. *Journal of Experimental Psychology: General*, 117, pp. 227–47.

Goldstein, I. and Papert, S. (1977). Artificial intelligence, language, and the study of knowledge. *Cognitive Science*, 1, pp. 84–123.

Gopnik, A. (1993). How we know our minds: the illusion of first-person knowledge of intentionality. *Behavioral and Brain Sciences*, 16, pp. 1–14.

Gordon, W. J. (1961). *Synectics*. New York: Harper.

Gorman, Michael E. (1986). How the possibility of error affects falsification on a task that models scientific problem solving. *British Journal of Psychology*, 77, pp. 85–96.

Gorman, Michael E. and Gorman, Margaret E. (1984). A comparison of confirmatory, disconfirmatory and control strategies on Wason's 2–4–6 task. *Quarterly Journal of Experimental Psychology*, 36A, pp. 629–48.

Gorman, Michael E., Gorman, Margaret E., Latta, M. and Cunningham, G. (1984). How disconfirmatory, confirmatory and combined strategies affect group problem solving. *British Journal of Psychology*, 75, pp. 65–79.

Gorman, Michael E., Stafford, A. and Gorman, Margaret E. (1987). Disconfirmation and dual hypotheses on a more difficult version of Wason's 2–4–6 task. *Quarterly Journal of Experimental Psychology*, 39A, pp. 1–28.

Goswami, U. (1992). *Analogical Reasoning in Children*. Hove, East Sussex: Lawrence Erlbaum Associates.

Goswami, U. and Brown, A. L. (1989). Melting chocolate and melting snowmen: analogical reasoning and causal relations. *Cognition*, 35, pp. 69–95.

Grice, H. P. (1975). Logic and conversation. In P. Cole and J. L. Morgan (eds), *Syntax and Semantics*, Vol. 3: *Speech Acts* (pp. 41–58). New York: Seminar Press.

Griffin, D. and Tversky, A. (1992). The weighting of evidence and the determinants of confidence. *Cognitive Psychology*, 24, pp. 411–35.

Griggs, R. A. and Cox, J. R. (1982). The elusive thematic-materials effect in Wason's selection task. *British Journal of Psychology*, 73, pp. 407–20.

Groen, G. J. and Parkman, J. M. (1972). A chronometric analysis of simple addition. *Psychological Review*, 79, pp. 329–43.

Groen, G. J. and Resnick, L. B. (1977). Can pre-school children invent addition algorithms? *Journal of Educational Psychology*, 69, pp. 645–52.

Gruber, H. E. (1981). *Darwin on Man: A Psychological Study of Scientific Creativity* (2nd edn). Chicago: University of Chicago Press.

Guilford, J. P. (1950). Creativity. *American Psychologist*, 5, pp. 444–54.

Guilford, J. P. (1956). Structure of intellect. *Psychological Bulletin*, 53, pp. 267–93.

Guilford, J. P. (1967). *The Nature of Human Intelligence*. New York: McGraw-Hill.

Guilford, J. P. (1986). *Creative Talents: Their Nature, Uses and Development*. Buffalo, NY: Bearly.

Guyote, M. J. and Sternberg, R. J. (1981). A transitive-chain theory of syllogistic reasoning. *Cognitive Psychology*, 13, pp. 461–525.

Hadamard, J. (1949). *The Psychology of Invention in the Mathematical Field.* Princeton, NJ: Princeton University Press.

Hardy, G. H. (1979). *The Collected Papers of G. H. Hardy* (vol. 7). Oxford: Clarendon Press.

Harlow, H. (1949). The formation of learning sets. *Psychological Review,* 56, pp. 51–65.

Harris, P. L. (1992). From simulation to folk psychology: the case for development. *Mind and Language,* 7, pp. 120–44.

Heider, E. R. and Olivier, D. C. (1972). The structure of the color space in naming and memory for two languages. *Cognitive Psychology,* 3, pp. 337–54.

Henle, M. (1962). On the relation between logic and thinking. *Psychological Review,* 69, pp. 366–78.

Hintzmann, D. L. (1976). Repetition and memory. In G. H. Bower (ed.), *The Psychology of Learning and Motivation* (Vol. 10, pp. 47–91). New York: Academic Press.

Hitch, G. J. and Baddeley, A. D. (1976). Verbal reasoning and working memory. *Quarterly Journal of Experimental Psychology,* 28, pp. 603–21.

Holding, D. H. (1985). The psychology of chess skill. Hillsdale, NJ: Lawrence Erlbaum Associates.

Holding, D. H. and Reynolds, R. J. (1982). Recall or evaluation of chess positions as determinants of chess skill. *Memory and Cognition,* 10, pp. 237–42.

Hollan, J. D. (1975). Features and semantic memory: set-theoretic or network model? *Psychological Review,* 82, pp. 154–5.

Holland, J. H., Holyoak, K. J., Nisbett, R. E. and Thagard, P. R. (1986). *Induction: Processes of Inference, Learning and Discovery.* Cambridge, MA: MIT Press.

Holyoak, K. J. (1985). The pragmatics of analogical transfer. In G. H. Bower (ed.), *The Psychology of Learning and Motivation* (Vol. 19, pp. 59–87). New York: Academic Press.

Holyoak, K. J. and Koh, K. (1987). Surface and structural similarity in analogical transfer. *Memory and Cognition,* 15, pp. 332–40.

Holyoak, K. J. and Nisbett, R. E. (1988). Induction. In R. J. Sternberg and E. E. Smith (eds), *The Psychology of Human Thought* (pp. 50–91). Cambridge: Cambridge University Press.

Howe, M. J. A. (1989). *Fragments of Genius: The Strange Feats of Idiots Savants.* London: Routledge.

Howe, M. J. A. (1990). *Sense and Nonsense about Hothouse Children: A Practical Guide for Parents and Teachers.* Leicester: British Psychological Society Books.

Howe, M. J. A. and Smith, J. (1988). Calendar calculating in 'idiots savants': how do they do it? *British Journal of Psychology,* 79, pp. 371–86.

Hsu, F-h., Anantharaman, T., Campbell, M. and Nowatzyk, A. (1990). A grandmaster chess machine. *Scientific American,* 263, 4, pp. 18–24.

Hudson, L. (1966). *Contrary Imaginings.* London: Methuen

Hudson, L. (1987). Creativity. In R. L. Gregory (ed.), *The Oxford Companion to the Mind* (pp. 171–2). Oxford: Oxford University Press.

Hughes, M. (1981). Can preschool children add and subtract? *Educational Psychology*, 1, pp. 207–19.

Hughes, M. (1986). *Children and Number*. Oxford: Blackwell.

Hughes, M. (1988). What is difficult about learning arithmetic? In K. Richardson and S. Sheldon (eds), *Cognitive Development to Adolescence* (pp. 279–96). Milton Keynes: Open University Press.

Hunter, I. M. L. (1957). The solving of three-term series problems. *British Journal of Psychology*, 48, pp. 286–98.

Jeffries, R., Polson, P. G., Razran, L. and Atwood, M. E. (1977). A process model for missionaries–cannibals and other river crossing problems. *Cognitive Psychology*, 9, pp. 412–20.

Jenkins, H. H. and Ward, W. C. (1965). Judgment of contingency between responses and outcomes. *Psychological Monographs*, 79 (1, whole no. 79).

Jennings, D. L., Amabile, T. M. and Ross, L. (1982). Informal covariation assessment: data-based versus theory-based judgments. In D. Kahneman, P. Slovic and A. Tversky (eds), *Judgement under Uncertainty: Heuristics and Biases* (pp. 211–30). Cambridge: Cambridge University Press.

Johnson-Laird, P. N. (1972). The three-term series problem. *Cognition*, 1, pp. 57–82.

Johnson-Laird, P. N. (1983). *Mental Models: Towards a Cognitive Science of Language, Inference, and Consciousness*. Cambridge: Cambridge University Press.

Johnson-Laird, P. N. (1986). Conditionals and mental models. In E. C. Traugott, A. ter Meulen, J. S. Reilly and C. A. Ferguson (eds), *On Conditionals* (pp. 55–75). Cambridge: Cambridge University Press.

Johnson-Laird, P. N. (1988). Freedom and constraint in creativity. In R. J. Sternberg (ed.), *The Nature of Creativity: Contemporary Psychological Perspectives* (pp. 202–19). Cambridge: Cambridge University Press.

Johnson-Laird, P. N. (1989). Analogy and the exercise of creativity. In S. Vosniadou and A. Ortony (eds), *Similarity and Analogical Reasoning* (pp. 313–31). Cambridge: Cambridge University Press.

Johnson-Laird, P. N. (1993). *Human and Machine Thinking*. Hillsdale, NJ: Lawrence Erlbaum Associates.

Johnson-Laird, P. N. (in press, a). A model theory of induction. *RISSEST*.

Johnson-Laird, P. N. (in press, b). Mental models and probabilistic thinking. *Cognition*.

Johnson-Laird, P. N. and Anderson, T. (1988). Common sense inference. Unpublished Manuscript, MRC Applied Psychology Unit, Cambridge, UK.

Johnson-Laird, P.N. and Bara, B. (1984a). Syllogistic inference. *Cognition*, 16, pp. 1–61.

Johnson-Laird, P. N. and Bara, B. (1984b). Logical expertise as a cause of error: a reply to Boolos. *Cognition*, 17, pp. 153–4.

Johnson-Laird, P. N. and Byrne, R. (1991). *Deduction*. Hove, East Sussex: Lawrence Erlbaum Associates.

Johnson-Laird, P. N. and Byrne, R. (1992). Modal reasoning, models, and Manktelow and Over. *Cognition*, 43, pp. 173–82.

Johnson-Laird, P. N. and Byrne, R. (1993). Authors' response: mental models or formal rules? *Behavioral and Brain Sciences*, 16, pp. 368–76.

Johnson-Laird, P. N. and Steedman, M. (1978). The psychology of syllogisms. *Cognitive Psychology*, 10, pp. 64–99.

Johnson-Laird, P. N. and Wason, P. C. (1970). Insight into a logical relation. *Quarterly Journal of Experimental Psychology*, 22, pp. 49–61.

Johnson-Laird, P. N., Byrne, R. and Schaeken, W. (1992). Propositional reasoning by model. *Psychological Review*, 99, pp. 418–39.

Johnson-Laird, P. N., Legrenzi, P. and Legrenzi, M. S. (1972). Reasoning and a sense of reality. *British Journal of Psychology*, 63, pp. 395–400.

Jones, G. V. (1982). Stacks not fuzzy sets: an ordinal basis for prototype theory of concepts. *Cognition*, 12, pp. 281–90.

Kahneman, D. and Tversky, A. (1972). Subjective probability: a judgement of representativeness. *Cognitive Psychology*, 3, pp. 430–54.

Kahneman, D. and Tversky, A. (1973). On the psychology of prediction. *Psychological Review*, 80, pp. 237–51.

Kahneman, D. and Tversky, A. (1979). Prospect theory: an analysis of decision making under risk. *Econometrica*, 47, pp. 263–91.

Kahneman, D. and Tversky, A. (1984). Choices, values and frames. *American Psychologist*, 39, pp. 341–50.

Kamp, H. (1973). Free choice permission. *Proceedings of the Aristotelian Society*, 74, pp. 57–74.

Karmiloff-Smith, A. and Inhelder, B. (1974). If you want to get ahead, get a theory. *Cognition*, 3, pp. 195–212.

Keane, M. T. (1987). On retrieving analogues when solving problems. *Quarterly Journal of Experimental Psychology*, 39A, pp. 29–41.

Keeney, R. L. and Raiffa, H. (1976). *Decisions with Multiple Objectives*. New York: John Wiley & Sons.

Keil, F. C. (1979). *Semantic and Conceptual Development: An Ontological Perspective*. Cambridge, MA: Harvard University Press.

Keil, F. C. (1984). Mechanisms in cognitive development and the structure of knowledge. In R. Sternberg (ed.), *Mechanisms of Cognitive Development* (pp. 81–99). New York: Freeman.

Keil, F. C. (1989). *Concepts, Kinds, and Cognitive Development*. Cambridge, MA: MIT Press/Bradford Books.

Keynes, J. M. (1921). *A Treatise on Probability*. London: Macmillan.

Klahr, D. and Robinson, M. (1981). Formal assessment of problem-solving and planning processes in preschool children. *Cognitive Psychology*, 13, pp. 113–48.

Klahr, D., Fay, A. L. and Dunbar, K. (1993). Heuristics for scientific experimentation: a developmental study. *Cognitive Psychology*, 25, pp. 111–46.

Klayman, J. and Ha, Y-W. (1987). Confirmation, disconfirmation, and information in hypothesis testing. *Psychological Review*, 94, pp. 211–28.

Koestler, A. (1964). *The Act of Creation*. London: Hutchinson.

Kolers, P. A. (1966). Interlingual facilitation of short-term memory. *Journal of Verbal Learning and Verbal Behavior*, 5, pp. 314–19.

Kolers, P. A. (1968). Bilingualism and information processing. *Scientific American*, 218, 3, pp. 78–86.

Kosslyn, S. M. (1975). Information representation in visual images. *Cognitive Psychology*, 7, pp. 341–70.

Kosslyn, S. M. (1980). *Image and Mind*. Cambridge, MA: Harvard University Press.

Kosslyn, S. M., Ball, T. M. and Reiser, B. J. (1978). Visual images preserve metric spatial information: evidence from studies of image scanning. *Journal of Experimental Psychology: Human Perception and Performance*, 4, pp. 47–60.

Kripke, S. A. (1972). Naming and necessity. In D. Davidson and G. Harman (eds), *Semantics of Natural Language* (pp. 253–355). Dordrecht: Reidel.

Kuhn, D. (1989). Children and adults as intuitive scientists. *Psychological Review*, 96, pp. 674–89.

Kuhn, D. (1991). *The Skills of Argument*. Cambridge: Cambridge University Press.

Kuhn, D., Amsel, E. and O'Loughlin, M. (1988). *The Development of Scientific Thinking Skills*. Orlando, FA: Academic Press.

Kuhn, T. S. (1970). *The Structure of Scientific Revolutions* (2nd edn). Chicago: Chicago University Press.

Labov, W. (1970). The logic of nonstandard English. In F. Williams (ed.), *Language and Poverty* (pp. 153–89). Chicago: Markham.

Laird, J. E., Newell, A. and Rosenbloom, P. S. (1987). SOAR: an architecture for general intelligence. *Artificial Intelligence*, 33, pp. 1–64.

Lakoff, G. (1987). *Women, Fire, and Dangerous Things: What Categories Reveal about the Mind*. Chicago: University of Chicago Press.

Langley, P., Simon, H. A., Bradshaw, G. L. and Zytkow, J. M. (1987). *Scientific Discovery: Computational Explorations of the Creative Processes*. Cambridge, MA: MIT Press.

Lantz, D. and Stefflre, V. (1964). Language and cognition revisited. *Journal of Abnormal and Social Psychology*, 69, pp. 472–81.

Larkin, J. H. (1979). Information processing models and science instruction. In J. Lochhead and J. Clement (eds), *Cognitive Process Instruction* (pp. 109–18). Philadelphia: Franklin Institute Press.

Larkin, J. H. (1983). The role of problem representation in physics. In D. Gentner and A. L. Stevens (eds), *Mental Models* (pp. 75–98). Hillsdale, NJ: Lawrence Erlbaum Associates.

Larkin, J. H. and Simon, H. A. (1987). Why a diagram is (sometimes) worth ten thousand words. *Cognitive Science*, 11, pp. 65–99.

Larkin, J. H., McDermott, J., Simon, D. and Simon, H. A. (1980). Models of competence in solving physics problems. *Cognitive Science*, 4, pp. 317–45.

Lave, J. (1988). *Cognition in Practice*. Cambridge: Cambridge University Press.

Lave, J., Murtaugh, M. and de la Rocha, O. (1984). The dialectic of arithmetic in grocery shopping. In B. Rogoff and J. Lave (eds), Everyday *Cognition: Its Development in Social Context* (pp. 67–94). Cambridge, MA: Harvard University Press.

Lemmon, E. J. (1965). *Beginning Logic*. London: Nelson.

Lenat, D. B. and Guha, R. V. (1990). *Building Large Knowledge-Based Systems: Representation and Inference in the Cyc Project*. Reading, MA: Addison-Wesley.

Leslie, A. M. (1982). The perception of causality in infants. *Perception*, 11, pp. 173–86.

Leslie, A. M. and Thaiss, L. (1992). Domain specificity in conceptual development: neuropsychological evidence from autism. *Cognition*, 43, pp. 225–51.

Lichtenstein, S. and Slovic, P. (1971). Reversal of preferences between bids and choices in gambling decisions. *Journal of Experimental Psychology*, 89, pp. 46–55.

Lichtenstein, S. and Slovic, P. (1973). Response-induced reversals of preference in gambling: an extended replication in Las Vegas. *Journal of Experimental Psychology*, 101, pp. 16–20.

Lichtenstein, S., Slovic, P., Fischhoff, B., Layman, M. and Combs, B. (1978). Judged frequency of lethal events. *Journal of Experimental Psychology: Human Learning and Memory*, 4, pp. 551–78.

Lindsay, R., Buchanan, B. G., Feigenbaum, E. A. and Lederberg, J. (1980). *Applications of Artificial Intelligence for Chemical Inference: The DENDRAL Project*. New York: McGraw-Hill.

Littlewood, J. E. (1953). *A Mathematician's Miscellany*. London: Methuen.

Loomes, G. and Sugden, R. (1982). Regret theory: an alternative theory of rational choice under uncertainty. *Economic Journal*, 92, pp. 805–24.

Luce, R. D. Raiffa, H. (1957). *Games and Decisions*. New York: John Wiley & Sons.

Luce, R. D. and Tukey, J. W. (1964). Simultaneous conjoint measurement: a new type of fundamental measurement. *Journal of Mathematical Psychology*, 1, pp. 1–27.

Luchins, A. W. (1942). Mechanisation in problem solving: the effect of Einstellung. *Psychological Monographs*, 54 (248).

Luria, A. R. (1959). The directive function of speech in development and dissolution, Part 1. *Word*, 15, pp. 341–52.

McGarrigle, J. and Donaldson, M. (1975). Conservation accidents. *Cognition*, 3, pp. 341–50.

McGonigle, B. O. and Chalmers, M. (1977). Are monkeys logical? *Nature*, 267, pp. 694–6.

MacKinnon, D. W. (1962). The nature and nurture of creative talent. *American Psychologist*, 17, pp. 484–95.

McShane, J. (1991). *Cognitive Development*. Oxford: Blackwell.

Mani, K. and Johnson-Laird, P. N. (1982). The mental representation of spatial descriptions. *Memory and Cognition*, 10, pp. 181–7.

Manktelow, K. I. and Evans, J. St. B. T. (1979). Facilitation of reasoning by realism: effect or non-effect? *British Journal of Psychology*, 70, pp. 477–88.

Manktelow, K. I. and Over, D. E. (1990a). *Inference and Understanding: A Psychological and Philosophical Perspective*. London: Routledge.

Manktelow, K. I. and Over, D. E. (1990b). Deontic thought and the selection task. In K. Gilhooly, M. Keane, R. Logie and G. Erdos (eds), *Lines of Thinking: Reflections on the Psychology of Thinking* (Vol. 1, pp. 153–64). Chichester: John Wiley & Sons.

Manktelow, K. I. and Over, D. E. (1991). Social roles and utilities in reasoning with deontic conditionals. *Cognition*, 39, pp. 85–105.

Marcus, M. P. (1980). *A Theory of Syntactic Recognition for Natural Language*. Cambridge, MA: MIT Press.

Markman, E. M. (1989). *Categorization and Naming in Children: Problems of Induction*. Cambridge, MA: MIT Press/Bradford Books.

Markovits, H. (1985). Incorrect conditional reasoning among adults: competence or performance? *British Journal of Psychology*, 76, pp. 241–7.

Marr, D. (1982). *Vision: A Computational Investigation into the Human Representation and Processing of Visual Information*. San Francisco: Freeman.

Mayer, R. E. (1992). *Thinking, Problem Solving, Cognition* (2nd edn). New York: Freeman.

Meadow, A., Parnes, S. J. and Reese, H. (1959). Influence of brainstorming instruction and problem sequence on a creative problem solving test. *Journal of Applied Psychology*, 43, pp. 413–16.

Medin, D. L. (1983). Structural principles in categorization. In T. J. Tighe and B. E. Shepp (eds), *Perception, Cognition, and Development: Interactional Analyses* (pp. 203–30). Hillsdale, NJ: Lawrence Erlbaum Associates.

Medin, D. L. and Schaeffer, M. M. (1978). Context theory of classification learning. *Psychological Review*, 85, pp. 207–38.

Medin, D. L. and Smith, E. E. (1981). Strategies and classification learning. *Journal of Experimental Psychology: Human Learning and Memory*, 7, pp. 241–53.

Mednick, S. A. (1962). The associative basis of the creative process. *Psychological Review*, 69, pp. 431–6.

Meehl, P. E. (1954). *Clinical Versus Statistical Prediction: A Theoretical Analysis and a Review of the Evidence*. Minneapolis: University of Minnesota Press.

Michalski, R. S. (1983). A theory and methodology of inductive learning. *Artificial Intelligence*, 20, pp. 111–61.

Michalski, R. S. and Chilausky, R. L. (1980). Learning by being told and Learning from examples: an experimental comparison of the two methods of knowledge acquisition in the context of developing an expert system for soybean diagnosis. *International Journal of Policy Analysis and Information Systems*, 4, pp. 125–61.

Michie, D. (1987). Computer chess. In R. L. Gregory (ed.), *The Oxford Companion to the Mind* (pp. 155–7). Oxford: Oxford University Press.

Michie, D. and Johnston, R. (1984). *The Creative Computer: Machine Intelligence and Human Knowledge*. Harmondsworth, Middlesex: Viking.

Miller, G. A. (1956). The magical number, seven plus or minus two: some limitations on our capacity for processing information. *Psychological Review*, 63, pp. 81–97.

Miller, G. A. and Johnson-Laird, P. N. (1976). *Language and Perception*. Cambridge: Cambridge University Press.

Miller, G. A., Galanter, E. H. and Pribram, K. H. (1960). *Plans and the Structure of Behavior*. New York: Holt, Rinehart & Winston.

Mitchell, T. M. (1982). Generalization as search. *Artificial Intelligence*, 18, pp. 203–26.

Mitroff, I. I. (1974). *The Subjective Side of Science*. Amsterdam: Elsevier.

Mooney, R. L. (1963). A conceptual model for integrating four approaches to the identification of creative talent. In C. W. Taylor and F. Barron (eds), *Scientific Creativity: Its Recognition and Development* (pp. 331–40). New York: John Wiley & Sons.

Moxey, L. M. and Sanford, A. J. (1987). Quantifiers and focus. *Journal of Semantics*, 5, pp. 189–206.

Moxey, L. M. and Sanford, A. J. (1993). *Communicating Quantities: A Psychological Perspective*. Hove, East Sussex: Lawrence Erlbaum Associates.

Moxey, L. M., Sanford, A. J. and Barton, S. B. (1990). Control of attentional focus by quantifiers. In K. Gilhooly, M. Keane, R. Logie and G. Erdos (eds), *Lines of Thinking: Reflections on the Psychology of Thinking* (Vol. 1, pp. 109–24). Chichester: John Wiley & Sons.

Murphy, A. H. and Winkler, R. L. (1984). Probability of precipitation forecasts. *Journal of the American Statistical Association*, 79, pp. 391–400.

Murphy, G. L. and Medin, D. L. (1985). The role of theories in conceptual coherence. *Psychological Review*, 92, pp. 289–316.

Murray, H. G. and Denny, J. P. (1969). Interaction of ability level and interpolated activity in human problem solving. *Psychological Reports*, 24, pp. 271–6.

Mynatt, C. R., Doherty, M. E. and Tweney, R. D. (1977). Confirmation bias in a simulated research environment: an experimental study of scientific inference. *Quarterly Journal of Experimental Psychology*, 29, pp. 85–95.

Mynatt, C. R., Doherty, M. E. and Tweney, R. D. (1978). Consequences of confirmation and disconfirmation in a simulated research environment. *Quarterly Journal of Experimental Psychology*, 30, pp. 395–406.

Newell, A. (1980). Physical symbol systems. *Cognitive Science*, 4, pp. 135–83.

Newell, A. (1981). Reasoning, problem solving and decision processes: the problem space as a fundamental category. In R. Nickerson (ed.), *Attention and Performance VIII* (pp. 693–718). Hillsdale, NJ: Lawrence Erlbaum Associates.

Newell, A. (1990). *Unified Theories of Cognition: The 1987 William James Lectures*. Cambridge, MA: Harvard University Press.

Newell, A. and Simon, H. A. (1963). GPS, a program that simulates human thought. In E. A. Feigenbaum and J. Feldman (eds), *Computers and Thought* (pp. 279–93). New York: McGraw-Hill.

Newell, A. and Simon, H. A. (1972). *Human Problem Solving*. Englewood Cliffs, NJ: Prentice-Hall.

Newell, A., Shaw, J. C. and Simon, H. (1957). Empirical explorations with the Logic Theory Machine. *Proceedings of the Western Joint Computer Conferece*, 15, pp. 218–39.

Newell, A., Shaw, J. C. and Simon, H. (1963). Chess-playing programs and the problem of complexity. In E. A. Feigenbaum and J. Feldman (eds), *Computers and Thought* (pp. 39–70). New York: McGraw-Hill.

Newstead, S. E. (1989). Interpretational errors in syllogistic reasoning. *Journal of Memory and Language*, 28, pp. 78–91.

Newstead, S. E. (1990). Conversion in syllogistic reasoning. In K. Gilhooly, M. Keane, R. Logie and G. Erdos (eds), *Lines of Thinking: Reflections on the Psychology of Thinking* (Vol. 1, pp. 73–84). Chichester: John Wiley & Sons.

Newstead, S. E. and Griggs, R. A. (1983). Drawing inferences from quantified statements: a study of the square of opposition. *Journal of Verbal Learning and Verbal Behavior*, 22, pp. 535–43.

Newstead, S. E. and Griggs, R. A. (1992). Thinking about THOG: sources of error in a deductive reasoning problem. *Psychological Research*, 54, pp. 299–305.

Newstead, S. E., Pollard, P., Evans, J. St. B. T. and Allen, J. (1992). The source of belief bias effects in syllogistic reasoning. *Cognition*, 45, pp. 257–84.

Nickerson, R. S., Perkins, D. N. and Smith, E. E. (1985). *The Teaching of Thinking*. Hillsdale, NJ: Lawrence Erlbaum Associates.

Nisbett, R. E., Fong, G. T., Lehman, D. R. and Cheng, P. W. (1987). Teaching reasoning. *Science*, 238, pp. 625–31.

Nisbett, R. E., Krantz, D. H., Jepson, C. and Kunda, Z. (1983). The use of statistical heuristics in everyday inductive reasoning. *Psychological Review*, 90, pp. 339–63.

Noelting, G. (1976). Stages and mechanisms in the development of the concept of proportion in the child and adolescent. In M. K. Poulsen, G. I. Lubin, and J. F. Magary (eds), *Piagetian Theory and the Helping Professions* (Vol. 5, pp. 302–11). Los Angeles: USC Press.

Norman, D. A. (1988). *The Design of Everyday Things*. New York: Doubleday.

Nosofsky, R. M. (1986). Attention, similarity, and the identification-categorization relationship. *Journal of Experimental Psychology: General*, 115, pp. 39–57.

Oakhill, J. V. (1984). Why children have difficulty reasoning with three-term series problems. *British Journal of Developmental Psychology*, 2, pp. 223–30.

Oakhill, J. V. and Garnham, A. (1985). Referential continuity, transitivity, and the retention of relational descriptions. *Language and Cognitive Processes*, 1, pp. 149–62.

Oakhill, J. V. and Garnham, A. (1993). On theories of belief bias in syllogistic reasoning. *Cognition*, 46, pp. 87–92.

Oakhill, J. V. and Johnson-Laird, P. N. (1984). The representation of spatial descriptions in working memory. *Current Psychological Research and Reviews*, 3, pp. 52–62.

Oakhill, J. V. and Johnson-Laird, P. N. (1985). The effects of belief on the spontaneous production of syllogistic conclusions. *Quarterly Journal of Experimental Psychology*, 37A, pp. 553–69.

Oakhill, J. V., Garnham, A. and Johnson-Laird, P. N. (1990). Belief bias effects in syllogistic reasoning. In K. Gilhooly, M. Keane, R. Logie and G. Erdos (eds), *Lines of Thinking: Reflections on the Psychology of Thinking* (Vol. 1, pp. 125–38). Chichester: John Wiley & Sons.

Oakhill, J. V., Johnson-Laird, P. N. and Garnham, A. (1989). Believability and syllogistic reasoning. *Cognition*, 31, pp. 117–40.

Oaksford, M. and Chater, N. (1991). Against logicist cognitive science. *Mind and Language*, 6, pp. 1–38.

O'Brien, D. P., Noveck, I. A., Davidson, G. M., Fisch, S. M., Brooke Lea, R. and Freitag, J. (1990). Sources of difficulty in deductive reasoning: the THOG task. *Quarterly Journal of Experimental Psychology*, 42A, pp. 329–51.

Osborn, A. F. (1953). *Applied Imagination*. New York: Scribners.

Osherson, D. N. and Smith, E. E. (1981). On the adequacy of prototype theory as a theory of concepts. *Cognition*, 9, pp. 35–58.

Osherson, D. N., Smith, E. E. and Shafir, E. B. (1986). Some origins of belief. *Cognition*, 24, pp. 197–224.

Osherson, D. N., Smith, E. E., Wilkie, O., Lopez, A. and Shafir, E. B. (1990). Category-based induction. *Psychological Review*, 97, pp. 185–200.

Paivio, A. (1971). *Imagery and Verbal Processes*. New York: Holt, Rinehart & Winston.

Palmer, S. E. (1978). Fundamental aspects of cognitive representation. In E. H. Rosch and B. B. Lloyd (eds), *Cognition and Categorization* (pp. 259–303). Hillsdale, NJ: Lawrence Erlbaum Associates.

Parnes, S. J. and Meadow, A. (1963). Development of individual creative talent. In C. W. Taylor and F. Barron (eds), *Scientific Creativity: Its Recognition and Development* (pp. 311–20). New York: John Wiley & Sons.

Pascual-Leone, J. (1970). A mathematical model for the transition rule in Piaget's developmental stages. *Acta Psychologica*, 32, pp. 301–45.

Patrick, C. (1935). Creative thought in poets. *Archives of Psychology*, 178.

Patrick, C. (1937). Creative thought in artists. *Journal of Psychology*, 4, pp. 35–73.

Payne, J. W. (1976). Task complexity and contingent processing in decision making: an information search and protocol analysis. *Organizational Behavior and Human Performance*, 16, pp. 366–87.

Payne, J. W., Bettman, J. R. and Johnson, E. J. (1988). Adaptive strategy selection in decision making. *Journal of Experimental Psychology: Learning, Memory, and Cognition*, 14, pp. 534–52.

Pennington, N. and Hastie, R. (1993). Reasoning in explanation-based decision making. *Cognition*, 49, pp. 123–63.

Penrose, R. (1989). *The Emperor's New Mind: Concerning Computers, Minds, and the Laws of Physics*. Oxford: Oxford University Press.

Perkins, D. N. (1981). *The Mind's Best Work*. Cambridge, MA: Harvard University Press.

Perkins, D. N. (1985). Reasoning as imagination. *Interchange*, 16, pp. 14–26.

Perkins, D. N. (1988). The possibility of invention. In R. J. Sternberg (ed.), *The Nature of Creativity: Contemporary Psychological Perspectives* (pp. 362–85). Cambridge: Cambridge University Press.

Perkins, D. N. (1989). Reasoning as it is and could be: an empirical perspective. In D. M. Topping, D. C. Crowell and V. N. Kobayashi (eds), *Thinking*

Across Cultures: The Third International Conference on Thinking (pp. 175–94). Hillsdale, NJ: Lawrence Erlbaum Associates.

Perkins, D. N., Farady, M. and Bushey, B. (1991). Everyday reasoning and the roots of intelligence. In J. F. Voss, D. N. Perkins and J. W. Segal (eds), *Informal Reasoning and Education* (pp. 83–105). Hillsdale, NJ: Lawrence Erlbaum Associates; Ann Arbor: University of Michigan Press.

Perner, J. (1991). *Understanding the Representational Mind.* Cambridge, MA: MIT Press/Bradford Books.

Peterson, C. R. and Beach, L. R. (1967). Man as an intuitive statistician. *Psychological Bulletin*, 68, pp. 29–46.

Piaget, J. (1951). *Play, Dreams and Imitation in Childhood.* New York: Norton.

Piaget, J. (1952). *The Origins of Intelligence in Children.* New York: International Universities Press.

Piaget, J. (1954). *The Construction of Reality in the Child.* New York: Basic Books.

Piaget, J. and Inhelder, B. (1956). *The Child's Conception of Space.* London: Routledge & Kegan Paul.

Pittenger, J. B. and Runeson, S. (1990). Paolo Bozzi's studies of event perception: a historical note. *ISEP Newsletter*, 4, 3, pp. 10–12.

Platt, J. R. (1964). Strong inference. *Science*, 146, pp. 347–53.

Politzer, G. and Braine, M. D. S. (1991). Responses to inconsistent premisses cannot count as suppression of valid inferences. *Cognition*, 38, pp. 103–8.

Pollard, P. (1990). Natural selection for the selection task: limits to social exchange theory. *Cognition*, 36, pp. 195–204.

Pollard, P., Hunter, B. and Service, V. (1992). A comparison of adult and children's understanding of relative quantifiers. Paper presented at the 2nd International Conference on Thinking, Plymouth, July 1992.

Popper, K. R. (1959). *The Logic of Scientific Discovery.* London: Hutchinson.

Potts, G. R. (1972). Information processing strategies used in the encoding of linear orderings. *Journal of Verbal Learning and Verbal Behavior*, 11, pp. 727–40.

Premack, D. (1976). *Intelligence in Ape and Man.* Hillsdale, NJ: Lawrence Erlbaum Associates.

Premack, D. and Premack, A. J. (1983). *The Mind of an Ape.* New York: Norton.

Preston, M. S. and Lambert, W. E. (1969). Interlingual differences in a bilingual version of the Stroop colorword task. *Journal of Verbal Learning and Verbal Behavior*, 8, pp. 295–301.

Priest, A. G. and Lindsay, R. H. (1992). New light on novice–expert differences in physics problem solving. *British Journal of Psychology*, 83, pp. 389–405.

Pullum, G. K. (1989). The great Eskimo vocabulary hoax. *Natural Language and Linguistic Theory*, 7, pp. 275–81.

Putnam, H. (1975). The meaning of 'meaning'. In K. Gunderson (ed.), *Language, Mind and Knowledge: Minnesota Studies in the Philosophy of Science VII* (pp. 131–93). Minneapolis: Minnesota University Press.

Pylyshyn, Z. W. (1973). What the mind's eye tells the mind's brain: a critique of mental imagery. *Psychological Bulletin*, 80, pp. 1–24.

Pylyshyn, Z. W. (1981). The imagery debate: analogue media versus tacit knowledge. *Psychological Review*, 88, pp. 16–45.

Quillian, M. R. (1968). Semantic memory. In M. Minsky (ed.), *Semantic Information Processing* (pp. 216–70). Cambridge, MA: MIT Press.

Quinlan, J. R. (1983). Learning efficient classification procedures and their application to chess end games. In R. S. Michalski, J. G. Carbonell and T. M. Mitchell (eds), *Machine Learning: An Artificial Intelligence Approach* (pp. 463–82). Los Altos, CA: Morgan Kaufmann.

Rapoport, A. and Chammah, A. H. (1965). *Prisoner's Dilemma*. Ann Arbor: University of Michigan Press.

Reason, J. (1990). *Human Error*. Cambridge: Cambridge University Press.

Resnick, L. (1983). A developmental theory of number understanding. In H. Ginsburg (ed.), *The Development of Mathematical Thinking* (pp. 109–51). New York: Academic Press.

Revlin, R. and Leirer, V. (1978). The effect of person biases on syllogistic reasoning: rational decisions from personalized representations. In R. Revlin and R. E. Meyer (eds), *Human Reasoning* (pp. 51–80). Washington, DC: Winston-Wiley.

Rips, L. J. (1975). Inductive judgements about natural categories, *Journal of Verbal Learning and Verbal Behavior*, 14, pp. 665–81.

Rips, L. J. (1983). Cognitive processes in propositional reasoning. *Psychological Review*, 90, pp. 38–71.

Rips, L. J. (1988). Deduction. In R. J. Sternberg and E. E. Smith (eds), *The Psychology of Human Thought* (pp. 116–52). Cambridge: Cambridge University Press.

Rips, L. J., Smith, E. E. and Shoben, E. J. (1975). Set-theoretic and network models reconsidered: a comment on Hollan's 'Features and semantic memory'. *Psychological Review*, 82, pp. 156–7.

Robinson, J. A. (1965). A machine-oriented logic based on the resolution principle. *Journal of the Association for Computing Machinery*, 12, pp. 23–41.

Roe, A. (1952). A psychologist examines sixty-four eminent scientists. *Scientific American*, 187, 5, pp. 21–5.

Rogoff, B. (1984). Introduction: thinking and learning in social context. In B. Rogoff and J. Lave (eds), *Everyday Cognition: Its Development in Social Context* (pp. 1–8). Cambridge, MA: Harvard University Press.

Rosch, E. (1974). Linguistic relativity. In A. Silverstein (ed.), *Human Communication: Theoretical Perspectives* (pp. 95–121). New York: Halstead Press.

Rosch, E. and Mervis, C. B. (1975). Family resemblances: studies in the internal structure of categories. *Cognitive Psychology*, 7, pp. 573–605.

Rosch, E., Mervis, C. B., Gray, W. D., Johnson, D. M. and Boyes-Braem, P. (1976). Basic objects in natural categories. *Cognitive Psychology*, 8, pp. 382–439.

Ruffman, T., Olson, D. R., Ash, T. and Keenan, T. (1993). The ABCs of deception: do young children understand deception in the same way as adults? *Developmental Psychology*, 29, pp. 74–87.

Ruffman, T., Perner, J., Olson, D. R. and Doherty, M. (1993). Reflecting on scientific thinking: children's understanding of the hypothesis–evidence relation. *Child Development*, 64, pp. 1617–36.

Rumain, B., Connell, J. and Braine, M. D. S. (1983). Conversational comprehension processes are responsible for reasoning fallacies in children as well as adults: IF is not the biconditional. *Developmental Psychology*, 19, pp. 471–81.

Rumelhart, D. E. (1980). Schemata, the building blocks of cognition. In R. J. Spiro, B. J. Bruce and W. F. Brewer (eds), *Theoretical Issues in Reading Comprehension* (pp. 33–58). Hillsdale, NJ: Lawrence Erlbaum Associates.

Russell, J. (1981). Children's memory for the premises in a transitive measurement task assessed by elicited and spontaneous justifications. *Journal of Experimental Child Psychology*, 31, pp. 300–09.

Saariluoma P. (1985). Chess players' intake of task-relevant cues. *Memory and Cognition*, 13, pp. 385–91.

Savage, L. J. (1954). *The Foundations of Statistics*. New York: John Wiley & Sons.

Schaeffer, B. and Wallace, R. (1969). Semantic similarity and the comprehension of word meanings. *Journal of Experimental Psychology*, 82, pp. 343–6.

Schank, R. (1972). Conceptual dependency: a theory of natural language understanding. *Cognitive Psychology*, 3, pp. 552–631.

Schauble, L. (1990). Belief revision in children: the role of prior knowledge and strategies for generating evidence. *Journal of Experimental Child Psychology*, 49, pp. 31–57.

Scribner, S. (1984). Studying working intelligence. In B. Rogoff and J. Lave (eds), *Everyday Cognition: Its Development in Social Context* (pp. 9–40). Cambridge, MA: Harvard University Press.

Scribner, S. (1986). Thinking in action: some characteristics of practical thought. In R. Sternberg and R. Wagner (eds). *Practical Intelligence: Nature and Origins of Competence in the Everyday World* (pp. 13–30). Cambridge: Cambridge University Press.

Shafer, G. (1976). *A Mathematical Theory of Evidence*. Princeton, NJ: Princeton University Press.

Shafer, G. (1986). Savage revisited. *Statistical Science*, 1, pp. 463–85.

Shafer, G. and Tversky, A. (1985). Languages and designs for probability judgement. *Cognitive Science*, 9, pp. 309–39.

Shafir, E. and Tversky, A. (1992). Thinking through uncertainty: nonconsequential reasoning and choice. *Cognitive Psychology*, 24, pp. 449–74.

Shanks, D. R. (1990). Connectionism and the learning of probabilistic concepts. *Quarterly Journal of Experimental Psychology*, 42A, pp. 209–37.

Shanks, D. R. and Dickinson, A. (1991). Instrumental judgement and performance under variations in action-outcome contingency and contiguity. *Memory and Cognition*, 19, pp. 353–60.

Shannon, C. E. (1948). A mathematical theory of communication. *Bell System Technical Journal*, 27, pp. 379–423.

Shepard, R. and Metzler, J. (1971). Mental rotation of three-dimensional objects. *Science*, 171, pp. 701–3.

Shortliffe, E. H. (1976). *MYCIN: Computer-Based Medical Consultations*. New York: Elsevier.

Siegler, R. S. (1976). Three aspects of cognitive development. *Cognitive Psychology*, 8, pp. 481–520.

Siegler, R. S. (1981). Developmental sequences within and between concepts. *Monographs of the Society for Research in Child Development*, 46 (whole no. 189).

Siegler, R. S. (1991). *Children's Thinking* (2nd edn). Englewood Cliffs, NJ: Prentice-Hall.

Siegler, R. S. (1993). Children's thinking: how does change occur? Paper presented at the annual SRCD Conference, New Orleans, Louisiana, March 28, 1993.

Simon, H. A. (1955). A behavioral model of rational choice. *Quarterly Journal of Economics*, 69, pp. 99–118.

Simon, H. A. (1966). Scientific discovery and the psychology of problem solving. In R. G. Colodny (ed.), *Mind and Cosmos: Essays in Contemporary Science and Philosophy* (pp. 22–40). Pittsburgh: University of Pittsburgh Press.

Simon, H. A. (1978). Rationality as a process and product of thought. *American Economic Review*, 68, pp. 1–16.

Simonton, D. K. (1984). *Genius, Creativity, and Leadership*. Cambridge, MA: Harvard University Press.

Sloboda, J. A. (1991). Musical expertise. In K. A. Ericsson and J. Smith (eds), *Toward a General Theory of Expertise: Prospects and Limits* (pp. 153–71). Cambridge: Cambridge University Press.

Slovic, P. and Tversky, A. (1974). Who accepts Savage's axioms? *Behavioral Science*, 19, pp. 368–73.

Slowiaczek, L. M., Klayman, J., Sherman, S. J. and Skov, R. B. (1992). Information selection and use in hypothesis testing: what is a good question, and what is a good answer? *Memory and Cognition*, 20, pp. 392–405.

Smedslund, J. (1977). Piaget's psychology in practice. *British Journal of Educational Psychology*, 47, pp. 1–6.

Smith, E. E. (1988). Concepts and thought. In R. J. Sternberg and E. E. Smith (eds), *The Psychology of Human Thought* (pp. 19–49). Cambridge: Cambridge University Press.

Smith, E. E. and Medin, D. L. (1981). *Categories and Concepts*. Cambridge, MA: Harvard University Press.

Smith, E. E. and Osherson, D. N. (1984). Conceptual combination with prototype categories. *Cognitive Science*, 8, pp. 357–61.

Smith, E. E., Shoben, E. J. and Rips, L. J. (1974). Structure and process in semantic memory: a feature model of semantic decisions. *Psychological Review*, 81, pp. 214–41.

Smith, E. E., Osherson, D. N., Rips, L. J. and Keane, M. (1988). Combining prototypes: a selective modification model. *Cognitive Science*, 12, pp. 485–527.

Smoke, L. L. (1932). An objective study of concept formation. *Psychological Monographs*, 42 (Whole No. 191).

Smyth, M. M. and Clark, S. E. (1986). My half-sister is a THOG: strategic processes in a reasoning task. *British Journal of Psychology*, 77, pp. 275–87.

Sodian, B., Zaitchik, D. and Carey, S. (1991). Young children's differentiation of hypothetical beliefs from evidence. *Child Development*, 62, pp. 753–66.

Soloway, E. and Ehrlich, K. (1984). Empirical studies of programming knowledge. *IEEE Transactions on Software Engineering*, 10, pp. 595–609.

Sosniak, L. A. (1990). The tortoise, the hare, and the development of talent. In M. J. A. Howe (ed.), *Encouraging the Development of Exceptional Abilities and Talents* (pp. 149–64). Leicester: British Psychological Society Books.

Spelke, E. S. (1991). Physical knowledge in infancy: reflections on Piaget's theory. In S. Carey and R. Gelman (eds), *The Epigenesis of Mind: Essays on Biology and Cognition* (pp. 133–69). Hillsdale, NJ: Lawrence Erlbaum Associates.

Sperber, D. and Wilson, D. (1986). *Relevance: Communication and Cognition*. Oxford: Blackwell.

Stein, M. I. (1969). Creativity. In E. F. Borgatta and W. W. Lambert (eds), *Handbook of Personality Theory and Research* (pp. 900–42). Chicago: Rand McNally.

Stenning, K. and Oberlander, J. (in press). Spatial containment and set membership: a case study of analogy at work. In J. Barnden and K. J. Holyoak (eds), *Analogical Connections*. Hillsdale, NJ: Lawrence Erlbaum Associates.

Sternberg, R. J. (1985). *Beyond IQ: A Triarchic Theory of Human Intelligence*. Cambridge: Cambridge University Press.

Sternberg, R. J. (1988). A three-facet model of creativity. In R. J. Sternberg (ed.), *The Nature of Creativity: Contemporary Psychological Perspectives* (pp. 125–47). Cambridge: Cambridge University Press.

Stevens, A. and Coupe, P. (1978). Distortion in judged spatial relations. *Cognitive Psychology*, 10, pp. 422–37.

Stich, S. (1983). *From Folk Psychology to Cognitive Science: The Case Against Belief*. Cambridge, MA: MIT Press.

Strawson, P. (1952), *An Introduction to Logical Theory*. London: Methuen.

Sugarman, S. (1982). Developmental change in early representational intelligence: evidence from spatial classification strategies and related verbal expressions. *Cognitive Psychology*, 14, pp. 410–49.

Tardif, T. Z. and Sternberg, R. J. (1988). What do we know about creativity? In R. J. Sternberg (ed.), *The Nature of Creativity: Contemporary Psychological Perspectives* (pp. 429–40). Cambridge: Cambridge University Press.

Taylor, D. W., Berry, P. C. and Block, C. H. (1958). Does group participation when using brainstorming facilitate or inhibit creative thinking? *Administrative Science Quarterly*, 3, pp. 23–47.

Thaler, R. H. (1985). Mental accounting and consumer choice. *Marketing Science*, 4, pp. 199–214.

Thayer, E. S. and Collyer, C. E. (1978). The development of transitive inference: a review of recent approaches. *Psychological Bulletin*, 85, pp. 1327–43.

Thompson, K. (1986). Programs that generate endgame data bases. *End Game*, 83, p. 2.

Thomson, R. (1968). *The Pelican History of Psychology*. Harmondsworth, Middlesex: Penguin.

Thorndyke, P. W. (1981). Distance estimation from cognitive maps. *Cognitive Psychology*, 13, pp. 526–50.

Torrance, E. P. (1966). *Torrance Tests of Creative Thinking*. Princeton, NJ: Personnel Press.

Torrance, E. P. (1988). The nature of creativity as manifest in its testing. In R. J. Sternberg (ed.), *The Nature of Creativity: Contemporary Psychological Perspectives* (pp. 43–75). Cambridge: Cambridge University Press.

Trabasso, T. (1977). The role of memory as a system in making transitive inferences. In R. V. Kail and J. W. Hagen (eds), *Perspectives on the Development of Memory and Cognition* (pp. 333–66). Hillsdale, NJ: Lawrence Erlbaum Associates.

Trabasso, T., Rollins, H. and Shaughnessy, E. (1971). Storage and verification stages in processing concepts. *Cognitive Psychology*, 2, pp. 239–89.

Truscott, H. (1966). Joseph Haydn and the rise of the classical symphony. In R. Simpson (ed.), *The Symphony* (Vol. 1, pp. 17–49). Harmondsworth: Penguin.

Tversky, A. (1969). Intransitivity of preferences. *Psychological Review*, 76, pp. 31–48.

Tversky, A. (1972). Elimination by aspects: a theory of choice. *Psychological Review*, 79, pp. 281–99.

Tversky, A. (1977). Features of similarity. *Psychological Review*, 84, pp. 327–52.

Tversky, A. and Kahneman, D. (1971). Belief in the law of small numbers. *Psychological Bulletin*, 76, pp. 105–10.

Tversky, A. and Kahneman, D. (1973). Availability: a heuristic for judging frequency and probability. *Cognitive Psychology*, 5, pp. 207–32.

Tversky, A. and Kahneman, D. (1974). Judgement under uncertainty: heuristics and biases. *Science*, 125, pp. 1124–31.

Tversky, A. and Kahneman, D. (1981). The framing of decisions and the psychology of choice. *Science*, 211, pp. 453–8.

Tversky, A. and Kahneman, D. (1982a). Evidential impact of base rates. In D. Kahneman, P. Slovic and A. Tversky (eds), *Judgement under Uncertainty: Heuristics and Biases* (pp. 153–60). Cambridge: Cambridge University Press.

Tversky, A. and Kahneman, D. (1982b). Judgments of and by representativeness. In D. Kahneman, P. Slovic and A. Tversky (eds), *Judgement under Uncertainty: Heuristics and Biases* (pp. 84–98). Cambridge: Cambridge University Press.

Tversky, A. and Shafir, E. (1992a). The disjunction effect in choice under uncertainty. *Psychological Science*, 3, pp. 305–9.

Tversky, A. and Shafir, E. (1992b). Choice under conflict: the dynamics of deferred decision. *Psychological Science*, 3, pp. 358–61.

Tversky, A., Sattath, S. and Slovic, P. (1988). Contingent weighting in judgement and choice. *Psychological Review*, 95, pp. 371–84.

Tversky, B. and Hemenway, M. (1984). Objects, parts and categories. *Journal of Experimental Psychology: General*, 113, pp. 169–93.

Tweney, R. D., Doherty, M. E., Worner, W. J., Pliske, D. B., Mynatt, C. R., Gross, K. A. and Arkkelin, D. L. (1980). Strategies of rule discovery on an inference task. *Quarterly Journal of Experimental Psychology*, 32, pp. 109–23.

VanLehn, K. (1990). *Mind Bugs: The Origins of Procedural Misconceptions*. Cambridge, MA: MIT Press.

Vera, A. H. and Simon, H. A. (1993). Situated action: a symbolic interpretation. *Cognitive Science*, 17, pp. 7–48.

von Ferson, L., Wynne, C. D. L., Delius, J. and Stadden, J. E. R. (1991). Transitive inference formation in pigeons. *Journal of Experimental Psychology: Animal Behavior Processes*, 17, pp. 334–41.

von Neumann, J. and Morgenstern, O. (1944). *Theory of Games and Economic Behavior*. Princeton, NJ: Princeton University Press.

Vygotsky, L. S. (1986). *Thought and Language* (rev. edn). Cambridge, MA: MIT Press.

Wagner, R. and Sternberg, R. (1986). Tacit Knowledge and intelligence in the everyday world. In R. Sternberg and R. Wagner (eds), *Practical Intelligence: Nature and Origins of Competence in the Everyday World* (pp. 51–83). Cambridge: Cambridge University Press.

Wallas, G. (1926). *The Art of Thought*. London: Cape.

Wason, P. C. (1960). On the failure to eliminate hypotheses in a conceptual task. *Quarterly Journal of Experimental Psychology*, 12, pp. 129–40.

Wason, P. C. (1965). The contexts of plausible denial. *Journal of Verbal Learning and Verbal Behavior*, 4, pp. 7–11.

Wason, P. C. (1966). Reasoning. In B. Foss (ed.), *New Horizons in Psychology* (pp. 135–51). Harmondsworth: Penguin.

Wason, P. C. (1968). Reasoning about a rule. *Quarterly Journal of Experimental Psychology*, 20, pp. 273–81.

Wason, P. C. (1983). Realism and rationality in the selection task. In J. St. B. T. Evans (ed.), *Thinking and Reasoning: Psychological Approaches* (pp. 44–75). London: Routledge & Kegan Paul.

Wason, P. C. and Brooks, P. G. (1979). THOG: the anatomy of a problem. *Psychological Research*, 41, pp. 79–90.

Wason, P. C. and Evans, J. St. B. T. (1975). Dual processes in reasoning? *Cognition*, 3, pp. 141–54.

Wason, P. C. and Green, D. W. (1984). Reasoning and mental representation. *Quarterly Journal of Experimental Psychology*, 36A, pp. 597–610.

Wason, P. C. and Johnson-Laird, P. N. (1972). *Psychology of Reasoning: Structure and Content*. London: Batsford.

Wason, P. C. and Shapiro, D. A. (1971). Natural and contrived experience in a reasoning problem. *Quarterly Journal of Experimental Psychology*, 23, pp. 63–71.

Weisberg, R. W. (1988). Problem solving and creativity. In R. J. Sternberg (ed.), *The Nature of Creativity: Contemporary Psychological Perspectives* (pp. 148–76). Cambridge: Cambridge University Press.

Wellman, H. M. (1990). *The Child's Theory of Mind*. Cambridge MA: MIT Press/Bradford Books.

Wertheimer, M. (1945). *Productive Thinking*. New York: Harper & Row.

Whitehead, A. N. and Russell, B. (1910–13). *Principia Mathematica* (3 vols). Cambridge: Cambridge University Press.

Whorf, B. L. (1956). *Language, Thought and Reality: Selected Writings of Benjamin Lee Whorf* (ed. J. B. Carroll). Cambridge, MA: MIT Press.

Wilkins, M. C. (1928). The effect of changed material on the ability to do formal syllogistic reasoning. *Archives of Psychology*, 16 (whole number 102).

Willats, P. (1984). The stage IV infant's solution of problems requiring the use of supports. *Infant Behavior and Development*, 7, pp. 125–34.

Wimmer, H. and Perner, J. (1983). Beliefs about beliefs: representations and constraining function of wrong beliefs in young children's understanding of deception. *Cognition*, 13, pp. 103–28.

Winston, P. H. (1975). Learning structural descriptions from examples. In P. H. Winston (ed.), *The Psychology of Computer Vision* (pp. 155–209). New York: McGraw-Hill.

Wittgenstein, L. (1922). *Tractatus Logico-Philosophicus*. London: Routledge & Kegan Paul.

Wittgenstein, L. (1953). *Philosophical Investigations*. Oxford: Blackwell.

Woods, S. S., Resnick, L. B. and Groen, G. J. (1975). An experimental test of five process models for subtraction. *Journal of Educational Psychology*, 67, pp. 17–21.

Woodworth, R. S. (1938). *Experimental Psychology*. New York: Holt.

Woodworth, R. S. and Sells, S. B. (1935). An atmosphere effect in formal syllogistic reasoning. *Journal of Experimental Psychology*, 18, pp. 451–60.

Younger, B. A. and Cohen, L. B. (1983). Infant perception of correlations among attributes. *Child Development*, 54, pp. 858–67.

Zadeh, L. (1965). Fuzzy sets. *Information and Control*, 8, pp. 338–53.

Zaitchik, D. (1990). When representations conflict with reality: the preschooler's problem with false beliefs and 'false' photographs. *Cognition*, 35, pp. 41–68.

Name Index

Subject Index

abduction, 80, 120–1, 258, 267;
  see also induction, specific
accommodation, 294
ACT*, 204, 279
addition, 327–30
  min model, 329–30
  sum model, 329–30
adversary problems, see game
  playing
affirming the consequent, 87
AI, 7, 13, 16, 44, 72, 120, 202,
  208, 228, 279
algorithms, 203
  see also neo-Darwinian
  algorithms for creativity;
  neo-Lamarckian algorithms for
  creativity
Allais paradox, 189–90
alpha-beta pruning, 221–2
analogy, 202, 215–17, 256, 258,
  264, 289, 315, 341
  structure-mapping hypothesis
  (Gentner), 216–17
analytic processes, see dual process
  theory of reasoning
anchoring and adjustment, 163–4
AND/OR trees, 214–15

anti-realism, 20, 42–3
appearance–reality distinction,
  338
arithmetical problem solving,
  268–72
arithmetic, formal code of, 328
artefacts, 21
artificial intelligence, see AI
artificial science studies, 149–51
assimilation, 294
association, see creativity
associationism, 3–6
atmosphere, see syllogistic
  reasoning
attributes in decision making, see
  MAUT
autism, 233, 338
autobiography, see creativity,
  biographical and
  autobiographical approaches
automatization, 302
availability, 126, 158, 162–3, 177
axioms, 62–4, 99

back propagation, 7
balance beam problems, 298–302,
  312